FREDERICK DOUGLASS

THE NEGRO
IN OUR HISTORY

BY
CARTER G. WOODSON, Ph.D.

*Editor of the Journal of Negro History, Author of the Education
of the Negro Prior to 1861, a Century of Negro Migration, the
History of the Negro Church, the Mind of the Negro as
Reflected in Letters, Negro Orators and their Orations,
and Free Negro Heads of Families in the United
States in 1830.*

FIFTH EDITION
(Further Revised and Enlarged)

THE ASSOCIATED PUBLISHERS, INC.
WASHINGTON, D. C.

Printed in the United States of America

To

MY BROTHER

ROBERT HENRY WOODSON

PREFACE TO THE FIRST EDITION

THIS book was written five years ago and would have been published at that time, had not the high cost of printing during the World War rendered its manufacture too expensive. A few pages have been added to bring the work nearer to the present date, but the leading facts as set forth herein appear as they were originally written.

The purpose in writing this book was to present to the average reader in succinct form the history of the United States as it has been influenced by the presence of the Negro in this country. The aim here is to supply also the need of schools long since desiring such a work in handy form with adequate references for those stimulated to more advanced study.

In this condensed form certain situations and questions could not be adequately discussed, and in endeavoring thus to tell the story the author may have left unsaid what others consider more important. Practically all phases of Negro life and history have been treated in their various ramifications, however, to demonstrate how the Negro has been influenced by contact with the Caucasian and to emphasize what the former has contributed to civilization.

The author is indebted to Mr. David A. Lane, Jr., who kindly assisted him in reading the entire proof.

CARTER G. WOODSON.

Washington, D. C.
April, 1922.

PREFACE TO THE THIRD EDITION

As the first edition of this book was written almost a decade ago and the second was more of a revision than an enlargement of the first, the author has found it advisable to expand the treatment of certain topics and to add three chapters. The new material is intended not so much to illuminate briefly mentioned facts as to develop certain topics which, because of the unsettled state of things, could not be adequately treated when the first edition was produced.

In this edition considerable attention has been given to causes and their results which have had their play since the beginning of this century. For example, segregation is one of the most important topics treated. What has been done for the advancement of the Negro in his sequestered sphere, moreover, and how he is working out his salvation along economic lines have been proportionately discussed. Another important topic treated is the effort of the Negro to help himself by agitative methods supported by organized effort.

Some minor changes should likewise be noted. The last two pages of the chapter on "Reconstruction" have been rewritten, the statistics of the chapter on "Achievements in Freedom" have been revised according to figures of the census of 1920, and a number of illustrations have been added. In fact, that portion of the book following page 280 is practically new material.

The cordial welcome which this sketch of the Negro in history has received has surpassed the expectations of the author. He realizes that this success has been due primarily to the urgent need for a work giving in succinct form the salient facts of this neglected aspect of our history. Knowing that this work is not without fault, however, he has carried out some valuable suggestions of friends who have so kindly received this volume.

Washington, D. C.   CARTER G. WOODSON.
June, 1924.

PREFACE TO THE FOURTH EDITION

This edition of *The Negro in Our History* is to supply
an increasing demand for a single volume giving the leading facts of Negro achievement and the influence of the
race on the history of the world. Most of the space herein
is devoted to the Negro in this country. Some attention,
however, has been given to the African background and
to the European contact with that continent. Inasmuch as
the public is generally uninformed as to the early history
of Africa, and is not yet particularly interested in what
the Negro has accomplished in America, a volume presenting such an account in detail might not be acceptable.

It has, therefore, been thought best to let this volume develop by various editions in the direction in which the
public desires help. In the proportion as Americans and
Europeans become removed from such nonsense as the
Nordic myth and race superiority, they will increase their
interest in the history of other peoples who have accomplished just as much good as they have. So long handicapped by this heresy, however, they still lack the sense
of humor to see the joke in thinking that one race has
been divinely selected to do all of the great things on
this earth and to enjoy most of its blessings. For this
reason a large work on Negro history is not yet in demand,
but there has been much progress in this direction.

Having these thoughts in mind, the author has included
in this edition four or five times as much about the Negro
in Africa as appeared in the first three editions, and he has
given in more detail certain important facts of the Negro

Preface

history in cases where international influences and causes were at work. This volume, therefore, which was first intended for the average reader, still lies within his grasp; but at the same time, it supplies the need of those who, having the spirit of inquiry, desire to look far enough into the subject to appreciate the Negro as one of the advanced races of the world.

CARTER G. WOODSON.

WASHINGTON, D. C.,
January, 1927.

PREFACE TO THE FIFTH EDITION

THE Fifth Edition of the *NEGRO IN OUR HISTORY* is the result of the increasing demand which this book has served throughout the country during the last six years. It has supplied the need for a work of general information with respect to the Negro. At the same time it has been used extensively as a textbook for advanced high school and college students. Wherever the achievements of the Negro are given serious attention in courses in social sciences some reference is made to or some use is made of this work.

In further revising the book several parts of it have been expanded and a new chapter has been added. The additional matter deals largely with the recognition recently received by the Negro in art. The reason for this change in the attitude of the public toward the æsthetic contribution of the Negro and the effort to evaluate it constitute the important points developed in this chapter. Additional illustrations, together with those already in the work, will facilitate the study of the Negro in fine art.

For much of this treatment of the Negro in fine art we are indebted to the articles and books published by the Barnes Foundation of Merion, Pennsylvania. These advanced thinkers have done much to direct attention to the study of African civilization and its influence in the modern world.

CARTER G. WOODSON.

Washington, D. C.
September, 1928.

CONTENTS

CHAPTER   PAGE

I. THE UNKNOWN AFRICAN ORIGIN . . . 1

II. AFRICAN INSTITUTIONS A BACKGROUND . . 22

III. AFRICANS IN HISTORY WITH OTHERS . . . 37

IV. FOREIGN AGGRESSION 53

V. THE SITUATION IN TROPICAL AMERICA . . 71

VI. SLAVERY IN A STRUGGLE WITH SERVITUDE . 82

VII. SLAVERY IN ASCENDANCY 100

VIII. THE NEGRO AND THE RIGHTS OF MAN . . 117

IX. INDEPENDENT EFFORTS 141

X. THE REACTION 161

XI. SELF-ASSERTION 177

XII. A DECLINING ANTISLAVERY MOVEMENT . . 199

XIII. SLAVERY AT ITS WORST 216

XIV. THE FREE NEGRO 243

XV. BLAZING THE WAY 259

XVI. COLONIZATION 279

XVII. SCHEMES FOR DEPORTATION 294

XVIII. ABOLITION 306

XIX. FURTHER PROTEST 319

XX. SLAVERY AND THE CONSTITUTION 332

XXI. THE IRREPRESSIBLE CONFLICT 345

XXII. THE NEGRO IN THE CIVIL WAR 361

XXIII. RECONSTRUCTION 382

Contents

CHAPTER   PAGE

XXIV. POLITICAL RECONSTRUCTION UNDONE . . 409

XXV. FINDING A WAY OF ESCAPE 425

XXVI. ACHIEVEMENTS IN FREEDOM 446

XXVII. IN THE COURT OF THE GENTILES . . . 474

XXVIII. THE TENDER MERCIES OF THE WICKED . 494

XXIX. THE NEGRO IN THE WORLD WAR . . . 511

XXX. THE NEGRO IN SOCIAL JUSTICE . . . 534

XXXI. COURAGEOUS EFFORTS 548

XXXII. NEGRO ART IN ITS NATURAL SETTING . . 565

APPENDIX 577

INDEX 607

ILLUSTRATIONS

PAGE

FREDERICK DOUGLASS . . . . *Frontispiece*
SLAVERY AMONG THE ANCIENTS 2
A CONGO NATIVE 3
AN AFRICAN YOUTH 4
A CHAIR 5
CONGO POTTERY 8
A NATIVE 9
A SCENE ON THE NIGER 11
A CONGO CHIEF 12
CAPTIVES TO BE ENSLAVED 13
AN AXE OF AUTHORITY 15
IMPLEMENTS OF THE STONE AGE 17
A PRODUCT OF THE STONE AGE 18
ONE OF THE TYPES 19
KNIVES 20
AN AFRICAN LYRE 21
A POWDER FLASK 23
AN ANTELOPE HORN TRUMPET 24
INTERESTING ROCK PAINTING 24
A BANTU DANCE—ROCK PAINTING 25
A DAGGER 26
A KNIFE 27
ANOTHER SORT OF DANCE 28
AN AFRICAN STOVE 30
POTTERY 31
AN ANT HILL 38
AN AFRICAN HOME 39
A HANGING LAMP IN BRONZE FROM BENIN 40
BRACELETS IN BRONZE FROM BENIN 41
A CUSTOM—ROCK PAINTING 43
A MYTH—ROCK PAINTING 44
ARMS AND ORNAMENTS 48
A CYLINDRICAL VESSEL 49
A CHOPPER 50
A SHIELD 51
AN ORNAMENTAL VESSEL IN BRONZE FROM BENIN 52

xiii

PAGE

An African Forge 54
Timbuctoo 55
An African Village 57
Kano 65
Inspecting a Captive 66
Branding a Negro Woman Slave 67
A Chain Gang 73
The Dash for Liberty 83
Granville Sharp 101
An Advertisement of a Runaway Slave 105
The Faithful Slave 108
The Punishment of a Runaway Slave 109
Entertainment 112
The Death of Crispus Attucks in the Boston Massacre . 122
Peter Salem at Bunker Hill 124
Facsimile of an Honorable Discharge of a Negro Soldier
     from Washington's Army 127
Gustavus Vasa 135
     A Talented African.
Phyllis Wheatley 136
Benjamin Banneker's Almanac 137
Prince Hall 143
Peter Ogden 145
Richard Allen 147
James Varick 150
Christopher Rush 152
Lemuel Haynes 158
Benjamin Franklin 163
     An Advocate of Freedom.
Toussaint Louverture 168
An Early Cotton Gin 171
Nat Turner 181
Black Wolf, An Indian Chief 185
Indian Man and Woman in Dancing Dress 188
Four Legs, An Indian Chief 191
An Indian Family 192
Negro Abraham 194
An Indian Warrior 195
Osceola 197
Another Sort of Slavery 204
Thomas Jefferson 205
     An Antislavery Reformer.

Illustrations

THE NEGRO CALLS A HALT 210
THE MOTHER AND CHILD 213
JOSIAH HENSON 218
    Prototype of Uncle Tom's Cabin.
A SLAVE AUCTION 220
A PLANTATION 224
N. RILLIEUX'S EVAPORATING PAN 229
THE PURSUIT 233
HARRIETT TUBMAN 235
NEW YORK AFRICAN FREE SCHOOL No. 2 254
    Built a Century Ago.
A SECONDARY SCHOOL IN MERCER COUNTY, OHIO 260
    Admitting Negroes in 1842.
ELLEN CRAFT 263
    A Fugitive disguised as her Master.
WILLIAM STILL 264
    An Agent of the Underground Railroad.
MYRTILLA MINER 265
DR. JAMES McCUNE SMITH 266
FREE NEGROES IN THE CRISIS 267
    Charles L. Reason.
    Phillip A. Bell.
    William Whipper.
    Charles B. Ray.
WILLIAM WELLS BROWN 268
A NEGRO NEWSPAPER EDITED A CENTURY AGO 271
ALEXANDER CRUMMELL 274
HENRY HIGHLAND GARNETT 275
J. W. C. PENNINGTON 276
SAMUEL R. WARD 277
HARRIET BEECHER STOWE 278
PAUL CUFFE 284
    The First Actual Colonizer.
LOTT CARY 286
JOHN B. RUSSWURM 288
    First Negro to receive a Degree from an American Col-
    lege.
ROBERT PURVIS 291
WILLIAM WILBERFORCE 295
    The Antislavery Leader in England.
MARTIN R. DELANEY 297
    An Author, Physician, and Leader before the Civil War.

PAGE

THE MESURADO LAGOON 299

MONROVIA 304

WM. LLOYD GARRISON 307

LEWIS TAPPAN 308

WENDELL PHILLIPS 309

ANTISLAVERY APOSTLES 311
    Abby Kelly Foster.
    Lucy Stone.
    Stephen S. Foster.
    George Thompson.

PRUDENCE CRANDALL 312

LUNSFORD LANE 313
    A Native of North Carolina, who lectured in the North
    against Slavery.

LUCRETIA MOTT 314

CHARLES LENOX REMOND 315

SOJOURNER TRUTH 316

FREDERICK DOUGLASS 317

SOUTHERN ABOLITIONISTS 321
    Benjamin Lundy.
    John G. Fee.
    James G. Birney.
    Daniel R. Goodloe.
    Cassius M. Clay.

GERRIT SMITH 322

WHITE MARTYRS IN THE CAUSE OF ABOLITION 327
    Daniel Drayton.
    Calvin Fairbank.
    L. W. Paine.
    Charles T. Torrey.

SENATOR JOHN P. HALE 330

JOHN QUINCY ADAMS 333
    The Champion of Free Speech.

JOHN C. CALHOUN 336

JOSHUA R. GIDDINGS 337

WILLIAM H. SEWARD 338

FRIENDS OF THE FUGITIVES 339
    John Needles.
    Grace Anne Lewis.
    Abigail Goodwin.
    Daniel Gibbons.

Illustrations

PAGE

PROMOTERS OF THE UNDERGROUND RAILROAD 341
   William Wright.
   J. M. McKim.
   Wm. H. Furniss.
   E. F. Pennypacker.
   John Heman.
   Bartholomew Fussell.
   Samuel Rhoads.
   John Henry Hill.
JOSEPH CINQUE 346
CHARLES SUMNER 347
   A Fearless Advocate of Democracy.
HENRY WARD BEECHER 351
   A Champion of Freedom.
THE DISTRIBUTION OF THE NEGRO POPULATION IN 1860 . . . 357
   By permission of the United States Bureau of Census.
BENJAMIN F. WADE 358
   The Defier of the Secessionists.
ABRAHAM LINCOLN 362
NEGROES IN THE SERVICE OF THE CONFEDERATES 364
U. S. GRANT 365
FACSIMILE OF THE ORIGINAL DRAFT OF THE EMANCIPATION
   PROCLAMATION 371
ROBERT GOULD SHAW LEADING THE FIFTY-FOURTH MASSA-
   CHUSETTS REGIMENT 373
COL. THOMAS W. HIGGINSON 375
   A Commander of Negro Troops.
BISHOP DANIEL A. PAYNE 377
   An Educator and Churchman active during the Civil
   War.
GEN. O. O. HOWARD 383
   Head of the Freedmen's Bureau and Founder of Howard
   University.
GEN. SAMUEL C. ARMSTRONG 385
   A Friend in War and Peace.
TEACHING THE FREEDMEN 386
RICHARD DEBAPTISTE 388
W. H. MILES 389
J. W. HOOD 390
JAMES POINDEXTER 392
SOME FACTORS IN THE RECONSTRUCTION 399
   William P. Fessenden.

Frederick T. Frelinghuysen.
Samuel Shellabarger.
Thaddeus Stevens.
Carl Schurz.
JOHN M. LANGSTON 402
JOHN R. LYNCH 403
A Member of Congress.
SOME NEGRO CONGRESSMEN 404
Robert B. Elliott.
Robert C. DeLarge.
Josiah T. Walls.
Richard H. Cain.
H. R. REVELS 405
U. S. Senator from Mississippi.
B. K. BRUCE 406
U. S. Senator from Mississippi.
JOSEPH H. RAINEY 407
A Member of Congress.
JAMES T. RAPIER 408
A Member of Congress.
BISHOP L. H. HOLSEY 410
A Factor in Reconstruction through the Church.
W. R. PETTIFORD 412
A Reconstructionist in the Church.
THE NEW FREEDOM 417
The First Mixed Jury in the District of Columbia.
THREE SURVIVORS OF THE RECONSTRUCTION 420
M. W. Gibbs.
P. B. S. Pinchback.
James Lewis.
W. J. SIMMONS 423
A Reconstructionist in Education.
R. T. GREENER 430
J. C. PRICE 431
KELLY MILLER 432
BISHOP H. M. TURNER 434
A Fearless Spokesman for his People.
BOOKER T. WASHINGTON 440
W. E. B. DuBois 442
OSWALD GARRISON VILLARD 443
MOORFIELD STOREY 444
President of the National Association for the Advance-
ment of Colored People.

PAGE

A NEGRO COUNTRY SEAT 448
    The Home of Scott Bond.
THE RESIDENCE OF MADAME C. J. WALKER 450
PROMINENT CHURCHMEN OF THEIR TIME 451
    Bishop G. C. Clement.
    Bishop R. E. Jones.
    Bishop R. A. Carter.
    Bishop B. F. Lee.
JULIUS ROSENWALD 455
ANDREW CARNEGIE 456
    The Donor of $600,000 to Tuskegee. The first philan-
    thropist to set the example of giving large sums of money
    for the elevation and development of the Negro race.
JOHN D. ROCKEFELLER AND HIS SON 457
R. R. MOTON 458
    The Principal of Tuskegee.
FACTORS IN THE ECONOMIC PROGRESS OF THE NEGRO . . . 460
    Mrs. A. E. Malone.
    Heman E. Perry.
    John Merrick.
    Samuel W. Rutherford.
AN ILLUSTRATION SHOWING THE MODELS MADE BY MATZELIGER
    FOR HIS INVENTIONS 463
GRANVILLE T. WOODS 465
H. O. TANNER'S CHRIST AND NICODEMUS 468
PAUL LAURENCE DUNBAR 470
NEGROES OF CREATIVE GENIUS 476
    Mrs. G. D. Johnson.
    Egbert Austin Williams.
    Roland Hayes.
    Charles S. Gilpin.
COWORKERS IN VARIOUS CAUSES 482
    George E. Haynes.
    C. W. Chesnutt.
    E. K. Jones.
    W. S. Braithwaite.
L. K. WILLIAMS 483
    A prominent Factor in Socializing the Church.
CLAUDE McKAY 484
BISHOP JOHN HURST 487
    Distinguished by Services for Freedom within and without
    the Church.

Illustrations

PAGE

W. M. TROTTER 489
  A Fearless Opponent of Segregation.
OFFICEHOLDERS BECAUSE OF MERIT 495
  William H. Lewis.
  Robert H. Terrell.
JOHN R. HAWKINS 499
  A Business Man, an Educator, and a Factor in the Church.
EDUCATORS IN CHARGE OF LAND GRANT COLLEGES 507
EDUCATORS OTHERWISE INTERESTED 509
  Mordecai W. Johnson.
  John Hope.
  W. G. Pearson.
  James E. Shepard.
THE PERCENTAGE OF NEGROES IN THE POPULATION OF THE
  UNITED STATES IN 1920 513
A RESULT OF THE MIGRATION 516
  A Negro Teacher with Pupils of both Races.
COL. CHARLES YOUNG 522
  The Highest ranking Negro Graduate of West Point.
THE NEW YORK FIFTEENTH IN THE WORLD WAR 525
MAJOR JOEL E. SPINGARN 529
  An Enemy of Prejudice in the Army.
FIRST SEPARATE BATTALION OF THE DISTRICT OF COLUMBIA
  RECEIVING THE CROIX DE GUERRE IN FRANCE 531
JAMES WELDON JOHNSON 536
  Secretary of the National Association for the Advance-
  ment of Colored People.
MARY WHITE OVINGTON 538
  Chairman of the Board of Directors of the National Asso-
  ciation for the Advancement of Colored People.
F. J. GRIMKÉ 540
  A Preacher of the New Democracy.
A. H. GRIMKÉ 543
  "A Defender of His People."
CARTER GODWIN WOODSON 547
REPRESENTATIVE WOMEN 549
  Mary Church Terrell.
  Mary M. Bethune.
  Mary Talbert.
  Nannie H. Burroughs.
ROBERT S. ABBOTT 553

Two New Factors in Business 557
    Anthony Overton.
    C. C. Spaulding.
Scholars of National Standing 559
    Ernest E. Just.
    Charles H. Turner.
    George W. Carver.
    Julian H. Lewis.
A Julius Rosenwald School taking the Place of a Ramshackle Structure 561
Entrance to an African Palace 566
Art as the African Understands It 567
An African Idea 568
Leslie Pinckney Hill 569
Ivory Utensils 571
Nathaniel Dett 572
Masks 574
Langston Hughes 575

INTRODUCTION

By KELLY MILLER

DR. CARTER GODWIN WOODSON, the author, was born of ex-slave parents near New Canton, Buckingham County, Virginia, December 19, 1875. His father was James Henry Woodson, and his mother Anne Eliza (Riddle) Woodson. As he was one of a rather large family of nine children, his parents, who started life in poverty, could not provide him with the ordinary comforts of life and could not regularly send him to the five-months district school taught alternately by his two uncles, John M. and James B. Riddle. In this rural atmosphere, however, he managed largely by self-instruction to master the fundamentals of the common school subjects by the time he was seventeen.

At this age, in 1892, he went with his brother Robert Henry Woodson to West Virginia, to which his parents were induced to move the following year. They settled at Huntington, but the young Woodson had to accept employment in the coal fields in Fayette County. There he labored as a miner for six years, while spending a few months annually in school in Huntington, West Virginia.

In 1895 he entered the Douglass High School of that city. In this school the young man came under the instruction of William T. McKinney, who inspired him to aspire to higher things. He completed the course in less than two years. He next entered Berea College in Kentucky. This institution was famous at that time because of its coeducation of the two races. He studied there a part of two years. He then began teaching at Winona, Fayette County, West

Virginia, in 1898. From Winona he was called to the principalship of the Douglass High School, of Huntington, from which he had been graduated four years before. He then spent his summers studying at the University of Chicago. There he later obtained the degree of Bachelor of Arts.

He traveled and studied a year in Asia and Europe, spending one semester at La Sorbonne, the University of Paris, under the instruction of Professors Aulard, Diehl, Lemonnier, and Bouché-Leclerc. In France he not only did graduate work in history, but in having contact with French as it is spoken, he learned to speak the language as fluently as he had already learned abroad to speak Spanish.

Returning to the United States, he resumed his studies at the University of Chicago. From this institution he received the degree of Master of Arts in 1908. After studying a little further at Chicago, he went to Harvard to continue his graduate work in history and political science. He specialized under Professors Charles Gross, Ephraim Emerton, W. B. Munro, and Edward Channing. In 1909 he accepted a position as instructor in Romance Languages in the Washington High Schools that he might engage in research in the Library of Congress. In this way he wrote his doctoral dissertation, *The Disruption of Virginia*, which was accepted at Harvard in 1912, in fulfillment of the requirements for the degree of Doctor of Philosophy.

Dr. Woodson served in the Washington Public School System ten years. During the last two years of this service he was an instructor in English and the History of Education at the Myrtilla Miner Normal School and principal of the Armstrong Manual Training High School. In 1919 he became Dean of the School of Liberal Arts of Howard University but resigned at the close of the year because he could not agree with the policies of the administration. From 1920 to 1922 he served as Dean of the West Virginia Collegiate Institute, mainly to reorganize the college department.

The restrictions of the school room, however, did not furnish free scope to exploit his specialty implied in the degree "Doctor of Philosophy in History." In the meantime his life purpose was taking shape and direction in his mind. His dominant purpose was to turn his historical training and preparation to the best racial account. At the expiration of this last service, Dr. Woodson retired from teaching to devote all of his time to research in connection with the Association for the Study of Negro Life and History.

This Association was born in the brain of Carter G. Woodson. Its conception, inspiration, growth, and development are the outgrowth of his personal genius and energy. It was organized by him in Chicago on September 9, 1915, with only five persons. It was incorporated under the laws of the District of Columbia on the third of the following October. The purpose of this undertaking is to preserve and publish the records of the Negro that the race may not become a negligible factor in the thought of the world. The Association has endeavored to publish such materials in scientific form that facts thus properly set forth may tell their own story.

An important purpose of the Association is the publication of *The Journal of Negro History,* a quarterly scientific review of more than 100 pages of current articles and documents giving facts generally unknown. This publication has been regularly issued since January, 1916, and has reached its eleventh volume. In bound form it constitutes a veritable encyclopedia of information concerning the life and history of the Negro in this country and abroad. It circulates among scholars throughout the civilized world. It appeals especially to colleges and universities of both races as a desirable aid to social workers and students carrying on research.

During these years of painstaking research, Dr. Woodson has written a number of books dealing with neglected aspects of Negro history. The first of these, *The Education of the Negro Prior to 1861*, appeared in 1915. It evoked from the leading organs of thought in the United States most favorable comment to the effect that it showed both original treatment and independent research. His next work was *A Century of Negro Migration*, brought out in 1918 at the time of the culmination of the exodus of the Negroes to the North. Recently, Dr. Woodson has published through the Associated Publishers two very popular works, *The History of the Negro Church*, and *The Negro in Our History*. The former has reached its second edition and the latter its fourth, in a revised and enlarged form. Dr. Woodson has recently produced also three important source books, *Negro Orators and Their Orations, Free Negro Heads of Families in the United States in 1830* and *The Mind of the Negro as Reflected in Letters written During the Crisis, 1800-1860*. He is now engaged in writing a comprehensive history of the Negro in six volumes. He is endeavoring to make this the monumental work of his life.

The importance of Dr. Woodson's work is better appreciated when we reflect that the literature of the race problem abounds mainly in propaganda based upon opinion and argumentation. The importance of collecting and collating exact and accurate material has not yet received the recognition which it deserves. We are so anxious to solve the race problem, that we do not take time to study it. Infallible assumption and passionate dogma take the place of carefully ascertained fact and calm analysis. The largest measure of our admiration is due to the Negro

who can divest himself of momentary passion and prejudice, and with self-detachment, devote his powers to
searching out and sifting the historical facts growing out
of race relationship and present them to the world, just as
they are, in their untampered integrity.

The social importance of history, or perhaps, I had better
say, the importance of social history, has become but
recently appreciated. As a school boy, I used to read in
the textbooks that history was a record of the deeds and
doings of important personages and people. Distinguished
achievements and spectacular performances monopolized
the entire field of recorded human action. The ordinary
deeds and doings of ordinary people did not rise to the
level of the historian's concern. But in more recent time
we are beginning to recognize that any performance, individual or en masse, which influences the course of human
progress or retrogression is deemed a contributory factor
of history. If no single slave ever rose above the benumb-
ing drudgery of hewing wood and drawing water, nevertheless, slavery and the slave could not be omitted from
any trustworthy account of the civilization of the South,
and indeed, of the nation. Dr. Woodson has somewhere
made a sharp distinction between the history of the Negro
and the Negro in history. Too often the artist makes the
mountain peaks suffice for the whole landscape. The in-
finite smaller eminences and depressions are apt to be
ignored by the painter bent on exploiting dominant features. But not so with the scientific historian. The
battle may be lost for the want of the horseshoe nail as
well as for lack of the imperious general. It is said that
the loss of the Battle of Waterloo, which turned the tide
of European history, might have been attributable to the
careless cook whose tough beefsteak affected Napoleon's
usual alertness and enabled the Duke of Wellington to take
advantage of his momentary dullness. Henson, the black

attendant, accompanied Peary to the North Pole. The menial part played by this sable attendant was an important and essential part in polar discovery. Dr. Woodson is concerned in digging out every significant rôle which the Negro has played in the world's drama. This makes our history, not only full and complete, but true to the actualities of history happenings.

The Negro is often forced to feel that there is a conspiracy of silence to ignore his best deeds and to exploit his imperfections. If a Negro athlete takes the world's sprinting record, the feat is exploited, while his race is ignored. But if a Negro commits a crime its heinousness is enhanced by reason of the color of the criminal. The reputation of the race suffers seriously by the exploitation of its vices and the suppression of its virtues. The true historian holds the balance true between good and evil. To him the deeds of Judas are as full of historical meaning as those of John. His function is to present the facts.

The Negro's pride of race is humiliated when he contemplates the great drama of this continent and finds that he is accorded no honorable part in the performance. The tendency is always to glorify the white man and to debase the Negro. The effect upon the spirit of the Negro is deplorably oppressive. If he must forever dwell upon a picture in which all worthwhile deeds are ascribed to white men and none to his own race, whence can he derive spirit and inspiration? So strong has been the tendency towards race belittlement, that even Negroes affect to disdain their own contributions. Some are even ashamed to study about themselves and the doings of their race. Negro students have been known to feel ashamed of the songs which welled from the heart of their race as the trill from the throat of the bird. How much more ennobling they feel to read about "how Achilles injured the Greeks" than to recount the lesser exploits of their own blood! But thanks to Dr. Woodson and the Association for the Study of Negro Life and History, all of this is being changed. The story of one's own blood and breed is naturally of keener interest and zest than the story of an alien. Every Jewish boy's heart feels a little bigger when he reads of the part his race has played in the drama of mankind. Not a single fact creditable to Jewry is ever allowed to escape his attention. See how the women delight to extol the part played by their sex; how the Catholics exploit the achievements of their co-religionists; and so the Negro must learn to know his own story and to love it.

Dr. Woodson is furnishing the material which will be of incalculable value to students and scholars of race relations, not only in the immediate future but in the remoter years to come. His work possesses what might be termed a strategic timeliness. America is just acquiring the scientific method of handling historical material. Dr. Woodson is, I believe, the second member of his race to receive complete university training and equipment for scientific historical inquiry. The facts involved in the contact of the African with the Western World are scattered throughout many sources which are growing less and less available as the years go by. Like the Sibylline books, the value increases as the volumes decrease. Many private libraries contain invaluable material, which will be disseminated or destroyed unless it is utilized during the lifetime of the compilers. Much invaluable material is now confirmable by living memory, which, within a few years, will pass beyond reach of consultation. Now is the time of all times to gather up the documents and to collect and collate the racial material which they contain. It is fortunate that some one has had vision enough to do this thing.

Dr. Woodson has made every possible sacrifice for the cause to which he is devoted. In the beginning of the movement he beggared himself that the work might succeed. The work of the Association for the Study of Negro Life and History soon approved itself to the historical scholars of the country. The historical departments of both Harvard and Chicago, where Dr. Woodson has studied, at once recognized the importance of what he was endeavoring to do. A few philanthropists began to find out what was being accomplished and furnished substantial assistance. Among those making personal donations to the cause we find such well-known Americans as Jacob H. Schiff, William G. Wilcox, Morefield Storey, James J. Storrow, Frank Trumbull, Cleveland H. Dodge, Morton D. Hull, and Julius Rosenwald. The work has been assisted, too, by the Carnegie Corporation and the Laura Spelman Rockefeller Memorial.

With funds obtained through these sources the Association has been studying the Free Negro prior to the Civil War and the Negro in the Reconstruction of the Southern States. The project has gone far beyond the ability of one man to operate. Dr. Woodson has on his staff several carefully trained Negro students in present-day historical method through whom, under his direction, much of this research work has already been accomplished. In this effort, too, the investigation is not restricted to the Negro in the United States. The Association has an investigator working in the Archives of the Indies, in Seville, Spain, one making an investigation in the British Museum and the Public Record Office in London, and still another in Hayti studying folklore. The Association has thereby been enabled to accomplish worthwhile work which speaks for itself.

THE NEGRO IN OUR HISTORY

CHAPTER I

THE UNKNOWN AFRICAN ORIGIN

MOST historians know practically nothing about the
Negroes in Africa prior to their enslavement, and there
has been little systematic effort to study them.[1] The world
has long looked at Africa "through the eyes of human
sentiment or dividends." Men have invented   **Africa**
all sorts of arguments based upon estimates   **unknown.**
of "physical phenomena as conceived by phrenology and
physiognomy, using signs and symbols to describe every
part of the man—from the heel to the skull—to prove the
mental and moral inferiority of the Negro." There have
been few to enlarge upon the physical inferiority of the
Negro, however, inasmuch as the Negro is regarded as
belonging to the most vigorous portion of the human
family.

The fact is that we know less about Africa than about any
other part of the world. With the exception of Egypt
and the Red Sea shore, Africa is difficult of access because
of its plateau formation and unnavigable rivers. The

[1] For more extensive treatment see W. Z. Ripley's *Races of
Europe*, J. Deniker's *Races of Men*, J. Finot's *Race Prejudice*,
F. Ratzel's *The History of Mankind*, Franz Boas's *The Mind of
Primitive Man*, Spiller's *Inter-Racial Problems*, C. Bucher's *Indus-
trial Revolution*, Casely Hayford's *Ethiopia Unbound* and his
Native Institutions, James Bryce's *Impressions of South Africa*,
Leo Frobenius's *The Voice of Africa*, and G. Sergi's *The Mediter-
ranean Race*; David Randall-Maciver, *Medieval Rhodesia*; E. W.
Blyden, *African Life and Customs*; J. P. Johnson, *The Stone Im-
plements of South Africa* and *The Prehistoric Period in South
Africa*.

1

ancients knew more about Africans who came into the
Mediterranean world than they knew of the Africans in
Access   their home. Homer mentions the Ethiopians
difficult.   as "the farthest removed of men." Herodotus said that the Phœnicians visited parts of the continent

SLAVERY AMONG THE ANCIENTS

as far as the equator six centuries before Christ. About
450 or 500 B.C. the Carthaginians established trading
posts on the Atlantic Coast of Morocco and probably
reached Sierra Leone and the Gold Coast. Frequent in-

ternational commercial intercourse took place on the Nile and the Red Sea. The East Coast as far as Zambesi was known to the ancient Europeans. Ptolemy's geography indicates that the ancients had almost accurate knowledge of the Nile from its very source. Then there appeared evidences of closer contact in the permanent settlements like the Greek colonies, Cyrene and nearby cities, and those of the Phœnicians at Utica and Carthage. These figured conspicuously in the history of the ancient world, but did not penetrate the continent. The slave trade made Africa uninviting; and, on the other hand, the fight on the slave trade attracted attention thereto. Mohammedanism, disputing the progress of Christianity, also kept out the modern explorer.

A CONGO NATIVE

Until about 1850, Africa in the mind of the modern world was a series of coast lines. **A series of coast lines.** Americans and Europeans are still practically on the outside looking at the continent through a glass darkly. The coast contact, such as it was, figured in the history of the world. The East Coast of Africa was early visited by Arabs. Then came the slave traders of the Mohammedans as a result of the rise of Moslems. They took Northern Africa by the eighth century and threatened Europe, only to lose their foothold there and some of their conquest in the southern Mediterranean. They crossed the Sahara into the Soudan, and pushed their way as far as the Zambesi, roughly speaking, to ten degrees north latitude. Christian slave traders succeeded the Mohammedans but their traffic restricted them to the coast. Neither Europe nor America had any definite knowledge of the interior of Africa until after 1870 when Stanley had explored the back country.

It is only recently that there has been a tendency to study the African and his continent scientifically, and scholars in large numbers have not as yet turned in this direction. For this reason **Superiority Myth.** a majority of the people of Europe and America still regard the African as a heathen below the lowest of the human family. The supposedly low depths of the native Africans emphasize the so-called heights which the whites have attained. As a matter of fact, however, the African civilization does not suffer in comparison with the civilization of other members of the human family. All

AN AFRICAN YOUTH

have intermingled and borrowed, the one from the other. In science, then, there is no such thing as race. In anthropology and psychology there are no such myths as inferiority and superiority of races. Because of lack of opportunity in an unhealthy environment, some may not have accomplished as much as others more favorably circumstanced; but, wherever the climatic conditions and the opportunity for development have been similar, the cultures of various members of the human families have tended to be very much alike. Even in the case of different climatic conditions the record of man tends to support this parallelism. The early civilization of the African, for example, did not differ much from that of the primitive Greeks or that of the early Romans. Looking at the native African through a glass darkly, however, the American or European is apt to conclude that because the African is physically unlike the white man he is not worth while and his achievements are not significant. This wrong impression has come from innumerable books of travelers, officeholders, and missionaries presenting more misinformation than truth.

Travelers in Africa have been largely casual observers who go through the country rapidly. Because of its infelicitous climate and strange civilization differing so widely from that of their home countries they have not wanted to tarry there long. Very few of **Misrepre-** them have seen much of the interior of the **sentations.** continent. What they have to say about Africa, then, is very much like that of the Pullman car observations of tourists spending a few hours among the Negroes in our own South only to return home to pose as authorities on the race question.

A CHAIR

Public functionaries, as a rule, have been less dependable than the travelers. While having the opportunity for more careful observation, they have been biased by their position. If the political institutions of the natives differ **Misconception** very much from those of the mother country, **of Africa.** the natives have not shown capacity for political organization. If their industrial system does not harmonize with the projected exploitation by the conquerors, the natives are lazy and shiftless. If the victims of their greed do not readily wear the foreign yoke, they are cruel savages who should be destroyed that the interlopers may have full sway without the mischievous interference of the aborigines.

From the missionaries, whom we must concede as being disposed to be an honest and upright class, we cannot expect any more truth about Africa than we obtain from travelers and public functionaries. In a few of these missionaries' accounts, however, one does see some tendency toward fair-mindedness and an effort to rise unto the appreciation of the African's contribution to civilization. But some of these authors use exaggerating language, contradicting themselves in praising the natives in one place and denouncing them in another. They often blame the natives for the faults of a system decaying in the transition to another under European occupation. Furthermore, it would be unwise to expect that partisans of a certain religious **Unscientific** system seeking to uproot another can be **accounts.** depended upon to report definitely on the virtues of the people whom they would proselyte. The missionary is the very sort of man who would be more than apt to go to the extreme of denying the existence of anything significant in the civilization of the so-called heathen. If he had a favorable impression of the natives' religion and morals he would thereby be disqualified for missionary effort. The missionary naturally thinks that what the heathen is to-day is the very thing which he should not be, and that the mission of the apostle is to make him what he ought to be. The books written by most of these missionaries, therefore, are largely worthless in arriving at an appreciation of African culture. Peeved because of the meager results in converting the heathen, missionaries too often condemn the stubborn-hearted as hopeless pagans.

The missionaries do not realize that they are often trying to supplant a system superior to their own.

The trouble in this case results from the belief that differences in culture imply superiority or inferiority. The Africans do not build their houses, tend their flocks, herd their cattle, train the youth, or appease the **Differentness** gods in the same way as the Europeans or **misunderstood.** the Americans. Then, they must be inferior beings fit only for the exploitation of their so-called superiors or swept from the face of the earth if they resist the interlopers. It seldom has occurred to these foreigners that some achievements of modern civilization now referred to as steps forward in the development of the human race may be rued to-morrow as a backward stride toward barbarism. A hundred years from to-day many of the present customs of Europeans and Americans will be ridiculed and lamented by their descendants. Even to-day the modern world is rising like a seething mass to overthrow the present economic system to go back to the communistic basis of society so well worked out among the Africans.

In view of what has been said above, one might naturally inquire as to what is the African civilization. "Nothing," the majority of Europeans and Americans would reply, "except a backward culture leavened here **An important** and there with ideas from abroad." No state- **inquiry.** ment, however, can be farther than this from the truth. It is an evidence of ignorance to think that all parallelism in culture shows borrowed ideas. Groups of persons in the same climate and similarly circumstanced will develop very much alike, although the one may be ten thousand miles removed from the other. The pottery, tools, weapons, and musical instruments of the one resemble those of the other. As one writer has well said, one bereaved in Berlin would tend to express his grief very much in the manner in which a native of Oceania would give vent to this feeling except that the former might evince a command of more beautiful language. Equalize the circumstances of the two and the method of expression will show more parallelism. Unable to understand this, pseudo-scientists have tried to trace migrations of culture from the "higher" to the "lower" races when they have no facts whatever to support their fallacies.

CONGO POTTERY

Most assuredly one group has borrowed from another; but the fact must be established by satisfactory evidence. **Foreign influences.** For example, scholars say that the Negro taught the Mediterranean world the use of iron. It has been established that Africans near the heart of the continent were the first to learn the use of the valuable metal. It has also been proved that these Africans had commercial intercourse with the seats of civilization around the Mediterranean. It is reasonable to conclude then, that the Africans gave this unusual impetus to early progress. The missionary was wrong, however, when he claimed that the Muganda natives in Central Africa had learned bathing from the English. Promptly asked by one of them what is the English custom, he replied: "A bath every day." The native rejoined: "Well, a Muganda has one every evening as well." As a matter of fact some Europeans and Americans do not bathe more than once in six months. Yet this missionary thought that the Muganda habit of cleanliness was borrowed from the English.

The foreigner here, too, often makes the mistake of confusing advance in culture with brain improvement. On this false ground most of the argument for superiority or inferiority of races is made. Environment and opportunity have been the large factors in developing culture. Scientists have proved that one stock has no more mental capacity than any other. "The mind," says one authority, "is nothing but a means of manipulating the outside world. Number, time, and space conceptions and systems become more complex and accurate, not as the human mind grows in capacity, but as activities become more varied and call for more extended and accurate systems of notation and measurement." Unable to see virtue in the civilization of these natives, however, Europeans proceed to remake them or kill them off. While they may not be

Mistakes so easy in observations.

A NATIVE

killed in warfare, they are just as easily killed off by the disruption of their socialistic, communistic manner of life, without which the native cannot exist. Many African tribes, therefore, have thus been exterminated very much in the same manner in which the Red Men in America have met their fate.

To understand Africa, moreover, the continent itself must be studied. In considering the forces effective in making the civilization of Africa it is well to note that **Features of Africa.** although it is the second continent in size, it has such few inlets that it has the shortest coastline of all. Some historians will therefore inform us that owing to this lack of good harbors, Africa, through commerce, has not had sufficient contact with the outer world to keep its civilization abreast with that of other continents. Although Africa has valuable land, it suffers from the handicap of being in the main a high elevated tableland with rapids and falls, rendering difficult the approach from the outer world; and the four great rivers, the Zambesi, the Niger, the Congo, and the Nile, are not sufficent to furnish facilities for transportation even in the interior. Africa lies in the part of the tropical world where, because of its peculiar location with reference to the directions of the winds, the climate is unusually warm and dry except in the region drained by the Congo. There the abundant rainfall produces conditions very much like those in other parts of the torrid zone.

Because of these peculiar geographic conditions there exist various civilizations determined largely by the areas in which they have developed. For general purposes Africa **African civilizations.** may be divided into three zones. Stretching from a little above the equator to the south of that circle is the region of the heaviest rainfall and consequently the most abundant vegetation. There may be found swelling streams flowing through forests teeming with animals, natural crops, and an abundance of fruits serving as food for man. On that account there is no struggle for life. Above and below this zone are two others of less rainfall and consequently less vegetation. There it is necessary for man to cultivate the fields in order to make a living. Still farther beyond the limits of the

A Scene on the Niger

last-named zones are areas of much less vegetation. In the North, there is practically none at all on account of the lack of rain. In the sections of little rainfall man must earn

A Congo Chief

a living by pasturing cattle and the like.

What, then, are these various civilizations which have sprung up in these respective zones as a result of environment? Those Africans who have lived under the equator where there is no struggle for life have not made much advancement. In that section it has not been possible for necessity to become the mother of invention. Those living in the areas requiring cultivation of the soil have made the most progress of all. It has been necessary for them to bring under their control certain **Environment as a factor.** forces of nature to increase the food supply which nature in that zone niggardly yields. The dwellers in the arid regions are handicapped by being restricted to merely one industry from which returns are obtained with increasing difficulty. While under such circumstances the achievements of the people may in one or two respects reach a high stage, they must remain a backward stock for lack of proper environment and opportunity.

This situation throws much light on slavery and its concomitants in Africa. As there is not very much of an effort to earn a living in the region under the equator, slavery in that section seldom extends beyond that of women who are usually attached to men as wives. A rich man in need of labor secures additional wives to supply that need, and a wife is easily obtained in a land where every woman is supposed to be attached to some man. In the case of wars, too, when male

Slavery in Africa.

CAPTIVES TO BE ENSLAVED

captives are taken they can be easily disposed of as slaves for the reason that they are not needed in the economy of the country. Some few of such captives are sacrificed because they are not accustomed to work and cannot be trusted to fight for a new nation. Foreign slave trade found an opportunity here.

In the zone farther north there is much demand for the labor of slaves. A living is obtained there with more difficulty than in the equatorial zone. The effort on the part of one to shift arduous labor to the shoulders of another results in the enslavement of the weak to do the work of the strong. In the arid zone a slave class is not considered indispensable, since it cannot easily maintain itself there and at the same time support superiors. As all of the population must work, free rather than slave labor is the rule.

The people of Africa inhabiting these various zones are commonly known as the black race. Yet, because of climatic differences, men in these parts became widely different from each other. Later they have tended to blend in various migrations. We are told that there was a movement of peoples and of civilizations from Asia into Egypt and from Egypt up the Nile into the interior of Africa, and again from Egypt westward to the Atlantic near the Gulf of Guinea. There was, too, a backward movement from the West to the East, causing a conflict, a fusion, and a destruction of cultures. Out of this chaos developed the Bantu, self-styled "the people," a warlike nation which imposed its sway and language on all of Southern Africa.

The movement of peoples.

In the north the controlling forces centered for some centuries in Egypt. Although commonly regarded as a country of Asiatic civilization, Egypt, like other parts of Africa, was molded in this crucible of cultures. It was the land of mixed breeds or persons comparable to Negroes passing in this country as people of color. One-third of the Egyptians, however, were distinctly black. History seems to indicate that that country was first settled by a Negro tribe that mingled later with the Mediterranean people coming from the north. There came into contact with them the Greeks, the Italians, and Carthaginians. The Greeks were thereby influenced to the extent that investigators contend that the civilization of Greece had African rather than European origin.

Egypt and the North.

Some scientists are even of the opinion that original man evolved in Africa rather than in Asia. The African, moreover, has left traces of a very early culture. Recent studies based upon actual excavation in Africa have **Primitive** led to startling conclusions. There have been **man in** discovered from place to place relics indica- **Africa.** tive of an interesting culture in this continent during prehistoric times.

Leo Frobenius believes that on the west coast of Africa there developed in the prehistoric era the Atlantes, an advanced nation of superior culture. This nation had a civilization very much like that of ancient Greece and Rome.

AN AXE OF AUTHORITY

All of Africa, however, just as most of other parts of the world, was not settled by people of exactly the same type. The records of archæologists indicate that the primitive African was not necessarily black, but of an Asiatic type of Negroid features. There are certain records which lead to the conclusion that at one time the **African** peoples of Africa were largely of the mulatto **peoples.** type. To-day the natives of Africa are not generally black but exhibit in their racial characteristics many of the divergencies found among the people of color in the United States. There are in the main such types as the small primitive stock, the larger forest Negro in the center and on the west coast, and the tall blacks in the Soudan.

In the course of time people tend to become a hybrid group just as it has happened in Europe and America. The efforts to promote racial integrity have begun too late. All Africans except those in the extreme North, however, were Negroes. This means that they were persons who, although not purely black, nevertheless had a larger percentage of Negro blood than that of any other stock. Biased investigators referring to these, however, identify them as whites if they happen to discover evidences of advanced culture even if such persons have a small percentage of Caucasian blood. The inconsistency of the position is that these Negroid persons brought into contact with Europeans and Americans elsewhere are all designated as Negroes and treated as an inferior group when they aspire to economic and social equality among whites. It can be proved that neither the majority of the Egyptians nor of the natives in Northern Africa were actually black people. In the same sense it can be established that the so-called Negroes of America are not actually black people, or that because of their interbreeding with Indians and Negroes Americans are not thoroughly white. If the Egyptians and the majority of the tribes of Northern Africa were not Negroes, then, there are no Negroes in the United States. If the biased writers must claim connection with the early tribes in Northern Africa they should be equally as willing to do the same with respect to the so-called Negroes of America.

Races in Africa.

In Central and Southern Africa, however, there can be no question as to the existence of the typical black man. The Pygmies, a primitive stock, lived in Central Africa. These primitive people are said to have covered the country from the Sahara to the Zambesi-Congo and from the coast to the Atlantic. They were a dwarf-like people of from 4 feet 2 inches to 4 feet 6 inches in height. They lived largely by hunting with bows

The Pygmies.

and arrows. It is thought that they represented a culture anterior to that of the Stone Age; but this requires further proof.

Other primitive peoples of prehistoric age were the Bushmen and Hottentots in South Africa. They have left striking evidences of their culture showing that they were among the first of men to advance in civilization. The Bushmen lived on the flesh of animals. They did not cultivate the soil. They hunted game with poisoned arrows. Relying largely upon these

Bushmen.

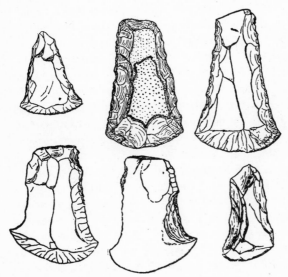

IMPLEMENTS OF THE STONE AGE

means to find a subsistence, they became masters of the knowledge of poisons and antidotes. They were not cannibals. They dwelt in caves. Because of their artistic turn of mind they painted the walls of the caves in which they lived. Some of this rock painting is still preserved. Their music showed progress in rhythm. They had a folklore exhibiting thought and poetical fancy. As a people they were said to have wonderful power of endurance, remarkable alertness, keenness of vision, and a highly developed sense of hearing. In government the political organization did not extend beyond that of a clan ruled by a chief. Their religion was a fetishism. They practiced monogamy rather than polygamy.

The Hottentots appeared in Southern Africa later than the Bushmen. They were of a larger stature than the Bushmen. They were noted for their buoyancy of spirit and fitfulness of feeling. For this reason it is

Hottentots. not surprising that they were given to merry-making, singing, and dancing. At the appearance of the new moon, it is said that members of this tribe danced and sang without intermission the whole night and poured

A PRODUCT OF THE STONE AGE

forth libations in honor of Phœbus. They possessed unusual power of imagination. They had also a lore of heavenly bodies to which they assigned names. Like the Bushmen, they were remarkable for their hardihood and power of endurance. They also used the poison arrow in hunting and in war. But they did not develop this to the degree observed among the Bushmen. Unlike the Bushmen, they were pastoral in their habits. They lived largely upon the horned cattle, sheep, and goats rather than altogether upon hunting. Yet they were not disinclined to the chase. They kept dogs for this particular purpose, both for the

sport of it and for providing themselves with a variety
of food.

In the pastoral stage the Hottentots, of course, enjoyed
food of a higher class than that of the Bushmen. The Hottentots feasted on the milk and the flesh of domestic animals. They also ate roots,
wild fruits, and certain
vegetables. In dress the
Hottentot was restricted to
skins and fur karosses of
animals. These extended
from the waist to about the
level of the knees. Like
the Bushmen, too, they
had no use for permanent
dwellings, inasmuch as
they went from place to
place to find pasturage for
their cattle. Their houses,
therefore, consisted of huts
made of sticks, set in the
ground and then bent and
bound together and cov-

ONE OF THE TYPES

ered with mats and rushes. Settled in a place for considerable time, they had a form of government consisting of
tribes and clans under separate chiefs. The Hottentots
and the Bushmen suffered from the rise of the powerful
Bantu. The Bushmen were practically destroyed by the
Dutch when they established their colonies in South Africa.

The Bantu, the most important stock that developed in
South Africa, consists of three ethnical groups of tribes.
The details do not interest us here. They were **The Bantu.**
the result of an extensive admixture of the
various tribes of Africa and possibly had some infusion
from invaders from Asia. They are, therefore, re-

ferred to by some scientists as a hybrid group. In most cases they have preserved valuable traditions of families, tribes, and clans except where certain wars have destroyed their records and dismembered the nations. They trace their history without much difficulty. This, of course, is not possible to get through books but by means of tradition and the monuments of the country.

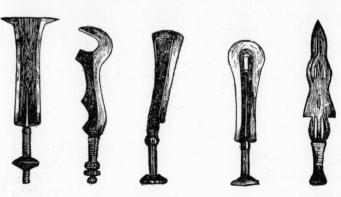

KNIVES

The chief occupation of the Bantu is agriculture. They raise principally millet, Kaffir corn or Indian corn. Africans, it is said, introduced it into America as they did **Occupations** tobacco centuries before the whites ever **of the Bantu.** reached the Western Hemisphere. They also raise pumpkins, melons, the sweet reed, sugar cane, and beans. Business developed among them to the extent that exchange was necessary. In their transactions they used cattle, sheep or goats as a medium of exchange. Their agriculture was largely primitive, however, and was carried on mainly by women inasmuch as the men devoted themselves to warfare. The weapons which they generally used were the spear and the shield.

The government of these people was strictly patriarchal,

very much like that in tribes governed by a sort of king. He was the chief magistrate, the military commander, the supreme justice, and the most high priest. Under him served petty chiefs of the clans making up the tribe. Under these were the heads of the families which in their local jurisdiction exercised practically the same powers as the chief of the tribe. This social order was very much like that of the early Greeks and Romans. The Bantu tribes, however, never had a strong centralized government like those of modern times. The Bantu lived in village communities ranging from 50 to 500 and sometimes to 1,000 persons. Each village was independent of the others socially, economically and politically. The head of the community was a headman, a viceroy representing the supreme ruler of the tribe. The village in which the chief lived, of course, was the metropolis of the nation. Other Africans showed more capacity for political organization and welded the tribes into nations of village communities.

Institutions.

AN AFRICAN LYRE

CHAPTER II

AFRICAN INSTITUTIONS A BACKGROUND

THE ease with which the Negro thrives in centers of modern civilization, in contradistinction to the destructive effect of this influence on the belated peoples like the Indians, has evoked admiration and comment. In the beginning of the treatment of the rôle played by **The African background.** the Negro in our history, then, it may be well briefly to examine the situation in Africa with a view to determining exactly what accounts for the facility with which the culture of the Negroes brought to Europe and America has so easily fused with the culture generally known as that of the white man. Has the culture of the Negro anything in common with that of the modern nations, or is the Negro merely imitative, as is often asserted by many writers?[1] History says that the African is the father of civilization.

A thorough knowledge of African institutions, therefore, is essential to understanding the African's contribution. Let us direct attention, then, to this neglected aspect of the story. In some parts of Africa the state has reached an advanced stage. Among the military tribes of the East the **African government** tends to be despotic inasmuch as **ernment.** a dictator is necessary in time of war. Such is not the situation where the people lead a peaceful life.

[1] The best authorities on African institutions are the following: E. W. Blyden's *African Life and Customs;* Casely Hayford's *Gold Coast Native Institutions;* S. M. Molema's *The Bantu, Past and Present;* and Leo Frobenius's *The Voice of Africa* in two volumes. Hundreds of other persons have written on African institutions, but most of them could not understand what they saw or heard.

The king, therefore, does not rule with absolute sway in all parts of the continent, as so many writers on African institutions have tried to make the world believe. The king is often a limited monarch. His position is sometimes hereditary, but in many cases he is chosen by a council of state. For proper cause, in some of these parts, the people through their chosen representatives may depose the king and choose another. The king's power, however, is real. The head of each community or province belonging to the state must respect the authority of the king. He is the commander-in-chief of the forces of the state and he is the arbiter of all

A Powder Flask

disputes arising among the provinces of his jurisdiction. But the local governments of his province seldom suffer from interference on the part of the king.

The king, surrounded by courtiers, maintains himself with usual pomp in his home. His household is controlled by a number of chieftains performing various functions like those of stool-bearers, sword-bearers, criers, butlers, huntsmen, farmers, and physicians. Then   **The King.** there are the body-guard of the king and other military bodies functioning through a sort of a department of war. It must not be thought, however, that the African king is merely a war chieftain. His problem is rather that of maintaining the peace. The peace is often disturbed by interference with national institutions. Most of the wars in Africa are fought to prevent such tampering with the customs of the country. Travelers and others in misrepresenting Africa, however, have said that these wars have been waged merely to supply the demand for slaves. Captives in war have been sold as slaves, but the wars were not waged for such a purpose. The selling of captives as slaves is a sequel rather than a cause of war.

The same may be said about the sacrifices of human be-

AN ANTELOPE HORN TRUMPET

ings in ancient Africa. Among some Africans there are certain religious ceremonies involving the sacrifice of human beings. Victims thus offered up, however, consist of **The sacrifice.** criminals convicted of certain infractions of the law and kept for execution in connection with religious rites. These are supposed to have a deter-

INTERESTING ROCK PAINTING

rent effect upon those permitted to witness the ordeal. While innocent persons have been thus dispatched to appease the gods, there is no general custom of sacrificing unoffending people. Here the Africans do no more than the Hebrews when "Samuel hewed Agag in pieces before the Lord or when David delivered to the Gibeonites the seven sons of Saul to be hanged before the Lord."

The institutions of the Africans are worked out on the socialistic basis. In keeping with the customs of the village community of the ancient world, strict communism or socialism is carried out on the family basis. The clan is merely a family expanded. All males of the same blood dwell to-

A BANTU DANCE—ROCK PAINTING

gether. They bring their wives to live with their kindred rather than separate on marrying. This means that the village is made up of several **Interesting customs.** joint families each occupying a distinct ward, at the head of which is the oldest male member of the family group. Just as the village is a coöperative union of families, so is the tribe a coöperative village of families. The underlying principle of the whole scheme is that of brotherhood established on social and economic equality. All institutions exist for the good of the many rather than for the benefit of the few.

In this system, therefore, no labor is requited. Everybody is supposed to work and everybody has the right of enjoying the fruits of the common labor. There can be **Equality.** no extremely rich, and there can be no extremely poor. Such a thing as capitalism or pauperism cannot exist in this society. Individualism has no place here. Collectivism is the underlying law of the communistic and socialistic system. Private property, however, does exist in these parts. While land is free to all, some things like cattle are subject to private ownership. Yet, inasmuch as all of these things come under the protection of the tribe, they are regarded as belonging in a sense to the chief. The owner considers himself merely a sort of steward enjoying the use of a possession of the king. What he gains in excess of the average share may be distributed among his relatives; but on his death the clan often decides the question of inheritance.

A DAGGER

Africans have a system of education with much merit. Leo Frobenius had never been in a country where he heard so much of education, and he never saw a place where it was more systematically carried out. There is no formal school training in native Africa except the discipline of two societies found in most communities. The one for the boys is under the direction of a fatherly old man, and that for the girls under a trustworthy matron. They are **Methods of** carefully instructed in physiology and hy-**instruction.** giene with special reference to fatherhood and motherhood. It is the ambition of every male to produce offspring. It is the desire of every woman to become a mother. As the clan or tribe needs strong men for its protection, this tendency is encouraged.

Early in life, about the regular school age in modern countries, the African boy begins his education. He is required to look after the kids, the young goats, and to make observation in agricultural methods. The boy is required later to tend larger animals and finally to herd cattle. He also undergoes circumcision very much like that of the Hebrews. The girls of the same age begin the study of household and domestic duties such as supplying the family with water, cleaning the house, pounding the corn, and preparing food. They continue at this sort of training until they reach the age of becoming housewives. After having been under strict supervision of matrons who have instructed them in the rudimentary instructions of motherhood and have taught them the duty of wives to their husbands, the course terminates with ceremony. This consists mainly of dancing. In preparation for this dance, a thing which is a part of the training, they paint their faces with bewildering colors.

A KNIFE

In marrying the African youth has an eye single to the good of the communistic state. In keeping with the custom among most people of such a stage of civilization, the ceremony is arranged after the contract is made by the parents of the young people. They themselves have very little to do with it. The groom is accustomed to give a number of cows, goats,

Marriage.

sheep, or the like, to the parents of the girl he has chosen. These, however, are not intended as an actual purchase of the wife, as maligners of Africans often say. They are rather intended as a means of securing the wife against ill treatment. If ill used, she can leave her husband and return to her father, but these gifts are not returned. Of course, there are cases of an actual purchase of women as happens

in any slaveholding country like the Southern United
States before the Civil War. There is no more of an actual
purchase in such marriage arrangements in Africa, however, than in some of the dowry contracts common in
Europe and America to-day.

The marriage ceremony, like others, is usually celebrated
with dancing. The most of this festive performance is

ANOTHER SORT OF DANCE

not according to any particular rhythm, but resembles
rather a confused and independent jumping in which all
participate. Members of the families concerned, however,
are accustomed to stage also a more graceful exercise in
keeping with the art, the description of which has found its
way into modern literature. The musical instruments are
drums, horns, reed and stringed instruments.

Connected with marriage sometimes, too, is polygamy.

As women do most of the work to release the men for hunting and the protection of the state, a man's wealth may be determined by the number of wives he has. The husband, however, usually concentrates his attention on one of the group. She is his household manager. The others are treated mainly as servants. This also has been misunderstood and referred to as backward- **Polygamy.** ness when compared with the monogamy supposed to be practiced among the Christians. As a matter of fact, however, polygamy is not found among all Africans. Where it is found, all men are not economically prepared to indulge in it. A man cannot easily support more than one wife. Polygamy, then, is restricted largely to the official class and the well-to-do, as it illegally exists to-day among such elements in modern countries. Some tribes, moreover, practice monogamy in preference to polygamy.

Polygamy, moreover, grows out of their peculiar social-istic system. Because of frequent wars so many soldiers are killed off that there are more women than men. Polygamy is practiced, then, because of the benefit resulting to the state in the production of sufficient able-bodied men to protect it. As a rule a woman must attach herself to some man. Polygamy in Africa, moreover, renders impossible spinsterhood and prostitution, which exist among the so-called civilized people. The Africans practice openly what Europeans and Americans practice clandestinely. There are no loose women among the people of Africa. Every woman has her own marital connection and recognizes the tie as binding. There are cases of moral lapses, but no evidence of a general profligacy of sexes. Delinquents are deterred therefrom by the strict laws punishing adultery with maiming, mutilation, or death.

In another way, too, the Africans have often been misunderstood. Travelers have occasionally referred to them as thieves and liars. Examples of their mendacity consist

mainly of efforts to mislead the foreigner whom they sus-
pect as desirous of doing some injury to them or to their
Morals of tribe. If, for example, the foreigner inquires
Africans. as to the right road to the house of the chief,
the native invariably sends him in the contrary direction.
If he wants to know the distance to a certain town, the
native informs him that it is about twice or three times as

AN AFRICAN STOVE

far as it actually is; and
when he has gone as far
as directed another na-
tive may inform him
that he is on the wrong
road. To weaken their
enemies, moreover, peo-
ple in this stage are ac-
customed to take cattle,
goats, sheep, or other
property; for while they
weaken the tribe from
which they are taken
they strengthen their
own particular group.
Any person able to contribute thereby to the welfare of
the tribe is considered a leader of worth, and may rise to
the chieftaincy of the tribe. These things were customary
among the American Indians and the Americans find
them so to-day among the Filipinos. The custom differs
little, too, from that of Europeans and Americans; for
they have one code of law and ethics which they follow
when dealing with other races and a different code in dealing with their own kind.

In their own group, living among themselves, the Africans consider an untruth a sin. Any one disturbing the
property of another, moreover, becomes a criminal, subject
to the severe penalty of a fine, imprisonment or even death.

In fact, locks and safes which are necessary in America and
Europe are not required among the uncontaminated natives of Africa. The patterns of morality of the Hebrews
and certain Africans, the Kaffirs, for example, are strikingly coincident. The Kaffirs have laws to meet every
crime committed. "Theft is punished by restitution and
fine; injured cattle, by death or fine; false witness, by a
heavy fine; adultery, by fine or death; rape, by fine or
death; poisoning or witchcraft, by death and confiscation
of property; murder, by death or fine; treason or deser-
tion from the tribe, by death and confiscation."

POTTERY

Running throughout the system underlying the life of
the African native is his religion. He adheres to this,
even to the very letter of the law as handed down by his
forefathers. Roughly speaking, we may say this religion
is a belief in a world of spirits and an effort to be guided
by them. The African believes in God. He **African**
believes that man is immortal. His spirit **religion.**
can never die. Since the beginning of time, then, the
world has become filled with spirits. Man can therefore
commune face to face with the spirits of the departed.
Referring to the custom on the Gold Coast, Casely Hayford

says: "You should watch him as he takes offerings of food and drink to the graveside. There he carefully sets a chair for the dear one gone before, then places the meal in order, and pours out a libation, addressing the spirit of the departed the while. He earnestly believes that the spirit of the departed relative hovers around him by day as well as by night, and he has both the physical and the spiritual sense to perceive its presence. He sees in the mammiferous bat, winging its flight from room to room at night in the home once dear to the loved one, who is supposed to dominate it, a kindly providence which does not leave him all forlorn in his grief, but sends the spirit of the departed back occasionally to watch and to protect. He even speaks to it in endearing terms at times, and would fain believe that it understands and is in full sympathy with him. You may sneer at the seeming simplicity of the native mind, but the Aborigines believe that there are mysteries in this world yet unrevealed to man. He, the Native, implicitly believes in ghosts, and has many an authentic story to tell of some strange visitation which he has experienced. Nay, more, his sense of smell detects the presence of a ghost in a house."

Speaking further on this wise, the same author says: "Mark you, he does not look to communion with the gross, material matter that lies mouldering in the grave; but he looks to that indefinable something beyond which has defied the reason of mankind for all time. He looks beyond his present squalid surroundings to a world hereafter where he will meet every member of his family, and particularly those whom he has dearly loved, and where he will meet with them in joyous intercourse as he has done in this world. It matters not what happens to-day, since to-morrow may find him in the grave and at rest with his forefathers. In this happy frame of mind he goes through life contentedly, free from

Communion with the spirit.

carking care, and wonders sometimes at all the excitement
and ado of men of another race. And as for a material hell,
the scarecrow of the missionaries, he merely smiles at such
a suggestion. Is there not trouble enough in this world?
God knows there is. Why should God add trouble to
trouble?"[1]

In Africa one finds a varying conception of God. Among
some strictly African natives, in Yorubaland, however,
Leo Frobenius found these ideas of divinity: "The idea
of the generative and fertilizing godlike force is so persistent that it is not confined to human beings; but, on
the contrary, the first-fruits of every spring-   **God in**
sowing, the firstlings of stock-raising without   **Africa.**
any exception, again become the share of the deity in the
form of sacrificial offerings in return for having been by
him begotten. And not only so, many other things go to
prove the significance and inevitability of the idea that
the Deity must necessarily be the originator of all succes-
sive generations. And, therefore, almost all the prayers of
Yorubans, all their rituals, always culminate in the petition
for fruitfulness of their fields, the blessings of children in
their families, and aid in every kind of propagation.

"Now, an Orisha (a god) can just as well have his home
on a grand altar, rich in symbolic ornamentation, as in a
naked, little hut. He is manifest in it and to no lesser degree than in the control of the natural agencies in which he
mythologically dwells. The River God is not the river;
he only animates it, he is effective in it, proceeds from it.
And the Sun God is not the actual sun; the   **Nature**
divinity lives in the sun. Every Orisha has   **as God.**
taken up his abode in his natural attributes, and may, if
he so will, leave them, move about amongst his family, and
there plant the seeds of blessing and abundance of increase.
Precisely in the same way he can inspire, i.e., enter into,

1 Casely Hayford, *Gold Coast Native Institutions*, 101-103.

those specially destined to receive him, so that they behave
as though possessed.'' [2]

[2] The African story of the creation, although found in various
versions, differs little from that of the Hebrews. In it appears also
the idea of the fall and redemption of man. Leo Frobenius found
in Africa one running like this: "At first there was no earth.
There was Okun (or Olokun), the ocean, a water stretched over
all things. Above it was Olorun. Olorun, the Orisha of the sky, and
Olokun, the Orisha of the sea, were coeval. They contained (or
possessed) all that there was. Olorun had two sons. The first
one's name was Orishalla (the same as Ostaballa, who here is
also simply called Orisha); the younger's, Odudua. Olorun summoned Orisha. He gave him some earth. He gave him a hen with
fingers (? claws) (Adje-alesse-manu). He said to him, 'Climb down'
(or, go down to earth), 'and make the earth upon Okun.' Orisha
went. On the way he found some palm-wine. He began to drink
and got drunken. Then he slumbered. Olorun saw this. Then
Olorun summoned Odudua and said to him: 'Thy (elder) brother
has got drunken on his way down below. Go thou, take the sand
and the hen with five fingers and make the earth upon Okun.'
Odudua went. He took the sand. He went down and laid it on
the sea. He put the hen with five fingers on it. The hen began
to scratch and spread the sand about and forced the water aside.
Ilife was the spot where this took place, round, which, at first,
the sea still flowed. Odudua ruled the land of Ilife as its first
king. The sea of Ilokun grew less and less and ran away through
a small hole from there a hole from which to this day one can
fetch the holy water—much water and it never fails. It is called
Osha. Now, Orisha was very wrath that he had not created the
earth; he began to wage war against Odudua. They contended
for a long time, but then made peace. They both went underground and were never seen again."
A second version runs thus:
"In the beginning the earth was not. There was only water.
Olorun sent down Oshalla. He gave him a ball of sand on his
way. He said: 'Spread this out upon the face of the waters.'
Oshalla went. On the road Oshalla picked up a flask of palm-
wine. He tasted it and said: 'This is good.' He drank while
going. Whenever he was athirst he drank a mouthful. He
drank the first mouthful very early. Then he grew weary, went
to sleep and forgot what Olorun had bidden him. Then the
other Orishas took a mirror (Awo-aje), looked into it and saw
that Oshalla had been drinking down below, gone to sleep and
forgotten Olorun's behest. Thereupon Olorun sent Odudua, saying: 'Do thou what I told Oshalla to do.' Odudua was a strong
man. He took a ball of earth with him. He descended. He made
the earth and pushed the water aside. Olorun then gave Odudua
a hen, called Adje-alesse-mahun; it was a hen with five fingers;
it pushed the water back so that it became the sea. When Odudua
and Oshalla had finished their work, they went into the earth

This religion is administered by a priestcraft of which the king himself is head. However, the actual administration of the system is not generally interfered with by the king. With this religious effort the priests unite the function of the medicine men. Working in this   **African** way the priests treat both mind and body.   **priestcraft.** The training of the priest begins in early childhood by sending him to another community to undergo training for a number of years. This consists of the study of things spiritual and also the use of herbal remedies. The completion of this training is celebrated with an exciting dance in which the fetish is said to come upon him. Some of these medico-priests have been known to cure diseases which have baffled the skill of European physicians. They are experts in herbal treatment. These medico-priests, however, like most of those operating among primitive people, clothe their operations with sufficient secrecy to make the people believe in their power to do many things which are impossible. Although the laity may detect the imposition, the office of the priest is so sacred among the Africans that they do not expose them when caught.

Studying the religious system, in which there is so much good in spite of the irrational ideas involved, one can see the reasons for the ease with which the Negro has accepted Christianity. The religion of Jesus is an Oriental production. It easily appeals to the mind of the Negro, which is also Oriental. The mind of the white man is Occidental. He has, therefore, failed to understand and appreciate Christianity. The study of the African religion, too, leads one to understand how it is the greatest impediment to the missionary work in that continent. It is extremely

at Ilife where they had begun their labors, and were turned to stone. Since then men worshiped these stones. Oba-diu is the high priest of Oshalla. Odudua is greatly feared. So powerful is this Godhead that before the people in Ilife can speak the name of Odudua, they must slay a sheep and drink its blood."

difficult for the native to abandon his own religion when it so permeates the life of the people that to do so means a declaration of hostility to the king, the most high priest, **Difficulties of** and a repudiation of all of the traditions of **missionaries.** the native's forefathers. It is almost impossible to change the religion of a man without changing the other elements in his civilization. For this reason it has been said that one railroad is worth a thousand missionaries. But such an innovation as a railroad or steamboat brings many evils in its train. In thus changing the civilization of these people by foreign aggression they fall victims to social diseases, intemperance, prostitution, and race hate.

CHAPTER III

CONSIDERED from the continental point of view, however, the life of the African is complicated. Being the second largest continent with various sorts of climate, Africa presents all of the aspects of life in **Occupations** other regions. Above we have tried to indi- **of Africans.** cate the chief interests of the people by the designation of certain zones. While this is helpful, there are so many exceptions to be made that we should not consider these terms as absolutely conclusive. Africans have been and are now doing things very much in the same manner as we find them done by other peoples similarly circumstanced. In a short sketch like this, moreover, it is impossible to figure out accurately the occupations or industries of all the people of a continent. Considered as a whole, however, there are certain pursuits which may be thought of as typical of large areas of that continent. Cattle raising is one of the chief industries of Africa. This is marked by the kraal, or cattle pen, found in almost every village of the cattle zone. This is a sort of center of the commercial life of the people. The majority of Africans look upon their cattle, sheep, or goats as the most valuable property. They often use them in exchange as we do money. Some sort of farming, too, is general among most Africans, although not that of modern times. They cultivate maize, rice, millet and vegetables. Nature enables them to produce easily

37

also yams, ground nuts, pumpkins, melons and beans. Such fruits as the plantain, banana, orange, and the mango flourish there as in other tropical countries. Coffee, too, may be produced in large quantities. Africans have not been generally interested in their mineral wealth except in making use of iron.[1]

In the construction of their homes the natives of the rainy region seem to have followed the model of the "ant hill." There the native, like the ant, has had to look out for himself in building his hut high enough to be beyond **Home** the reach of the rising water. The homes of **construction.** the natives are thatched huts built sometimes upon beams of hard wood like ebony or mahogany found in abundance in certain parts of Africa. Softer woods

AN ANT HILL

would be quickly destroyed by the maggots which feast thereupon in that climate. In their villages the homes of the tribal chiefs and wealthy may be more imposing structures. The arrangement of these homes in clusters or sometimes according to design presents an interesting picture.

In facing the forces of nature to wrest therefrom a livelihood, the African has given a lesson to the so-called

[1] For more extensive treatment see J. Deniker's *Races of Men,* J. Finot's *Race Prejudice,* F. Ratzel's *The History of Mankind,* Franz Boas's *The Mind of Primitive Man,* Spiller's *Inter-Racial Problems,* C. Bücher's *Industrial Revolution,* Casely Hayford's *Ethiopia Unbound* and his *Native Institutions,* James Bryce's *Impressions of South Africa,* Leo Frobenius's *The Voice of Africa,* G. Sergi's *The Mediterranean Race,* Felix DuBois's *Timbuctoo, the Mysterious;* Lady Lugard's *A Tropical Dependency,* and David Randall Maciver's *Medieval Rhodesia.*

civilized world. In the industrial arts they have shown conclusively that they were once the greatest metal workers of the world. Developing as such, the Africans were the first to smelt iron and use the forge. To this **Industrial** race, therefore, belongs the credit for the gift **arts.** of the most useful thing to man. Upon its use has been established the civilization of modern times. We cannot imagine ourselves without the use of iron unless we think of the most barbarous state of the prehistoric period when men dwelt in caves and lived by pillage and plunder. In the all-wise plan by which our des-tiny is determined every race has the capacity for certain definite contribu-tions. The discovery of iron is the outstanding contribution of the Negro.

AN AFRICAN HOME

It is a grave error to think of Africans altogether as people working in the rough. In the use of metals the Africans have not restricted themselves to crude methods. By practically all persons who have made a study of the industrial arts of the African, we have a high estimate of what they have produced. Their pottery, **Metal** basketry, implements, and weapons show the **workers.** highest of skill and the keenest appreciation of the beau-tiful. Although deprived of foreign contact, they have shown here a capacity in industrial arts beyond that of anything contemporaneous in Europe. Their cutlery not only compares favorably with that of Sheffield, but even shows workmanship and inventive genius unexcelled in the modern world.

Advancing still further, the African, even with limited evidence available, has sufficient to show that he has equaled if not excelled the world in fine arts. In evidence **Fine** the archæologists **arts.** offer the figures of Sherbro and the megaliths of Gambia. These indicate a superior culture which we have seldom considered as possible among Africans. Further evidence has been supplied in the discoveries of stone implements belonging to the prehistoric period in South Africa. Other discoveries in Rhodesia are decidedly convincing as to the unusually artistic mind of the African. According to evidences brought to light by such investigators as Schliemann, Sir Arthur Evans, Giuseppe Sergi and Count de Gobineau, the stimulus to Greek art came from Africa. Probably the most striking of all these discoveries is that of the antique works of art of Benin described by Pitt Rivers and Felix von Luschan. These works were brought to light as a result of the punitive expedition sent upon this town

A Hanging Lamp in Bronze
from Benin

at the mouth of the Niger River in 1897. They represent
a fine art of such an early stage that there is no actual
record as to the date of its production. In characteristic
style Europeans thought of this art as resulting from
European influence. Further investigation, however, has

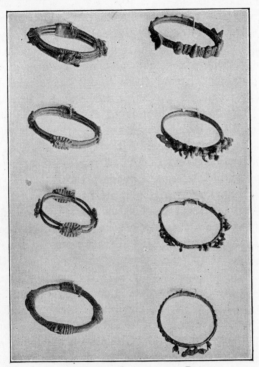

BRACELETS IN BRONZE FROM BENIN

shown that these productions are characteristically African. They could not have resulted from European influence because they belonged to an early period when Europeans were savages.

Although the Africans have made unusual contributions
to the dance, music, and sculpture, however, some of the

most advanced nations have not succeeded in political organization. Yet Africa itself is not a fair test of the political possibilities of the Negro. In the first place, as stated above, the continent is cut off from the rest of the world by an unbroken coast line of a plateau area permit-

Political ting few navigable rivers. Having had such
organization. little opportunity to profit by contact with other parts, Africa deserves unusual credit for the political institutions which it has independently developed. While immensely rich in vegetable oils, fibers, gums and hardwoods, foreigners found those things too accessible elsewhere to warrant the hardships necessary for invading the all but impenetrable interior of Africa. At that time, moreover, little difference in the situation resulted from the gold and diamonds which to-day crown Africa as one of the richest of the continents. These are treasures which have come into their own in modern times.

In the interior of Africa itself nature provided other handicaps to political organization. Both the climate and the physiographic features of the continent indicate the difficulty of developing political institutions. On the West

Handicaps to Coast, for example, most of the land is so
progress. low and marshy, so full of small streams and prodigious growth that travel is decidedly difficult. Road building is almost impossible in this section, and in the case of clearing a path, nature is so prolific here that in a few days the rapid growth will close up the thoroughfare. Unsuitable, too, for horses and mules, which easily fall victims of the tsetse fly, the problem of transportation is still more complicated. The highest form of political organization attainable under such circumstances, therefore, is that of a tribe ruled by the chief. Occasionally, too, there may arise a chieftain with sufficient following to bring under his sway a number of these tribes to form a kingdom.

On the East Coast, however, nature renders possible a more extensive development of political institutions. While the climate is the same, the country is somewhat open and the means of communication are far better **African** than on the West Coast. This is true of the **kingdoms.** Sudan and also of Dahomey. Northeast of Dahomey, the Fulahs, similarly circumstanced, established a number of kingdoms which manifested evidences of ability to endure.

A CUSTOM—ROCK PAINTING

Near the head of the Niger, the Mandingan Negroes showed much capacity for government in founding the Wassula kingdom, of much influence and power in that section. In the East there appeared also the Hausa kingdom resembling a federation very much like that of Switzerland. West of Lake Tchad developed the kingdom of Bornu, which has enjoyed its growth largely since the invasion of the Mohammedans, about the year 1000.

It will no doubt be interesting, therefore, to trace briefly the rise and fall of some of these empires. The highest of these civilizations centered in the Nile region, with Ethiopia around the head waters of that river and **The Negro in** Egypt along the lower. "Ancient Egypt **the Empires.** knew the Negro, both bond and free," says Chamberlain, "and his blood flowed in the veins of not a few of the mighty Pharaohs. Nefertari, the famous Queen of Aahmes, the King of Egypt, who drove the Hyksos from the land and founded the 18th Dynasty (*ca.* 1700 B.C.), was a Negress of great beauty, strong personality, and re-

markable administrative ability. She was for years associated in the government with her son, Amen-hotep I, who
succeeded his father. Queen Nefertari was highly venerated and many monuments were erected in her honor; she
was venerated as 'ancestress and founder of the 18th
Dynasty' and styled 'the wife of the God Ammon,' etc.
Another strain of Negro blood came into the line of the
Pharaohs with Mut-em-ua, wife of Thothmes IV, whose

A MYTH—ROCK PAINTING

son, Amen-hotep III, had a Negroid physiognomy. Amen-
hotep III was famous as a builder and his reign (*ca.* 1400
B.C.) is distinguished by a marked improvement of Egyptian art and architecture. He it was who built the great
temple of Ammon at Luxor and the colossi of Memnon.
Besides these marked individual instances, there is the fact
that the Egyptian race itself in general had a considerable
element of Negro blood, and one of the prime reasons why
no civilization of the type of that of the Nile arose in
other parts of the continent, if such a thing were at all
possible, was that Egypt acted as a sort of channel by
which the genius of Negro-land was drafted off into the
service of Mediterranean and Asiatic culture. In this
sense Egyptian civilization may be said, in some respects,
to be of Negro origin. Among the Semitic peoples whose
civilizations were so numerous and so ancient on the shores
of the Mediterranean and throughout Western Asia, the

Negro, as in Egypt, made his influence felt, from the lowest
to the highest walks of life, sometimes as a slave, sometimes
as the freest of citizens. As cup-bearer, or confidential
adviser, he stood next to kings and princes and as faithful
eunuch he enhanced and extended the power of the
other sex in lands where custom confined them to the four
walls of their dwellings, or restricted to the utmost their
appearance and their actions in public. And women from
Ethiopia, 'black but comely,' wives or favorite slaves of
satraps and of kings, often were the real   **Influence**
rulers of Oriental provinces and empires.   **abroad.**
Nor have the Negroes in these Asiatic countries been absent from the ranks of the musician and the poet, from
the time of Solomon to that of Haroun al Raschid and
beyond in the days of emirs and sultans. One must not
forget the Queen of Sheba, with her dash of Negro blood,
said, together with that of the great Solomon, to have been
inherited by the sovereign of Abyssinia. When under the
brilliant dynasty of the Ommiades (661-750 A. D.), the
city of Damascus was one of the glories of the world, its
galaxy of five renowned poets included Nosseyeb, the
Negro. And we can cross the whole of Asia and find the
Negro again, for, when, in far-off Japan, the ancestors of
the modern Japanese were making their way northward
against the Ainu, the aborigines of that country, the leader
of their armies was Sakanouye Tamuramaro, a famous
general and a Negro.'' [2]

The story of the Negro restricted to Africa is still more
interesting. Ethiopia and Egypt were at first united, but
in the course of time separated as two distinct empires.
There were various wars between the Egyp-   **Ethiopia and**
tians and the Ethiopians when the former   **Egypt.**
were trying to wrest the country from the invaders of the

[2] *Atlanta University Studies, Select Discussions of Race Problems,* pp. 86-87.

north. The affairs of the Ethiopian and Egyptian empires did not apparently become separate until during the Middle Empire of Egypt, when Nepata and Meroe became centers of a largely native civilization. The new empire, however, continued its wars against the Ethiopians and gradually incorporated the country, until Ethiopia finally became subject to that land. In the course of time, however, Ethiopia asserted itself, easily overran Egypt, and appointed a son of the king of Ethiopia to rule the land of the Pharaohs.

The Negro was then at his best as a constituent factor in the affairs of the Egypto-Ethiopian empire. When, however, the country was conquered by the Assyrians and then by the Persians, Egypt became subject to the invaders from Asia, whereas Ethiopia continued its way. Ethiopia was again invaded by a Greek influence from the East and the influence of the tribes from the Soudan on the West, but the Ethiopian language and government tended to endure. Ethiopians persistently gave trouble **The Egypto-Ethiopian empire.** to the Romans, who undertook to subdue them and failed thoroughly to do so because of their interior position. This country lay asleep during the Middle Ages. In later years it took the name of Nubia. After having experienced various conquests and subjugations resulting in changes which have not yet succeeded in blotting out altogether its ancient civilization, it finally became known as Abyssinia.

With the exception of what the historian Herodotus has left in fragmentary form, not much is known about the early nations established on the Niger or the Soudan. They **Soudan and the Niger.** are connected in history with Ethiopia and Egypt as centers of culture distinctly African. The first extensive accounts date from the approach of the Mohammedans about the year 1000. The Mohamme-

dans came largely as traders and gave much stimulus to
the rise of commerce among these people. The invaders
did not utterly change the civilization, but they influenced
the life and history of the people. Drawing no color line,
these Arabs accepted the blacks as equals and carried
some of them to Arabia. This gave rise to the Arabised
blacks represented by Antar. In Arabia he became the
military hero and one of the great poets of Islam. Carrying their civilization later into Spain, the Africans attained distinction there also. A Negro poet resided at
Seville, and a Negro founded a town in lower Morocco.

In the eleventh century the Moslems found in the west
the far advanced kingdom of Ghana, which they conquered
after much resistance. The natives had an army of two
hundred thousand men and sufficient wealth **The Kingdom**
to support it. When this kingdom declined **of Ghana.**
in the thirteenth century, Melle superseded it and added
greatly to its wealth by the expansion of its commerce
through welcoming the Mohammedan traders. The Mohammedans found evidence of advanced civilizations even
in the Congo, and learned that the Zulu chiefs, whose
armies swept southeastern Africa, exhibited unusual power
of military organization.

Among the city states where this exceptional culture
was discovered was that of Jenne. From this the modern
name Guinea has been obtained. This city experienced,
as usual, migrations and movements frequent **The State**
in other parts of Africa, resulting in the de- **of Jenne.**
struction of many of the evidences of civilization. But,
according to several travelers, there was found an advanced
culture in their terra-cotta industry, in their achievements
in clay, stone and iron, in their glass beads, earthen and
glassware, and in the dexterity of their weaving. This
civilization shows the city group like that around Timbuctoo

and Hausa. These cities had a government largely like that

Timbuctoo. of an autonomy of modern times—what we would call the social and industrial state, but of an essentially democratic order. These achievements so impressed the world that in keeping with other claims based on prejudice, biased men have undertaken to accredit whites with this culture.

There developed also the states commonly known as the Ashanti and Dahomey. In their orgies of war and sacrifice of human beings, these states exhibited a striking **Ashanti and** contrast to the **Dahomey.** city democracy of "elevated religious ideas, organized industry and noble art." So far as known, however, the white race has not yet made a strenuous effort to prove that this civilization was Caucasian. Backward conditions rendered the country so weak that it finally developed into a region of internecine wars which paved the way for the lucrative slave trade carried on by the Christian nations.

ARMS AND ORNAMENTS

In the regions of the Great Lakes flourished other centers of civilization. There were found evidences of advanced culture in the mining of silver and gold and in trade in precious stones. These Africans were the first to smelt iron and to use it as the great leverage of civilization. **The Lake** They had useful iron implements, erected **Region.** well-constructed buildings and fortifications, made beautiful pottery, and worked extensively in the

various metals. As indicated by their utensils and implements, they had made much more advancement in religion
than some of the other tribes. They had temples of significance comparing favorably with those of the Greeks and
Romans. The government established was based on

slavery. The people devoted themselves to
agriculture and other industries.

There emerged, too, the large kingdom of
Songhay, covering the period from the year
700 to 1335 A. D. This nation, according to
Es-Sadi, the author of the *Tarikh Es-Soudan,*
had three well-connected dynasties distinguished by great warriors who extended the
territory of the empire, and statesmen who
distinguished themselves in ad- The Kingdom
ministering its affairs. After of Songhay.
resisting the Mohammedans for some time,
the sixteenth king was converted to their faith
about the year 1000. Among the greatest of
these rulers was Soni Ali, noted for his military exploits and his success as a statesman.

A CYLINDRICAL
VESSEL

The country again saw something like a
return to a golden age under another distinguished ruler called Mohammed Askia. He brought the
country into contact with Egypt and the outer world, and
finally marched against neighboring empires, which he
conquered and ruled with a provincial system very much
like that of Rome. He established schools of learning and
promoted the study of law, literature, the natural sciences,
and medicine.

In the end, however, this empire fell into the hands of
undesirable rulers. According to the pious annalist, ''All
was changed in a moment. Danger took the place of seren-
ity, destitution of abundance; trouble, calamities and

violence succeeded to tranquillity. Everywhere the populations began to destroy each other. In all places and in every direction rapine became the law, war spared neither life nor property, nor the position of the people. Disorder was general, and it spread everywhere till it reached at last the highest degree of intensity." "Things continued thus," adds the historian, "until towards the moment in which the Songhay dynasty approached its end, and

A Chopper

its empire ceased to exist. At this moment faith was exchanged for infidelity; there was nothing forbidden by God which was not openly done. Men drank wine, they gave themselves up to vice. . . . Because of these abominations, the Almighty in His vengeance drew down upon the Songhay the victorious army of the Moors, whom he brought through terrible sufferings from a distant country. Then the roots of this people were separated from the trunk, and the chastisement they underwent was exemplary."

All of these facts set forth, however, show that African culture prior to the exploitation of the New World was in many respects like the culture of Europe. The natives **African culture.** far removed from the equator had reached the stage of easily earning a subsistence by using iron implements. European nations were late in learning this. In art and architecture they had advanced far beyond the primitive stage, in literature their achievements attained the rank of the world's best classics in the *Tarikh Es-Soudan,* and in religion and morals most of them kept abreast with the times. In government the Africans united the best in democracy and monarchy. Theirs was a slave society, but there was a healthy sentiment against the exploitation of men. With the thinking class, birth did not differ from birth; "as the freeman was born so was the slave." "In the beginning," said a pious African, "our Lord created all; with Him there is neither slave nor freeman, but every one is free." "To love a king," the African thought, "is not bad, but a king who loves you is better." And it sounds a little socialistic to hear the proverbs, "If thou art poor do not make the rich man thy friend," "If thou goest to a foreign country, do not alight at a rich man's house," or "It is better to be poor and live long than rich and die young."

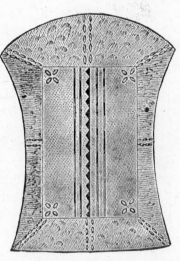

A SHIELD

The African mind, too, exhibited evidences of philosophy not to be despised. The native philosopher found three friends in "courage, sense and insight." The African realized that "the lack of knowledge is darker than night," that "an ignorant man is a slave," and that "whoever works without knowledge works uselessly." "Not to know," he believed, "is bad;

African proverbs.

not to wish to know is worse." Adhering to a high standard of morals, the African taught the youth that "there

is no medicine for hate" and that "he who bears malice is a heathen; he who injures another brings injury to himself." To emphasize opportunity the moralist reminded his fellows that "the dawn does not come twice to wake a man." To teach politeness he asserted that "bowing to a dwarf will not prevent your standing erect again." In emphasizing the truth, he asserted that "lies, however numerous, will be caught by truth when it rises," and "the voice of truth is easily known." The selfish man was warned that "if you love yourself, others will hate you; if you humble yourself, others will love you." Among the Africans there was a feeling that "a man with wisdom is better off than a stupid man with any amount of charm and superstition." Such sentient expressions as "A butterfly that brushes against thorns will tear his wings," and "He who cannot move an ant and yet tries to move an elephant shall find his folly," have the ring of the plantation philosophy developed in the United States. The proverbs "When the fox dies, fowls do not mourn," and "He who goes with a wolf will learn to howl," exhibit more than ordinary mental development.

AN ORNA-
MENTAL VESSEL
IN BRONZE
FROM BENIN

CHAPTER IV

FOREIGN AGGRESSION

IT happened that centuries ago, when the civilization of the blacks was not unlike that of the emerging modern Europe, Africa was disturbed within by migrations and from without by foreign aggression. Such a movement overthrew the Roman Empire and destroyed **Disorder in** its civilization. Being too weak to resist **Africa.** invaders while dealing with enemies at home, Africa yielded to the attacks of the restless nations. When the Bantu hordes had destroyed the peace of the African empires, there appeared the Mohammedans on the East Coast in quest of slaves to supply their harems and armies.[1]

During the seventh and eighth centuries the Mohammedan religion well established itself in Western Asia and began to take over Northern Africa. At first Africans already enslaved were bought from their masters and used in war, as was the custom throughout Europe and Asia. When, however, there came a demand for a larger number of slaves than could thereby be supplied, they were seized by well-planned methods involving the enslavement and depopulation of large districts of Africa. This led to the overthrow of African nations long since established as centers of culture and the rise of other states committed to the policy of profiting by the lucrative slave trade.

[1] For this aspect of the subject the following are helpful: Sir Charles Lucas's *The Partition of Africa;* T. K. Ingram's *History of slavery and Serfdom;* John R. Spear's *The American Slave Trade;* F. H. Buxton's *The African Slave Trade;* and T. Clarkson's *African Slave Trade.*

This trade finally reached the very interior of the continent and became the most cruel traffic in human flesh theretofore known to the world.   It is only of late that it can
be said that this Mohammedan slave trade has been actually
Mohammedan checked.   It remained as a disgrace to certain
slavery.   Eastern nations during the latter part of the
nineteenth century and even into the twentieth.   Slavery
among the Mohammedans, however, was not altogether a

AN AFRICAN FORGE

hopeless condition.   If the slave professed faith in Islam
he might become a communicant in that connection, enjoying equality with the richest and the best, accepted on the
principle of the brotherhood of man.

Finally came Europeans, too, working their way to the
Far East and Australia by way of the Cape of Good Hope.
Marco Polo's account of Cipango or Japan was a stimulus.
This undertaking was a conspicuous development of the
Renaissance which resulted in the discovery of America.

Foreign Aggression

TIMBUCTOO

The moving spirit in the early enterprise was Prince Henry of Portugal, who sent out men to trade in gold dust and Negro slaves. They proceeded sometimes under **Coming of the** the pretext of converting the heathen. Prince **Portuguese.** Henry died in 1460; but others pushed the exploration as far as the Equator by 1471 and reached the Congo by 1484. Two years later Diogo Cam went a thousand miles south of the Equator and "set up a stone cross on the border of Hottentot land. Then came Bartholomew Diaz, who was driven by storm beyond the Cape of Good Hope in 1486. Vasco da Gama doubled the Cape in 1497 and explored the coast as far as Mombasa and Melinde. He proceeded thence to Calicut in India in 1498. The Portuguese established strongholds on the bay of Arguin and at Elmina on the Gold Coast. They extended their influence into Angola and Mozambique and even learned something about parts of the interior of Africa.

The French, following close upon the Portuguese, if not preceding them, made a settlement in the Canaries in 1402. They later entered the region of the Senegal. The English made an unsuccessful attempt to trade with the Guinea coast in 1481. William Hawkins, the father of Sir **Other** John Hawkins, ventured to trade in slaves **troubles.** on the coast from 1530 to 1532 and in 1553. Then came his son, Sir John Hawkins, who in 1562 took more than a hundred slaves from Guinea to Santo Domingo. Uniting religion with the slave trade, he ordered his crews to "serve God daily" and "to love one another." He went first to Hispaniola with three hundred Negroes whom he traded for pearls, hides, and other products. The second voyage was more hazardous, and he failed in the third. In spite of his murderous plundering, however, his chronicler entreats that "his name be praised forevermore, Amen."

An African Village

Yet men of the type of Hawkins are not to be unsympathetically condemned. In that day there was no sharp distinction between a pirate and an honorable seaman. Some of the sea rovers held commissions of their "God-fearing sovereigns" who promoted these popular enter-

Piracy and commerce. prises. Most races, moreover, have not yet emerged from the stage of primitive civilization when right was restricted to one's blood kin. If strangers within the gates could not be murdered, there was no moral law restraining one from abusing the subjects of non-Christian nations. Menendez believed that his slaughter of captives was for the glory of God. Francis Drake, the notorious plunderer of his time, commended his lieutenant "to the tuition of Him that with His blood redeemed us."

This importation of the Negroes, however, was not their first contact with the Western Hemisphere. Long before the Teutonic elements established a claim to North America the Africans had visited its shores and penetrated

The Negro and the discovery of America. the interior. According to Leo Wiener, of Harvard University, the Africans were the first to discover America. He has found in the American language the early African influence in words like "canoe," "buckra," and "tobacco." They could not have been brought from any other part of the world. African fetishism, too, resembling a custom among the American Indians, has been considered another reason for believing that Africans saw the shores of America centuries before the Teutons had developed sufficiently to venture so far on the high seas. Inasmuch as scientists now claim that there once existed on the western coast of Africa a very advanced people who influenced even the civilization of the Mediterranean World, they have little doubt of their having extended their culture across the Middle Passage. Africa, it will be remembered, is nearer to America than Europe.[2]

Negroes, moreover, have a place among the exploits of the European pioneers who many years later explored North and South America. Pedro Alonso Niño, a pilot of the fleet of Columbus, has been referred to as a Negro, but this has not been proved. Voyages with Cristobal de la Guerra and Lúis de la Guerra are also accredited to Niño. In the discovery of the Pacific Ocean, Balboa carried with him thirty Negroes, including Nuflo de Olano. In the conquest of Mexico, Cortez was accompanied by a Negro, who, finding in his rations of rice **The Negro** some grains of wheat, planted them as an **with the Span-** experiment and thus made himself the pioneer **ish explorers.** in wheat raising in the Western Hemisphere. Negroes assisted in the exploration of Guatemala and the conquest of Chile, Peru, and Venezuela. Negroes accompanied Ayllon in 1526 in his expedition from the Florida Peninsula northward and figured in the establishment of the settlement of San Miguel near what is now Jamestown, Virginia. They accompanied Narvaez on his ill-fated expedition in 1527 and continued with Cabeza de Vaca, his successor, through what is now the southwestern part of the United States. They went with Alarcon and Coronado in the conquest of New Mexico.[3] They were ordered to be imported by De Soto, the explorer of the lower Mississippi.

One of these Negroes wrote his name still higher in the hall of fame. This was Estevanico, or Little Stephen, the explorer of New Mexico and Arizona. Estevanico was a

---

[2] *Journal of Negro History*, IX, 1-17; Channing's *A History of the United States*, I, 116-117.

[3] By 1540 a Negro in Quivira, Mexico, had attained the priesthood. At Guamanga in 1542 Negroes constituted a brotherhood of the True Cross of Spaniards.

member of the unfortunate expedition of Narvaez who undertook to reduce the country between Florida and the Rio
Little de las Palmas, in Mexico. Overcome by mis-
Stephen. fortune, only four of the expedition survived. One of these survivors was Estevanico. Referring to Cabeza de Vaca's instructions to this Negro, Channing says, "He ordered him to proceed in advance for fifty or sixty leagues and to report the probability of success by sending back wooden crosses. If the news which the Negro gathered was of moderate importance only, he was to send back a cross the size of the palm of his hand; if the news were better, the cross might be larger. Four days later an Indian came into camp with a cross as tall as a man. With him was another Indian, who fold the friar of seven large cities with houses of stone and lime, some of them four stories in height. The portals of the principal houses, he said, were ornamented with designs in turquoise. Other crosses greeted Fray Marcos, another member of the expedition, as he journeyed onward. Instead of awaiting the coming of his chief at the appointed distance, Estevanico pushed on to the wonderful city, where he was at once murdered. Indian traditions still tell of his coming and his going; of how he related to those in the city that he was the messenger of two white men, one of whom was skilled in things of the heavens. The Indians at once made up their minds that he was a liar, for it was incredible that a black man should be the agent of two white men. They set him down for a deceiver and also found that he was greedy, without morals, and a coward. Seeking to escape, they fell upon him and killed him; if they had got hold of the white men and the attendant Indians, they would doubtless have massacred them also—"a curious slaughter of red, white, and black."

The Negroes followed with the French close upon the trail of Cartier and Champlain. They appeared with the

Jesuits in Canada and the Mississippi Valley during
the seventeenth century. They later consti-   **Negroes and**
tuted a considerable element of the pioneers   **the French.**
in Louisiana. In these regions as elsewhere the Negro
assisted in the exploration of the country and contributed
much to the establishment of legal claims by actual settlement.

The chief interest of the whites here, it must be remembered, was the enslavement of the blacks. The ''Christians,'' like the Mohammedans, justified their enslavement
of foreigners taken as captives in war. But   **Christian**
in the eighteenth and nineteenth centuries,   **slavery.**
when the Europeans were engaged in the exploitation of
the New World, slaves were no longer merely taken over as
a sequel of war but became also an object of commerce to
supply the colonies with cheap labor. This change of attitude was justified by the Christian world on the ground
that, although it was contrary to an unwritten law to enslave a Christian, this principle was not applicable to the
unconverted Negroes. Driven later from this position
when numerous Negroes accepted Christianity, they salved
their consciences by a peculiar philosophy of the officials
of the church. These ecclesiastics held that conversion did
not work manumission in the case of the Negro who differed so widely from the white man. The substance of this
was soon incorporated into the laws of the colonies and
the decrees of the Bishop of London, the spiritual head of
the colonial church.

An important stimulus to these developments was the
slave trade. Europe was in the midst of a commercial
revolution. They wanted new routes, new methods, and
new commodities. Slaves were considered an important
commodity. Prior to the operation of the slave trade for
the purpose of exploitation, however, there had been suffi-

cient infiltration of the Negroes into southern European countries to make their presence no exception to the rule.

African slaves in Europe. African slaves were brought to Spain, and this trade was further extended by the Portuguese when they conquered the Mohammedans of North Africa. After the extensive explorations of Prince Henry, the Portuguese ships were bringing to that country more than seven or eight hundred slaves every year to serve as domestic servants and to work the estates evacuated by the Moors. Slaves were so common in the city of Seville in 1474 that Ferdinand and Isabella nominated a celebrated Negro, Juan de Valladolid, as the "mayoral of the Negroes" in that city.[4]

This slavery in the Iberian peninsula, of course, was of a mild form. Despite the suggestions of men commercially inclined, the Christian Queen Isabella had refused to permit the traders to embark upon the enterprise as a commercial one. Furthermore, to prevent the spread of heathenism and to promote religion, she allowed only **Slavery in Spain.** Christian Negroes to be carried to the colonies.[5] At the death of Isabella, however, King Ferdinand, who was less interested in the Negroes than was his companion, gradually yielded to the requests of the merchant class, and allowed the importation of unconverted Negroes into the Spanish colonies. But Ferdinand did not give extensive privileges to all persons desiring to bring in Negroes. At times he undertook to check the trade. In the reign of Charles V, Bishop las Casas urged a plan for importing Negroes to take the place of the enfeebled Indian slaves. This plan, once adopted, became the policy of the Spaniards in dealing with the Negroes in their colonies. When the Spaniards became committed

[4] W. E. B. DuBois, *The Negro*, p. 146.
[5] C. G. Woodson, *The Education of the Negro Prior to 1861*, p. 19.

to the policy of slaveholding, however, they found themselves handicapped by having no foothold in Africa. They had to depend on the slave traders of other nations, especially the English. This explains the "Asiento," one of the important provisions of the Treaty of Utrecht in 1713. In closing the War of the Spanish Succession, this agreement secured to the English for a number of years the monopoly of the slave trade with the colonies of Spain.

The English, however, never got a foothold on the African coast until they established their authority on the Gambia about 1618. The Dutch made a voyage to Guinea in 1595. In 1617 they took possession of the island of Goree and in 1624 obtained their great desideratum in establishing a fort on the Gold Coast. The Danes reached the Gold Coast probably about 1650 and built Christiansborg Castle. Near the close of the seventeenth century a Brandenburg company built one or more forts on the Gold Coast. After holding them for two generations they disposed of them to the Dutch.

The Portuguese influence in Africa, however, was predominant during these years. The Spaniards, on the other hand, ruled in Central and Southern America by virtue of the Papal Bull and the Treaty of Tordesillas, which divided the newly discovered lands between these nations. Other nations were in Africa on sufferance **The Portuguese** only. Thus the power of the Portuguese **predominant.** continued until it was broken by the Dutch in the wars culminating in 1637. They then took Elminia on the Gold Coast and drove the Portuguese from West Africa north of the Equator except from Gambia and certain islands. At the same time the Portuguese were being driven south by the Arabs on the east coast. By 1700 they lost all of their territory there except Mozambique. They were able to keep only Angola on the west coast. The Dutch trading companies then had their day during the first half of the seventeenth century. The Dutch East India Company was the most successful corporation of its kind in existence. One of the ships of the Dutch brought upon this country an evil when in 1619 it sold the colonists at Jamestown, Virginia, twenty Negroes. The Dutch West India Company followed in 1621 for further exploitation in America.

The Dutch, however, were not permitted to come into permanent possession of all they had taken over from the Portuguese. The English made inroads here as a result of the naval war successfully closed with the Peace of **The Dutch on** Breda in 1667; and a war between the French **the coast.** and the Dutch in 1672 ended with the transfer of Gorée to France. The English slave trade then became an organized business operated by special companies beginning with such a grant as early as 1618. Another was made to a company of this sort in 1631. In 1662 there was chartered the Royal Adventurers trading into Africa. This corporation was reorganized in 1672 as the Royal African Company with the monopoly of the slave trade between the Gold Coast and the American colonies. So profitable did the trade become, however, that as a result of a general demand the trade was thrown open to all English vessels. This brought in vessels from New England, especially from Boston and Newport. The slave-trading corporations maintained a line of vessels plying between America and certain forts established on the Guinea coast. The French operated in the region of the Senegal, the **Slave-trade** English on the Gambia, and the Dutch and **corporations.** English on the Gold Coast. At first the task of obtaining the slave cargo was largely that of the captain. On landing, he traded his trinkets or rum for slaves. He sometimes kidnaped Africans, even the princes, who drove their captives in war to the coast to be sold. This led to hazardous encounters with armed Africans. They found it necessary thereafter, then, to systematize the buying by

KANO

establishing factories along the coast to have the slaves on hand before arrival. In the course of time the slave trade in the interior of Africa was highly developed. Wars being waged at that time supplied captives offered as slaves for the market. When captured they were brought to the coast and sold to the representatives of the companies with vessels in port for their exportation. They

INSPECTING A CAPTIVE

were not usually natives of the countries along the coast. In fact, Africans of these ports were seldom sold for this purpose except when a rival nation captured the slaves of the masters living in a hostile section. Some of the slaves supplying this demand were brought from the distant countries in the interior of Africa.

The commodities given in exchange for these slaves were generally sent out from manufacturing centers like Newport and Boston in New England, and from Bristol and

Liverpool in England. In 1726 Bristol, Liverpool and London had 171 ships engaged in the slave traffic. These vessels carried iron bars, rum, cloth, shells, crystal beads, brass pans, and foreign coins, to be exchanged for slaves. The slaves thus purchased had been driven to the coast in coffles, sometimes for distances of more than one thousand miles. They had to cross a country which had practically no facilities for transportation except those with which nature had endowed it. As it was necessary to go most of the way walking, and as the means of subsistence were not always to be secured, many of the captives dropped dead from thirst and famine. Those who succeeded in surviving the

BRANDING A NEGRO WOMAN SLAVE

ordeal of this drive to the coast were presented for sale on arrival only to face other horrors of the "Middle Passage." Sometimes forced into a crouching position, sometimes compelled to lie **Horrors of the Slave Trade.** down, captives accepted as valuable were shackled and herded together like cattle in ships. The space generally allowed for the standing room of a slave was just a few square inches. Ventilation was usually inadequate, clothing was limited, the water was insufficient, and the food was spoiled. Crowded thus together in the lower parts of an unsanitary vessel, many of these unfortunates died of various complaints before reaching America. Occasionally the trusted Negroes on board would start a riot to liberate themselves by killing their captors, but the system was finally reduced to such a safe procedure that little fear therefrom was experienced. After the slave trade was declared criminal the traffic became most inhuman. Prior to this time a slaver had to exercise some care with these captives, for a loss of too many would have made the voyage unprofitable. But the restriction on the trade so increased the price of slaves thereafter that a loss of some of them could be more easily borne.

These slaves, however, were not brought in large numbers directly to the continental ports. Slave labor did not at first seem very profitable along the Atlantic. In the West Indies, devoted to the production of cane sugar so much in demand at that time, African slaves were welcomed. In these islands they were exchanged mainly for such raw materials as molasses. They could secure a slave in Africa for about 100 or 120 gallons of rum valued at about $50 or $60. They would sell him in the West Indies for from $100 to $200 or for molasses worth this amount. Brought by the slavers to our ports, the molasses was manufactured into rum. To supply this demand for rum manufacture Newport had twenty-two dis-

Slaves carried to the West Indies. tilleries. With this rum the ships set out to Africa again on their triangular route connecting with the commercial centers in three widely separated parts of the world.

In the West Indies the Negroes were successfully exploited so as to make those islands the wealthiest colonies of the world. In the course of time, however, after having been well broken in, and in some cases after having taken over a considerable portion of the western civilization, a number of these slaves were brought from the West Indies to the United States. Some of them had then learned to read and write two or three modern languages. When, however, such mentally developed Negroes proved to be the source of discontent and insurrections, the American colonists deemed it wiser to import slaves directly from Africa in their crude form.

As to exactly how many Negroes were thus brought away from Africa, authorities widely differ. When the slave trade was in full swing 50,000 or 100,000 were brought over every year. Some authorities believe that not more than 5,000,000, while others contend that 10,000,000 Africans were expatriated. But to figure out the extent to which this process of depopulation **The enormity of the trade.** affected Africa, one must bear in mind that for every slave imported into America at least four or five others had to meet death in the numerous wars, in the inhuman drive to the coast, and in the cruel shipment in unsanitary ships hardly suitable for importing hogs. Africa probably lost more than 50,000,000 natives. When we think of how the World War conscription of 4,000,000 men upset the economic and social life in our own country, we can easily estimate the effect of the loss to Africa of 50,000,000 of its inhabitants. This, to some extent, accounts for its decline.

The source of these Negroes will be of much interest. They came in the main from Guinea and the Gold Coast. Very few came from the West Coast of Africa. The slave trading nations did not control that part of the continent. Among these slaves were a few of the most intelligent of the Africans, the Senegalese, with an infusion of Arabic blood. They were especially valuable for their work as mechanics and artisans. Then there were the **Sources of the slaves.** Mandingoes, who were considered gentle in demeanor but "prone to theft." The Coromantees brought from the Gold Coast were hearty and stalwart in mind and body. For that reason they were frequently the source of slave insurrections. It was said, however, that the Coromantees were not revengeful when well treated. Slavers brought over some Whydahs, Nagoes and Paw

Paws. They were much desired by the planters because they were lusty, industrious, cheerful and submissive. There came also the Gaboons. They were physically weak and consequently unsuited for purposes of exploitation. The colonists imported, too, some Gambia Negroes, prized for their meekness. The Eboes brought from Calabar were not desired, because they were inclined to commit suicide rather than bear the yoke of slavery. The Congoes, Angolas and the Eboes gave their masters much trouble by running away. Among the Negroes thus imported, too, there were a few Moors and some brown people from Madagascar.

Sometimes an African of high social standing was thus kidnaped and brought over. In the possession of Michael Denton of Maryland there was found a slave who observed the custom of praying five times a day according to the requirements of the Mohammedan religion. An ignorant white boy, seeing him kneel and bowing in the direction of Mecca, threw sand in his eyes and so impaired his sight as to invite an investigation of his habits. It was discovered that he was an orthodox Mohammedan and an Arabic scholar. Hearing this, James Oglethorpe interceded in his behalf, had him liberated and taken to England. There he was accorded all of the honors due a man of learning. He was associated with a professor of Cambridge in the translation of oriental manuscripts and through him he was introduced to some of the most desirable people of England. This was probably the record of Job, a slave in Maryland in 1731-1733, a Fula, brought from Futa in what is now French Senegal. He could write Arabic and repeat the whole Koran.[6]

6 Thomas Bluett, *Some Memoirs of the Life of Job the Son of Solomon the High Priest of Boonda in Africa;* London 1816. Francis Moore, *Travels into the Inland Parts of Africa,* London 1738.

CHAPTER V

THE SITUATION IN TROPICAL AMERICA

THE lot of the slave in tropical America was most unfortunate. Owing to the absentee ownership, the inefficient management of the plantations, and the paucity of white women to serve as restraining influences on masters, the system of slavery developed in the West Indies proved to be of a cruel sort. The slaves were treated more as brutes subjected to a process known as "breaking in." Some were assigned to work among well-seasoned slaves, and a few were given individual tasks. When they became well "broken in" they were grouped by families in separate quarters. These were surrounded by small tracts of land on which they were required to raise their own food. Such things as clothing, dried fish, molasses, rum and salt, which they could not easily produce, were issued from the plantation commissary. They went to work in gangs, some cultivating sugar cane, some toiling in the mills and stills, some laboring at handicrafts. Others were placed in domestic service.[1] On the continent their lot was a little easier.

As few implements had been introduced and the planters

The slave in the West Indies.

---

[1] The conditions in the tropics facilitating the increase in the slave trade are treated in T. K. Ingram's _History of Slavery and Serfdom_, John R. Spear's _The American Slave Trade_, W. E. B. DuBois's _Suppression of the African Slave Trade_, B. Mayer's _Captain Canot or Twenty Years of an African Slaver_, R. Drake's _The Revelations of a Slave Smuggler_, Bryan Edwards' _West Indies_, T. Clarkson's _History of the Abolition of the Slave Trade_, 2 Volumes, and the _Journal of Negro History_, XI, 584-668.

of that day did not easily take to labor-saving devices, most of the cultivation of the crops was done with the hoe. This **Drudgery fatal.** required the hardest of labor. Under these conditions the slaves could not develop into a robust class. Worst of all, many of them died as a result of this drudgery. While the death-rate was unusually high, the birth-rate was exceptionally small. There was no provision for taking care of the African newborn. Speaking of Jamaica, a surgeon said that one third of the babies died in the first month, and few of the imported women bore children. A contemporary said that more than a quarter of the babies died within the first nine days of "jaw fall," and another fourth before they passed their second year. The Negro women had to work hard and the planters themselves encouraged them in sexual promiscuity. Such a habit is not conducive to reproduction. This meant that the colonies had to depend on the importation of new African slaves. The slave trade to supply the demand for such labor was thereby stimulated. The planters ceased therefore to purchase male and female slaves in equal numbers, as had been the custom, inasmuch as the breeding of slaves there apparently failed.

Negroes, moreover, proved to be susceptible to the diseases of white men. Lacking time to establish an immunity against such maladies, the unseasoned slaves died in large numbers. They suffered especially from colds and measles **Ravages of diseases.** which, considered ordinary complaints in the case of the white men, proved fatal to these Africans. Travelers and planters mention in their accounts such other troublesome diseases as lockjaw, yaws, cocoa-bag, guiney worms, smallpox, leprosy, hereditary venereal diseases, menstrual obstructions, promiscuous venery and ulcers. The excessive use of new rum aggravated these complaints and contributed to the sterility of the early slave population. To supply this need, an authority estimated that a planter with 100 slaves would have to import six a year. Others estimated it at a figure as high as from a third to two-thirds. This, of course, varied according to the treatment of the slave with respect to food, housing conditions, and alloted labor. Toward the end of the eighteenth century, however, the average life of the slave was estimated at from fifty to sixty years.

A CHAIN GANG

The treatment of the slaves in Tropical America is reflected by the code developed there. Among the English the slave was early declared by law as the personal property of his master. The child followed the condition of his mother. Slaves had no right of locomotion except subject to the will of their owner. The patrol system authorized all persons to punish slaves absent from their **Law of slavery.** plantation without required passes. In the course of time this penalty for running away was so increased that in some cases the fugitives would suffer death.

In the case of mutiny or rebellion, they were subject to the rigors of martial law. Slaves were not allowed to have weapons, nor to assemble in public meetings. For striking a Christian, the slave could be subjected to severe corporal punishment. For unusual crimes they suffered death. There were cases of punishment by being mutilated, broken on the wheel, or burnt alive. The sale of alcoholics to slaves was prohibited.

Certain precautions as to the comfort of slaves were taken, moreover, for otherwise they might prove unprofitable to their masters. They were by law allowed so much clothing and at least as much as a specified quantity of food. There had to be drawers and caps for the men and petticoats and caps for the women. Such regulations as these were especially featured in the slave code of Barbados, which decidedly influenced the slave codes of the Southern States. Barbados was the first prosperous slaveholding colony of the English.

The lot of the slave in Tropical America, too, was aggravated by absentee ownership. The overseers in charge of the plantations were required to produce the largest crop possible. This in turn, of course, necessitated their **Evils of absentee ownership.** driving the slaves to the utmost in order to secure the largest return from their labor. The owners of these plantations residing in Europe might sometimes be won to the idea of reform, but the good words which they might periodically utter out of compassion for the slave had little effect in improving the economic situation far away in the New World. In the course of time, however, the lot of the slave under the English in Tropical America seemed to improve. The tendency was from slavery unto serfdom. Some of the cruel measures fell into desuetude. Planters, becoming more kindly disposed toward their slaves, permitted them to acquire property. They sometimes owned not only hogs, cattle and sheep, but also land. The custom of the country permitted masters to bequeath to their slaves some of the property which had been accumulated as a result of their faithfulness to their owners. This change was effected as a result of the humanitarian movement in England which took the form of agitation for the abolition of the slave trade and the improvement of the condition of the slave. West Indian slaves, then, sometimes tended to become servants.

Among the Portuguese, Spanish and French colonists the condition of the blacks became still more favorable. The very letter of the slave law among the Latins resembled that of the English; but the home countries in these three cases insisted on humane treatment of the slaves and were more generous than the English in offering bondmen opportunities to toil upward. The slaves as such fared much better than they did on the English planta- **The enlight-** tions. Whereas, the English never treated **enment of** the slaves with familiarity, nor smiled upon **the slaves.** them, nor spoke to them except when compelled, the Latins addressed them with mildness, handled them kindly, and treated them as members of the human family. The tendency of the Latins to interbreed with the blacks and their custom of recognizing and elevating their mulatto offspring, moreover, offered a way of escape to a large number of Negroes. But some of the English actually sold their offspring by Negro women. A large number of bondmen in Latin-America, too, secured their manumission by meritorious service and thereafter had the status of freemen.

Among these fortunate Negroes there was in Guatemala, in the seventeenth century, a freedman who had accumulated much wealth. He had secured his liberty by paying his kind master a handsome sum for his freedom. Thereafter he bought a large farm and considerably increased his holdings by making other purchases.   He lived in Agua

A thrifty freedman in Guatemala.
Caliente, a little Indian village on the road to the city of Guatemala.   This was that part of the country then said to abound with gold, a treasure which the Spaniards had for many years sought in vain.   Although the sources of this Negro's wealth were cattle, sheep, goats, and his trade in butter and cheese with the City of Guatemala, the Spaniards persisted in believing that his wealth came from the hidden treasure.[2]

In his travels through this tropical region, Sir Thomas Gage found a still more interesting Negro of this class. While sailing along the Atlantic coast of Costa Rica, Gage's

The Black Corsair.
ship was captured by two corsairs under the flag of the Dutch, who were then struggling against Spain for their freedom.   The commander of this ship was a mulatto named Diaguillo, a native of Havana. His mother lived there.   Because of maltreatment by the Governor of Campeche, to whom he was attached as a servant, this mulatto desperately ventured to swim to one of the Dutch ships near by.   Offering himself to serve the Dutch against those who had abused him, he easily ingratiated himself into their favor.   Soon thereafter he married a Dutch girl and arose to the position of captain of a vessel under the command of the famous and dreadful commander named Pie de Palo.   Coming aboard the ship on which Gage was sailing, the corsair took four thousand pesos' worth of jewelry and pearls and deprived the individuals of their personal belongings.   But because of Gage's ministerial profession Diaguillo permitted him to retain some books, pictures and clothes.   He said to Gage: "If fortune to-day is on my side, to-morrow it will be on

---

[2] *The Journal of Negro History,* Vol. I, p. 395; and Sir Thomas Gage's *Voyages,* Part 3, Ch. II.

yours, and what I have won to-day, that I may lose to-
morrow.'' Diaguillo then prepared a luxurious dinner,
to which he invited Gage. Thanking the crew for the
good luck they had procured him, the corsair took leave
of the captives.[3]

The most interesting example of the enlightened Negro
of this class in the West Indies was Francis Williams. He
was the son of one John Williams, liberated in 1708, and
ranked among those persons in the island   **Francis**
against whom slave testimony was forbidden.   **Williams,**
These same privileges were later extended to   **the scholar.**
other members of his family. Consequently they were
respected by the whites among whom they socially moved.
We have much more information about the son, Francis.
The family was of such good report, and the youth Francis
had exhibited so many evidences of mental capacity, that
early in the eighteenth century the Duke of Montague,
desiring to put to test some of his opinions about the capabilities of the Negro, had Francis instructed in an elementary school in Jamaica. He then sent him to an
English grammar school to prepare for Cambridge University. After some years Francis Williams completed his
education at that institution and returned to Jamaica between 1738 and 1748.

Impressed more than ever with the truth that a Negro
trained in the same way as a white man will exhibit the
same intellectual attainments, the Duke of Montague sought
further to advance his protégé by securing for him a seat
in the Jamaica Council. This proposition,   **The Duke of**
however, was opposed by Governor Trelawny.   **Montague.**
He contended that admitting a black man to the Council
would excite restlessness among the slaves. Whether or not

[3] *The Journal of Negro History*, Vol. I, p. 395; and Sir Thomas
Gage's *Voyages*, Part 3, Ch. II.

the governor was diplomatic or prejudiced is not known. He did add a Negro detachment to the army employed in Jamaica, but he never permitted the ambitious youth to sit in the Council. Williams settled in Spanish Town, the capital of the island, and during the rest of his life conducted a classical school. In this position he made a reputation for himself as a schoolmaster and figured somewhat prominently as a poet. The only evidence of his attainments in this field, however, consists of a Latin poem which conforms in most respects to the standard of that age. It seemed, however, that the poet was not very popular among his own people, as he was regarded as haughty and opinionated. He treated his fellow blacks with contempt and entertained a rather high opinion of his own knowledge. He was also charged with being a sycophant and racial toady who said and did much to the detriment of his race.[4]

This better situation of a few Negroes was due also to the fact that a large number of slaves in remote parts of the West Indies and Latin-America asserted themselves **The Maroons.** and escaped to uninhabited districts to declare and maintain their independence. In parts where the Negroes were as numerous as the whites, these fugitives often jeopardized the very life of the colony. As such, they were known as Maroons. They had few arms that the primitive man did not possess, but because of their resourcefulness and power in military organization they became a source of much terror throughout Latin-America.[5] In the small colony of Guatemala in the seventeenth century there were as many as three hundred such Negroes.

[4] The career of Francis Williams is treated in *The Journal of Negro History*, Vol. II, pp. 146-159. A better account may be found in William James Gardner's *History of Jamaica*, p. 31; and in Edward Long's *History of Jamaica*, p. 234.

[5] Dallas, *History of Maroons*, p. 26.

They had resorted to the woods and could not be subdued by the forces sent against them.

The greatest enterprise of the Maroons, however, was exhibited by the little Negro Republic in Brazil, Palmares. Professor Charles E. Chapman calls it the Negro Numantia, because its career resembles **The Negro Numantia.** so much that of Numantia against which the Romans fought for a number of years before they could invade the beleaguered city. Because of the self-asserting spirit of certain Portuguese slaves, many of those imported from Guinea escaped to the forests. They established there villages called *quilombos,* the type to which Palmares, in the Province of Pernambuco, belonged. It was not long, however, before this town extended its sway over a number of others settled by persons of the same antecedents. At one time it was reported to have a population of twenty thousand, with ten thousand fighting men. Palmares, the name also of the capital of the republic, was surrounded by wooden walls made of the trunks of trees and entered by huge gates. It was provided with facilities for wide surveillance and sentry service.

In the course of time the population of this village gradually increased because of the eagerness of slaves and freemen to try their fortunes in the forests. In the beginning they maintained themselves by a sort **The rise of** of banditry, taking food, slaves and women, **the republic.** whether mulatto, black, or white. They later settled down to agriculture, and established seemingly peaceful trade relations with the Portuguese settlements in the less hostile parts of Brazil. Palmares then developed into a sort of nation, uniting the desirable features of the republican and monarchical form of government. It was presided over by a chief executive called the *Zombe,* who ruled with absolute authority during life. ''The right to candidacy,'' says Professor Chapman, "was restricted to a group recognized as composing the bravest men of the community. Any man in the state might aspire to this dignity providing he had Negro blood in his veins. There were other officers, both of a military and a civil character. In the interest of good order the *Zombes* made laws imposing the death penalty for murder, adultery and robbery. Influenced by their antecedents, they did not discontinue slavery, but they put a premium on freedom. Every Negro who won his freedom by a successful flight to Palmares remained free, whereas those who were captured as slaves continued as such in Palmares."

This Negro Republic, however, was an unnatural growth in the eyes of the Portuguese. It was considered a resort for undesirable aliens who constituted an ever-increasing danger to the prosperity of Brazil. In 1698, therefore, **The destruction of Palmares.** Governor Caetano de Mello of Pernambuco ordered an expedition to proceed against the city. These brave blacks met the invading forces and indisputably defeated them. Returning later, however, with a formidable army of seven thousand men under the command of a more competent soldier and provided, too, with adequate artillery, the Portuguese reached the city after some difficulty and placed it in a state of siege. The defense of this city was heroic. "After the Portuguese had breached the walls in three places," says the annalist, "their infantry attacked in force. They entered the city, but had to take it foot by foot. At last the defenders came to the center of Palmares where a high cliff impeded further retreat. Death or surrender were the only alternatives. Seeing that his cause was lost beyond repair, the *Zombe* hurled himself over the cliff, and his example was followed by the most distinguished of his fighting men. Some persons were taken, but it is perhaps a tribute to Palmares, though a grewsome one, that they were all put to death; despite the value of their labor it was not safe to enslave these men. Thus passed Palmares, the Negro Numantia, most famous and greatest of the Brazilian *quilombos.*" [6]

[6] *The Journal of Negro History,* Vol. III, pp. 31-32.

CHAPTER VI

SLAVERY IN A STRUGGLE WITH SERVITUDE

THE cruel system of exploiting Africans in Tropical America did not reach the slave States until the cotton gin and other mechanical appliances instrumental in effecting the industrial revolution made slavery seemingly profitable.[1] The first Negroes brought to the continental colo-

Slavery patriarchal. nies were few, and they served largely as indentured servants so closely attached to the homes of their masters that they were treated like members of the families. They had the same status as that of the white felons and convicts imported into this country to serve a definite period. After serving their master a few years the indentured servant could become free. This happened in the case of some of the first twenty Negroes brought to Jamestown in 1619. It has been said, moreover, that Anthony Johnson, probably one of these Negroes, not only gained his freedom but became a slaveholder himself. Between slavery and servitude there was no clear distinction in the English language at that time. A man described as a servant might be a slave, and vice versa. The status of a slave was unknown to English law. Slavery gradually evolved in America by custom. It has been shown conclusively that the Negroes were gradually debased from

[1] Slavery in its first form is briefly treated in Channing's *History of the United States*, II, 336-400. The slaves' opportunities for enlightenment are presented in C. G. Woodson's *The Education of the Negro Prior to 1861*, 18-150. See also Bryan Edwards' *History of the West Indies;* Sir Harry Johnston's *The Negro in the New World;* and the *Journal of Negro History*, I, 132-150, 163-216, 243-264, 399-435; II, 78-82, 105-125, 186-191, 229-251, 411-422, 429-430; III, 1-21, 22-28, 33-44, 45-54, 55-89, 211-328, 335-353, 381-434.

indentured servitude to slavery.[2] Slavery as such was not
legally recognized in Virginia until 1661. At that time
the Negro was considered as held to the permanent service
of his master, "incapable of making satisfaction for the
time lost in running away by addition of time."

The importation of Negroes gradually increased, however. Negroes were brought from the West Indies to

THE DASH FOR LIBERTY

Massachusetts probably as
early as 1636. The rec-
ords show the actual im-
portation of Negroes in
1638, and Massachusetts
passed her first regulation
in regard to slavery in
1641. It was Coming of
restricted to Negroes.
the forced servitude of
lawful captives taken in
just wars. In 1646,
however, Massachusetts
rather set its face against
slavery when she ordered
returned to Africa at
public expense two slaves brought in by one cruel John
Smith from the Guinea Coast. Connecticut had no special
interest in slavery during the earliest period. The colony
merely used it as punishment for Indians in providing that
those incurring the public displeasure should be shipped
out and exchanged for Negroes. In developing its attitude
toward slavery, Rhode Island provided in 1652 that all
slaves brought into the colony should be liberated after
serving ten years. In 1703 and 1708, however, Rhode
Island legally recognized slavery in penalizing vagrancy
and taxing the trade. This colony became the chief slave-

[2] *Journal of Negro History*, VIII, 247-281.

trading center in the country. New Hampshire was largely passive in this respect. In 1714 it enacted a measure respecting the conduct of slaves and masters.

The Dutch West India Company introduced slavery into the New Netherlands about 1650. By indentured service arrangement, however, some of them became free. In the hands of the English in 1664 there came some restrictions in New York in the new code of laws providing **Slaves in** that no Christians could be held as slaves ex-**the colonies.** cept when adjudged thereunto by authority or when selling themselves. Such regulations were abrogated later, however, when slaves rather rapidly became Christians. The Bishop of London, the head of the colonial church, and the lawmaking bodies of the colonies came to the rescue with decrees and ordinances to the effect that although the Negro might accept Christianity, his conversion would not work manumission.

New Jersey seems to have followed the fortunes of New York in accepting slaves from the Dutch. The colony took legal action in sanctioning the institution in 1664. Delaware had slaves during these years, too; but the colony did not formally recognize the institution until 1721. Maryland definitely legalized permanent slavery at the session of its legislature of 1663-1664.

We hear of Negroes in Pennsylvania as early as 1639; but by a provision in its Charter to the Free Society of Traders in 1682 they had an outlet to freedom through the expiration of terms of indentured service. In 1688, **The German-** moreover, their lot was doubtless improved **town protest.** by the protest of the Germantown Quakers against slavery.[3] Although nothing definite was then done,

---

[3] This document was signed by Gerhard Hendricks, Franz Daniel Pastoruis, Dirck Op den Græff, and Abraham Op den Græff. Nothing definite, however, was done.

the Quakers renewed their opposition in 1696. By 1700, however, the Negro seemed definitely on the decline from servitude to slavery and his status as such was recognized by law that year. While the lawmaking body prohibited the selling of Negroes out of the colony it determined their status as slaves. Importation was checked by a duty on slaves brought in after 1700 and the tax was doubled five years later. Unsuccessful attempts were made in 1712 and 1715 to prevent importation altogether by excessive duties, but these were disallowed in England.

Farther south the development was not so very different. North Carolina, like some of the other colonies, had slavery before it knew it as such. The colony took cognizance of the institution in 1715 when it established a system of slave control. Slaves came into **Slaves in the** South Carolina so rapidly after its sanction **Lower South.** in 1682, however, that there was fear that, outnumbering the whites, the slaves might rise against their masters. This happened in 1720 and several times thereafter. Importation, therefore, was checked by prohibitive duties as in the case of 1740. At the same time white immigration had to be encouraged. The treaty of Utrecht, granting the English a monopoly of the slave trade, opened the way for such large importations that some of the colonies were in danger of being "Africanized." Georgia, therefore, was to be a free frontier colony because in this important position it needed free labor and could not spare time to guard both the frontier and Negroes. But apparently outstripped in economic development by slaveholding colonies, Georgia began importing slaves in 1749. In 1755 and 1765 Georgia worked out a regular slave code.

This sketch above brings out the fact that slavery as a system of exploitation was not seriously thought of in the colonies until near the end of the seventeenth cen-

tury. England had not then a strong foothold on the West
Coast of Africa and had not the monopoly of the slave

**Slow
expansion
of slavery.**
trade conceded in the Treaty of Utrecht.
Furthermore, the development of the colonies
during the early years was not so rapid as to
require much more cheap labor than what could be supplied by the white indentured servants. The economic
urge, moreover, required time to overcome the scruples of
the early settlers with respect to man-stealing. Some colonies tried to forbid the traffic. Americans trading in slaves
during the early years, too, left most of them in the
West Indies. English slave traders still farther removed
from the effects of an excessive slave population, however,
had no such sentiments as those of some Americans with respect to the trade. The British administration regarded
slaves as essential to a colony. Measures enacted by the
original thirteen to prohibit the traffic were abrogated by the home Government on the ground that the
colonies had no authority to interfere with a trade so
profitable to Englishmen.

At the same time, too, the other European nations
championed the traffic and supplied their colonies accordingly. Negroes, as we have observed above, were with the
Spanish and Portuguese settlers throughout Latin America.
They were brought in as constituents of the very first

**Slave trading
popular.**
settlement of Florida at St. Augustine. Certain Negro fugitives taken over from the
English plantation of St. George, in South Carolina, were
settled just outside of St. Augustine as a community known
as the settlement of Gracia Real de Santa Teresa de Mose.
They had their own public officers, their priest, and their
own militia to defend the settlement. There they tended
to develop into freemen rather than continue as slaves.

In Louisiana under the French, moreover, the Negroes
also increased. Here, as in Spanish America, there was

not so much of that fear of the Teuton that he might be overcome by the slave. Because of the more favorable attitude of the Latins the Negroes could **Negroes in** become free and race prejudice did not al- **Louisiana.** ways prevent him from rising to equality in the community. In 1721 there were 600 Negroes in Louisiana and 2,020 in 1745. In 1729 Governor Perier wrote of prodigies of valor performed by fifteen Negroes armed to fight the Indians. The very next year, however, we hear of Negroes there, who, realizing their prowess in arms, turned the tide the other way. They were plotting with the Indians to annihilate the whites and take over the country. The plan failed. Samba, the leader, and several of his companions were broken on the wheel; and a woman, charged with being their accomplice, expiated her offense on the gallows.

The slave, as it will appear elsewhere, was rebelling against being reduced lower and lower in the social order until he constituted the lowest element in society with no social or political rights which the others needed to respect. Slaves tended to be regarded as property, taxed and disposed of by will as other chattels. Indentured servants were subject to poll tax, and the contracts under which they served rather than themselves were considered as property. In 1748 and 1753 Virginia defined slaves as imported non-Christians but provided that the definition should not apply to Turks and Moors on good terms with England and with proof that they were free **The slave** in that country. According to this code, **code.** moreover, conversion to Christianity could not result in the freedom of the slave. Intermarriage of the races was forbidden. Manumission was restricted to liberation for meritorious service. A Negro could not enslave any other person than one of his own color. Dealings with slaves could be had only through their masters. Both fugitive servants and slaves could be apprehended, imprisoned, and advertised for as any other property lost or stolen, and they could be whipped for escaping from their masters. Slaves rebelling, conspiring with free Negroes or indentured servants, or administering medicine, should be put to death. The right of assembly was restricted. Slaves who would not abandon "evil habits" might be dismembered. Any Negro who lifted his hand against a white man received thirty lashes on his bare back. Testimony of Negroes was admissible only in the case of a capital offense charged to a slave. Even in that case the judge warned the witness beforehand that if he falsified he would be pilloried, his ears would be cut off, and he would get thirty-nine lashes. Negro criminals were tried by special courts without the assistance of a jury.

This code of Virginia tended to become the law of all of the slaveholding colonies, modified to suit local conditions. In 1693 the government of Philadelphia ordered the constable to arrest all Negroes "gadding about" on the first day of the week. Such offenders were to be imprisoned until the following morning and given thirty-nine lashes. South Carolina and Pennsylvania followed Virginia in providing special courts for Negroes charged with burglary, murder, and the like. They might be whipped, branded, deported, or put to death.

Politically the Negro in the colonies was almost a nonentity. In colonial days few colonists could exercise the right of suffrage or hold office unless they had a certain acreage or some other property, belonged to a particular church, or met a special requirement. Only one white man out of every fifteen in this country could vote, even as late **Political** as 1800. Some few free Negroes comply-**rights.** ing with these conditions exercised this right. These distinctions were then based on economic conditions and not on color. When race discrimination required that the Negroes be deprived of the right to hold office and to

vote it had to be done by special enactments. Such a
code had to be worked out step by step. During the
increase of race prejudice and the debasement of the
majority of Negroes to a lower status, the colonies
gradually restricted the civic and social rights to the whites.
In this the colonies generally followed the English laws
for vagrants and servants and the Barbadian slave code.
In most colonies Negroes were excluded from the militia.
The laws generally provided, however, that the child should
follow the condition of its mother. This meant that a child
born of a slave would be a slave although his father might
be free, and that a child born of a free mother would be
free although his father might be a slave. Some of the
colonies, however, were late in taking the extreme position
of antagonism to the Negro, and several never had this
attitude altogether. For example, Negroes voted in North
Carolina until 1834.

In the course of this debasement, too, an effort was made
to degrade the Negro below the Indian. A law of Virginia
in 1670 made distinction between the slavery of Negroes
and that of Indians. The measure provided that when
Indians were sold the terms should be such as applied in
the case of selling Englishmen into service **The Negro and**
and it secured to the Indians the protection **the Indian.**
of the laws of England. Although the Indian himself
gradually lost favor, the laws of this same colony tended
nevertheless to give him a higher social and civic position
than that of the Negro. This tendency continued in all
colonies until the Indians caused the whites so much trouble
by such uprisings as that giving rise to Bacon's Rebellion in
1676 that they were no longer considered more desirable
than Negroes. This was especially true after they began to
join with the Negroes in conspiracies against the whites.
The Indian as a slave, however, was not tractable and the
colonies tended to refrain from enslaving them. The laws

of Massachusetts and Pennsylvania in 1712, of New Hampshire in 1714, and of Rhode Island in 1715, will show this point of view.

Out of the association of these reds and blacks subjected to the whites came a class of Negroes commonly known as the mustees, or mestizos, and it became necessary for laws and legal documents citing persons of color to give **Mustees and** in detail all of these various designations. **mestizos.** No distinction was later made between them and other persons of color, however, and they passed as a part of the free Negro population. Evidences of their presence in Virginia appeared at an early date. In 1734 John Dungie, an Indian of King William County, married Anne Littlepage, a mulatto daughter of the wealthy Edmund Littlepage. He himself was occupied as a sailor, and his wife, a free woman, was the heir of considerable wealth. It was difficult to hold the Indian in the status of slavery. The Indian tended to find equal privileges or to be regarded a troublesome foe.

Because of the numerous uprisings of Negroes, too, the colonies began to think of the Negroes as being as untractable as the Indians. The former not only joined with **Early** the latter in conspiracies against the whites **uprisings.** but started insurrections themselves. This danger became pronounced after the wholesale importation of slaves brought enough of the unyielding Africans to start easily an uprising in the interest of freedom. This was one of the reasons why the colonies prohibited or restrained the importation of slaves. The disturbances of the unconquerable African recruits caused them to live in eternal dread of servile insurrection.

Some of these early uprisings deserve mention here. In 1730 a Negro in Malden, Massachusetts, plundered and burned his master's home because he was sold to a man in Salem, whom he disliked. In 1731, slaves being imported from Guinea by George Scott of Rhode Island, asserted themselves and murdered three of the crew. Captain John Major of Portsmouth, New Hampshire, in charge of a cargo of slaves, was thus **Blows at sea.** murdered with all of his crew the following year. Captain Beers of Rhode Island, and all his unfortunate co-workers except two, suffered the same fate when on a similar voyage a few years later. Before leaving the West Coast of Africa in 1735 captives on the *Dolphin* subdued the crew and by explosion destroyed both their enslavers and themselves in the effort to escape.

In the colonies themselves this rebellious spirit in the Negro continued. In the Northern Neck of Virginia in 1687 and in Surry County in that State in 1710 Negroes worked out plots for the overthrow of slavery. In 1722 two hundred Negroes assembled in a church near the mouth of the Rappahannock River, Virginia, to kill the white people. When the plot was discovered they **Troubles in** fled. Hearing that Governor Spotswood **Virginia.** would free all Christianized Negroes on his arrival there, certain of them started an insurrection in Williamsburg, Virginia, in 1730.

Escaping from their masters in South Carolina in 1711, a number of armed Negroes maintained themselves by marauding expeditions from their base on the frontier. The Governor of the colony, terrified by their raids, advocated amending the Negro act to cope with the aggravated situation and offered a reward of £50 **Uprisings in** for Sebastian, their Spanish Negro leader. **South Carolina.** His final capture brought relief to the whites. There was a small uprising in that State in 1720, resulting in the execution of three Negroes. In 1730 there was to be organized warfare between the races. Each slave was to kill his master and then the Negroes would proceed to dispose of all other white persons whom they met. For

this effort the leaders met the usual fate. In 1739, however, three other such plots developed in that State in St.
Paul's Parish, in St. John's, and in Charleston. With this,
however, the Spaniards seemed to have had some connection. They were at that time embarrassing in every way
possible the British plantations to the north of them. In
the conflicts which took place twenty-five Negroes were
killed. The Negro leaders and others to the number of 34
were shot, hanged, or gibbeted alive. Not deterred by this
drastic punishment, the Negroes in the same section staged
a repetition of this in 1740. The leader was a shrewd man
named Cato. They proceeded from place to place, taking
possession of firearms and burning houses. After they had
successfully performed their mission in terrorizing the
whites in a radius of ten miles they were overpowered by
the militia where they halted to indulge in drinking, singing, and dancing. More than 20 white persons were killed
and, as a result, the leaders were all put to death. A special
act of the State in 1740 checked the importation of Negroes.
by imposing a duty of £100 on Africans and £150 on
the Negroes from the colonies. Even this did not put an
end to such uprisings, for in 1754, C. Croft, of Charleston,
had two of his female Negroes burned alive because they
set fire to his buildings. In 1755, Mark and Phillis, slaves
of John Codman of Charleston, having learned that their
master had made them free by his will, poisoned him to
expedite matters. Mark was hanged and Phillis was
burned alive.

Believing that the necessity for maintaining surveillance
over Negroes at the time of combating the Indian on the
frontier was sufficient reason for preventing the importa-
The Georgia tion of slaves, Georgia soon had reasons for
situation. regretting that it had receded from this position. In 1728 a plan to kill the whites of Savannah brought
into the field a body of militant Negroes. Because of dis-

sension in the ranks they met defeat. Soon thereafter, however, the colony contrived to meet the exigencies of this situation.

Farther north, where we do not now think of the Negroes as being numerous, there were sufficient of them for such an effort. In 1712 New York was shocked from its very foundation by the discovery of the Negro plot to destroy the whites with fire and sword. The school of Elias Neau, maintained for the education of the Negroes, **Plots in** had to be temporarily closed. The excitement **New York.** did not subside until it was known that eighteen of the leaders had been hanged and others deported or broken on the wheel. In 1741 the Negroes repeated the effort in New York City. They proceeded to the slaughter by burning the city to kill the white people to get possession of their property and free the Negroes. Four white persons implicated were executed. Of the one hundred and twenty-five Negroes arrested, thirteen were burned, eighteen hanged, and seventy-one deported. In 1723 some desperate Negroes planned to burn the City of Boston. So much fear was experienced that the city had to take precaution against "Indians, Negro or Mulatto Servants, or Slaves." The Negro tended, then, to be regarded as a slave to be exploited or an outcast to be dreaded.

This apparently fixed attitude toward the Negro continued in the leading colonies. By the end of the seventeenth century the Negroes were abandoned to develop the best they could in their isolation in the New World. As agricultural interests of the colo- **The Negro** nies attracted the larger number of slaves **on his own** they were gradually removed from close con- **initiative.** tact with the masters and therefore had but little opportunity for improvement as did those who continued as house servants. In this neglected condition the master class ceased to think of the Negroes as capable of spiritual or mental development. Some never thought of the Negro as possessing a mind or soul. In 1756 Andrew Burnaby reported that the people of Virginia hardly regarded the Indians and Negroes as human beings, and that it was almost impossible to convict a white man for killing a Negro or an Indian.[4]

Against this system, which held the blacks in perpetual servitude and prevented the elevation of free persons of color to the dignity of citizenship, persons of sympathetic tendencies persistently protested.[5] There was some anti-

Antislavery sentiment. slavery sentiment from the very beginning of the introduction of slavery into the original thirteen. Here and there in the colonies there were persons who seriously objected to the rigor to which the slaves were subjected in the development of the industries of the New World. These first protests, however, were largely on religious grounds. The objection was that the exploiting methods gave the Negroes no time for mental development or religious instruction. Men who had at first accepted slavery as a means of bringing these heathen into a Christian land where they might undergo conversion to the faith, bore it grievously that selfish masters ignored the right of the Negroes to be enlightened.

This antislavery sentiment, however, was not due primarily to cruel treatment of the slaves. In fact, the first Negro slaves were largely house servants, enjoying the treatment usually received among the ancient patriarchs. Some of them were indentured for a certain period, and

---

[4] Andrew Burnaby, *Travels Through North America*, p. 31.

[5] The early antislavery movement has been well treated in M. S. Locke's *Antislavery in America from the Introduction of the African Slaves to the Prohibition of the Slave Trade*, in Alice D. Adams' *Neglected Period of Antislavery in America*, and in the annual reports of *The American Convention of Abolition Societies*.

even the slaves during the eighteenth century had many opportunities for obtaining freedom. The free Negroes had a social status of equality with that of **Mild attack** the poor whites, but the latter had little **on slavery.** chance for full citizenship. A bold attack on slavery, therefore, did not follow, for most of the objections raised during the eighteenth century were economic or political rather than sentimental. Certain antislavery advocates considered slavery prejudicial not only to the interests of the slaves themselves but to those of a country desirous of economic and political development. Efforts were first made to keep the institution out of Georgia because slaves were not vigorous enough to furnish defense for a frontier colony and would starve the poor white laborers. William Usselinx proposed to prohibit its introduction in the Swedish settlements because African slave labor would be less profitable than that of the European.

More striking than these arguments were those of the Puritans and Quakers, based on religious principles.[6] The religious element believed in slavery as connected in some way with religion. Although not advocates of social equality for the blacks, the New England colonists **Puritans.** believed in equality before God and, therefore, in the freedom of the body. The Puritans thought that slavery was the particular offense that called down the avenging wrath of God; but not wishing to make money of it, they sought at first to restrict it to lawful captives taken in just wars. They felt that it was an impediment to salvation in that the souls of the captives were often neglected. ''Remember,'' said Richard Baxter, whose

[6] For a lengthy discussion see M. S. Locke's *Antislavery in America from the Introduction of the African Slaves to the Prohibition of the Slave Trade*, pp. 1-157, and C. G. Woodson's *The Education of the Negro Prior to 1861*, Ch. III. Valuable information may be obtained from *The Journal of Negro History*, Vol. I, pp. 49-68; Vol. II, pp. 37-50, 83-95, 126-138.

thought influenced the Puritan, "that they are of as good a kind as you; that is, they are reasonable creatures as well as you, and born to as much natural liberty. If their sins have enslaved them to you, yet Nature made them your equals. To go as pirates and catch up poor Negroes or people of another land, that never forfeited life or liberty, and to take them slaves, and sell them, is one of the worst kinds of thievery in the world." Having the same idea, Roger Williams protested against the enslavement of Pequot Indians in 1637. John Eliot and Cotton Mather attacked the institution because of its abuses. In 1701 Justice Sewell presented his convincing argument against it in his essay entitled *The Selling of Joseph.*

Among the Quakers, who unlike the Puritans, believed in social equality as well as equality before God, the antislavery movement met with more success. The Quakers **Quakers in earnest.** noticed especially the cruel treatment of slaves and the vices resulting from the system. They also endeavored to prove that the system was prejudicial to the interests of all in that it prevented the poor whites from finding employment, promoted idleness among the rich, cut off the immigration of industrious Europeans, and precluded the prosperity of whites already in the land.

These religious antislavery attacks, of course, were met by various other arguments. Some said that Negroes were slaves because of the curse of Canaan; others because they **Proslavery and antislavery arguments.** were ignorant and wicked. They might, therefore, rejoice over their opportunity to be led to Christ through enslavement by the Christian white race. Ralph Sandiford inquired: "If these Negroes are slaves of slaves, whose slaves must their masters be?" [7] Elihu Coleman, replying to the argument that Negroes should be enslaved because of their wicked-

[7] Ralph Sandiford, *Brief Examination,* Ch. IV, p. 5.

ness, said: "If that plea would do, I believe that they need not go far for slaves as now they do."[8]   Seeing that the difference of race was the main thing, the Quakers of Germantown, Pennsylvania, said in 1688: "Now, though they are black, we cannot conceive there is more liberty to have them slaves, than it is to have other white ones. There is a saying that we shall do to all men like as we will be done to ourselves, making no difference of what generation, descent or color they are. Here is liberty of conscience which is right and reasonable. Here ought also to be liberty of the body."[9]   This argument was further elaborated by George Keith, John Hepburn, William Burling and Benjamin Lay. All of these were men of influence in shaping the thought of the Quakers with respect to slavery.

This protest against slavery tended to become more and more religious. Sandiford said: "Shall we go to Africa for bread and lay the burden which appertains to our bodily support on their shoulders? Is this washing one another's feet, or living by the Gospel, or maintaining liberty and property? And to live on another's labor by force and oppression, is this loving mercy? And to keep them slaves to us and our posterity to all eternity, is this walking humbly with God?"[10]   Denouncing all slaveholders as sinners, Benjamin Lay said: "Slaves are bound to them; so are they to the Devil, and stronger, for as death loosens one, it fastens the other in eternal Torment if not repented and forsaken." He styled as a sort of devils that preached to hell rather than to Heaven those ministers who, in leaving their homes on Sunday to preach the "Gospel of glad tidings to all men and liberty to the captives,

Ralph Sandiford's attack.

Benjamin Lay.

[8] Elihu Coleman, *Testimony*, p. 17.
[9] Germantown Friends' Protest Against Slavery in A. B. Hart's *American History Told by Contemporaries*, Vol. II, Section 102, pp. 291-293.
[10] Ralph Sandiford, *Brief Examination*.

directed the slaves to work to maintain them in pride, idleness, laziness and fullness of bread, and sins of Sodom.''[11]

These arguments were not merely empty protests but ideas translated into action by the Quakers. They promoted manumission by individual owners, and by 1713 worked out a definite scheme for the liberation of the Afri-

Manumission promoted.

cans and their restoration to their native land, after having been prepared beforehand by instruction in religion and the fundamentals of education. Their protests against the purchase of Africans seriously impaired the market for slaves in Philadelphia by 1715, and decidedly checked the importation of slaves into Pennsylvania in 1743.

In this effort there figured two important characters among the Quakers, Anthony Benezet of Philadelphia and John Woolman of New Jersey. Born of Huguenot parents persecuted as heretics in France, Benezet readily sympa-

Benezet and Woolman.

thized with the oppressed Negroes in America. He considered the world his country and all mankind his brethren. In several treatises he warned the world of the calamitous state of the enslaved Negroes, endeavoring to show that such a practice is inconsistent with the plainest precepts of the Gospel, the dictates of reason, and every common sentiment of humanity. In the struggle for the rights of man he boldly advocated the emancipation of the slaves and their elevation through practical education and religious instruction. John Woolman, his contemporary, and Quaker to the manner born, was no less courageous in his attack on the institution. Having traveled through the colonies where slavery was pronounced, he became embittered against the institution. Wherever he went he bore eloquent testimony against ''slavekeeping, preaching deliverance of the captive.'' He refused to eat food or wear clothes produced by slave

[11] Benjamin Lay, *All Slave-Keepers Apostates*, pp. 92-93.

labor. Living up to his high ideals of freedom, he refrained from accepting the hospitality of slaveholders. He actually retired to seclusion in Pennsylvania and led a most eccentric life.

In later years the work of the Quakers became more effective. Most of the slaves of Quakers in New England and the Middle States were manumitted by moral suasion and religious coercion by the time of the American Revolution. The same followed among the Quakers **Results** in the Southern States not long after the close **among the** of the century. No such effective work was ac- **Quakers.** complished by any other body of Christians. Among the Congregationalists there were heard such protests as that of Samuel Hopkins of Newport and that of Ezra Stiles, later the president of Yale College. Samuel Webster of Salisbury, and Nathaniel Niles and William Gordon, of Roxbury, also attacked the evil, but at that time their group did not make an organized effort for the extermination of the system.

CHAPTER VII

In spite of these conditions, however, the slave population continued to increase. There were about 6,000 Negroes in Virginia in 1700, and they so rapidly multiplied as factors in the widely extending tobacco culture that in 1760 one-half of the inhabitants of that colony were blacks. To supply the need for cheap labor in the production of rice and indigo, the blacks increased so fast in South Carolina after 1730 that Negroes soon exceeded the whites and outnumbered them two to one in 1760. This increase tended to degrade the position of the white servant, to "cause pride and ruin the industry of our white people, who, seeing the race of poor creatures below them, looked down upon them as if they were slaves." [1]

There were not many Negroes in the northern part of the United States. Pennsylvania had a considerable number, however, for William Penn himself owned slaves. A **Few slaves in** few toiled on the farms along the Hudson, **the North.** and the number in the city of New York reached 6,000 when the whole population was 40,000. Boston was one of the centers in New England to which some Negroes were brought, but a still larger number doubtless landed at the ports connecting more closely with the West Indies. Many of these went to Newport and thence they gradually scattered to other points. In 1748 South Kingston had 1,405 whites, 381 Negroes and 193 Indians. New

---

[1] Almost any of the monographs on slavery of the various States contain useful information on early slavery in America. *The Journal of Negro History*, I, pp. 163 to 216; VIII, pp. 247-283, however, is especially helpful there.

England, however, because of its economic condition, never became the home of many slaves. In 1770, when there were 697,624 slaves in the thirteen States, only 3,763 of these were in New England. At that time 36,323 of the slave population lived in the Middle States and 656,538 in the South.

This result was not strange; for the colonies were merely commercial enterprises, and the slave trade was profitable to the European promoters. In 1770 there were in England itself not less than 15,000 slaves brought in by traders as attendants and servants. There was no decided check to this influx until the famous Somerset decision. Somerset had run away from his master **Slavery in England.** in Virginia. When captured he was to be shipped to Jamaica, where he was to be sold.

GRANVILLE SHARP

A writ was procured by Granville Sharp, however; and there followed a hearing which finally brought the question before Lord Mansfield. He gave the opinion that the state of a slave is so odious that it can be supported only by positive law **The Somerset** to that effect. Such law did not exist in **decision.** England.[2] He therefore ordered the slave to be discharged. Liberal as this decision was, however, it did not seem to have any effect on the colonies, although the subsequent struggle for the rights of man in this country

[2] Hurd, *Freedom and Bondage*, I, 189-191.

tended to do much to direct attention to the condition of the Negro.

There were then in the American colonies many slaves whose condition constituted an exception to the rule. The slaves as a whole were much better treated at that time than they were during the nineteenth century. Most of them were then given some opportunity for enlightenment **Exceptional** and religious instruction. Embracing these **slaves.** opportunities, many of them early established themselves as freemen, constituting an essential factor in the economic life of their communities. Some became artisans of peculiar skill; others obtained the position of contractors; and not a few became planters themselves who owned extensive estates and numbers of slaves. Sir Thomas Gage found a number of such planters of color in Guatemala in the seventeenth century; the mixed breeds of Louisiana produced a number of this type. Even the English colonies along the coast were not always an exception to this rule. Anthony Johnson, probably one of the Negroes brought over by the Dutch in 1619, became an owner of slaves in Virginia. Andrew Bryan, a Negro Baptist preacher, was widely known as a slaveholder in Savannah, Georgia, before 1790.

These exceptions resulted largely from the few white men who became interested in the welfare of the Negroes during the seventeenth and eighteenth centuries. Among these **The clergy** were Paul le June, a Jesuit missionary in Can- **and** ada, Le Petit and François Phillibert Watrum **the blacks.** of the same sect in Louisiana, Alphonso Sandoval in Havana, Morgan Goodwyn in Virginia, Thomas Bacon in Maryland, and George Keith in Pennsylvania. Some of these liberal workers coöperated with the Society for the Propagation of the Gospel in Foreign Parts, to which the Negroes were indebted for most of their early enlightenment. These reformers contended that the gospel was sent also to the slaves and that they should be prepared by mental development to receive it. With the increasing interest in education it became more restricted to the clergy and such other well-chosen persons recommended by them and attached to the churches.

It was soon evident, however, that little could be effected in the enlightenment of these blacks without first teaching them the English language. In almost every case, therefore, during the eighteenth century, when the clergy undertook the teaching of the gospel among the blacks, it involved also instruction in the fundamentals of education, that their message might have the desired effect.[3] In fact, in some of the colonies, the Negroes were about as well provided with schools as the whites.[4] The first school for the education of the whites in the Carolinas was established in 1716, and a school for the education of the Negroes was established in 1744. There were in a few colonies, schools not only for free Negroes but for slaves. They were sometimes taught in the classes with the children of their masters. In some cases, when the Negroes experienced sufficient mental development to qualify as teachers themselves, they were called upon to serve their masters' children in this capacity. In the eighteenth century there were schools for Negroes in almost all of the cities and towns where they were found.[5]

It was fortunate for the Negroes that many schools of the middle colonies were conducted by the indentured servant class of low estate. It looks rather strange that our fathers should commit such an important task **Convicts as** to the care of the convicts taken from the **teachers.** prisons in England and indentured in America. Yet this

[3] *The Journal of Negro History,* I, 87, 233, 361, and 492, and II, 51.
[4] Woodson, *Education of the Negro Prior to 1861,* Chapter II.
[5] *Ibid.,* 10-150.

was the case. Jonathan Boucher said, in 1773, that two-thirds of the teachers in the colony of Maryland were such felons.[6] As these were despised by the whites of the higher classes, they were forced to associate with the Negroes. The latter often learned from them how to read and write, and were thereby prepared to enlighten their own fellow men. Negro apprentices, moreover, as in the case of David James, a free Negro bound out in Virginia in 1727, had the right to instruction in the rudiments of learning and the handicrafts.

The location of some of these schools established for Negroes will be of much interest. Samuel Thomas undertook the instruction of certain Negroes in the Goose Creek Parish in Charleston, South Carolina, in 1695. A school **Early schools** for the more extensive instruction of the **for Negroes.** Negroes was established there in 1744, with Harry and Andrew. These young men were the first of the Negro race to be employed as teachers in America. Further interest was shown in the enlightenment of the slaves in that section by gentlemen and ladies of consequence. This was especially true of Eliza Lucas, later the wife of the renowned Justice Pinckney. Encouraged by the appeal of Benjamin Fawcett in behalf of the instruction of the slaves, the Rev. Mr. Davies devoted much of his time to this work among the Negroes in Virginia. So did Hugh Neill and William Sturgeon, ministers in Pennsylvania. Elias Neau had a school for Negroes in New York as early as 1706. Anthony Benezet began to hold evening classes for them in Philadelphia in 1750. The settlers of New England then tolerated the instruction of the slaves along with their own children.

The evidences of the mental development of the Negroes

[6] Jonathan Boucher, *A View of Causes and Consequences of the American Revolution*, 39.

of that day are found in the words of the masters themselves. In offering slaves for sale and advertising for fugitives, masters spoke of their virtues as **Intellectual development.** well as their shortcomings. Judging from what they said about them in these advertisements, one must conclude that many of the eighteenth-century slaves had taken over modern civilization and had made themselves useful and skilled laborers. Some of them had a knowledge of the modern languages, the fundamentals of

AN ADVERTISEMENT OF A RUNAWAY SLAVE

mathematics and science, and acquaintance with some of the professions. It was a common thing to refer to a slave as being smart and exhibiting evidences of having experienced most of that mental development which usually results from what we now call a common school education. Some spoke "good English," in contradistinction to others who spoke "very much broken English." In other cases the fugitive would be credited with speaking "proper English" or speaking "very properly."

Brought in from the West Indies, where they had been in contact with all nationalities of Europe and had not been restricted in their development, many of these slaves had picked up more than the mere fragments of education.

Slaves with some knowledge. It was not unusual to find a slave speaking Spanish, French and English—and exceedingly good English. William Moore had a slave who spoke Swedish and English well. Philip French of Philadelphia had another who spoke Dutch and good English; and John Williams, of the same state, owned a Negro who spoke very good English and was very fluent in his talk. Another type of this sort was a slave who escaped from Charleston in 1799. He spoke both French and English fluently, was very artful, and succeeded in passing as a freeman. A better example was a slave of Thomas May of Maryland, whom his master considered plausible and complacent. He could speak good English, a little French and a few words of High Dutch. He had been in the West Indies and in Canada, serving as a waiting-man to a gentleman, and had thereby had the opportunity of getting acquainted with the different parts of America.

In addition to the mere knowledge of how to express themselves fluently in the modern tongues, a considerable number of the fugitives advertised in some parts had

Slaves able to read and write. learned to read and write. Advertising for a Negro, named Cato, Joseph Hale said that "he speaks good English and can read and write." Another said: "he is an artful fellow and can read and write, and it is probable that he may endeavor to make his escape out of the Province." And still another was described in the terms: "He can read and write and it is likely that he may have a counterfeit pass." An examination of hundreds of advertisements for fugitive slaves during the eighteenth century shows that almost a third of them could read and write.[7]

---

[7] For a treatment of the eighteenth-century slave see *The Journal of Negro History,* I, 175-189.

Another evidence as to the favorable condition of the Negroes during the eighteenth century is their economic condition. The kind of garments they wore and the manner in which they lived throw much light on this situation. In some cases they lived in houses, enjoying the same comforts as their masters. In other cases their quarters were much better than those then provided for the poor whites in Europe and for the indentured servants in the colonies. Some masters did not take much care of the latter, since, when their term of service expired, they would no longer be of use to them.

According to the testimony of most masters in the advertisements for fugitives, they were well attired. For example, a master of Philadelphia in 1721 said that his slave escaped, wearing "a dark brown colored coat and jacket, a pair of white fustian breeches, a gray milled **Slaves** cap with a red border, a pair of new yarn **well dressed.** stockings with a pair of brown worsted under them or in his pockets." A slave owner in Maryland spoke of another fugitive as having "a black cloth coat, a high hat, white flannel waistcoat, a checked shirt, a pair of everlasting breeches, a pair of yarn stockings, a pair of old pumps, a worsted cap, an old castor hat, and sundry other clothes." A Boston master in 1761 lost a slave, who had, "when he went away, a beaver hat, a green worsted coat, a close-bodied coat with a green narrow frieze cape, a gray coat, a black and white homespun jacket, a flannel checked shirt, gray yarn stockings, a flannel shirt, a bundle of other clothes, and a violin." White persons at that time were not generally better clad.[8]

In not a few other cases these fugitives are mentioned as persons who had not only an ample supply of clothing, but considerable money. John Dulin, of Baltimore, advertised

[8] *The Journal of Negro History*, I, 203.

in 1793 for a slave supplied with ample funds. The context of the advertisement indicates that the money was earned by the slave while hiring his time. Referring to another fugitive, a master said: "As I expect he has a sum of money with him, probably he may get some one to forge a pass for him and pass as a free man." Some Negroes were widely

Slaves in good circumstances.

THE FAITHFUL SLAVE

known, as they were serving as mechanics and artisans. A few of them became contractors on their own account, overseers for their masters, and finally freemen established in business for themselves.[9]

In the absence of restrictions which characterized the oppressive slavery of the following century, they had entered many of the higher pursuits. Some of these Negroes were serving as teachers and preachers, and a few were en-

9 *Ibid.*, 203.

gaged in such practice of medicine as was then common in this country. Referring to one of his slaves, in 1740, James Leonard of Philadelphia said he could "bleed and draw teeth, pretending to be a great doctor and very religious, and he says he is a churchman." In 1797 James George of Charleston, South Carolina, had a slave who passed for a doctor among

Slaves in higher pursuits.

THE PUNISHMENT OF A RUNAWAY SLAVE

his people and, it was supposed, practiced in that capacity about town. Negroes were serving as privateers and soldiers in the army during the colonial wars and had learned so much about the military contests for possession in the New World that the English feared the close relations between the French in the West and the slaves of the colonies along the coast. This might eventually lead to an understanding between the French and the slaves to the effect that the latter might cross the mountains into French territory.

Probably the most striking evidences of the favorable situation of the slaves during the eighteenth century is their close relation with the poor whites. The most of these, at that time, were indentured servants. Reduced to **Slaves and** the same social status by common lot in servi- **poor whites.** tude, these two classes were equally treated in many parts. This was especially true of the colonies around the Chesapeake Bay. The slaves and the indentured servants followed the same occupations, had the same privileges and facilities, and experienced together the same pleasures. Living on this common plane, these two classes soon proceeded to intermarry. In 1720 Richard Tilghman of Philadelphia complained that his mulatto slave, Richard Molson, had run away in company with a white woman named Mary, who, it was supposed, passed as his wife, and with a white man named Garrett Choise, and Jane, his wife. A mulatto servant man in Philadelphia named Isaac Cromwell absconded with an English servant woman named Anne Greene in 1745. Two years later, Ann Wainrite, a servant woman of New Castle County, escaped, taking with her a negro woman.[10]

These close relations between the blacks and the indentured servants later caused unusual dissatisfaction. Laws were therefore enacted to prevent this interbreeding of the races. In 1661 the preamble of such a law in Maryland **Dissatis-** said, "And forasmuch as divers free-born **faction.** *English* women, forgetful of their free condition, and to the disgrace of our nation, do intermarry with negro slaves, by which also divers suits may arise, touching the issue of such women, and a great damage doth befall the master of such Negroes, for the prevention whereof, for deterring such free-born women from such shameful

[10] *The Journal of Negro History*, I, 206.

matches, *be it enacted:* That whatsoever free-born women
shall intermarry with any slave, from and after the last
day of the present assembly shall serve the master of such
slave during the life of her husband; and that all the issues
of such free-born women so married, shall be slaves as
their fathers were. *And be it further enacted:* That
all the issues of *English,* or other free-born women, that
have already married Negroes shall serve the master of
their parents, till they be thirty years of age and no
longer.'' [11]

This, however, did not seem to prevent the miscegenation of the two races. Planters sometimes married white
women servants to Negroes in order to transform such servants and their offspring into slaves. This happened in
the case of Irish Nell, a servant woman **Miscege-**
brought to Maryland by the proprietor and **nation.**
sold later to a planter when he returned to England. The
proceedings instituted to obtain freedom for her offspring
by her Negro husband occupied the attention of the courts
of Maryland for a number of years. The petition was
finally granted. This procedure was especially legislated
against in 1681, by a measure which penalized this custom
then obtaining among the planters. The interbreeding of
the races continued, however, in spite of the laws against
it. The public was burdened with so many illegitimate
mulatto children that it became necessary to frame laws
to compel the persons responsible to maintain these unfortunate waifs, and to make the Negroes or the white
persons concerned servants or slaves for a certain number
of years.

In Virginia it was necessary to take the same action.
Hugh Davis was whipped there in 1630 because he was
guilty of defiling his body by lying with a Negro. In 1622

[11] This social status is more extensively treated in *The Journal of
Negro History*, I, 206-216, and II, 335-353.

the colony imposed fines for fornication with a Negro, but
did not restrict intermarriage until 1691.   According to

**Efforts to
separate
the races.**

this law, if any free English woman should
have a bastard child by a Negro or mulatto,
she should pay the sum of fifteen pounds
sterling.   In default of such payment she should be taken
into the possession of the church wardens and disposed of

ENTERTAINMENT

for five years.   Such illegitimate children should be bound
out as servants until they reached the age of thirty.   If the
woman in question happened to be already in servitude, five
years were added to the term for which she was then bound.
This same law was further elaborated and extended by the
Virginia law of 1753.   Here, however, it developed, just as
in the case of Maryland, that these laws failed to remedy
the prevailing evil.   That State also found itself with an

unusually large number of illegitimate mulatto children on its hands. The officials hit upon the plan of binding them out. This was done in the cases of David James in 1727, one Malachi on a plantation, and another free Negro in Norfolk county in 1770.

North Carolina also undertook to put an end to this miscegenation. That colony provided in 1715 for the usual laws restricting the intercourse of the two races. Clergymen officiating at mixed marriages were penalized. These precautions, however, failed to meet the requirements. The custom continued in North Carolina just as it had elsewhere, in spite of the fact that the law of 1741 legislated against "that abominable mixture and spurious issue, which hereafter may increase in this government by white men and women intermarrying with Indians, Negroes, Mulattoes or Mustees." It was enacted that if any man or woman, being free, should intermarry with such persons, he should be fined fifty pounds for the use of the parish, and any white servant woman found guilty of such conduct should have two years of service in addition to the time for which she was already bound out.

This custom obtained in other parts where the Negroes were found in smaller numbers. Because of the scarcity of such population it was checked with greater difficulty. Massachusetts enacted a law against it in 1705. Pennsylvania took action in 1725. These laws were **Difficulties in separating the races.** extended and made more rigid in the course of time, as the custom gave more and more dissatisfaction. It was a long time, however, before it had very much effect in New York, and still longer in Pennsylvania. This intermixture endured. The anti-miscegenation law was repealed in Pennsylvania in 1780, and mixed marriages became common. But when the ardor of the revolutionary leaders had become much diminished towards the close of the eighteenth century, there set in

a decided reaction against miscegenation. It was therefore extensively agitated throughout communities where
Negroes were found in large numbers, and various petitions came from those sections praying that intermarriage
of the whites and blacks be prohibited.

Persons who professed seriously to consider the future
of slavery, therefore, saw that miscegenation, and especially the concubinage of white men with their female
slaves, introduced a mulatto race whose numbers would
become dangerous if the affections of their
The danger of white parents were permitted to render them
miscegenation free. The Americans of the future would
to slavery. thereby become a race of mixed breeds rather than a white
and a black population. As the lust of white persons for
those of color was too strong to prevent race admixture, the
liberty of emancipating their mulatto offspring was restricted in the slave States, but the custom of selling them
became common.

These laws, therefore, eventually had their desired
effect. They were never intended to prevent the miscegenation of the races, but to debase to a still lower status the
offspring of the blacks. In spite of public opinion they
might under other circumstances intermarry with the poor
Laws finally white women. The more important objective,
effective. too, was to leave the women of color without
protection against white men. They might use them for
convenience, while white women and black men would
gradually grow separate and distinct in their social relations. Although thereafter the offspring of blacks and
whites did not diminish, instead of being gradually assimi-
lated to the type of the Caucasian, they tended to constitute a peculiar class, commonly called people of color.
This class had a higher social status than that of the blacks
but became finally classified, with all other persons of
African blood as Negroes.

These various elements of the so-called Negro population were at first designated according to the custom in the West Indies. "The Kingston parish register of baptisms," says Prof. Pitman, "mentions black or Negro, mulatto, sambo, quadroon, mustee or mestee, brown, 'of color,' and Indian. The mulatto was the offspring of a white man and a black woman; the mulatto and a black produced a sambo; from the mulatto and a white came the quadroon; from the quadroon and white the mustee; the child of a mustee by a white man was called a musteefino. The children of a musteefino in Jamaica were free by law and ranked as white persons to all intents and purposes." Others there, as on the American continent, suffered from the pagan requirements of caste in a frontier country advertised as Christian.

There were made efforts also to restrict contact of slaves with the free Negroes. One means employed was the embittering of one against the other. The free Negro was encouraged to think himself better than the slave. On the other hand, the slave was taught to hate the free Negro because of his haughtiness in his superior position. The poor whites, another undesirable class in the slave society, were handled very much in the same way. The Negroes, therefore, continued to become a hopeless class doomed to exploitation by the whites.

In the lowest status possible in the social order the slave-holder could content himself with the thought that the Negro thus debased could not rise from the position assigned him. The gap was to be widened by improving the whites while leaving the Negro to his fate. He must be left out of the political and social order. Little account was taken of the Negro then except in a few liberal centers. Slaves were not even required to marry according to law. Morals were vitiated by the breaking of home ties in this operation of the slave trade and by remating in the interest of the masters. Even when married according to form it was an extra legal ceremony of words of caution as to how to conduct themselves in the interest of their owners. This was sometimes followed by a feast in the kitchen of the plantation house, or a collation no more expensive than a morsel and cup of tea or coffee.

CHAPTER VIII

THE NEGRO AND THE RIGHTS OF MAN

THE case of the Negro, however, was not hopeless. Efforts in behalf of the race became more successful in later years. This was due not altogether to the forceful preachments of the sects, but also to the new impetus given the movement by forces set to work during the period following the French and Indian War and culminating in the spread of the nascent social doctrine which effected the American Revolution.[1] The British, as a result of the military triumph of Wolfe at Quebec and Clive in India, had come into possession of vast territory. Parliament, under the leadership of Grenville, Townshend and North, hoped to incorporate these conquests into the empire. These ministers hoped to defray the expenses incident to the execution of the plan by enforcing the Navigation Acts, which had all but fallen into desuetude. Long since accustomed to freedom from such restraint, the colonists began to seek in law and history facts with which they disputed the right of Parliament to tax America, and on the basis of which they set forth theories justifying the religious, economic and political freedom of man.

During this period the colonists of the more democratic

---

[1] For a lengthy discussion see M. S. Locke's *Antislavery in America from the Introduction of the African Slaves to the Prohibition of the Slave Trade*, pp. 1-157; and C. G. Woodson's *The Education of the Negro Prior to 1861*, Ch. III. Valuable information may be obtained from *The Journal of Negro History*, Vol. I, pp. 49-68; Vol. II, pp. 37-50, 83-95, 126-138.

order obtained first toleration and finally religious freedom for their more popular sects. These were the Quakers,

Toleration and the Negro. Methodists, Baptists and Presbyterians. Most of these at that time accepted the Negroes as human beings and undertook to accord them the privileges of men. For the Negroes this meant larger opportunities for religious development and intellectual progress, and finally, citizenship in the more liberal colonies. Political leaders, imbued with the idea of the unalienable rights of man, joined these religious bodies in the struggle for the freedom of the Negroes. These efforts of religious groups, formerly operating independently along parallel lines, finally culminated as one united movement. Political leaders, impelled by the spirit of universal liberty, joined hands with theologians and humanitarians to translate these theories into vigorous action.

In this struggle appeared some of the most forceful and logical protagonists. They united the religious protests with that of the rights-of-man theory justifying universal

The rights of Man. liberty. In 1767 Nathaniel Appleton insisted that the slaves should not only ''be treated with a respect agreeable'' but that the institution should be abolished. If the West Indies, as some then contended, could not be cultivated without slave labor, ''let them sink then,'' said he, ''for it is more honorable to seek a support by begging than by theft.'' [2]

Playing their part in the anti-slavery drama, the Presbyterians took the position that slavery was wrong because it subjected the will of the slave to that of the master. The

Presbyterians. Baptists often attacked the institution with such zeal that some of them became known as the Emancipating Baptists. The Methodist Episcopal Church, influenced by John Wesley, declared at its conference in 1786: ''We view it as contrary to the golden law of

[2] Nathaniel Appleton, *Considerations on Slavery*, p. 19.

God and the prophets, and the unalienable rights of mankind, as well as every principle of the Revolution, to hold
in deepest abasement, in a more abject slavery than is perhaps to be found in any part of the world, except America,
so many souls that are capable of the image of God.'' [3]
Strenuous efforts were then made to excommunicate slaveholders and especially those known as ministers. [4]

This success, however, was not necessarily due to the
work of the clergy of the liberal sects. It was their effort
supported by those political leaders who applied the principles of the Declaration of Independence to   **Political
the Negro. The same theological doctrines   leaders and
and political theories which impelled the colo-   the Negro.**
nists to rise against the home country to establish the free
government and religious liberty caused them also to contend that it was wrong for the whites to exploit the blacks.
In many cases the foremost advocates of the rights of the
colonists were also advocates of the freedom of the Negroes.
However, there were some who contended that the principles of the Declaration of Independence did not apply to
the Negroes, as slaves were not constituent members of our
society.

Finding it difficult to harmonize their holding men in
bondage with the assertion of the right of all men to be
free, however, the revolutionary leaders boldly met the
question. When James Otis was arguing the   **Meeting
case of the Writs of Assistance, showing the   the issue.**
immunity of the colonists from such violation of the laws
of nature, he did not forget the Negroes. He said they
should also be freed. It is little wonder, then, that John

[3] Lucius Matlack, *History of American Slavery and Methodism*,
p. 29.
[4] While the Quakers, however, discouraged the growth of the institution among their people, and actually exterminated it, the other
sects kept the question in its agitated state until it finally divided
several of them before the Civil War.

Adams, who heard the argument, shuddered at the doctrine taught and the consequences that might be derived from such premises. Patrick Henry soon discovered that his own denunciation of the clergy and other agents of royalty in America was broad enough to establish the right of the Negro to freedom, and later expressed himself accordingly.

Thomas Jefferson, the philosopher of the Revolution, found among other grounds for the justification of the re-**The position** volt against Great Britain that the King had **of Jefferson.** promoted the slave trade. Jefferson incorporated into his original draft of the Declaration of Independence an indictment of George III to the effect that he had violated the ''most sacred rights of life and liberty of a distant people, who never offended him, captivating them into slavery in another hemisphere or to incur miserable death in their transportation thither.'' Though not so outspoken, there stood with Jefferson almost all of the fathers of the American Revolution, even those in the South, like Henry Laurens, George Wythe, George Mason, and George Washington. These men supported Jefferson in 1776 in the immortal declaration ''that all men are created equal, that they are endowed by their Creator with certain unalienable Rights, that among these are Life, Liberty and the pursuit of Happiness.''

This new interest in the Negro during the American Revolution secured to the race an appreciable share in defending the liberty of the country.[5] One cause of the **The new** Boston Massacre was that a slave, out of love **freedom and** of country, insulted a British officer. Ne-**the Negro.** groes were in front rank of those openly protesting against the quartering and billeting of British

[5] This military history is well treated in W. B. Hartgrove's *The Negro Soldier in the American Revolution,* in *The Journal of Negro History,* Vol. I, pp. 110-131.

soldiers in Boston to enforce the laws authorizing taxation in the colonies. In the clash itself Crispus Attucks, another Negro, was one of the first four to shed blood in behalf of American liberty. During the war numbers of Negroes, like Lemuel Haynes, served as minute men and later as regulars in the ranks, side by side with white men. Peter Salem distinguished himself at Bunker Hill by killing Major Pitcairn, a number of other Negroes heroically rescued Major Samuel Lawrence, and Salem Poore of Colonel Frye's regiment acquitted himself with such honor at the battle of Charlestown that fourteen American officers commended him to the Continental Congress.

The organization of Negro soldiers on a larger scale as separate units soon followed after some opposition. The reasons for timidity in this respect were various. Having the idea that the Negroes were savages who **Negro units** should not be permitted to take part in a **proposed.** struggle between white men, Massachusetts protested against the enlistment of Negroes. The Committee of Safety, of which John Hancock and Joseph Ward were members, had this opinion. They contended that inasmuch as the contest then between Great Britain and her colonies respected the liberties and privileges of the latter, the admission of any persons but freemen as soldiers would be inconsistent with the principles supported and would reflect dishonor on the colony. Although this action did not apparently affect the enlistment of free persons of color, Washington, in taking command of the army at Cambridge, prohibited the enlistment of all Negroes. The matter was discussed in the Continental Congress and as a result Washington was instructed by that body to discharge all Negroes, whether slave or free. When the enlistment of Negroes came up again in the council of the army, it was unanimously agreed to reject slaves and by a large majority to refuse Negroes altogether. By these instructions Washington, as commander of the army, was governed late in 1775.

Many of the colonists who desired to avail themselves of the support of the Negroes were afraid to set such an example. They were thinking that the British might outstrip them in playing the same game and might arm both the Indians and Negroes faster than the colonies could. A few were of the

Fear of arming Negroes.

THE DEATH OF CRISPUS ATTUCKS IN THE BOSTON MASSACRE

opinion that the Negroes, seizing the opportunity, might go over to Great Britain. On this account the delegates from Georgia to the Continental Congress had grave fears for the safety of the South. They believed that if one thousand regular troops should land in Georgia under a commander and with adequate supplies, and he should proclaim freedom to all Negroes, twenty thousand of them would join the British in a fortnight.

As a matter of fact, they had good reason for so thinking. When Lord Dunmore, Governor of Virginia, was driven from the colony by the patriots, he summoned to his support several hundred Negroes to assist **Negroes armed by British.** him in regaining his power. He promised such loyalists freedom from their masters. The British contemplated organizing a Negro regiment in Long Island. Sir Henry Clinton proclaimed in 1779 that all Negroes in arms should be purchased from their captors for the public service and that every Negro who might desert the "Rebel Standard" should have security to follow within the British lines any occupation which he might think proper.

These plans, moreover, were actually carried out in some parts. The British made an effort to embody two Negro regiments in North Carolina. Between 1775 and 1783 the State of South Carolina lost 25,000 Negroes, **Negroes with the British.** who went over to the British. Probably three-fourths of all the Negroes then in Georgia were lost to the Americans. One-third of the men by whom Fort Cornwallis was garrisoned at the siege of Augusta were Negroes loyal to the English. A corps of fugitive slaves calling themselves the King of England's Soldiers harassed for several years the people living on the Savannah River, and there was much fear that the rebuffed free Negroes of New England would do the same for the colonists in their section.

It was necessary, therefore, for the leaders of the country to recede from this position of refusing to enlist Negroes. Washington within a few weeks revoked his order prohibiting their enlistment. The committee in the **Negroes enlisted.** Continental Congress considering the matter recommended the reënlistment of those Negroes who had served faithfully, and Congress, not wishing to infringe upon what they called States' rights, was disposed to leave the matter to the commonwealths. Most men of foresight, however, approved the recognition of the Negro as a soldier. James Madison suggested that the slaves be liberated and armed. Hamilton, like General Greene, urged that slaves be given their freedom with the sword, to secure their fidelity, animate their courage, and influence those remaining in bondage by an open door to their emancipa-

PETER SALEM AT BUNKER HILL

tion. Henry Laurens of South Carolina, then in eternal dread of the disaffection of the slaves, said he would ad-

Proposal of Henry Laurens.

vance those who are unjustly deprived of the rights of mankind to a state which would be a proper gradation between abject slavery and perfect liberty, and would have a corps of such men uniformly clad and equipped to operate against the British. John Laurens, the son of Henry Laurens, was permitted by the Continental Congress to undertake such enlistment in South Carolina, but when he brought his plan before the legislature he was defeated by a "triple-headed

monster that sheds the baneful influence of avarice, prejudice and pusillanimity in all our assemblies.'' [6]

In other parts of the country, however, the interest in
the Negro was such that they regained their former standing in the army. Free Negroes enlisted in Virginia, and so
many slaves deserted their masters for the   **Negro soldiers**
army that the State enacted in 1777 a law   **in Virginia.**
providing that no Negro should be enlisted unless he had
a certificate of freedom. But later many Virginia slaves,
with the promise of freedom, were sent to the army as
substitutes for freemen. To prevent masters of such Negroes from reënslaving them, the State passed an act of
emancipation, proclaiming freedom to all who had enlisted
and served their term faithfully, and empowered them to
sue in *forma pauperis,* should they thereafter be unlawfully held.

In his strait at Valley Forge, Washington was induced
by General Varnum to enlist a battalion of Negroes in
Rhode Island to fill his depleted ranks. The   **Solving the**
Rhode Island assembly acceded to this re-   **problem in**
quest. The State gave every effective slave   **the States.**
the liberty to don the uniform on the condition that upon
his passing muster he would become absolutely free and
entitled to all the wages, bounties, and encouragements
given to any other soldier. Connecticut undertook to raise
a Negro regiment, and New York in 1780. The latter promised masters the usual bounty land to purchase their slaves
and proclaimed freedom to all bondsmen thus enlisting for
three years. This sort of action governed the enlistment of
Negroes in New Hampshire. There it tended to exterminate slavery. In 1781 Maryland resolved to raise 750
Negroes to be incorporated with the other troops. At the
suggestion from Thomas Kench, Massachusetts considered
the question of organizing in separate battalions the Ne-

[6] Sparks, *Writings of George Washington,* VIII, 322, 323.

groes serving in the ranks among white men. It was believed that in units by themselves they would exhibit a better *esprit de corps* and that a larger number would enlist; but, as the suggestion led to a heated debate in the legislature and to blows in the coffee houses of Boston, nothing definite was done.

In estimating the services rendered by the black troops of the American Revolution, observers and officers were loud in their praise. Speaking of the valor displayed by the Rhode Island regiment, the Marquis de Chastellux said: "At the passage of the ferry I met a detachment of the Rhode Island regiment, the same corps we had with us last summer, but they since have been recruited and clothed. The greater part of them are Negroes or mulattoes; but they are strong, robust men and those I have seen had a very good appearance." Referring to the behavior of Negroes who fought under General Greene, Lafayette said that in trying to carry the commander's position the enemy repeated the attempt three times and was often repulsed with great bravery. One hundred and forty-four of the soldiers holding this field were Negroes. Speaking of the troops who took part in the battle of Long Island, Dr. Harris, a veteran, said: "Had they been unfaithful or even given way before the enemy, all would have been lost. Three times in succession they were attacked with more desperate valor and fury by well-trained disciplined troops and three times did they successfully repel the assault, and thus preserved our army from capture." Negro troops sacrificed themselves to the last man in defending Colonel Greene in 1781, when he was attacked at Point Bridge, New York. Referring to the Battle of Monmouth, Bancroft said, "Nor may history omit to record that of the Revolutionary patriots who on that day offered their lives for their country more

Opinions as to Negro bravery.

The Negro and the Rights of Man

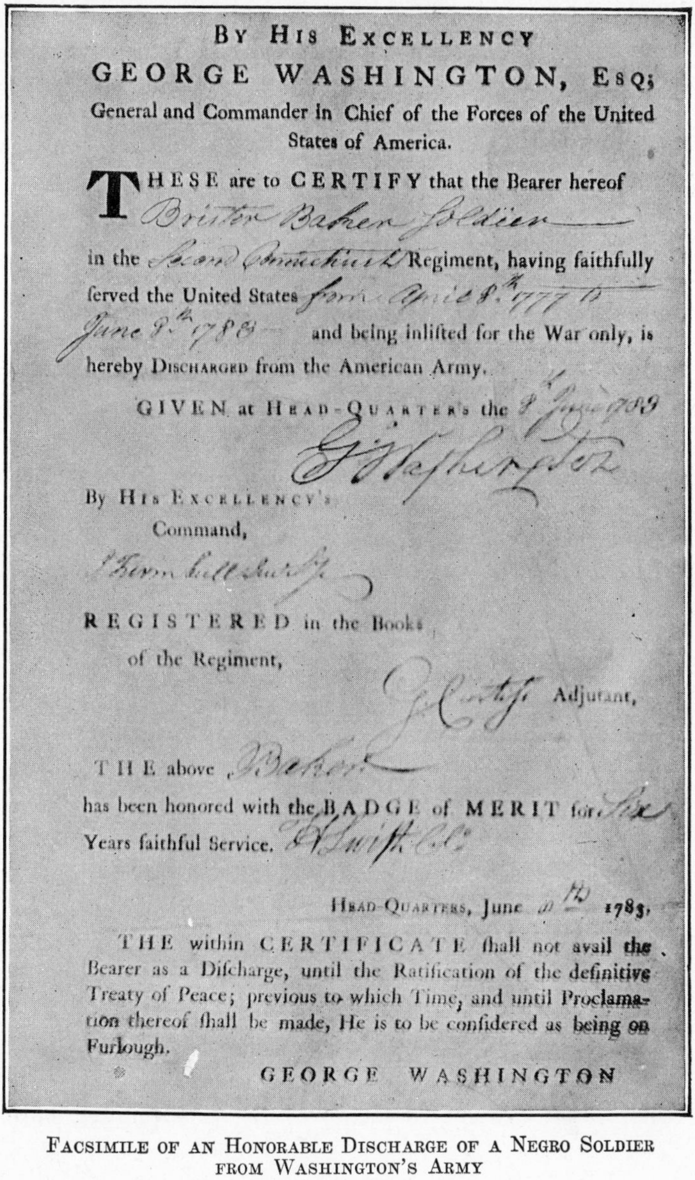

BY HIS EXCELLENCY
GEORGE WASHINGTON, ESQ;
General and Commander in Chief of the Forces of the United States of America.

THESE are to CERTIFY that the Bearer hereof Britton Baker Soldier in the Second Connecticut Regiment, having faithfully served the United States from April 8th 1777 to June 8th 1783 and being inlisted for the War only, is hereby DISCHARGED from the American Army.

GIVEN at HEAD-QUARTERS the 8th June 1783

G Washington

By HIS EXCELLENCY'S
Command,

Jonth Trumbull Jun Secy

REGISTERED in the Books
of the Regiment,

J Curtiss Adjutant,

THE above B Baker has been honored with the BADGE of MERIT for Six Years faithful Service. H Swift Col

HEAD-QUARTERS, June 11th 1783,

THE within CERTIFICATE shall not avail the Bearer as a Discharge, until the Ratification of the definitive Treaty of Peace; previous to which Time, and until Proclamation thereof shall be made, He is to be considered as being on Furlough.

GEORGE WASHINGTON

FACSIMILE OF AN HONORABLE DISCHARGE OF A NEGRO SOLDIER FROM WASHINGTON'S ARMY

than 700 black men fought side by side with the white.''
According to Lecky, ''the Negroes proved excellent soldiers
in a hard-fought battle that secured the retreat of Sullivan
when they three times drove back a large body of Hes-
sians.''

Some of these Negro soldiers emerged from the Revolution as heroes. A Negro slave of South Carolina rendered
Governor Rutledge such valuable services in this war that
by special act of the legislature in 1783 his wife and children were liberated. Because of his unusual fortitude and
valor in many skirmishes in the South, the State and the
people of Georgia honored Austin Dabney. Fighting under
Elijah Clark, he was severely wounded by a bullet which in
passing through his body wounded him for life. He received a pension from the United States Government and
by an act of the legislature of Georgia was given a tract
of land. He subsequently accumulated considerable property, attained a position of usefulness among his white
neighbors, had the respect and confidence of high officials,
and died mourned by all.

The result of the increasing interest in the Negro was
soon apparent. The Continental Congress prohibited the
importation of slaves. With the exception of South Carolina and Georgia, a general effort in the extermination of

The progress of emancipation. slavery was made during the revolutionary
epoch. The black codes were considerably
moderated and laws facilitating manumission
were passed in most of the colonies. In 1772 Virginia repealed a measure forbidding emancipation except for military service. About the same time Maryland prohibited
the importation of slaves and in like manner facilitated
emancipation. New York, New Jersey and Pennsylvania
prohibited the slave traffic. Vermont, New Hampshire and
Massachusetts exterminated slavery by constitutional pro-

vision; Rhode Island, Connecticut, New Jersey, New York and Pennsylvania washed their hands of the stain by gradual emancipation acts; and the Continental Congress excluded the evil from the Northwest Territory by the Ordinance of 1787.[7] So sanguine did the friends of universal freedom become that they thought that slavery of itself would later gradually pass away in Maryland, Virginia and North Carolina.

To prepare the freedmen for this new opportunity, schools were established in almost all large groups in towns and cities. Efforts were made to apprentice such blacks to trades, to place them in the higher pursuits **Preparation for** of labor, and to develop among them a class **emancipation.** of small farmers who might be settled on unoccupied lands west of the Alleghenies. The friends of the Negro looked to education and religion as the leverage by which they might be elevated to the status of white men. Here and there there had been some effort in the education of the Negroes during the colonial period; but, after the revolutionary movement was well on its way, this undertaking became more systematized. It was, therefore, productive of more satisfactory results. There was an actual education for the social betterment of practically all of the Negroes who thus became free.

---

[7] This prohibitory clause was:
There shall be neither slavery nor involuntary servitude in the said territory, otherwise than in the punishment of crime, whereof the party shall have been duly convicted: *Provided always,* That any person escaping into the same, from whom labor may be lawfully claimed in any one of the original States, such fugitive may be lawfully reclaimed and conveyed to the person claiming his or her labor or service as aforesaid.

Be it ordained by the authority aforesaid: That the resolutions of the 23d of April, 1784, relative to the subject of this ordinance, be, and the same are hereby, repealed, and declared null and void.

Done by the United States, in Congress assembled, the 13th day of July in the year of our Lord 1787, and of their sovereignty and independence the twelfth.

Education was regarded as a right of man. Dr. McLeod
seriously objected to the holding of slaves because it de-
Education a   stroyed their intellectual. powers.   David
right of man.   Rice in attacking the institution complained
that the master thereby deprived them of the opportunity
to have instructing conversation and for learning to read.
Thomas Jefferson, having in mind the gradual emancipation
of slaves, hoped that the masters would permit them to be
prepared by instruction and habit for self-government,
the honest pursuit of industrial and social duty. Negroes
were voting and holding office. In fact, this was the
halcyon day of the Negro race prior to the Civil War.
Never had so much been done before in behalf of the blacks,
never had there been such opportunities for developing
their power to function as citizens. So much impetus was
then given to the cause of the Negroes that, despite the
reaction following this epoch, they retained their citizenship intact in most parts of the North and even late in
parts of the South. Negroes voted in North Carolina until
1834.

The strongest impulse to general improvement of the
Negroes, however, came through the new religious bodies.
In this social upheaval they attained not only toleration
Religious   but freedom. As there was less ground for
freedom.   antagonism to the development of the Negroes
in this direction, many of them became socially equal with
the white communicants; and some Negro churchmen,
trained by pious persons, preached to audiences of the
Caucasian race. Among these was Jacob Bishop. He so
impressed his co-workers that near the close of the
eighteenth century he was made pastor of the first Baptist church (white) of Portsmouth, Virginia. William
Lemon was at this time preaching to a white congregation
at Pettsworth or Gloucester, Virginia. Some recognition
by whites was given during these years to Henry Evans

and Ralph Freeman of North Carolina, to Harry Hosier
of Philadelphia, Black Harry of St. Eustatius, and Lemuel
Haynes, an intelligent Negro preacher to white people in
New England. Andrew Bryan, contemporary with Jacob
Bishop, preached occasionally to the whites, but devoted
his life to religious work among his own people. He was
the successor to George Liele, who, under the   George Liele
rule of the British in Savannah, had founded   and Andrew
the first Baptist church of that city. Liele   Bryan.
went with them to Jamaica, where he established the first
Baptist church in that colony. Bryan's task, however, was
not so easy as that of Liele. The Americans who succeeded
the British in authority at Savannah persecuted Bryan.
They whipped him whenever he attempted to preach. In
the course of time, however, he obtained the support of a
few kind-hearted whites, who interceded in his behalf and
secured for him the permission to preach without interruption. His work thereafter made progress, and extended
to Augusta through the coöperation of Henry Francis and
others.

During these years, too, thanks to this religious influence,
the liberation of the slaves and their elevation to a more
important position in society assumed a form different from
that of emancipation through military service. The struggle for the rights of man resulted in the organization of the
first abolition society in Pennsylvania in 1775. The membership of this organization consisted largely of Quakers.
The movement did not gain much force during the Revolutionary War for the reason that abolition was being worked
out to some extent along other lines. The very   Abolition
next year after the signing of the treaty of peace   Societies.
closing the war, abolition interest among the Quakers and
their co-workers was renewed. With John Jay as president
the New York Manumission Society was established in 1785
to promote the liberation of slaves and to protect those al-

ready freed. They had in mind here the liberation of those kidnaped and unlawfully held in bondage. The Pennsylvania Abolition Society started in 1775 was reorganized in 1787 with Benjamin Franklin as president. As many as twelve such organizations were reported in 1791. New Jersey organized another in 1792. Seeking to concentrate their efforts upon the sources of authority in this country, nine of these abolition societies delivered to Congress on December 8, 1791, a memorial inveighing against the slave trade. Undaunted by the refusal of Congress to take action in this case and encouraged by the faith of those within their ranks, these nine local bodies organized in 1794 the American Convention of Abolition Societies. Their two important objectives were to increase the zeal and efficiency of the individual societies, and to assume the responsibility in regard to national matters.

Operating locally, these societies became a fighting force in behalf of the Negro. In cases of oppression they appealed to the courts for the relief of this despised class. Negroes unjustly imprisoned and kidnaped, and illegally held in bondage, were freed here and there wherever these abolition societies operated. Not restricting their efforts to **The method of** the freedom of the slave, they undertook also **abolitionists.** to prepare them for the duties of citizenship. Negroes were taken into the meetings of the Quakers and other abolitionists to undergo religious instruction. Some were placed in school or apprenticed to trades. When properly equipped they were turned over to a committee charged with placing them in positions of usefulness and in settling them in comfortable homes in the community. They were freely advised from time to time as to how to conduct themselves in such manner as to win the favor of the public. They were told to attend church, to acquire the rudiments of education, to learn trades, to deal justly with their fellow men, to be simple and frugal in all their habits, to refrain from the use of alcoholics, to avoid frolicking and idle arguments, to marry according to legal requirements, to save their earnings, and to demean themselves in proper manner toward their respective communities.

In this effort for the uplift of the Negroes these friends had the moral support of reformers abroad. Fighting for the abolition of the slave trade and for the improvement of the Negroes in the British colonies had for some years been an important concern of Thomas Clarkson, William Wilberforce, Granville Sharp, and Zachary Macaulay in England. They organized there a society for the abolition of the slave traffic in 1787. Influenced by the example of these men there started in France the following year the Society of the Friends of the Blacks. Among the persons coöperating then were Le Comte de Mirabeau, Le Marquis de Lafayette, Condorcet, Jean Pierre Brissot, Clavière, and later Sieyés, Pétion, Grégoire, Robespierre, and the Duke de la Rochefoucauld.

The idea of improving the Negro as a preparation for emancipation had some weight even in the distinctly slaveholding areas when connected with the idea of colonization. Some larger slaveholders agreed with Thornton, Fothergill and Granville Sharp in the plan for educating Negroes for colonization in Africa. Others believed with Anthony Benezet, T. Brannagan, and Thomas Jefferson, that after adequate instruction they might be settled upon the lands of the public domain west of the Allegheny Mountains. Men like Daniel Davis, and Benjamin Rush, however, insisted upon the right of the Negro to be educated whether he should remain here or be deported for colonization. Their position was immediately attacked by those who insisted that the Negro was   Interest mentally inferior to the white man, and,   in colonization. therefore, could not be equipped to function as a citizen. To this John Wesley replied that if they were dull, their

stupidity was due to the inhuman masters who gave them
no opportunity for improving their understanding, "for
the Africans were in no way remarkable for their stupidity
while they remained in their own country." William
Pinkney insisted that Negroes are no worse than white
people under similar circumstances, and that all the
Negroes need to disprove their so-called inferiority was an
equal chance with the more favored race. Buchanan informed these "merciless aristocrats" "that the Africans
whom you despise, whom you inhumanly treat as brutes
and whom you unlawfully subject to slavery with tyran-
nizing hands of despots are equally capable of improvement
with yourselves."

Franklin considered the idea of the natural inferiority
of the Negro as a silly excuse. He conceded that most of
the blacks were improvident and poor. He believed, however, that their condition was not due to deficient under-
Mental standing but to their lack of education. He
capacity. was very much impressed with their achievements in music. So disgusting was this notion of inferiority to Abbé Grégoire of Paris that he wrote an interesting
essay on "Negro Literature" to prove that people of color
have unusual intellectual power. In this sketch he made
honorable mention of Phillis Wheatley, Benjamin Banneker, "Othello," Angelo Solimann, Thomas Fuller, James
Derham, and others. He sent copies of this pamphlet to
leading men where slavery existed. Another writer dis-
cussing Jefferson's equivocal position on this question said
that one would have thought that "modern philosophy
himself" would not have the face to expect that the wretch,
who is driven out to labor at the dawn of day, and who
toils until evening with a whip over his head, ought to be
a poet. Benezet, who had actually taught Negroes, declared "with truth and sincerity" that he had found

among them as great variety of talents as among a like number of white persons. He boldly asserted that the notion entertained by some that the blacks were inferior in their capacities was a vulgar prejudice founded on the pride or ignorance of their lordly masters who had kept their slaves at such a distance as to be unable to form a right judgment of them.

Had these defenders of the Negro lived a few years later, they could have joined with Professor Alexander F. Chamberlain in referring to the Chevalier de Saint-George, knighted by Louis XVI, because of his unusual achievements as the director of the orchestra at the Grand Opera in Paris. They might have mentioned, too, Lislet Geoffrey, who attained such distinction as a man of thought that he was admitted to the French Academy. "Among the favorites of Peter the Great and his famous consort Catharine, was an Abyssinian Negro educated in France, to whom was attached the name of Hannivalov, who became a general and received other honors from the Russian government. He married the daughter of a Greek merchant, and his son became a general of artillery, who built the harbor and fortress of Cherson. The grandson of Hannivalov was A. S. Pushkin (1799-1837), perhaps the greatest of all Russian poets.[8] In Spain, where, besides, some diluted Negro blood came in with the Moors, we find a remarkable remembrance of the black man in the field of art. In one of the churches of Seville are to be seen four beautiful pictures (Christ bound to a column,

GUSTAVUS VASA, a talented African

[8] For further information on Pushkin see *The Journal of Negro History*, VIII, 359-366.

with St. Peter kneeling at his side; St. Joseph; St. Anne; Madonna and Child), the work of a mulatto, Sebastian Gomez, the slave, then the pupil, the companion and the equal of his master, the great painter Murillo, who had him made a free citizen of Spain, and at his death (1682), left him part of his estate.''[9]

In the circle of intellectual Negroes there stood out two characters more prominent than most blacks in America. These were Phyllis Wheatley[10] and Benjamin Banneker.[11] Phyllis Wheatley was a slave in a Boston family that gave **Phyllis Wheatley.** her every opportunity for improvement. After receiving instruction for a few years she mastered the fundamentals of education and made unusual advancement in the study of Latin and History. In the very beginning of her career she exhibited the tendency to write poetry. Present-day criticism

PHYLLIS WHEATLEY

would hardly classify her as a poet. In her way, however, she was a writer of such interesting verse that she was brought into contact with some of the best thinkers of that period. All of them were not seriously impressed with her actual contribution to literature, but they had to concede

[9] *Atlanta University Publications,* No. 20; *Select Discussions of the Race Problem,* 87-88.
[10] R. R. Wright, *Phyllis Wheatley.*
[11] Henry E. Baker, *Benjamin Banneker* in *The Journal of Negro History,* Vol. III, pp. 99-118.

that she had decidedly demonstrated that Negroes had possibilities beyond that of being the hewers of wood and drawers of water for another race.

Benjamin Banneker was a character of more genius than that with which many of his white contemporaries were endowed. Born in Maryland, of a free mother and slave father, he was free. At that time, a Negro of this class exercised most of the privileges accorded white men. Banneker attended an elementary school. Upon the moving of the well-known Ellicotts to his neighborhood about the time he was reaching his majority, Banneker had made such advancement in science and mathematics that Mr. George Ellicott supplied him with books. Studying these works Banneker developed into one of the most noted astronomers and mathematicians of his time. He was the first of all Americans to make a clock, and he published one of the first series of almanacs brought out in the United States. These meritorious achievements made him so prominent that he was sought and received by some of the most prominent men of the United States. Among these were James McHenry, once Vice-President of the United States, and Thomas Jefferson. The latter was so impressed with his worth that he secured for him a place on the commission

Benjamin Banneker.

BENJAMIN BANNEKER'S ALMANAC

that surveyed and laid out Washington in the District of Columbia.

Banneker is otherwise known to fame.   Forestalling Woodrow Wilson [12] by 125 years, this unusual man

[12] "The Plan of this office is as follows:

"I. Let a Secretary of Peace be appointed to preside in this office, who shall be perfectly free from all the present absurd and vulgar European prejudices upon the subjct of government; let him be a genuine republican and a sincere Christian, for the principles of republicanism and Christianity are no less friendly to universal and equal liberty.

"II. Let a power be given to this Secretary to establish and maintain free schools in every city, village and township of the United States; and let him be made responsible for the talents, principles, and morals of all his school-masters. Let the youth of our country be carefully instructed in reading, writing and arithmetic, and in the doctrines of a religion of some kind; the Christian religion should be preferred to all others; for it belongs to this religion exclusively to teach us not only to cultivate peace with all men, but to forgive, nay more—to love our very enemies. It belongs to it further to teach us that the Supreme Being alone possesses a power to take away human life, and that we rebel against his laws, whenever we undertake to execute death in any way whatever upon any of his creatures.

"III. Let every family in the United States be furnished at the public expense, by the Secretary of this office, with a copy of an American edition of the Bible. This measure has become the more necessary in our country, since the banishment of the Bible, as a school-book, from most of the schools in the United States. Unless the price of this book be paid for by the public, there is reason to fear that in a few years it will be met with only in courts of justice or in magistrates' offices; and should the absurd mode of establishing truth by kissing this sacred book fall into disuse, it may probably, in the course of the next generation, be seen only as a curiosity on a shelf in Mr. Peale's museum.

"IV. Let the following sentences be inscribed in letters of gold over the door of every home in the United States:

The Son of Man Came into the World, Not to Destroy Men's Lives, But to Save them.

"V. To inspire a veneration for human life, and an horror at the shedding of human blood, let all those laws be repealed which authorize juries, judges, sheriffs, or hangmen to assume the resentments of individuals, and to commit murder in cold blood in any case whatever. Until this reformation in our code of penal jurisprudence takes place, it will be in vain to attempt to introduce universal and perpetual peace in our country.

"VI. To subdue that passion for war, which education, added to human depravity, has made universal, a familiarity with the instruments of death, as well as all military shows, should be care-

brought forward in 1793 the very principles of international peace now encouched in the League of Nations, an advanced step which Europeans and Americans are not far enough out of the brush to understand at this late date. Banneker pointed out that, while the Federal **International Peace.** constitution adopted in 1787 made provisions for war, it suffered from the glaring defect of not doing at least as much to promote and preserve perpetual peace. He therefore recommended the establishment of the office of Secretary of Peace in the Cabinet of the President of

fully avoided. For which reasons, militia laws should everywhere be repealed and military dresses and military titles should be laid aside: reviews tend to lessen the horrors of a battle by connecting them with the charms of order; militia laws generate idleness and vice, and thereby produce the wars they are said to prevent; military dresses fascinate the mind of young men, and lead them from serious and useful professions; were there no uniforms, there would probably be no armies; lastly military titles feed vanity, and keep up ideas in the mind which lessen a sense of the folly and miseries of war.

"In the seventh and last place, let a large room, adjoining the federal hall, be appointed for transacting the business and preserving all the records of this office. Over the door of this room let there be a sign, on which the figures of a lamb, a dove, and an olive-branch should be painted, together with the following inscriptions in letters of gold:
                    "Peace on Earth—Good-Will to Man.

Ah! Why Should Men Forget That They are Brethren? Within this apartment let here be a collection of plough-shares and pruning-hooks made out of swords and spears; and on each of the walls of the apartment the following pictures as large as life:

"1. A lion eating straw with an ox, and an adder playing upon the lips of a child.
"2. An Indian boiling his venison in the same pot with a citizen of Kentucky.
"3. Lord Cornwallis and Tippo Saib, under the shade of a sycamore tree in the East Indies, drinking Madeira wine out of the same decanter.
"4. A group of French and Austrian soldiers dancing, arm in arm, under a bower erected in the neighborhood of Mons.
"5. A St. Domingo planter, a man of color, and a native of Africa, legislating together in the same colonial assembly.

"To complete the entertainment of this delightful apartment, let a group of young ladies, clad in white robes, assemble every day at a certain hour, in a gallery to be erected for the purpose, and sing

the United States. He hoped that no objection would be made to the establishment of such an office while this country was engaged in a war with the Indians, inasmuch as the War Department had been established in the time of peace.

odes, and hymns, and anthems in praise of the blessings of peace.
"One of these songs should consist of the following beautiful lines of Mr. Pope:

"Peace o'er the world her olive wand extends,
And white-rob'd innocence from heaven descends;
All crimes shall cease, and ancient frauds shall fail,
Returning justice lifts aloft her scale." [1]

[1] Phillips, *Benjamin Banneker*.

CHAPTER IX

INDEPENDENT EFFORTS

PRIOR to the American Revolution the Negroes were not sufficiently well developed to be mutually helpful. The institutions of the country were in the hands of the whites. There was therefore little opportunity for concerted action among the Negroes. The American Revolu- **Negroes weak** tion, however, marked an epoch in the de- **at first.** velopment of the Negro in the United States. The struggle for the rights of man set working certain forces which all but indicated the dawn of a new era. In spite of the reaction which followed the Negro held this ground for years to come. In the considerable number of schools established for the education of the Negroes and the churches founded by them the race had its opportunity for independent thought and action. Granted larger economic opportunities in preparation for gradual emancipation, they could more easily carry out plans to supply their peculiar needs. Negroes readily manifested interest also in the efforts to manumit members of their race and to secure justice for those illegally held in bondage.[1]

In education they ceased to be altogether recipients of the favors of the whites. Now and then there appeared ambitious Negroes who had qualified themselves as teachers. As such they not only served their own particular group but also the whites. At that time **Showing** prejudice was one of caste rather than of **initiative.** race. Men were not generally restricted on account of color; and whatever the attitude of the government

[1] These facts are covered in detail in Woodson, *Education of the Negro Prior to 1861*, pp. 93-178, and *The History of the Negro Church*, pp. 40-121. See also *A Century of Negro Migration*, pp. 1-60.

might be in the matter that had little bearing on the question, inasmuch as education at that time was a private undertaking at the expense of the persons concerned. The Negro as a private school-teacher, moreover, had a social standing about as high as that of a teacher of any other group. Few persons otherwise engaged aspired to teach except from the missionary point of view. The profession was largely restricted to those suffering from physical handicaps or otherwise undesirable. In 1773, according to Jonathan Boucher, two-thirds of the school-teachers in Maryland were the imported felons and convicts brought from Europe to serve here as indentured servants.

The independence of the Negro manifested itself even in the form of the ambition to rise to usefulness in professions. As early as 1740 there was a Negro in Pennsylvania **Negroes in** advertised as qualified to bleed and draw **professions.** teeth "pretending to be a great doctor." In 1797 there was another in South Carolina posing as a doctor among his people and practicing in that capacity about town. Near the end of the century there appeared in Philadelphia a regularly recognized Negro physician known as James Derham. He was born in Philadelphia in 1762 where he was taught to read and write. Employed occasionally by his master to compound medicines, and to assist him with his patients, he learned the profession. Sold as a slave to Dr. George West, a surgeon in the 16th British regiment during the Revolutionary War, he further developed in the medical profession. At the close of the War he was sold to Dr. Robert Dove, of New Orleans, where he had still more opportunity in this line and obtained his freedom on liberal terms. He became so well grounded in the art of healing that he soon built up a business in New Orleans paying him $3,000 a year. Of him Dr. Benjamin Rush said: "I have conversed with him upon most of the acute and epidemic diseases of the country where he lives and was pleased to find him perfectly acquainted with the modern simple mode of practice on those diseases. I expected to have suggested some new medicines to him; but he suggested many more to me. He is very modest and engaging in his manners. He speaks French fluently and has some knowledge of the Spanish language.''

Endeavoring to provide for their own social life, too, the Negroes easily became interested in fraternal organizations. The pioneer in developing the Negro in this direction was Prince Hall, the father of Free Masonry among the Negroes in America. Hall was born September 12, 1748, at Bridge Town, Barbados, British West Indies. His f a t h e r, Thomas Prince Hall, was an Englishman and his m o t h e r a free woman of F r e n c h descent. He was apprenticed as a leather worker in which he made unusual progress. De-

Prince Hall and the Masons.

PRINCE HALL

sirous of visiting this country, he came to the United States in 1765 at the age of seventeen. Although in a foreign country where he had neither friends nor education to help him on his way he applied himself industriously at common labor during the day and studied privately at night. Upon reaching the age of twenty-seven he had acquired the fundamentals of education. Saving his earnings, he had

accumulated sufficient to buy a piece of property. He
joined the Methodist Church, in which he passed as an eloquent preacher. His first church was located in Cambridge, Massachusetts. There he built up a prosperous
congregation.

Desiring to learn the secrets of Free Masonry even
during revolutionary times, he found his way to the
quarters of General Gage on Cox Hill in Boston. He
was admitted to the military lodge and advanced to
the degree of Master Mason prior to the actual Revolution. Along with him there were associated others
who later obtained a charter under which they finally
operated with limited power. Their membership was increased from time to time by accessions from New York,
Pennsylvania, and foreign countries. Hoping to enter
into the full rights and powers in this country, Hall presented such a petition, which was refused on account of
color. He then turned to foreigners for what he had been
refused in his own country. The separation from England
intervened. He nevertheless entered actively in the war
and acquitted himself with credit. At the close of the
struggle he renewed his effort to secure a charter for the
Negro Masonic lodge. Addressing the Grand Lodge of
England with such a prayer on March 2, 1784, he received a
prompt reply granting the dispensation. The warrant was
delayed. It was not actually delivered until 1787. The
lodge was then organized and the officers duly installed.
From this organization there sprang up others which
soon necessitated the establishment of the Grand Lodge in
Massachusetts. In the multiplication of lodges, too, a similar need developed elsewhere. The movement was well es-
lished in Philadelphia and Rhode Island in 1797. It was
on its feet in New York in 1812 and the District of
Columbia and Maryland in 1825. This same movement led
to the organization of the Grand United Order of Odd

Fellows among Negroes in 1843. The society was established under a dispensation obtained by Peter Ogden from the order in England. Because of racial proscription in America these Negroes had **Peter Ogden.** been barred from the Independent Order of Odd Fellows, a purely American craft.

In the religious world the independent movement among

PETER OGDEN

Negroes had a better chance. The church was a more popular institution than the school or lodge. The majority of men in those days aspired to salvation. After the triumph of toleration and religious freedom, there were few to interfere with the institutions designed to prepare the multitude to this end. Prior to this change in the religious sentiment of the country, however, there was little thought as to the Negro in the administration of the church. The clergy of the sects dominant during the colonial **The church an** period were either inaccessible or unsym- **inviting field.** pathetic toward the Negro. The Anglicans succeeded by the Protestant Episcopalians would not countenance such a thought as that of a Negro rector; Catholics, more kindly disposed to the race, did not work in that direction; and neither did the Presbyterians nor the Quakers make sufficient inroads among them to justify the elevation of Negroes to commanding positions in these respective circles.

In the case of the Methodist and Baptist churches, however, the Negro had a better chance. These denominations socialized the Gospel. They presented it in such a simple form and with such a forceful appeal as to reach both the **Methodists** illiterate poor whites and the Negroes. Ex-**and Baptists.** tensively proselyting these elements, the Methodists and Baptists rapidly developed as national forces in the United States after the American Revolution. Later, however, a considerable number of these poor whites became rich and in some cases slaveholders. They thereupon easily lost their sympathy for the Negroes. In these once antislavery churches, then, the race problem soon had its first battle. There were those who desired to restrict the Negro merely to passive worship. He was merely to heed the word and live. Finally, they tended to restrict members of the race to certain pews, to a separate section of the church, or to a different building.

Having enjoyed for some time the boon of freedom in the church, moreover, the Negroes were loath to give up this liberty. The escape of a young Negro, a slave of Thomas Jones, in Baltimore County in 1793, is a case in evidence. Accounting for his flight his master said: "He **Reaction in** was raised in a family of religious persons com-**the church.** monly called Methodists and has lived with some of them for years past on terms of perfect equality; the refusal to continue him on these terms gave him offense and he, therefore, absconded. He had been accustomed to instruct and exhort his fellow creatures of all colors in matters of religious duty." Another such Negro, named Jacob, ran away from Thomas Gibbs of that State in 1800, hoping to enlarge his liberty as a Methodist minister. His master said in advertising him as a runaway: "He professed to be a Methodist and has been in the practice of preaching of nights." Another Negro preacher of this type, named Richard, ran away from Hugh Drummond in

Anne, Arundel County, that same year. Still another, called Simboe, escaped a little later from Henry Lockey of Newbern, North Carolina.

This was the beginning of something more significant. The free Negroes in the North began to assert themselves.

RICHARD ALLEN

They contended that they were not necessarily obligated to follow the fortunes of the white churches. Such self-assertion early culminated in the protest of Richard Allen, the founder of the African Methodist Episcopal Church. Richard Allen was the very sort of man to perform this great task. He was born a slave of Benjamin Chew of Phila-

Richard Allen.

delphia, but very soon thereafter he was sold with his whole family to a planter living near Dover, Delaware. There he grew to manhood. Coming under Christian influence, he was converted in 1777 and began his career as a minister three years later. Struck with the genuineness of his piety, his master permitted him to conduct prayers and to preach in his house. The master himself was one of the first converts of this zealous man. Feeling after his conversion that slavery was wrong, Allen's master permitted his bondmen to obtain their freedom. Allen and his brother purchased themselves for $2,000 in the depreciated currency of the Revolutionary War. Richard Allen then engaged himself

at such menial labor as a Negro could then find. He cut
and hauled wood while preaching at his leisure. Recognizing his unusual talent, Richard Watcoat on the Baltimore
circuit permitted Allen to travel with him. Bishop Asbury
frequently gave him assignments to preach. Coming to
Philadelphia in 1786, Allen was invited to preach at the St.
George Methodist Episcopal Church and at various other
places in the city. His difficulties, however, had just begun. Yet he could not but succeed, because he was a man
of independent character, strict integrity, business tact,
and thrifty habits. When he spoke a word, it was taken
at its face value. His rule was never to break a promise
or violate a contract.[2]

The special needs of his own people aroused him to
action in their behalf. He said, ''I soon saw a large
field open in seeking and instructing my African brethren
who have been a long-forgotten people, and few of them
attended public worship.'' Starting a prayer meeting in
Philadelphia, he soon had forty-two members. Encouraged
thus, he proposed to establish a separate place of worship
for the people of color, but was dissuaded therefrom by the
protest of the whites and certain Negroes unto whom he
ministered. Only three of them approved his plan.
Preaching at this church with such power as to move his
own people in a way that they had never been affected
before, however, he attracted so many that the management proposed to segregate the Negroes. The church
undertook to carry out this plan drastically even to the
extent of disturbing Richard Allen, Absalom Jones, and
William White by pulling them off their knees while
they were in the attitude of prayer. The Negroes, therefore, withdrew from the church in a body.

---

[2] When he purchased the property for the Bethel Church on Lom-
bard Street near Sixth the majority of the committee refused to
accept it. Allen, having given his word so to do, kept it at a great
personal loss.

This was the beginning of the independent Free African Society, organized by Richard Allen and Absalom Jones. At first, however, this organization was not so much a church as it was a social uplift organization. It appeared that Jones and Allen soon had differing plans; for the former finally organized the African Protestant Episcopal Church of St. Thomas, while the majority of the persons seceding from the St. George Methodist Episcopal Church followed the standard of Allen in effecting the independent body known as the Bethel Church. Allen purchased an old building for the Bethel Church and had it duly dedicated in 1794. He organized also a Sunday School and a day and night school, to which were sent regular ministers by the Methodist Conference. Allen was ordained deacon by Bishop Asbury in 1799. He later attained the status of elder. Negroes of other cities followed this example. They organized what were known as African Methodist Episcopal Churches in Baltimore, Wilmington, Attleboro, Pennsylvania, and Salem, New Jersey. Having maintained themselves independently for some time, these African societies soon developed sufficient leaders to effect the organization of a national church. A conference for this purpose was called in Philadelphia in 1816. The most important transaction of the Philadelphia meeting was the election of a bishop. Upon taking the vote the body declared Daniel Coker bishop-elect. But for several reasons he resigned the next day in favor of Richard Allen, who was elected and consecrated by regularly ordained ministers.

The first independent Negro Methodist church.

Much progress thereafter was noted. With the establishment of the New York conference the limits of the connection extended eastward as far as New Bedford, westward to Pittsburgh, and southward to Charleston, South Carolina. There-

Progress of separate churches.

after, however, there was little hope of success in the South. The African Methodists there met with some difficulty under the leadership of the Rev. Morris Brown, who established in Charleston a church reporting 1,000 members in 1817 and 3,000 in 1822. Because of the spirit of insurrection among Negroes following the fortunes of Denmark

JAMES VARICK

Vesey, who devised well-laid plans for killing off the masters of the slaves in 1822, these communicants were required to suspend operation. Their pastor, Morris Brown, was threatened a n d would have been dealt with foully, had it not been for the interference of General James Hamilton. He secreted Brown in his home until he could give him safe passage to the North. There Morris Brown very soon reached a position of prominence, even that of bishop in the African Methodist Episcopal Church.

Another secession of the Methodists from the white connection was in progress in other parts. A number of Negroes, most of whom were members of the John Street Methodist Episcopal Church, in New York City, took the first step toward separation from that connection in 1796. They had not been disturbed in their worship to the extent **Zionites separate.** experienced by Richard Allen and his co-workers in Philadelphia, but they had a "desire for the privilege of holding meetings of their own, where they might have an opportunity to exercise their spiritual gifts among themselves, and thereby be more useful to one another.'' Such permission was obtained from Bishop Francis Asbury by a group of intelligent Negro Methodists. Their white friends appointed as their adviser Rev. John McClaskey, who instructed them how to proceed in drawing up the articles of government. A charter was secured in 1801 and bears the signatures of Peter Williams and Francis Jacobs. This was the beginning of the African Methodist Episcopal Zion Church. A number of such congregations were established.

This church had not proceeded very far before there arose some dissension in the ranks. The supporters of Bishop Allen, moreover, appeared at the opportune moment, when the Zionites in New York City were without a building and were also without the direc- Causes for tion which they had formerly had from the doubt. white Methodists. The latter were disturbed by a schism resulting from differences as to church government and property. There soon came a time when it was necessary for the Zionites to decide exactly what they would do. This being the case, an official meeting was held on August 11, 1820, for the purpose of considering the serious state of the church. Being desirous, however, to proceed regularly rather than radically, these African Methodists sought ordination and consecration through some branch of the Christian Church. They sent a committee to make such a request of Bishop Hobart of the Episcopal Church, but he was unable to serve them. They then appealed to the bishop of the Methodist Church, but they were put off in one way or another. They thereafter appealed to Methodist conferences in Philadelphia and New York and were finally refused. The Zionites were then reduced to radical measures in that they finally had to ordain their own deacons and elders. Becoming thus aggressive, the

Zionites, like the Allenites, had taken the offensive. They extended their operations through missionaries. Under the leadership of such men as James Varick, George Collins, Charles Anderson, and Christopher Rush, they drew up

CHRISTOPHER RUSH

the doctrines and discipline of the African Methodist Episcopal Zion Church in America. They elected a number of elders, and finally organized in 1821 a national body, of which James Varick became the first bishop in 1822.

Before the Negro Methodists perfected their organization by which the influence of their churches might be permanently extended throughout the country, the Baptists had been locally trying to do the same thing. The Harrison Street Baptist Church was organized at Petersburg, Virginia, in **Early Baptist** 1776; and another Baptist Church at Wil- **churches.** liamsburg, Virginia, in 1785. The first African Baptist Church was established in Savannah in 1785, with the second Baptist Church in that City following fourteen years later. The African Baptist Church of Lexington, Kentucky, appeared in 1790. There was founded a mixed Baptist Church in the Mound Bayou, Mississippi district, in 1805, by Joseph Willis, a free Negro, born in South Carolina in 1762.[3] In the City of Phila-

---

[3] A man of fair education, Willis was a power in that State as early as 1798. We hear of him in Louisiana in 1804. Mississippi

delphia on May 14, 1809, thirteen Negro members who had for some time felt that it would be more congenial for them to worship separately, were dismissed to form the first African Baptist Church. On June 19, 1809, the use of the First Baptist Church (white) was given them for the meeting at which they were constituted an organized body. The main trouble with the First Baptist Church (white) seemed to be that it had suffered from having its antislavery ardor dampened during the reaction following the Revolutionary War.

When the African Baptist Church of Philadelphia was being organized, the same movement was culminating likewise in Boston. Prior to 1809 the Baptists of color had worshiped along with their white brethren. The church record of November 1, 1772, says: "After divine service, Hannah Dunmore and Chloe, a Negro woman belonging to Mr. George Green, were received into the church." Speaking about this relation, this document says: "Our records have many notices of baptisms and marriages among the Negro people and until early in the present century there was a large group of them in the church." But the desire for independence and a more congenial atmosphere so obsessed them that they sought to form an organization of their own. This was finally effected in 1809 under the leadership of the Rev. Thomas Paul, a native of Exeter, New Hampshire. His labors, however, were not restricted to that city. He frequently made preaching excursions into different parts of the country where his "color excited considerable curiosity." Being a person of very pleasing and fervid address, he attracted crowds. It was while he was pastor of the Church in Boston, that in 1808 he organized in New York City the congregation now known

Early workers Among Baptists.

sent two ministers to ordain him in Louisiana in 1812. He organized the Louisiana Baptist Association and was chosen as its moderator in 1837.

as the Abyssinian Baptist Church and served it from June to September of that year. After this Josiah Bishop and others had charge of this very promising work in the metropolis of the nation.[4]

That the independent church movement among Negroes should be directed toward Methodism and Baptism requires some consideration. In those parts of the country in which most Negroes were found, the dominant communicants among the whites were at first Episcopalians, the **Causes of the** successors to the rites and ceremonies of the **independent** Anglican Church. Among some of the best **movement.** friends of the Negroes, moreover, were the Presbyterians, who often extended the blacks the same hand of welcome as did the Quakers. Whether the failure of the Negro to be attracted to them was due altogether to the emotional nature of the Negroes to which the Baptists and Methodists appealed, to chance, or to the wisdom of the leaders of the independent church movement among the Negroes, is a much-mooted question.

The Episcopal Church, moreover, could hardly attract large numbers of Negroes. Its discipline was ill-suited to the undeveloped Negro. Its ministers had been among the first to offer the Negroes religious instruction, but it had lost favor by refusing to give Negroes the consideration

---

[4] Paul's interest in the Negro was not limited to those in this country. In 1823 he presented to the Baptist Missionary Society of Massachusetts a plan for improving the moral and religious condition of the Haitians. His plan was received with considerable enthusiasm and he was appointed as a missionary and sent to that country for six months. President Boyer of the Republic of Haiti and other public functionaries kindly received this missionary. There he soon met with some success in edifying a few pious people who seemed gratified beyond measure by his ministrations. Writing home, he frequently mentioned "the powerful precious soul-reviving seasons" which he and the few disciples on the island enjoyed. Because of his lack of knowledge of the French language, however, he could not reach a large number of the inhabitants of that island. He was, therefore, compelled to leave Haiti with the regret that he could not do more for its general welfare.

which they enjoyed among the Methodists and Baptists. Furthermore, the Episcopal churchmen refused to make slavery a matter of discipline. Consequently their work among the Negroes was restricted to such establishments as St. Thomas in Philadelphia, St. Philips, organized in New York in 1818, and the St. James, established later in Baltimore.

The independent movement among other Negro communicants was not so pronounced. In the first place there were not many of them, although various sects welcomed the Negroes and contributed much to their uplift. In the case of a more ritualistic church like the Catholics, to which Negroes **Negroes in ritualistic churches.** were attracted only in small numbers, there was no opportunity offered for the development of the Negro along independent lines. Among the Congregationalists were found most of the ardent friends of the Negro during the first half of the nineteenth century. Consequently, there was little reason for a separate establishment from their fellow white communicants. A separate church of this faith among the Negroes did not appear until 1829 when there was organized the Dixwell Avenue Congregational Church in New Haven.

There were many other Negroes who without very much independent organization to support them nevertheless accomplished much in demonstrating the initiative of the race. For more than a generation, Andrew Marshall continued the efficient work among the Baptists of Savannah begun by George Liele and **Henry Evans.** successfully developed by Andrew Bryan. For more than forty years, a pioneer Negro preacher, one "Uncle Jack," went from plantation to plantation in Virginia to preach to whites and blacks. Henry Evans, a free Negro preacher of Virginia, happened to stop at Fayetteville, North Carolina, while on his way to Charleston. Expounding the Gospel on Sunday while working at the trade of shoemaking during the week, he so stirred up the town that the officials prohibited him from preaching. He won so many friends, however, that this order was recalled. He developed the work there to the extent of having a sufficient following for a church by 1790. He labored successfully among both races in that field until 1810. At this time Black Harry, another Negro preacher, had so impressed the public that Dr. Benjamin Rush pronounced him the greatest orator in America. Bishop Asbury often took him as his companion because his forceful preaching attracted a larger audience than the bishop himself could draw, for, says John Ledman, "Harry was a more popular speaker than Mr. Asbury or almost any one else in his day."

Out of Tennessee had come another Negro preacher of this type. This was John Gloucester, who had been the body servant of Gideon Blackburn of that State. Moved by his unusual gifts as a scholar and a preacher, his master **John Gloucester.** liberated him that he might engage in the ministry. He came to Philadelphia where he began his life's work as a missionary exhorting from house to house. He then preached in a schoolhouse and finally had sufficient converts with whom to establish the First African Presbyterian Church in Philadelphia in 1807. This work he promoted with unusual success until 1822 when he passed away.

In this class of preachers there were those who accomplished certain definite things worthy of attention. Among these a prominent place should be given to John Stewart. **John Stewart, the apostle to the Indians.** He was born of free parents in Powhatan County, Virginia. There he received some religious instruction. On coming to Marietta, Ohio, he came under the influence of the Methodist Episcopal Church. Believing that it was his mission to serve the world as a preacher, he proceeded to the arduous task of converting the Indians of Lake Erie. After overcoming the opposition of William Walker, the Federal Agent, he returned to the Wyandot Indians, at Upper Sandusky. Filled with enthusiasm and preaching with unusual power in proselyting the Indians, the Methodist Episcopal Church granted him the support which his work required. A mission station was established, and actual education with instruction in mechanic arts and agriculture soon followed. With other workers coming to his assistance Stewart saw his efforts crowned with remarkable success as he, on account of unusual labor, began to decline in 1822. He had nevertheless made himself the pioneer of the Methodist Episcopal Church in its mission work among the Indians.

Still more ambitious was the work of Lemuel Haynes. He was the son of a Negro by a white woman. He was born in 1753. His mother, because of the stigma attached to her child of color, deserted Lemuel in infancy. He later became an apprentice in the family of **Lemuel Haynes, a preacher to whites.** a white man who transferred him to one David Rose, of Granville, Massachusetts. Lemuel was placed at school. Conspicuous in the curriculum which he had to follow was religious instruction. Before his education could be completed, however, he had to answer the call to the colors and served with distinction in the Revolutionary War. Upon returning to his home among his good people he was often called upon on Satday evenings to read from collections of sermons to prepare the minds of the family for the more serious worship on the Sabbath Day. Availing himself of the opportunity to study religious books, he soon developed much knowledge of things spiritual. One Saturday evening, therefore, when asked to read a sermon from one of the divines, he read one of his own. As this sermon had a new ring

and a thought that David Rose had never heard before
he inquired as to whose sermon it was. Lemuel had to
confess that it was his own sermon. The community, then,
realized that it had in Lemuel the possibility of an unusual
preacher. He was soon given the opportunity to exercise
this gift. However, there were those who were disinclined
to accept the ministry of a Negro. One white man who
came to a church to hear him preach out of curiosity

endeavored to show his
disrespect by keeping his
hat on. He confessed
thereafter, however, that
before Lemuel Haynes
had spoken five minutes
it seemed to him that the
greatest man he had ever
seen was preaching to him
from that pulpit. And
thus he was finally re-
ceived throughout that
section in New England.
He preached to the whites
at Torrington, West Rut-
land, Manchester, and at
Granville, in New York.

LEMUEL HAYNES

He served also as a missionary in the destitute sections of
New England. While thus engaged he showed his unusual ability in engaging in the theological discussions of
the times. This was about 1815. He was especially interested in that of the Stoddardian principle of admitting
moral persons with credible evidence of grace to the Lord's
Supper. Everywhere he acquitted himself with honor.
He is remembered to-day by the white people of that section in New England.[5]

[5] *The Journal of Negro History*, IV, 22-32.

Farther South during these years there was before the
public a Negro preacher of unusual distinction. He was
a full-blooded Negro of dark-brown color. He was born
in Oxford, Granville County, North Carolina, in 1763.
Making upon his hearers the impression of being unusually
gifted, they sent him to Princeton. Under Dr. Wither-
spoon he was educated there as a Latin   John Chavis, a
and Greek scholar. He devoted some time   preacher and
also to the study of Theology, and on his teacher.
return from Princeton engaged in the ministry. In 1801
the Presbyterians referred to him as a "black man of
prudence and piety, in the service of the Hanover Presby-
tery as a riding missionary under the direction of the General Assembly." We find him stationed in Lexington, Virginia, in 1805. Afterward he returned to North Carolina.
Referring to him as a man of that early day, Paul Cham-
eron, a white man of note, said: "In my boyhood life at
my father's home I often saw John Chavis, a venerable
old Negro man, recognized as a freeman and as a preacher
or clergyman of the Presbyterian Church. As such he was
received by my father and treated with kindness and consideration, and respected as a character." Mr. George
Wortham, a lawyer of Granville County, said: "I have
heard him read repeatedly. His English was remarkably
pure, containing no 'Negroisms'; his manner was impres-
sive, his explanations clear and concise, and his views, as
I then thought and still think, entirely orthodox. He was
said to have been an acceptable preacher, his sermons
abounding in strong common sense views and happy illustrations, without any effort at oratory or sensational appeals to the passions of his hearers." Thus he continued
as a minister in having the respect and coöperation of both
races until as a result of Nat Turner's insurrection, the
preaching of Negroes was prohibited. He thereafter engaged in teaching until the time of his death. In this

capacity he served the most aristocratic white people of that State in teaching their sons and daughters. In the end he counted among his former students W. P. Mangum, afterward United States Senator; P. H. Mangum, his brother; Archibald and John Henderson, sons of Chief Justice Henderson; Charles Manly, later Governor of that commonwealth, and Dr. James L. Wortham of Oxford, North Carolina.

CHAPTER X

THE REACTION

THE impetus given the uplift of the Negroes during the struggle for the independence of the country was gradually checked after 1783, when the States faced the problem of readjustment. In the organization of governments the States came to the conclusion that it was nec- **Emancipation** essary to restrain men to maintain order and **checked.** that they had to depart from some of the theories on which the Revolution was fought. In the elimination of the impracticable from the scheme of reconstruction after making peace with Great Britain, the proposal for the emancipation of the slaves was no longer generally heeded. In those colonies where the Negroes were not found in large numbers they were emancipated without much opposition and some of them were made citizens of the new States. But in those where the Negroes constituted a considerable part of the population there followed such a reaction against the elevation of the race to citizenship that much of the work proposed to promote their welfare and to provide for the manumission was undone.[1]

Certain States of the upper South did support the movement to abolish the slave trade. The prohibition of the slave trade in Delaware, Maryland, Virginia, **Slave trade** and North Carolina, however, did not neces- **in the South.**

[1] M. S. Locke, *Antislavery in America*, pp. 157-166; K. H. Porter, *A History of Suffrage in the United States*, Chs. II and III, C. G. Woodson, *The Education of the Negro Prior to 1861*, Chs. VI and VII; and A. D. Adams, *The Neglected Period of Antislavery in America*, *passim.*

161

sarily show a humanitarian trend. The reasons for such action were largely economic. Industry there had reached a settled state, and the influx of more slaves, they believed, would lead to a decrease in the value of slaves, cause the supply of Southern products to exceed the demand, drain the States of money, and constitute a sinister influence on Negroes already broken in. If imported in large numbers the trade might force upon the communities a larger number than could be supported, and instead of promoting slavery might make instant abolition necessary.

The country, moreover, was far from being antislavery. The Congress of the Confederation had very little to do with slavery, as it did not care to interfere with the rights of the States. Slavery as a national question, however, appeared in the adoption of the Ordinance of 1787, providing **Slavery and** for the organization of the Northwest Terri-**the Ordinance** tory. The sixth clause of that document **of 1787.** provided that neither slavery nor involuntary servitude, except for punishment of crime, should be permitted in the said territory. This was enacted, of course, prior to the adoption of the Constitution of the United States and may seem to have no bearing thereon; but as its legality was questioned on the ground that no such power had been granted to the Continental Congress by the States or by any provision in the Articles of Confederation, it requires special attention. It is of importance to note that it was defended on the untenable ground that it was a treaty made by the States forming the Confederation rather than an agreement of the States to be organized in this territory thereafter. The best which can be said for it, however, is that it was merely a legislative act of Congress.[2]

[2] All of these aspects of the Ordinance of 1787 are thoroughly discussed in J. P. Dunn's *Indiana; A Redemption from Slavery*, Ch. VI; and in Chas. Thomas Hickok's *The Negro in Ohio*, chapter on the Ordinance of 1787.

The Convention of 1787, called to frame the first constitution of the United States, desired to take very little interest in the antislavery movement in the organization of
the new government. Oliver Ellsworth of Connecticut and
Elbridge Gerry of Massachusetts thought the **The Conven-**
question of slavery should be settled by the **tion of 1787.**
States themselves. When this question came more prominently before this body, however, it had to be considered
more seriously. It was necessary to consider a regulation
for returning fugitive slaves, the prohibition of the slave
trade, and the apportionment of representation. When the
South wanted the Negroes
to be counted to secure
larger representation on
the population basis, al-
though it did not want
thus to count the blacks
in apportioning federal
taxes, some sharp debate
ensued. But the Northern
antislavery d e l e g a t e s
were not so much at-
tached to the cause of
universal freedom as to
force their opinions on
the proslavery group and
thus lose their support in
organizing a more stable form of government.[3] They
finally compromised by providing for representation of the
States by two Senators from each, and for the representation of the people in the House by counting all whites and
five Negroes as three whites. Another compromise was
made in providing for the continuation of the slave trade
until 1808, when it should be prohibited, and for a fugitive

BENJAMIN FRANKLIN, an advocate
of freedom

[3] *The Journal of Negro History*, Vol. III, pp. 381-434.

slave law to secure slaveholders in the possession of their peculiar property.

Immediately after the Federal Government was organized there seemed to be a tendency to ignore the claims of the Negro. In 1789 the Quakers, at their annual meeting **The Negro a** in Philadelphia and New York, adopted cer- **negligible** tain memorials praying the action of Congress **factor.** in adopting measures for the abolition of the slave trade and, in particular, in restraining vessels from being entered and cleared out for the purpose of that traffic. There came also a memorial to the same effect from the Pennsylvania Society for the Abolition of Slavery, bearing the signature of its president, Benjamin Franklin. This led to much discussion of the slavery question, but the memorials were, by a vote of 43 to 11, referred to a special committee which reported March 5, 1790. On the 8th the report was referred to the committee of the whole where it was debated a week. Several amendments were proposed and given consideration in the House. Finally, by a vote of 29 to 25, the reports of the special committee and of the committee of the whole house were ordered to be printed in the Journal and to lie on the table. The principle of non-interference with slavery set forth in this report determined for a number of years the reactionary attitude of Congress with respect to slavery.[4]

[4] The report of the Special Committee was: The committee to whom were referred sundry memorials from the People called Quakers; and also a memorial from the Pennsylvania Society for promoting the Abolition of Slavery, submit the following report:

That, from the nature of the matters contained in those memorials, they were induced to examine the powers vested in Congress, under the present Constitution, relating to the abolition of slavery, and are clearly of the opinion,

First, That the General Government is expressly restrained from prohibiting the importation of such persons "as any of the States now existing shall think proper to admit, until the year one thousand eight hundred and eight."

Secondly, That Congress, by a fair construction of the Constitution are equally restrained from interfering in the emancipation of

Congress refused also to intervene in behalf of certain manumitted Negroes of North Carolina, who after having been given their liberty by the Quakers were again reduced to slavery. The only action of this sort taken by Congress during its early operation was to pass the **Non-inter-** Fugitive Slave Law of 1793. This measure **vention by** provided that a master might seize his ab- **Congress.** sconding slave taking refuge in another State, carry him

slaves, who already are, or who may, within the period mentioned be imported into, or born within any of the said States.

Thirdly, That Congress have no authority to interfere in the internal regulations of particular States, relative to the instruction of slaves in the principles of morality and religion; to their comfortable clothing; accommodations, and subsistence; to the regulation of their marriages, and the prevention of the violation of the rights thereof, or to the separation of children from their parents; to a comfortable provision in cases of sickness, age, or infirmity; or to the seizure, transportation, or sale of free negroes; but have the fullest confidence in the wisdom and humanity of the Legislatures of the several States, that they will revise their laws from time to time, when necessary, and promote the objects mentioned in the memorials, and every other measure that may tend to the happiness of slaves.

Fourthly, That, nevertheless, Congress have authority, if they shall think it necessary, to lay at any time a tax or duty, not exceeding ten dollars for each person of any description, the importation of whom shall be by any of the States admitted as aforesaid.

Fifthly, That Congress have authority to interdict, or (so far as it is or may be carried on by citizens of the United States, for supplying foreigners) to regulate the African trade, and to make provision for the humane treatment of Slaves, in all cases while on their passage to the United States, or to foreign ports, as far as it respects the citizens of the United States.

Sixthly, That Congress have also authority to prohibit foreigners from fitting out vessels, in any port of the United Sates, for transportation of persons from Africa to any foreign port.

Seventhly, That the memorialists be informed, that in all cases to which the authority of Congress extends, they will exercise it for the humane objects of the memorialists, so far as they can be promoted on the principles of justice, humanity, and good policy.

REPORT OF THE COMMITTEE OF THE WHOLE HOUSE

The Committee of the Whole House, to whom was committed the report of the committee on the memorials of the People called Quakers, and of the Pennsylvania Society for Promoting the Abolition of Slavery, report the following amendments:

Strike out the first clause, together with the recital thereto, and

before any magistrate, and secure from that functionary authority to return the slave. Congress refused on this occasion to provide any safeguards to prevent the enslavement of free Negroes. No sympathy could then be expected from the North, for while that section considered the institution an evil, it had not in the least increased its love for the Negro; and evidences of unrest among Negroes did not make conditions more favorable. The North did not want the Negroes, and those southerners who had advocated their emancipation were confronted with the question as to what should be done with them when freed.

This problem was aggravated by the uprising in Santo Domingo. The successful rebellion of the Negroes in Santo Domingo brought such a dread of servile insurrection among the slaveholders that many of them opposed the continuation of the slave trade. And even in the radi-

---

in lieu thereof insert, "That the migration or importation of such persons as any of the States now existing shall think proper to admit, cannot be prohibited by Congress, prior to the year one thousand eight hundred and eight."

Strike out the second and third clauses, and in lieu thereof insert, "That Congress have no authority to interfere in the emancipation of slaves, or in the treatment of them within any of the States; it remaining with the several States alone to provide any regulations therein, which humanity and true policy may require."

Strike out the fourth and fifth clauses, and in lieu thereof insert, "That Congress have authority to restrain the citizens of the United States from carrying on the African trade, for the purpose of supplying foreigners with slaves, and of providing by proper regulations for the humane treatment, during their passage, of slaves imported by the said citizens into the States admitting such importation."

Strike out the seventh clause.

Ordered, that the said report of the Commitee of the Whole House do lie on the table.

See Text of both reports in the *House Journal*, 1st Cong., 2d Sess.; the report of the special committee is also in the *Annals of Congress*, 1st Cong., II, 1414, 1415, and in *Amer. State Papers, Miscellaneous*, I, 12. Full reports of discussions are in the *Annals*; condensed in Benton's *Abridgment*, I. See also von Holst's *United States*, I, 89-94; Parton's *Franklin*, II, 606-614; Wilson's *Rise and Fall of the Slave Power*, I, 61-67.

cally proslavery South, as in the case of South Carolina, it was specifically provided that no slaves should be imported from this disturbed area in the West Indies. As a matter of fact, however, many refugees from Haiti did come to the ports of Baltimore, Norfolk, **Refugees** Charleston, and New Orleans. They sowed **from Haiti.** seeds of discord from which came most of the uprisings of Negroes during the first three decades of the nineteenth century.[5]

The story of Toussaint Louverture made a deep impression on the minds of a few Negro leaders. The situation in Santo Domingo was a complication. The **Haitian** eastern end of the Island was Spanish and **revolution.** the western, French. Further difficulty resulted from having in this French portion 50,000 Creoles, an equal number of mulattoes and about a half-million Negroes of pure African blood. All elements desired to avail themselves of the equality guaranteed French citizens by the General Assembly of the French Revolution. The mulattoes first asked for the extension of these rights to them. After being baffled by the grant ambiguously phrased, they finally heard the decree extending to the people of color of free ancestry the rights and privileges of citizens. The whites, incensed by this liberality on the part of the French Republic, precipitated revolution in the island by espousing the cause of the French King.

Thereupon, the slaves struck for freedom on August 23, 1791, and killed off their masters in large numbers. Hoping to undo this work, the Conventional Assembly of France abrogated the order extending the rights of **The uprising.** citizens and sent troops to put down the in-

[5] These uprisings are set forth in Joshua Coffin's *An Account of the Principal Slave Insurrections.* See also Edwin V. Morgan's *Slavery in New York* (American Historical Association Report, 1895), pp. 629-673; and E. B. Green's *Provincial America* (The American Nation), Vol. VI, p. 240.

surrection. In the struggle which followed during the next
two years, the Negroes tended to join the mulattoes to
fight the master class. Thousands of persons were killed
in the meantime and much property was destroyed. San-
thonax, sent from France with Polverel to restore order,
thereupon issued a proclamation of freedom to all slaves
who would uphold the cause of the French Republic. This

TOUSSAINT LOUVERTURE

proclamation through the
coöperation of Polverel,
in charge at Port - au -
Prince, gradually spread
throughout the Island.

At this juncture there
forged ahead an unusual
character. This was
Toussaint Louverture, an
experienced soldier,
forty-eight years old. He
had been at first in com-
mand of royalist troops.
He abandoned the royal-
ist standard in 1794 to
serve the Republican
cause after the favorable

decree of the Assembly. He was promoted to the rank
of general of the brigade in 1796. The following year he
Toussaint   was put in full command in Santo Domingo.
Louverture.   Proceeding to handle matters efficiently, he
immediately forced the surrender of the English invading
the island. In somewhat similar fashion through the commercial aid of the United States, he expelled his rival
Rigaud from the country. He then cleared the way for
full civil military authority by imprisoning Roume, the
agent of the Directory. He next subdued the Spanish
part of the Island and proclaimed a constitution grant-

ing him power for life and the right of naming his successor.

This triumph of Toussaint Louverture upset one of the dreams of Napoleon Bonaparte. As First Consul, he was trying to make himself the head of a French empire. In 1800 he induced Spain to retrocede the Louisiana territory to France. Santo Domingo was to be a stepping stone in this direction. He sent his brother-in-law, General Le Clerc, with twenty-five thousand soldiers to enforce the claims of France in Haiti. Santo Domingo, thus upset by Toussaint Louverture, seemed to Napoleon an **Napoleon's** impediment of Republicanism tainted with **dream upset.** American ideas. As a matter of fact, however, the Government established by Toussaint Louverture was less democratic than that of Napoleon. Le Clerc appeared upon the scene in 1802. He betrayed Toussaint Louverture into a conference on a French vessel on which he was transported to France only to die of neglect in the prison of Joux. There was immediately proclaimed the annulment of the decree of liberty to the slaves. This, however, did not end the resistance to French Power. Toussaint Louverture's task of arousing his people had been too well done. The French Army was decimated not only by guerrilla warfare but the yellow fever. Before the end of the year 1802, six-sevenths of Le Clerc's army had perished, including the General himself. In the meantime, the much delayed retrocession of Louisiana by Spain was effected. The United States Government, moreover, was anxious to obtain this territory as an outlet to trade in the West. This had been often interfered with by the closing of the Mississippi to the trade of the Americans in the Middle West. Jefferson, through the negotiation of James Monroe, made a final effort to purchase this territory. In the unfortunate outcome in Haiti, the disaster in Egypt, and the inability to reach India, Napoleon could see his dream for a world empire a failure. He, therefore, disposed of the territory to the United States in 1803.

The slavery question was immediately brought prominently before the country in the effort of antislavery groups to exclude the institution from the new lands thus acquired. It was provided that in acquiring the territory of Louisiana from France the privileges and immunities enjoyed by those citizens under the government of the French would be guaranteed by the United States. This led to some future constitutional questions. Inasmuch as Louisiana was slaveholding prior to the purchase, the institution was thereby perpetuated in that territory. On the other hand, many of the Negroes of that territory belonged to the body of citizens exercising the same rights as the whites. When, a few years thereafter, Louisiana followed in the wake of the other reactionary States of the South and undertook to restrict the privileges of the free Negroes, it was contended that the action of the State conflicted with this treaty. Free persons of color who were citizens at the time of the purchase were guaranteed the full enjoyment of the privileges which they had under the French régime. On the occasion of the enforcement of a law of that state depriving certain free Negroes of the right to attend school, this question was brought up in Mobile, Alabama. At the time of the purchase this city belonged to the Louisiana territory. By special ordinance of the city council, therefore, these citizens were exempted from the operations of this law.

The chief cause of this reaction, however, was not fear of influences from without. The cause was primarily economic. During the second half of the eighteenth century, inventors, beginning with Watt, who built the first steam engine, brought out such mechanical appliances as the wool-combing machine, the spinning jenny, the power-loom, and finally Whitney's famous cotton gin. These revolutionized industries in the modern world. In facilitating the making of cloth these appliances so increased the demand for cotton as to expand the plantation system requiring a large increase in the importation of slaves. The cotton gin was a machine of revolving cylinders, one for tearing the lint from the seeds and another arranged to remove the lint from the first cylinder. It simplified the process of seeding cotton, and in releasing labor for production multiplied its output in a few years. Cotton cloth was thereby cheapened and the demand for it so rapidly increased that the South became a most inviting field in which was rooted one of the greatest industries of the world. Before the end of the second decade of the nineteenth century the States of the lower South became inalterably attached to slavery as an economic advantage in supplying the cheap labor it required. They began to denounce those who persisted in dubbing it an evil.

AN EARLY COTTON GIN

With this increase in the demand for slaves there came numerous petitions for the reopening of the African slave trade in the lower South. The Northern and Middle States early prohibited the slave traffic, holding it as a grievance against George III that they were not permitted to do so earlier. Maryland prohibited it in 1783. North Carolina checked it by a rather high import duty in 1789, and South Carolina proscribed it by law for sixteen years. Georgia alone took no action except to provide for its own security in prohibiting the importation of insurrectionary slaves from the West Indies, the Bahamas and Florida, and to require free

Increase in the demand for slaves.

Negroes to furnish certificates of their industry and honesty.

An early effort was made to repeal the prohibitory provision against the traffic in South Carolina, but it was defeated. Those interested in the trade proceeded to smuggle slaves along the coast, and the efforts to enforce the prohibitory law were without success. Finally, in 1805, after much persistence, the slave-traders in that State carried their point. They put through the bill to remove all African restrictions but continued the exclusion of Negroes from the West Indies and slaves from other States failing to have certificates of good character.

The action of South Carolina was interpreted as opening the door for all of the atrocities formerly practiced by the slave traders. North Carolina, New Hampshire, Vermont, **The slave** Maryland and Tennessee, therefore, requested **trade** their Congressmen to make an effort to have **objectionable.** the Constitution of the United States so amended as to prohibit the importation of Negroes from Africa and the West Indies. Congress refused to act in this case, not only because it had become reactionary, but because the time provided by the Constitution for the abolition of the slave trade would arrive in 1808. At the next session of Congress bills to prohibit the trade were introduced, but no action was taken.

In 1806 Jefferson took up the question in his annual message, urging Congress to interpose its authority to withdraw citizens of the United States from all further partici- **Jefferson on** pation in those violations of human rights **abolition.** which had been "so long continued on the unoffending inhabitants of Africa." [6] Senator Bradley of Vermont promptly introduced a bill with the provisions that interstate slave trade along the coast should be prohibited after the close of the year 1807 and that importa-

[6] *Annals of Congress*, 1806-1807, p. 14.

tion of slaves should be a felony punishable by death.[7]
In the House, where proslavery Congressmen managed
the framing of the bill, it prohibited importation, provided
fines and forfeitures of the slaves from abroad on board
such vessels, and authorized the sale at public auction of
slaves thus smuggled in. As it was evident that this bill
would not prevent the enslavement of the blacks concerned,
Mr. Sloane of New Jersey proposed to amend the measure
so as to free the slaves thus forfeited. This proposition
to turn loose in the South Negroes just from Africa evoked
from Early, of Georgia, the prophecy of the prompt extermination of such Negroes in the Southern States. But
speaking for his people, Smilie of Pennsylvania felt that
he could not tolerate the idea of making the Federal Government a dealer in slaves. Such an act, thought he, would
be unconstitutional. After some excitement, this provision
was stricken out.

An effort was then made to substitute imprisonment for
the death penalty, only to cause much more confusion.
After more exciting discussion the House laid aside its bill
for the one from the Senate, from which it **Efforts in**
promptly eliminated the death penalty and **behalf of**
provided a penalty of imprisonment of not **slave trade.**
less than five nor more than ten years. The prohibition
as to participation in coastal slave trade was also eliminated. The bill was then passed and sent back to the Senate.
The Senate accepted this with the modification that the
coastal trade provision be applied only to vessels of less
than forty tons. There was still some opposition from
Early of Georgia because he thought the bill in that form
futile for the prevention of smuggling from Florida. John
Randolph believed it interfered with a man's right of private property. The bill as passed penalized with imprison-

[7] The debate on the prohibition of the slave trade is treated in
W. E. B. DuBois's *Suppression of the African Slave Trade.*

ment the importation of slaves from abroad, prohibited the slave trade along the coast in vessels of less than forty tons, required of larger vessels conformity to certain stipulated regulations, and placed smuggled slaves, when seized, at the disposal of the State where they might be landed.

This law, of course, was a victory for the lower South then demanding an increase in the slave labor supply. With these evasive provisions favoring State control, the

Victory for the proslavery group. measure was never effective and the illicit trade flourished throughout the South without much interference. It was not long before the prohibition of the slave trade was very much like that of the prohibition of the sale of alcoholics in our day. It was an easy matter to smuggle slaves into the country at the Southern ports. This was especially true of Fernandina and Galveston. Through a well connected number of points reaching into the interior and crossing the Indian reservations, the Negroes were carried wherever they were desired. By connection with certain Spanish Islands in the West Indies, especially with Cuba, ships engaged in this traffic sailed under the Spanish flag. For convenience they might assume the colors of almost any nation, since these slave traders represented different nationalities. Madison complained of this trade in 1810 and Congress enacted in 1818 another measure prohibiting the traffic. The proslavery interests at that time, however, were so influential that the measure was so worded as to be weak and ineffective. This was the culmination of the reaction against the Negro. For economic reasons the South had pitted itself against the Constitution. That Negroes might be further exploited by the whites that section had finally secured a majority sufficiently lacking in moral courage to crush the spirit of the fundamental law. In the hands of persons out of sympathy with the Negro, it was impossible to secure a conviction under these laws until the Civil War.

From this stimulated traffic there followed not only the enslavement of a large number of helpless Africans, but also of some of the learned and most aristocratic of the tribes. One of these distinguished Africans brought thus into this country was Lahmen Kebby from Futa. He was liberated in 1835 after having been held as a slave for 40 years in South Carolina, Alabama, and other Southern States. In Africa he had served as a schoolmaster after having pursued a long course of preparatory studies. He said that his aunt was much more learned than he and "eminent for her superior acquirements and for her skill in teaching." "Schools," he said, "were generally established through the country, provision being made by law for educating children of all classes, the poor being taught gratuitously." [8] Finally there was another Fula, Omar ibn Said, sold into slavery in the Carolinas about 1807. At first he had a kind master, but at the death of his owner his lot was hard. He, therefore, became a fugitive. Arrested as a vagrant, he was imprisoned in Fayetteville. Writing in Arabic on some coals while confined in the Cumberland County jail, probably making thus an appeal for succor, he attracted attention as a remarkable man. General James Owen, brother of Governor John Owen, bought Omar and carried him to his home in Bladen County. There he was treated more as a distinguished freeman of color than as a slave. He was at first a devout Mohammedan and faithfully read the Koran that he might religiously live up to the principles of the Prophet; but Omar gradually became interested in Christianity. He later made a profession of faith in this religion and attended the country church near Owen's estate. He lived until after the Civil War. A slave of this type (it might

[8] *African Repository*, XIII, 204; *Methodist Review*, XLVI, 77-90.

have been Omar Ibn Said himself) was taken to the University of North Carolina, sometime before the Civil War, to instruct one of its professors in the Arabic language and literature.[9]

[9] *The American Historical Review*, XXX, 787-795.

CHAPTER XI

As a sequel and a cause of the reaction came the bold attempts of the Negroes at insurrection.[1] Unwilling to undergo the persecutions entailed by this change of slavery from a patriarchal to an exploitation system, a number of Negroes endeavored to secure relief by refreshing the tree of liberty with the blood of their oppressors. The chief source of these uprisings came from refugees brought to this country from Santo Domingo in 1793 Slave and from certain free Negroes encouraged insurrections. to extend a helping hand to their enslaved brethren. With the news of the first uprising of the blacks in that island in 1791 Negroes of Louisiana were emboldened to do likewise. On account of disagreement as to time and dissension in the ranks the plan failed. Twenty-three suspected slaves were hanged and exposed to public gaze to produce a deterrent effect on the minds of others.

The first effort of consequence was an insurrection in Virginia in 1800. The full name of the author of this plot was Gabriel Prosser. He was faithfully assisted by his brother named Martin and by Jack Bowler. They finally worked out a far-reaching plan with the first day of September as the date to assemble. The Negroes in and near Richmond were to march upon the city, seize the arsenal, strike down the whites, and liberate the slaves. This plan was frustrated by a fearful storm on the appointed day and by a slave who disclosed the secret to save the life of

[1] For additional information as to the rising of slaves see Joshua Coffin's *Slave Insurrections*, and Higginson's *Travelers and Outlaws*.

177

his kind master. However, there were echoes from it in a projected riot in Suffolk county and in some exciting scenes in Petersburg, Virginia, in Edenton, North Carolina, and in Charleston, South Carolina. Bowler surrendered without much resistance and Gabriel fell into the hands of his pursuers in a few weeks. Six of the accomplices were sentenced to execution on the twelfth of the month and five others on the eighteenth. Prosser himself was executed on the third of October. Twenty-four others, some of whom were innocent, suffered the same fate.

The uprising had been so deliberately planned that it was thought that white men were concerned with it; but, according to James Monroe, an investigation showed that there was no ground for such a conclusion. It was discovered, however, that the plotters had given orders not to destroy any of the French in the city. It was brought out, then, that these Negroes, through channels of information, had taken over the revolutionary ideas of France and were beginning to use force to secure to themselves those privileges so highly prized by the people of that country.[2]

The insurrectionary movement was impeded but could not be easily stopped. At Camden in 1816 a considerable number of Negroes planned another uprising. Betrayed also by a "faithful" slave, the Negroes saw themselves terror-stricken at the execution of six of their leaders. Some years later at Tarboro, Newberne and Hillsboro, North Carolina, there developed other such plots of less consequence. A plot to destroy the city of Augusta, Georgia, in 1819, resulted in the execution of the leader named Coot. For some years these outbreaks were **Other plots.** frequent around Baltimore, Norfolk, Petersburg, and New Orleans.

In 1822, however, Charleston, South Carolina, was the scene of a better planned effort. The leading spirit was

[2] *The New York Daily Advertiser*, Sept. 22 and Oct. 7, 1800.

Denmark Vesey, an educated Negro of Santo Domingo. His name was Telemaque, reduced later among illiterates to *Telmak* and finally to *Denmark*. He knew both English and French. With some money which he won in a lottery in 1800 he purchased himself from his owner, Captain Vesey, who had brought him to Charleston. He thereafter successfully established himself as a carpenter, and accumulated property to the amount of $8,000. From Santo Domingo he had brought new ideas as to freedom. He easily won the confidence of the slaves and for the next generation endeavored to inculcate in their minds discontent with their lot. Operating here in Charleston where free Negroes were to some extent a privileged class, many of them able to read and write, Vesey and his co-workers stirred up a considerable number. They often met in a church in Hampstead, one of the suburbs of Charleston. Instruction was given in things bearing on the struggle for liberty, literature styled incendiary was circulated, and the leader of the Santo Domingo revolt was probably approached for aid. These Negroes read with interest the debate on the Missouri Compromise. The official report was that "materials were abundantly furnished in the seditious pamphlets brought into the State by equally capable incendiaries, while the speeches of the oppositionists in Congress to the admission of Missouri gave a serious and imposing effect to his machinations."[3]

The recruiting of the Negroes for seventy or eighty miles around was to begin about the Christmas of 1821. On the second Monday in July, 1822, when most of the master class would be absent for the summer vacation, the attack was to be made. Lists of thousands of recruits were drawn up, money was raised to purchase arms, and a blacksmith

[3] See *The City Gazette and Commercial Daily Advertiser*, August 21, 1862; *The Norfolk and Portsmouth Herald*, August 30, 1822; *The Education of the Negro Prior to 1861*, pp. 156-158.

was engaged to make pikes and bayonets for the incipient attack. The conspirators hoped, however, to obtain a larger supply by raiding the arsenal in the city. Here again the history of Negro insurrections repeated itself. A slave hearing about it, told his master. Officials, at first, could hardly believe all that which was divulged. Some of those implicated were exonerated when first examined. By the day set for the rising, however, the plans had all been disclosed. The city then ran wild with excitement. And well might this be so, for by this time the authorities had learned that some of the most respectable free Negroes and slaves enjoying the highest confidence of the public were deliberately planning to kill all of the whites of the city. Denmark Vesey, Peter Poyas, Ned Bennett, Rolla Bennett, Balleau Bennett, Jesse Blackwood, Gullah Jack, and others, thirty-five in all, were hanged; forty-three were banished.

An extensive scheme for an insurrection, however, came in 1828 from David Walker of Massachusetts. In an address he appealed to slaves to rise against their masters. To bring out the causes of the intolerable condition of the Negroes Walker mentioned "our wretchedness in consequence of slavery, our wretchedness in consequence of ignorance, our wretchedness in consequence of the preachers of the religion of Jesus Christ, and our wretchedness in consequence of the colonization plan." Walker said: "For although the destruction of the oppressors God may not effect by the oppressed, yet the Lord our God will bring **David Walker's appeal.** other destruction upon them, for not unfrequently will he cause them to rise up one against the other, to be split, divided, and to oppress each other, and sometimes to open hostilities with sword in hand." [4]

The most exciting of all of these disturbances, however,

[4] David Walker's *Appeal.*

did not come until 1831. In August of that year Nat Turner, a Negro insurgent of Southampton County, Virginia, feeling that he was ordained of God to liberate his people, organized a number of daring blacks and proceeded from plantation to plantation to murder **Nat Turner's** their masters. His chief co-workers were **insurrection.** Henry Porter, Hark Travis, Nelson Williams, Samuel

NAT TURNER

Francis, and Jack Reese, Nat Turner was born the slave of Benjamin Turner, October 2, 1800, the very year in which perished Gabriel Prosser of like fame. Precocious as a youth, Nat Turner early learned to read and made progress in the study of the Bible and religious literature. He learned also to make paper, gunpowder, and pottery. He developed into a man of steady habits. He spent much time fasting and praying and communing with the spirit. Voices, he believed, spoke to him. He said he saw drops of blood on the leaves, and had visions of black and white spirits arrayed in a serious combat. In this mystified atmosphere he heard a voice saying: "The Serpent is loosed. Christ has laid down the yoke. You must take it up again. The time is at hand when the first shall be the last and the last shall be the first." [5]

An eclipse of the sun following close thereupon was

[5] Drewry, *Insurrections in Virginia;* and *The Journal of Negro History,* V, 208-234.

interpreted as the sign for the insurrection to begin. The slaying was ordered as soon thereafter as was convenient. They dispatched first the owners in that vicinity. Although they succeeded in carrying out their designs for the first night, most of the company frustrated their own plans by making noise resulting from intoxication. Nat Turner, himself, however, never indulged in strong drink; and he gave explicit instructions against committing outrages. They were decidedly weak the next day. After delaying they were dispersed by a company before they could reach Jerusalem, the county seat, to get the much needed arms and supplies. The following day the insurgents met another attack, and still another the next, when the group was finally dispersed. Nat Turner made another effort to assemble his men again, but did not succeed. With some provisions he then hid himself nearby under a fence from which he emerged only at night. Here for six weeks he evaded his pursuers, although State and Federal troops were scouring the country to find him. Detected by two Negroes attracted to the spot by a barking dog, Nat Turner had to change his hiding place for the less secure fields. Seen again by another on October 30, he surrendered. He was convicted on the fifth of November and executed on the eleventh. It is said: "He exhibited the utmost composure through the whole ceremony; and, although assured that he might, if he thought proper, address the immense crowd assembled on the occasion, declined availing himself of the privilege; and, being asked if he had any further confessions to make, replied that he had nothing more than he had communicated; and told the sheriff in a firm voice that he was ready. Not a limb or muscle was observed to move. His body, after death, was given over to the surgeons for dissection."

This uprising caused a reign of terror in Virginia. "Labor was paralyzed," says an author, "plantations abandoned, women and children were driven from their homes and crowded into nooks and corners. Negroes were tortured to death, burned, maimed, and subjected to nameless atrocities. Slaves who were distrusted were pointed out; and if they endeavored to escape they were ruthlessly shot down. In less than two days 120 Negroes were killed, most of them by ordinary man hunters who shot them as persons in pursuit of game. One individual rejoiced that he had been instrumental in killing between ten and fifteen.

"A party of horsemen started from Richmond with the intention of killing every colored person they saw in Southampton county. They stopped opposite the cabin of a free man of color engaged in cultivating his field. They called out: 'Is this Southampton County?' He replied: 'Yes, sir, you have just crossed the line by yonder tree.' They shot him dead and rode on.[6] A slaveholder went to the woods accompanied by a faithful slave who had been the means of saving his master's life during the insurrection. When they reached a retired place in the woods the man handed his gun to his master, informing him that he could not live a slave any longer and requested him either to free him or shoot him on the spot. The master took the gun in some trepidation, leveled it at the faithful Negro and shot him through the heart."[7] The Federal State troops under Lieutenant Colonel Worth, Brigadier General Eppes and General William H. Brodnax, called out to restore order, aided and abetted the slaughter of the Negroes instead of securing protection to all.

Only sixty-one white persons were killed by the conspirators. After the general slaughter fifty-three Negroes were arraigned, seventeen of them were convicted and executed, twelve convicted and transported, and ten ac-

---

[6] *Journal of Negro History*, V, 212; Higginson, *Outlaws*, 300.

[7] These quotations are all from the *Journal of Negro History*, V, 208-234.

quitted. Three of the four free Negroes subsequently tried were executed and one discharged. An effort was made to connect David Walker and William Lloyd Garrison with this rising, but no such evidence could be found. Garrison disclaimed any connection with the insurrection. Probably there would have been more consolation for the masters if they could have thought that slaves by themselves were incapable of concerted action.

The excitement beyond the borders of Virginia was almost as wild as in the State itself. There were conflicting rumors as to the deeds of Nat Turner and the supposed raids and attacks of various members of his band in places far removed from Southampton county. North Carolina was shaken to the very center by the rumor that Wilmington was to be burned. The excitement did not subside until four Negroes were shot down in cold blood and their heads were exposed to public gaze to terrify the Negro population. In Georgia there arose similar confusion from the report that Macon was to be attacked by a force of Negroes. In South Carolina, Governor Robert Y. Hayne, who had begun his fame in that State by suppressing the Denmark Vesey uprising of 1822, had to issue a proclamation to quiet the people. Alabama was disturbed by the rumor that the Indians and the Negroes were about to start an attack on the whites. New Orleans was likewise moved by the report that there were 1,200 stands of arms in a black man's home in that city.

The results from this uprising were far-reaching. There were those Virginians who looked upon slavery as an impossibility as long as Negroes would so willingly risk their lives for freedom. Such persons, therefore, advocated emancipation. Petitions to this effect were sent to the State legislature and the resolution to inquire into the expediency of gradual emancipation not only precipitated an interesting debate but the vote thereon showed that there was some antislavery sentiment in the State. Thinking people insisted that something had to be done when things had come to such a pass that "men with pistols in their hands had to lock their doors and open them in the morning to receive their servants to light their fires."

In other parts, where it was still believed that slavery was a safe and profitable institution, the result was the other way. This uprising had been sufficient to convince most of the South that if slavery was to be successful, the one thing needful was to close up the avenues of information to the Negroes. The first effort in this direction was to extend the slave code so as to penalize a number of deeds which theretofore had not been punishable by law. The majority of the slave states already had adequate regulations to keep down insurrections. But the fear resulting from this uprising had a direct bearing on other laws which followed. The Southern States enacted more stringent measures to regulate

BLACK WOLF, AN INDIAN CHIEF, 1827

Stringent measures in the South.

the travel of slaves, to make them ineffective in assembling for insurrectionary purposes or for information obtained through contact with other persons or from schools. These stringent measures applying to travel and assembly were not restricted to slaves but made applicable also to the free Negroes and mulattoes. The wording of these laws varied. They usually provided, however, that it would be unlawful for Negroes above a certain number, usually five, to assemble without the permission of their masters, not even for worship, unless the services were conducted by a recognized white minister or observed by "certain discreet and reputable persons."

Most of the State legislatures took some action in this respect at their next session. Governor McArthur of Ohio recommended that the legislature prohibit by law the influx of free people into that State. Maryland provided a board of managers to use a fund for the removal of the free people of color to Liberia. Delaware prevented the use of fire-arms by Negroes, revived the law against the coming of free Negroes and mulattoes into the State, prohibited the meetings of blacks after ten o'clock, and forbade non-resident Negroes to preach. Tennessee also forbade the immigration of free Negroes into that State. Georgia re-stricted the grant of credit to free Negroes, and prohibited all Negroes from preaching or carrying firearms. North Carolina, like Virginia, prohibited free Negroes from preaching. By constitutional provision in 1834 North Caro-lina prohibited Negroes from voting or holding office. Louisiana strengthened her slave code with respect to the instruction of mischievous slaves. Alabama prohibited free Negroes from settling in the State and provided a penalty for those who might teach Negroes to read and write. In 1834 South Carolina reënforced its law pro-hibiting the teaching of slaves to read and write and for-bidding the employment of a person of color as a salesman in any house, store, or shop, used for trading. In 1838 Virginia provided that any Negro leaving the State for the purpose of education should not return to the State as a resident.

In many of the Southern States, however, the effort was made not only to regulate the traveling and assem-

bling of the free Negroes but to get rid of them entirely.
Some States merely gave them so many days to leave.[8]
The Missouri General Assembly enacted in   **Free Negroes**
1819 a law providing that there should be no   **driven out.**
more assemblages of slaves or free Negroes or mulattoes,
mixing or associating with such slaves for teaching them
to read. When that State framed its constitution on being
admitted to the Union it incorporated a provision to prevent the immigration of free Negroes into that State.
Louisiana had prohibited the immigration of free persons
of color in 1814, and in 1830 excluded such persons from
the State. In 1830 Mississippi followed in the footsteps of
her sister State. In cases where free Negroes were not
driven out, certain stringent measures to safeguard the interests of the slaveholders materially interfered with the
personal liberty and economic welfare of these persons of
color. Not quite so much of this legislation disgraced the
statue books of Kentucky, Maryland and Tennessee, but
public opinion there sometimes had the same effect.

The resistance of the Negroes to established authority
during these years assumed also another form. Inasmuch as
the Indians were hostile to the whites who gradually forced
them to the West, a considerable number of Negroes of the
pioneer spirit continued to escape to their   **Negroes among**
settlements. The large majority of Negroes,   **Indians.**
uninformed as to the geography of the country and un-
acquainted with the Indian, of course, could not avail themselves of this opportunity. The infelicitous climate of the
mountains and swamps to which the Indians were driven
proved also to be another deterrent force in the mind of the
Negro. Yet from the very beginning there was much fear
that the Negroes might join with the Indians in the commonwealths near the Atlantic coast. But the expected did

[8] See C. G. Woodson's *A Century of Negro Migration*, p. 40; **and**
The Education of the Negro Prior to 1861, pp. 151-178.

INDIAN MAN AND WOMAN IN DANCING DRESS

The customs of the Indians resembled somewhat those of the Negroes in Africa. This supports the contention of those who believe that Africans visited the shores of America more than a thousand years ago and influenced the civilization of the aborigines of this continent.

not always happen. The number joining the Indians, however, became sufficiently considerable to justify mention here.[9]

In 1786 the Continental Congress adopted an ordinance systematizing Indian affairs through the organization of two large districts. One lay north of the Ohio and west of the Hudson and the other south of the Ohio and east of the Mississippi. The very next year an Indian reservation in Virginia was accused of harboring an "idle set of free Negroes." It was pointed out that the proportion of Africans with Indian blood seemed to be about equal, for Indian women were married to black men and Indian men were married to black women. About the same time Negro slaves were escaping from the Carolinas and Georgia across the frontier into Florida where they came under the protection of the Indians.

In the lower Indian district, south of the Ohio and east of the Mississippi, lying also west of certain seaboard slave States, there was considerable danger of the loss of slaves. Furthermore, the effort to return such slaves proved to be unusually difficult after the interbreeding had **Fugitives** gone to the extent of making these Negroes **demanded.** and their children important factors in the Indian communities. Sometimes when compelled to give up the Negro women who were thus reclaimed by the white slaveholders the Indians refused to give up their children by such women inasmuch as they were a part of their own blood. One of the charges brought against the British at the close of the Revolutionary War, and even at the end of the War of 1812, was that in connection with Indians they had thus encouraged the escape of the Negroes to their lines. This matter was not settled until 1828. Georgia

[9] The general facts of the Indian-Negro question are given in the following: John T. Sprague's *The Florida War;* Joshua R. Gidding's *Exiles of Florida;* Samuel G. Drake's *Aboriginal Races.*

filed such a complaint against the Creeks in 1789. This practice was continued from year to year very much to the discomfort of the colonists in the South. The matter finally came to a head in the case of the Creeks in 1813, when, advised by the British, they attacked Fort Mins on the Appalachicola River and massacred a large number of citizens. They were, therefore, attacked by Andrew Jackson, who decisively routed them in Alabama in 1814 and forced them to sue for peace. Further trouble came in 1815, when about 1,000 Negroes from Georgia took charge of the fort which the British commander abandoned upon his return to England. Strengthened by the accession of some Creeks, this Negro fort became a menace to the peace of the slaveholding settlements. The Spanish, in whose territory this fort was, were called upon to destroy it. As no satisfaction came from this source it was necessary for Jackson to order General Gaines to destroy it in 1816. This order he carried out in most disastrous fashion.

The conflicts with the Creeks became easily connected with a more serious trouble with the Seminoles in 1817. The next year Jackson invaded the Florida territory, destroying things as he passed, and almost brought this nation into a war with Great Britain by hanging unceremoniously two British subjects trading there with the Indians. Some relief was offered the whites in this quarter by the treaty of Indian Spring of 1821.

Conflicting troubles.

In this the Creeks ceded to the Federal Government in the interest of Georgia about 5,000,000 acres of land. One of the important provisions of this treaty with the Creeks, who received a stipulated sum, was that the Federal Government should hold therefrom a fund to pay for such slaves as had escaped from Georgia to the Creeks since the year of 1802. This fund was administered in dishonest fashion by deception and fraud, which left a dark blot on American Indian diplomacy. After the

Florida territory was finally turned over to this country in 1821, moreover, the same dishonor characterized our methods employed in moving the Indians from the most valuable lands. To carry out such a design the Federal authorities forced upon the Indians another treaty at Fort Moultrie in 1823. One stipulation was: "The chiefs and

FOUR LEGS, AN INDIAN CHIEF, 1827

warriors aforesaid, for themselves and tribes, stipulate to be active and vigilant in the preventing the retreating to, or passing through, the district of country assigned them, of any absconding slaves, or fugitives from justice; and further agree to use all necessary exertions to apprehend and deliver the same to the agent, who shall receive orders to compensate them agreeably to the trouble and expense incurred."

Instead of settling matters this treaty aggravated them. Certain Indian chiefs never consented to this treaty and suffered themselves rather to be driven into exile. Forced into this precarious position, moreover, the Indians were further harassed by white raiders seeking to reclaim fugitives and to enslave free Negroes living **Forced** among the Indians. Many of the Negroes born **treaties.** among the Indians and others whom they had purchased were snatched from them. Being unaccustomed to matters of business requiring receipts and contracts, they could not make a case when such a matter sometimes came before

AN INDIAN FAMILY

While Americanized Negroes did not enjoy so much the life of
the Indians, they found this lot much better than the drudgery of
slavery. The flight to the Indians was the only way of escape
available for the crude newcomers who had no opportunity to learn
anything about the interior.

the courts. Even before such tribunals neither the Indians nor the Negroes had any chance for justice. The inhuman raiders concerned, moreover, thought to get rid of the Indians in this district altogether by memorializing Congress for their complete removal beyond the Mississippi. Inasmuch as Humphreys, the Indian agent, had not been successful in turning over to the whites Negroes to whom they had no legal claim, his removal was effected by 1830. Andrew Jackson, too, although a staunch unionist with respect to nullification, supported state rights in protecting the supposed rights of these Georgians on the frontier. He was, therefore, a warm advocate of removal beyond the reach of the whites. The situation was further aggravated by the refusal of the Federal Government to sympathize in any way with the claims of the Indians. The only consideration they received was an explanation that the Federal Government desired to protect them only in the case that they were removed from the jurisdiction of these slave States. The agitation for the return of the Negro slaves, moreover, was kept up through this period, as a reason for removal, inasmuch as the Indians were disinclined to return fugitive Negroes who had become connected with them by ties of blood. In 1829 the Cherokees were induced by the Federal Government to go west. Three years later the Creeks found themselves compelled to do likewise.

There remained the Seminoles, however, still to be reckoned with. The complaint was that they had not returned fugitive slaves. The Seminoles were finally forced to sign the treaty for removal west of the Mississippi on the terms set forth in the Agreement of Payne's Landing in 1832. In that treaty Article VI says: "The Seminoles, **The Seminole** being anxious to be relieved from the repeated **War.** vexatious demands for slaves, and other property, alleged to have been stolen and destroyed by them, so that they may remove unembarrassed to their new homes, the United States stipulate to have the same property (properly) investigated, and to liquidate such as may be satisfactorily established, provided the amount does not exceed seven thousand ($7,000) dollars.'' An additional treaty was forced upon them at Fort Gibson, Arkansas, in 1833, when seven chiefs, according to agreement, examined the country. It is significant that along with the chiefs was the Negro interpreter known as Abraham. However, although the Senate of the United States ratified both treaties and urged the actual removal, the Seminoles repudiating the officiat-

Negro Abraham.

Negro Abraham

ing chiefs as deceivers, did not easily bestir themselves in that direction. This, together with the further reports of the slaveholders that the Seminoles were not returning fugitive slaves, irritated the Federal Government. It, therefore, prepared to force the removal of these Indians. This precipitated what is known as the Second Seminole War.

In this struggle there happened upon the scene one of the most distinguished characters in Indian-Negro history. This was Osceola. He was the child of an Indian chief and a woman of Negro blood. He was born a leader of men. He easily ingratiated himself into favor with all.

Osceola, a man of power. Although not legally a chief himself, he won upon all Indians with whom he came into contact and made himself the most important person in the

tribe. Arrayed against him, however, he had the Federal
Government, among the functionaries of which there was
little sympathy for the oppressed. One of them, however,
Congressman Giddings, from the Western Reserve, antici-
pating his later stand for freedom, said with respect to
this Florida trouble: ''I hold that if the slaves of Georgia
or any other State leave their masters the Federal Govern-

ment has no consti-
tutional authority to
employ our army or
navy for their re-
capture, or to apply
the national treas-
ure to repurchase
them.'' There could
be no question of the
fact that the war
was very largely one
over fugitive slaves.
To Giddings it
seemed a cruel pro-
cedure to return to
inhuman masters
slaves who had be-
come attached to the
Indians among

AN INDIAN WARRIOR

whom they had lived. Yet, it was earnestly insisted by the
slave power that the thing paramount in the removal of
the Seminoles was to prevent the increasing danger of
servile insurrection among the Negroes.

Cases of the actual stealing of innocent Negroes moreover are not wanting. The kidnapers openly did this
in the case of twenty slaves owned by Chief Kidnaping
Econchattimico. In 1835, John Walker, an Negroes.
Indian chief, spoke of other such raids upon his property

by whites from Columbus, Georgia. He began by inquiring, "Are the free Negroes and the Negroes belonging to this town to be stolen away publicly, and in the face of law and justice, carried off and sold to fill the pockets of these worse than land pirates?"

Appearing upon the scene when the agent of the Federal Government insisted upon the removal of the Indians in keeping with the forced treaties, Osceola urged them to take a definite stand against the encroachment of the **Second Semi-** whites. In fact, when threatened with the **nole War.** consequences resulting from such a refusal Osceola actually defied the Federal Government. To overcome the influence of Osceola, the agent made further efforts for inveigling the chiefs into signing other agreements which they themselves did not understand. As they could not be publicly induced to come to such an agreement the agent of the Federal Government accomplished the same by secret conferences. Certain restrictions were imposed upon the Indians to make their stay uncomfortable and the preparations for their removal were urged.

The crisis was reached, however, when a certain kidnaper carried back to captivity Osceola's wife, the daughter of a fugitive mulatto slave woman who had married an Indian chief. Reprimanding Thompson, the agent, for such an injustice, Osceola was arrested and imprisoned. By shrewdness, however, he effected his own release by deceiving Thompson to the extent of making him believe that Osceola had changed his point of view with respect to the removal and would induce the Indians to act accordingly. Osceola then hurried his preparations for war. The Indians themselves, however, became gradually divided into those in favor of the migration and protected by the Federal Government and those who, on the other hand, were ready to fight to death for their land. While some were preparing for removal, others were preparing for war.

Troops were soon upon the scene and Osceola himself had
his own soldiers lying in wait for Thompson. They finally
killed him one day while he was taking a walk. The die
was cast. At that very time other Indians, attacking
American troops led by Major Dade himself, annihilated
his command.

Our interest here in this story lies in the report that
Negroes were fearlessly fighting in the ranks of the Indians.
Then came the account that one lieutenant was tomahawked

OSCEOLA

by a Negro. Another
said that a Negro named
Harry had a band of 100
warriors. In **The Negro
always a**
all of these
engagements **fighter.**
the Negroes and Indians
fought bravely. Their
case, however, was hope-
less. After the coming of
Major General Thomas
Jessup, who believed in
uncivilized warfare, the
Seminoles and their allies
had no chance. This
commander resorted to
bloodhounds and hang-
ing. He authorized plunder on the grounds that all the
Indian property captured belonged to the corps or detachment making it. He even imprisoned an embassy from the
Indian lines seeking conference with the authorities to
devise means by which the removal might be worked out
satisfactorily. This shows the utter breakdown of the so-
called treatment of the Indians as independent nations and
furnishes striking evidence of the selfishness of the American whites. After this war the resistance of the Indian was

futile.   The Seminoles were soon compelled to take up
their abode on the other side of the Mississippi.   In this
position there could be little fear of servile insurrection of
the Negroes.   Most of their Indian allies were too far removed from the slave plantations.   The institution of slavery was further secured and the South could more
fearlessly face the country with its program to make cotton king.

CHAPTER XII

A DECLINING ANTISLAVERY MOVEMENT

THE early antislavery workers were not so aggressive as those of the second quarter of the nineteenth century, and they later lost some of their ardor. They did not contemplate instant abolition. The machinery for promoting the uplift of the Negroes, as further stated by them, had to do with methods of gradual emancipation.[1] According to their scheme, they raised funds to pur- Gradual chase slaves, encouraged their emancipation, emancipation. and provided for prospective freedmen opportunities for mental development and religious instruction that they might properly function in society on becoming citizens. These bodies maintained, moreover, a sort of vocational guidance committee in each locality to look out for apprenticing Negroes to trades and to find employment for them in the various fields when they had developed into efficient mechanics. The friends of the Negro, however, tended to diminish until few could be found.

The gallantry shown by the Negro soldiers in the War of 1812 added little to their desirability. Their record was soon forgotten by the exploiting and bloodthirsty class. This second war with England started from trade restrictions, the impressment of American seamen in the British service, and the failure to give up western forts

[1] The early antislavery movement has been well treated in M. S. Locke's *Antislavery in America from the Introduction of the African Slaves to the Prohibition of the Slave Trade*, in Alice D. Adams's *Neglected Period of Antislavery in America*, and in the annual reports of *The American Convention of Abolition Societies*.

as promised in the treaty of Paris and Jay's treaty. Additional hostility to England, however, was engendered by **The Negro** the outbreak of the Indian troubles in terri- **in the War** tory which white settlers going west desired. **of 1812.** The Americans had difficulty in holding the Indians at Tippecanoe in 1811 because they were supplied with munitions of war from Canada. The Negroes were then asked to play their part.

Negroes made a record for valor displayed in this struggle on land and sea. They fought bravely under Perry and Macdonough. An officer of this war writing of a naval engagement said: "The name of one of my poor fellows who was killed ought to be registered in the book of fame, and remembered with reverence as long as bravery is considered a virtue. He was a black man by the name of Johnson. . . . When America has such tars she has little to fear from the tyrants of the ocean."

Reduced to necessity of husbanding all resources, Andrew **Negro soldiers** Jackson appealed to the Negroes in prepar- **with Jackson.** ing for the battle of New Orleans. He said "Through a mistaken policy, you have heretofore been deprived of a participation in the glorious struggle for national rights in which our country is engaged. This no longer shall exist.

"As sons of freedom, you are now called upon to defend our most inestimable blessing. As Americans, your country looks with confidence to her adopted children for a valorous support, as a faithful return for the advantages enjoyed under her mild and equitable government. As fathers, husbands and brothers, you are summoned to rally around the standard of the Eagle, to defend all which is dear in existence." [2]

[2] He said also: "Your country, although calling for your exertions, does not wish you to engage in her cause without amply remunerating you for the services rendered. Your intelligent minds are not to be led away by false representations. Your love of

Three months after this proclamation when the battle of New Orleans had been successfully fought, Jackson could say: "To the Men of Color.—Soldiers! From the shores of Mobile I collected you to arms,—I invited you to share in the perils and to divide the glory of your white countrymen. I expected much from you; for I was not uninformed of those qualities which must render you so formidable to an invading foe. I knew that you could endure hunger and thirst, and all the hardships of war. I knew that you loved the land of your nativity, and that, like ourselves, you had to defend all that is most dear to man. But you surpass my hopes. I have found in you, united to these qualities, that noble enthusiasm which impels to great deeds.

"Soldiers! The President of the United States shall be informed of your conduct on the present occasion; and the voice of the Representatives of the American nation shall applaud your valor, as your General now praises your ardor. The enemy is near. His sails cover the lakes. But the brave are united; and, if he finds us contending among ourselves, it will be for the prize of valor, and fame its noblest reward."

The Negroes, too, had otherwise figured in the war. Inasmuch as the British Government followed the same policy of carrying away Negroes as in the case of the Revolutionary War, this question proved to be a trouble-

honor would cause you to despise the man who should attempt to deceive you. In the sincerity of a soldier and the language of truth I address you.

"To every noble-hearted, generous freeman of color volunteering to serve during the present contest with Great Britain, and no longer, there will be paid the same bounty, in money and lands, now received by the white soldiers of the United States, viz., one hundred and twenty-four dollars in money, and one hundred and sixty acres of land. The non-commissioned officers and privates will also be entitled to the same monthly pay, and daily rations, and clothes, furnished to any American soldier."

some one in the negotiations closing the second war with England. It was pointed out that many were induced to **Negroes with** run away and others were captured in battle. **the British.** From the Dauphin Islands, said to be without the limits of the newly acquired Louisiana territory, the British took many Negroes. A large number went over to the British ranks, also as a result of the proclamation of the British Admiral, Cochrane, proclaiming free all such fugitives. The first article of this treaty, therefore, provided that all possessions whatsoever taken by either party during the war or which might have been taken after the signing of this treaty shall be restored without delay and that these possessions should be destroyed. It specified, moreover, that artillery, public and private property originally captured in the forts of the United States should not be carried away. Negroes were carried away by the British even after the treaty had been signed. All of them were not declared free. The British sold some into the West Indies. The question was a difficult one because of difficult constructions of the clauses of the treaty by the representatives of the two different nations. It was not finally adjusted until 1828, when the claimants were awarded $1,197,422.18 largely for slaves whose indemnity a reactionary Federal Government had long sought.

The inevitable effect of the reaction was sectionalism. In proportion as there developed free labor in the North as a result of the industrial revolution, which at the same time, led to the extension of the plantation system, requir- **The results** ing more slaves, the South and the North **of the** became gradually estranged. The open viola- **reaction.** tions of the act prohibiting the African slave trade and the impetus given the domestic traffic to supply these plantations with Negroes, led to the bold attack on the institution during the first quarter of the nineteenth century. The cotton gin, although invented as early as

1793, had just then begun to do its work. During the first antislavery period there were no violent protests, as the workers concerned contented themselves with making an occasional speech or with writing for a newspaper an article inveighing against the institution and setting forth plans for exterminating the evil. A considerable portion of the abolition literature which influenced public opinion appeared in the *Genius of Universal Emancipation,* published by Benjamin Lundy. Through this organ the sentiments of a large number of antislavery people living in the Appalachian highland found expression. There were descendants of the Germans and Scotch-Irish immigrants who came to this country to realize their ideals of religion and government. They differed widely from those of the aristocratic planters who maintained a slavocracy near the coast. A few of these settlers of the uplands were gradually indoctrinated in the tenets of slavery in the proportion that the institution extended towards the mountains, but a large number of them continued even until the Civil War to work for the destruction of the institution. Out of this group developed a number of active manumission societies in North Carolina, Tennessee and Kentucky.

Later we see the tendency not only to regard the institution of slavery as an economic evil but to consider it as a sin of which the Christian people should be ashamed. In 1810 Louis Duprey informed professing **Slavery an** Christians that the great transgressions of **economic evil.** slave commonwealths would lead to overwhelming judgments of God. David Barrow, of Kentucky, denounced in a pamphlet the inconsistency in the use of religious formulas in connection with the bequests of slaves, and advocated immediate emancipation. About the same time, John D. Paxton, a preacher in Kentucky and Virginia, believed in the "moral evil of slavery and the duty of

Christians to aid slaves and free them.'' Daniel Raymond of Maryland branded slavery as a ''foul stain on our national escutcheon, a canker which is corroding the moral and political vitals of our country.'' Declaring slave traffic a curse to the master, John Randolph, of Virginia, said in Congress in 1816, ''Do as you would be done by.

ANOTHER SORT OF SLAVERY

Every man who leaves that great high road will have the chalice which he himself has poisoned—the chalice of justice, even-handed justice—put to his own lips by the God of nature, who does not require abolition societies to carry his purpose into execution.''

The strongest influence against slavery which had hitherto developed, as already observed, however, came from the Quakers. After ridding themselves of slavery they

were strenuously working to abolish the institution in other
parts during the first decade of the nineteenth century.
They had used passive means, however, in **Antislavery**
reaching their ends, and for that reason had **Quakers.**
not gained very much ground. Yet they had done effective
work in Virginia and North Carolina, and when they could
not operate there as they desired they sent their slaves and

others to the Northwest
Territory where they had
a new opportunity. It is
doubtless due to their influence in North Carolina
that a distinguished man
like Judge William Gas-
ton could call on the
State to extirpate slavery.
They, no doubt, had
much to do with the fact
that a proposal to abolish
slavery in the North
Carolina General Assem-
bly failed only by the
casting vote of the
speaker, and that the in-
stitution was strongly attacked in the Virginia

Thomas Jefferson, an antislavery
reformer

Convention in 1829-30, and in the legislature the following year.[2]

The spirit of antislavery, however, was declining in the
South throughout the first half century of the republic.
Free discussion of slavery was extended by the ardent
debate over the Missouri question from 1819 to 1821. In

[2] C. G. Woodson, *Education of the Negro Prior to 1861;* S. B.
Weeks, *Southern Quakers and Slavery,* and R. R. Wright, *Negro
Rural Communities* in *The Southern Workman,* Vol. XXXVII, pp.
158-166.

this contest the proslavery and antislavery forces for the
first time nationally clashed. The question then was

**Antislavery
cause in
the South.** whether or not slave territory should be extended. By that time it was evident that the
South was preparing to defend the institu-
tion, whereas the North, in the interest of free labor, had
unconsciously become radically opposed to the extension
of slavery. In so expressing itself in its defense of the institution, the South alarmed the whole country. Thomas
Jefferson, an uplander, said: "I tremble for my country
when I reflect that God is just." The thinking public was
impressed thereby with the idea that the country was then
face to face with a problem requiring serious consideration.
The United States had by this time developed a feeling of
nationalism.

These protests, however, were scattered and they had
little effect, for the abolition movement gradually became
a sectional one. The antislavery societies which held wide

**The decline of
the antislav-
ery movement.** sway until about the beginning of the nineteenth century lost ground from year to year.
The lower South early exterminated such
sentiments; and, in the Border States, where they had had
extensive influence, they soon claimed only a few adherents.
In 1827 there was one such society in Connecticut, none in
Delaware, two in the District of Columbia, twelve in Illinois, eight in Kentucky, eleven in Maryland, two in Massachusetts, one in New York, fifty in North Carolina, four in
Ohio, sixteen in Pennsylvania, one in Rhode Island,
twenty-five in Tennessee, eight in Virginia. Less than a
decade later almost all southern States in which most of
these societies had developed ceased to support them, and
the American Convention became largely a northern organization.

Against this system of oppression, however, a few prominent men of the South continued to protest. Judge J. B.

O'Neall of South Carolina felt that is was shameful to prevent the blacks from obtaining sufficient knowledge to read the Bible. Daniel R. Goodloe, of North Carolina, was of the same opinion. Southerners of the most radical type, moreover, did not like to live under the stigma with which they were branded by William Jay, who charged them with having closed up the Bible in denying the Negroes the revelation of God. Some opposition was, therefore, shown; and in certain parts it was found impossible to execute restrictive measures because of the healthy public opinion against them. The children of the sympathetic aristocratic slaveholders, and especially the wives and children of ministers, hardly ceased to teach Negroes to read as much as the Bible. Much was accomplished, however, by a new system called religious instruction. Among the earnest workers concerned were Robert Ryland and Bishop Meade of Virginia, Bishop Capers of South Carolina, Josiah Law and C. C. Jones of Georgia, and Bishop Polk of Louisiana. Under this system the Negroes were not permitted to learn to read and write, but were taught to commit to memory in catechetical form the principles of religion and instructive parts of the Bible.[3]

This reaction, however, was not peculiar to the slave States.[4] In the proportion that free Negroes, finding it impossible to live in the South, sought refuge in the North, race prejudice and friction increased. These culminated in race riots, easily developed in that section at the time when the country was receiving a number of Irish and German immigrants. They competed directly with the Negroes as laborers. Negroes were not

[3] See also C. G. Woodson's *A Century of Negro Migration*, pp. 39-60.

[4] This is extensively treated in C. C. Jones's *Religious Instruction of Negroes* and in C. G. Woodson's *Education of the Negro Prior to 1861*, Ch. VIII.

permitted to enter the academy thrown open to them at Canaan, New Hampshire, in 1834. The people of New Haven at a public meeting of their leading citizens strenuously protested against establishing there a manual labor school for the education of Negroes. The citizens of Canterbury actually imprisoned Prudence Crandall by securing special legislation to that effect because she persisted in admitting Negro girls to her seminary. It was feared that in becoming attractive to the Negroes there might be an increase in the colored population of that city to the displeasure of its white citizens.[5]

Riots of a graver sort were frequent throughout the North during these years. The first sanguinary conflicts of consequence took place in Ohio. In 1826 a mob under- **Race riots in** took to drive the Negroes out of Cincinnati. **the North.** In 1836 another mob not only attacked Negroes but broke up also the abolition press, which was supposed to encourage the influx of persons of that class. In 1841 there broke out in the same city a local race war which for a week disturbed that metropolis to the extent of resulting in the death of a number of persons and the expulsion of many Negroes from the place. On a "Black Friday," January 1, 1830, eighty of the two hundred Negroes living in Portsmouth, Ohio, were driven out of the city as undesirables. A mob of Germans drove John Randolph's Negroes from their own land in Mercer County, Ohio, where by will he had provided for their settlement and freedom.

The East offered no exception to this rule. The citizens of Philadelphia began to burn Negro homes in 1820, sought to expel the blacks from the city and State in 1830, and **Riots in** destroying their churches and other prop- **the East.** erty, cruelly mobbed them in 1834. In 1838 another conflict developed into a riot which resulted in the destruction of Pennsylvania Hall and the Colored Orphan Asylum in that city. When the Negroes in 1842 undertook to celebrate the abolition of slavery in the West Indies, another occasion was afforded for race conflict, which meant a loss of life and property to the Negroes. Pittsburgh, following the example of Philadelphia, had such a riot in 1839. In 1834, this rule of the mob in New York City and Palmyra led to riots during which the Negroes were attacked along the streets and driven from their homes.

The untoward condition of the Negro in the country resulted from the unusually rapid spread of cotton culture and the extension of slavery into the uplands of the South where it had been considered impracticable. The people of the frontier section, **Spread of cotton culture.** who had early constituted the opposition to the aristocratic pretensions of the slaveholders near the coast, gradually became indoctrinated in the tenets of the slaveholding aristocracy and began to develop the same thought as to politics and religion as obtained near the coast. In the seaboard States, the interior of which lay among rugged hills or beyond seemingly insurmountable mountains, the hopes of democracy lingered longer because of the difficulty experienced in extending slavery beyond these barriers; but even these parts had to yield ground to the growing evil, despite the warning given by statesmen in the prolonged debate resulting in the admission of Missouri.

In the same way the introduction of the culture of sugar in Louisiana accelerated the trade in that territory. By an additional act of Congress dealing with the prohibition of the slave trade in that State a loophole was **The sugar industry.** left in the law so that it was construed to permit the importation of slaves from the other parts of the United States. Slave traders in some of the Border States where the worn-out soil made the system unprofitable, moreover, supplied the Louisiana Territory in spite of restrictions to the contrary. They evaded the laws by purchasing slaves ostensibly for employment at home, but only to be sold later in Louisiana after a brief stay to comply with the letter of the legal requirements. The result was an influx of speculators buying sugar land and bringing in slaves. Before the nineteenth century was far advanced the increasing number of estates developed and their large production placed the culture of sugar in the front rank of the industries of the South.

THE NEGRO CALLS A HALT

In this situation, then, the South soon reached the position that slavery is not an evil and by no means a sin, and that the only use to be made of a Negro is to impress him into the service of the white man. No care was taken of the blacks as of persons to be elevated, for they were to be beasts of burden. Negro women were often worked too hard to bear children, and it mattered not if they did not, since it was deemed less expensive to drive an imported slave to

The situation in the South. death during a few years and buy another in his place, than to undertake to increase his efficiency by methods of improvement. They were herded in pens like cattle; they were sold to do hard labor from the rising to the setting of the sun; they were given quarters no better than the stables for animals; and they were fed upon the coarsest food known to be given to human beings. To prevent their escape, police control was effected by a patrol system. This governed their going and coming so as to prevent them from assembling for help or from securing assistance or advice from sympathetic white friends and free Negroes.

The extension of the cotton culture by the expansion of slavery was essentially connected with national development. Old political parties tended to pass away and national issues furnished the line of cleavage. Men were doing big things on a large scale. The main question was how to do them. While Northern pioneers were moving into the Middle West, South- **Cotton** erners and their slaves went into the South- **culture.** west. Some of the latter moved also into Southern Ohio, Indiana and Illinois. The opening up of these new lands relieved the seaboard slave States in two ways. It offered opportunity to the poor whites who could not easily compete with the large slaveholders living near the coast. It also solved the problem of relieving these States of the excess of slave population which could no longer be supported on the worn-out lands near the Atlantic. Unaccustomed to the scientific agriculture which requires fertilization and rotation of crops, these seaboard slave States found themselves trailing behind the progressively industrial North. Devising schemes, then, for the solution of this particular economic problem, southerners like James G. 'Birney, John G. Fee, Cassius M. Clay, and Daniel R. Goodloe, brought forward proposals for the abolition of slavery and the colonization of the Negroes. Such ideas tended to widen the gap between the uplanders and the rich planters near the coast.

In practically all of the seaboard slave States the

planters along the Atlantic, controlling the governments by virtue of their property, had persistently fought the liberal extension of suffrage and the reapportionment of representation. They were afraid that the mountaineers would tax slavery out of existence. When, however, the opening of the West brought this relief, the antislavery movement decidedly declined in that section. Many of the slaveholders, formerly thinking of slaves as a burden, replenished their purses, not only by selling off slaves in excess of those whom they actually needed, but also by breeding slaves for the market. In certain parts they paid special attention to the production of fine-looking mulatto Negro girls. These were very much in demand by young white slaveholders who moved into the Southwest without their families. It is said that in Tazewell County, Virginia, a slaveholder kept as many as four Negro women for each one of his three sons to supply this demand.

Exactly how important this movement was may be observed by noticing the rapid increase of the population in the Southwest. According to the census of 1790 there were in all the West, exclusive of Georgia, 109,368 inhabitants. In 1815 the same territory had a population of 1,600,000. Few immigrants could be included in this report, **Rapid development.** inasmuch as Europe was then at war. In 1791 only 38 bales of cotton were produced. In 1809 the production reached 218,723 bales. In 1816 the country exported $24,106,000 worth of cotton sold at the price of $0.28 a pound. With this rapid development it was soon possible for States carved from this territory to meet the requirements for admission to the Union. Indiana and Illinois came into the Union respectively in 1816 and 1818. They were practically accompanied by Alabama, and Mississippi to the south of them.

This, however, could not be worked out until an adjustment of certain claims was made with respect to the territory east of the Mississippi known as the lands of the Yazoo companies. In keeping with the claims to land lying directly west of the original thirteen, Georgia insisted that this was her territory. As the land had never been definitely surveyed, conflicting claims ensued. Much more trouble arose, however, from bribery and the **Yazoo land** corrupt deals entered into by the Govern- **claims.** ment with these land companies. In the midst of these

THE MOTHER AND CHILD

conflicting claims, of charges and counter-charges, Georgia ceded all of these lands to the United States in 1802. The State received in return a narrow strip of land just south of Tennessee, $1,250,000, from the proceeds of such sales of lands, and the assurance that the national government would extinguish the Indian titles in Georgia as early as the same could be peaceably accomplished on reasonable terms. The whole area was then organized as the Mississippi territory with the understanding that it would be admitted as a State as soon as it had 60,000 inhabitants. Having to grapple with the problem of removal from the territory, the Creek, Chickasaw, and Choctaw Indian population did not at first increase rapidly. Persons migrating went preferably to Georgia itself and to Louisiana. When this question of eliminating the Indians was finally adjusted by Jackson's victory over the Creeks in 1814 and the other victories over them in the first and second Seminole Wars, the territory became unusually inviting. As a result, therefore, there could be carved out of this territory the State of Mississippi in 1817 and Alabama in 1819.

This expansion of population stimulated national development along proslavery lines. The impetus given such nationalism by the outcome of the War of 1812 could not be counteracted by antislavery agitation. The average American's heart swelled with pride to know that his country was increasing its area by foreign aggression. The reminder that this eventually meant merely an extension of slavery was not sufficient to check **The purchase of Florida.** that movement. Such territorial growth, moreover, tended to strengthen the bonds of union in which the majority of the people of this country were beginning to believe. The first important step, thereafter, was the purchase of Florida from Spain in 1819 for $5,000,000.[6]

The most strenuous effort in this direction was the acquisition of Texas. The American Government made an unsuccessful effort to buy the country. Growing more rapidly than Mexico desired, Texas was able to establish its independence in 1836. The citizens of Texas then seemed to the slave States patriots fighting for liberty; **Texas question.** and numerous citizens of such commonwealths moved into the territory. Texas was easily recognized as an independent nation. The country as a whole, however, paid little attention to the immigration

6 For this acquisition there could be given many reasons. For a number of years Florida had been an asylum for fugitive slaves who found life much more satisfactory there among the Spanish and Indians than in the seaboard slave States. In trying to reduce the Seminoles there to order, moreover, Andrew Jackson had almost plunged the nation into a war with Great Britain by hanging two of its citizens supposedly implicated in troubles in that territory. Furthermore, the territory was needed for the expansion to a natural boundary in the Southeast. It was actually turned over in 1821.

of proslavery Americans into Texas and did not take so seriously the danger involved in the revolution so near to our border, which might lead to the expansion of slavery. When this proslavery country applied for admission to the Union, however, the matter became a formidable question. Andrew Jackson, who hoped to perpetuate his policy against the United States Bank by the election of Martin Van Buren to the Presidency, would not inject this question into the campaign of 1836. Thereafter, however, it was a burning issue which would not down. It helped the proslavery party somewhat to say that England and France were meddling in Texan affairs, and had induced Mexico to recognize its independence. However, it did not help the proslavery group very much to circulate the report that England was to advance money to free slaves in Texas in return for a guarantee of interest on a loan. Americans were not anxious of course to have any European country so near to our border, either as the owners of territory or promoters of trade. Several treaties for the annexation of the republic of Texas were presented, then, but all failed until 1845. As a result of the triumph of the Democratic party on an annexation platform in the election the previous year the republic was admitted as a State of the Union. To make good the annexation of this territory which Mexico had never given up, James Knox Polk actually picked a quarrel with Mexico not only to strengthen the claim to Texas, but to acquire other territory. This Mexican War **The Oregon** of two years, moreover, closed with the ces- **territory.** sion of territory in the Southwest, now included in as many as eight States. With the addition of the Oregon territory in 1846, the country had finally expanded to natural boundaries on the Rio Grande and the Pacific. Then came the contest of slave and free states for the extension of slave and free labor, respectively.

CHAPTER XIII

SLAVERY AT ITS WORST

THE plantation system resulting from the industrial **rev**-olution, the cause of the radical reaction, made slaveholding a business of apparently tremendous possibilities.

The rise of the plantation. Large sums were invested in the enterprise, and the South entered upon its career as a borrowing section. There was a rush of southern white men from the older States along the coast to the fertile cotton lands of the Gulf district as soon as they were opened for settlement. Many came almost empty-handed, but the majority of those taking up large tracts of land brought their slaves with them. The number of slaves increased forty or fifty per cent between 1810 and 1820, and they came thereafter in droves.[1]

On their way to the Southwest the slaves experienced the usual hardships of a long drive. The inhuman traders placed the children in wagons and forced the men and

The internal slave trade. women to walk from twenty-five to fifty miles a day. Often traders encountered on the way bought some of the slaves in transit, after subjecting them to such an examination of their teeth and other parts as to determine their age and health. Featherstonaugh mentions his meeting in southwestern Virginia a camp of Negro slave drivers just packing up to start. He said:

[1] A. B. Hart, *Slavery and Abolition*, Chs. IV, V, VI, and VII; U. B. Phillips, *American Negro Slavery*, pp. 151-401; W. E. B. DuBois, *The Negro*, Ch. IX; M. B. Hammond, *The Cotton Industry; Debow's Review;* Williams Wells Brown, *The Rising Son*, 265-318; G. W. Williams, *History of the Negro Race in America*, Vol. I, pp. 115-324; and J. B. McMaster's *History of the United States*, VII, pp. 238-370.

"They had with them about three hundred slaves who had bivouacked the preceding night in chains in the woods. These they were conducting to Natchez, on the Mississippi River, to work upon the sugar plantations in Louisiana. It resembled one of the coffles spoken of by Mungo Park, except that they had a caravan of nine wagons and single-horse carriages for the purpose of conducting the white people and any of the blacks that should fall lame. The female slaves, some of them sitting on logs of wood while others were standing, and a great many little black children, were warming themselves at the fire of the bivouac. In front of them all, and prepared for the march, stood in double files about two hundred men slaves, manacled and chained to each other." [2]

Referring to one of these parties, Basil Hall said: "In the rear of all came a light-covered vehicle with the master and mistress of the party. Along the roadside scattered at intervals we observed the male slaves trudg-   **A drove** ing in front. At the top of all, against the   **of slaves.** sky line, two men walked together apparently hand in hand, pacing along very sociably. There was something, however, in their attitude which seemed unusual and constrained. When we came nearer accordingly, we discovered that this couple were bolted together by a short chain riveted to broad iron clasps secured in like manner around the wrists." [3]

Josiah Henson, a Negro brought into this traffic said: "Men trudged on foot, the children were put into the wagon, and now and then my wife rode for a while. We went through Alexandria, Culpepper, Fauquier, **Josiah** Harpers Ferry, Cumberland, and over the moun- **Henson.** tains to the National Turnpike to Wheeling. In all the

[2] G. W. Featherstonaugh, *Excursion through the Slave States*, Ch. I, p. 120.

[3] Basil Hall, *Travels in North America*, Ch. III, pp. 128-129; and *Journal of Negro History*, VIII, 367-383.

taverns along the road were regular places for the droves of Negroes continually passing along under the system of internal slave trade. At the places where we stopped for the night, we often met Negro drivers with their droves,

JOSIAH HENSON, prototype of *Uncle Tom's Cabin*

who were almost uniformly kept chained to prevent them from running away. I was often invited to pass the evening with them in the bar-room—their Negroes in the meantime, lying chained in the pen, while mine were scattered around at liberty."[4]

Edwin L. Godkin said: "The hardships these Negroes go through who are attached to one of these migrant parties baffles description. They trudge on foot all day through mud and thicket without rest or respite. Thousands of miles are traversed by these weary wayfarers without their knowing or caring why,

Hardships. urged on by whip and in full assurance that no change of place can bring any change to them. Hard work, coarse food, merciless flogging, are all that await them, and all that they can look to. I have never passed them staggering along in the rear of the wagons at the close of a long day's march, the weakest furthest in the rear, the strongest already utterly spent, without wondering how Christendom, which eight centuries ago rose in arms for a sentiment, can look so calmly on

[4] Josiah Henson, *Uncle Tom's Story of His Life*, p. 53.

at so foul and monstrous a wrong as this American slavery.'' [5]

This migration, of course, had a disastrous effect on the seaboard States from which so many masters and their slaves were drawn. Industry was paralyzed on the lower Atlantic coast. There were the worn-out lands with deserted homes once characterized by abun- **The decline of** dance and luxury, ruined and distressed **the seaboard** debtors wondering how to find relief, hu- **States.** miliated planters with no way of escape but migration. Efforts at fertilization to rebuild the waste places were tried, and with this the slave States near the Atlantic experienced a sort of revival about the middle of the nineteenth century. This was due also, some think, to the demand for slaves as laborers on the railroads which at that time were being constructed to unite the South and to connect it with the West.

To supply the Southwest with slaves, however, the domestic slave trade became an important business, and the older States which suffered from the migration devoted themselves to slave breeding for this market. **Slave** In the work entitled *Slavery and the Internal* **breeding.** *Slave Trade in the South,* it is estimated that seven of the older States annually exported 80,000 to the South. These were Virginia, Maryland, North Carolina, Kentucky, Tennessee, Missouri and Delaware. Professor Asa Martin thinks that Kentucky furnished 5,000 a year. This flourished the more because of the restrictions on the African slave trade. One writer estimates the number of slaves exported from Virginia at 120,000. It is difficult to figure out numbers, however, for the documents bearing on the sale of slaves did not always determine exactly what their destination would be. Men sometimes bought them appar-

[5] *The North American Review,* Vol. CLXXXV, pp. 46, 47.

ently for private use, concealing their ultimate aim to sell them South. Except when forced by economic necessity or in the case of insubordination, some masters refused to sell their slaves if they knew that they would have to undergo the tortures of servitude in the cotton and sugar districts. It is also difficult to determine who were the interstate slave traders. Almost all commission merchants

A SLAVE AUCTION

dealt in slaves as in any other property, and they were not anxious to be known as being primarily interested in a work which was in no sense popular among the more nearly civilized slaveholders.

Some of these masters, in advertising slaves for sale, specifically stated that they were not to be sold out of the State. Persons who were bold enough to proclaim them-
Slaves selves as such traders were mentioned with
sold south. opprobrium in the older slave States.[6] The

6 I. E. McDougle, *Slavery in Kentucky* in *The Journal of Negro History*, Vol. II, pp. 226-230.

presence of such traders in Winchester, Virginia, in 1818, evoked the comment: "Several wretches, whose hearts must be as black as the skins of the unfortunate beings who constitute their inhuman traffic, have for several days been impudently prowling about the streets of this place with labels on their hats exhibiting in conspicuous characters the words, 'Cash for Negroes.'" Some time in the thirties of the last century a master of Danville, Kentucky, sold a Negro woman to a regular slave trader. Upon learning this, threats of a mob to do him violence compelled this master to go in quest of the trader, from whom he repurchased the woman at a decidedly increased price.[7] Yet, intense as this feeling was, Delaware was the only slave State to legislate against the interstate slave trade. Maryland, Kentucky and Louisiana undertook somewhat to regulate it.

This enlightened minority could not stop this traffic, and for a number of centers in the Border States it became a source of much revenue. Dealers bought up slaves in the local markets and confined them in jails, **A source of** taverns, warehouses or slave pens, while **revenue.** awaiting buyers from the Southwest. The average slave pen had an administration building for the slaves, a court for the women and one for the men, with gates, barracks, and eating sheds. Some of the slave pens, however, were no more than stables for cattle or horses. On the convenient day they were placed on the sales block and auctioned off to the highest bidder. The slaves themselves, sometimes for personal advantage in determining their buyers, aided or impeded the sale by singing their own praises or proclaiming their shortcomings. Thus they spent weeks and months until the owner drove a bargain with a trader, who removed them in coffles to their doom in the rising cotton kingdom.

[7] *The Journal of Negro History*, Vol. III, p. 229.

In this way the Negroes were made the means of exploiting the new Southwest by accelerating the westward movement from the South. The slaves were thereby taken from a declining section, where they had become such a burden that these States would have necessarily become antislavery, had they remained. These blacks were carried to the cotton district, where they were apparently profitable servants in developing a new industry. The 85,000,-000 pounds of cotton produced in 1810 doubled by 1820, doubled again during the next decade, and doubled still once more by 1840. This was then about two-thirds of the cotton production in the world. After that period there was no question as to our leadership in the production of this raw material.

What, then, was the plantation system, serving as the basis of this large cotton industry? This was the method of cultivating an estate of hundreds and sometimes thou-**The** sands of acres. The administration centered **plantation.** in the residence of the planter or, in case of absentee ownership, in the home of the manager of the estate. Nearby stood the stable, smoke-house, corn-house; and a little farther away appeared the garden, potato field, watermelon patch, and the like. Somewhat distant from this central building were the homes of the slaves, commonly known as quarters. In most cases these were rude huts, often with dirt floors and so poorly constructed as to furnish little protection from bad weather. Furniture was generally lacking unless the few stools and the beds of straw be worthy of such designation. In some cases the slaves were allowed to till a patch of ground on which they produced their own vegetables. Some few of them were permitted to raise chickens or hogs. They had to look after these personal affairs at night, on Sundays, or holidays, as their whole time was otherwise required in the service of their masters.

In the case of just a few slaves the master often worked with them. On larger plantations, however, slaves worked in gangs under masters or their overseers, if the owners had sufficient holdings to afford such supervision. **Slaves at** In the culture of rice the work could be so **work.** divided as to assign it as tasks by holding each slave responsible for a definite accomplishment. Some few plant-ers, like McDonogh of Louisiana, and Z. Kingsley of Florida, ran their plantations on something like the self-government basis. Slaves were thrown largely on their own initiative to earn what they could. The control was vested in courts, the personnel of which were slaves. The administrative officers were also bondmen carrying out the mandates of these tribunals. Isaiah T. Montgomery of Mound Bayou, Mississippi, was taught with white chil-dren and trained as an accountant to serve in this capacity on the Mississippi plantation of Joseph Davis, the brother of Jefferson Davis.

As a plantation was a community in itself, it had to be governed as such. On large plantations managed by men of foresight, definite rules were drawn up to determine the procedure of overseers and slaves. These were intended to maintain the government of the slaves, pro- **Plantation** duce the largest crop possible, and at the same **management.** time to exercise such care over the bondmen as not to lose any of them by unnecessarily harsh treatment and neglect of their health. On some plantations, however, masters either worked to their own detriment by driving their slaves to an untimely death, or accomplished the same through overseers in the case of absentee ownership. This was often true in cases in which overseers were paid by giving them a share of the crop. The abuses practiced by these managers caused many planters to brand them as being a negligent, selfish, and dishonest class. The situation was not any better when the slaves were placed under a Negro driver. Some say it was worse.

Slaves were not generally cared for when sick. Women in pregnancy were more neglected than ever, and some worked too hard to bear healthy children. Many slaves **The care** were not given sufficient of the simple corn-**of slaves.** bread, bacon and salt herrings they were allowed; and a still larger number were not adequately

A PLANTATION

clothed. Negroes supplemented their rations by hunting and trapping at night. Some of them, by working at night, accumulated means by which they added to the meager provisions for their families supplied by their masters. A few hoarded considerable sums with which they purchased their freedom and made their way to free States, if not permitted to remain after manumission. Others had to steal to obtain a subsistence, and were even encouraged to do so by parsimonious masters.

Above all, punishments were crude and abusive. Because it would be prejudicial to their own economic interests, masters no longer mutilated Negroes or destroyed them on the wheel, as in the eighteenth century, unless it was absolutely necessary; but flogging, unmerciful beating, and even burning at the stake sometimes followed. In cases of unruly Negroes they were sold **Punishments.** South, where they faced the alternative of either yielding or being punished to death. The runaway slaves were hunted with dogs. When brought back they were put in heavy iron shackles or collars and sometimes subjected to such tortures as drawing out the toe-nails. Those persisting in resisting their masters were occasionally murdered. These conditions, however, differed from plantation to plantation, according to the liberality of the masters.

Little relief from such a condition could then be expected when the church itself all but approved this régime. This was brought out in the case of Charleston, South Carolina, to which the African Methodists, after their **Restrictions** withdrawal from the whites, summoned Ne- **on religious** groes to be ordained to serve in that city. **affairs.** This freedom of action was too much for the South. The independent church movement there was stopped. Meetings were prohibited and the bishop, his exhorters, and immediate followers were ordered to be imprisoned if they did not depart from the State, while others were fined or given a number of lashes. (As Negroes were thereafter forced to accept what accommodations were given them in the white churches, they gradually yielded room to the increasing membership of the whites until the blacks were forced to the galleries or compelled to hold special services following those of the whites.) A refusal of Negroes to give up to the whites prominent seats long occupied by them in a church in Charleston, South Carolina, led to their ejection by a group of white youths. When criticized for this these young members behaved so unbecomingly that nine of them had to be expelled; but to show their attachment to caste one hundred and fifty others left with them.

Unsuccessful efforts were then made to establish separate churches for the slaves, like the Calvary Church in Charleston, and the African Baptist Church in Richmond. For **Negro churches.** feigned reasons the legal endorsement for the latter was not given until 1855, and then on the condition that a white minister be employed. In the churches in the cities in the Border States, however, there was more religious freedom among the slaves. There was a Baptist Church in Lexington, Kentucky, in 1830. George Bentley, a Negro minister of polemic distinction, was preaching to the most enlightened whites as well as blacks in Giles County, Tennessee, in 1859. Out of a debate on baptism lasting more than four days he emerged victor over a white minister in that county challenging him to a discussion of the principles of baptism. He numbered among his communicants the best white people of the community and received from them a salary of about $600 a year. In the large cities there was still more religious freedom. Washington Negroes had several churches early in the nineteenth century, and Baltimore had ten churches for slave and free Negroes in 1834. In the neglected districts, however, the Negro was left in his heathen state.

The awful lot of the Negro became more pronounced as the churches which formerly championed the cause of the Negro tended to become, according to James G. Birney, **Proslavery church.** "The Bulwarks of American Slavery." By 1836 the Methodist Church, which at first attacked slavery, took the position of disclaiming "any right, wish, or intention to interfere in the civil and political relation between master and slave, as it existed in the slaveholding states of the union." Northern churches here and there were closing up their Negro pews or gradually eliminating the Negro membership altogether.

There were, moreover, southern churchmen who were busy writing treatises on the inferiority of the Negro and the wisdom of Providence in subjecting them to servitude in keeping with the Noachian "Cursed be Canaan." Preaching to Negroes, they explained the ancient proclamation: Japheth shall dwell in the land of Shem and Ham shall be his servant. "Servants therefore, obey your masters." They were faithfully supported in this fallacy by an array of pseudo-scientists. Such misinformed authors were producing numerous books explaining in detail the various ways in which the "woolly-headed, flat-nosed prognathous race" differed from the divinely selected Caucasian. Such nonsense, however, should not detain the student of history except so far as it is necessary to note how near the public mind sometimes approaches insanity. No scholar now accepts any such theory as the inferiority or superiority of races.

As all of the members of the national churches could not easily come around to this point arrived at through fictitious ethnology and anthropology, there followed in these ranks a schism which was really the beginning of the disunion. If people can not coöperate along religious lines it is very difficult to find a point of agreement to supply the necessary cohesion **The schism.** of a united nation. The knell of the Union was sounded, then, not first in the bombardment of Fort Sumter, but in the separation of the churches into northern and southern jurisdictions. In 1844 and 1845 the Baptists divided on the question of sending out slaveholding missionaries. There followed about the same time a similar separation of the Methodists because of a difference of opinion as to whether James O. Andrew. who held the office of bishop, could at the same time remain in the possession of slaves whom he had acquired by marriage. Uniting slaveholding with the deeds of the just men to be made perfect, the cotton section said "yes" and proceeded to establish churches which could translate the souls of men who wrung their bread from the sweat of others' brows.

After this reaction the slaves were not generally allowed any chance for mental development; and, of course, they could not learn to appreciate Christianity. Planters in **Enlightenment** some parts, thinking that the teaching of **prohibited.** religion might lead to the teaching of letters, prohibited it entirely. The best slaves could then do for mental development was to learn by contact and by stealth. Many a sympathetic person taught slaves to read. In some cases private teachers were bold enough to maintain Negro schools This was actually done in Savannah, Charleston, and Norfolk.

How some of these slaves learned in spite of opposition makes a beautiful story. Knowing the value of learning as a means of escape and having a longing for it, too, be- **Stealing** cause it was forbidden, many slaves continued **learning.** their education under adverse circumstances. Some of them, like Frederick Douglass, had the assistance of benevolent whites who were a law unto themselves; others studied privately and even attended school. Children of the clergy, accustomed to teach slaves to read the Bible, were generally regarded as enjoying an immunity. Some private teachers among the whites encouraged Negroes to steal away to secret places where their operations were shielded from the zealous execution of the law.

The majority of these enlightened slaves, however, learned by contact, observation and dint of energy.[8] Many of them were employed at such occupations as to develop

[8] C. G. Woodson, *Education of the Negro Prior to 1861*, Ch. IX.

N. Rillieux

Evaporating Pan,

Nº 4,879

Patented Dec. 10, 1846

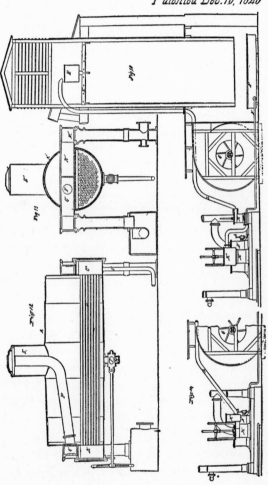

sufficient mental power to "read, write, and cipher."
"Blazon it to the shame of the South," said Redpath, "the
Learning by knowledge thus acquired has been snatched
contact. from the spare records of leisure in spite of
their honest wishes and watchfulness." Many, like Robert
Williams and Albert T. Jones, stole enough to enable them
to read with ease. Lott Cary heard a minister preach
from the third chapter of St. John, and on returning home
read that passage of scripture, although he had never before
been taught to read and had not hitherto made such an
effort. Dr. Alexander T. Augusta of Virginia learned to
read while serving white men as a barber. W. S. Scarbor-
ough, of Wilberforce, was taught by one J. C. Thomas,
a cruel slaveholder of the bitterest type living in Macon,
Georgia.

In spite of their circumstances a few slaves experienced
another sort of mental development. Being in a rapidly
growing country where the pioneers had to make use of the
Inventions forces of nature, here and there a slave be-
of slaves. came an inventor. According to the opinion
of Henry E. Baker, an examiner in the United States Patent Office, slaves made certain appliances, experimenting
with the separation of the seed from cotton, which, when
observed by Eli Whitney, were assembled by him as the
cotton gin. Freedmen, during these years, were more successful. While James Forten, a free Negro of Philadelphia,
was making a fortune out of his new device which he perfected for handling sails, Henry Blair, of Maryland, interested in labor saving, patented two corn harvesters in
1834 and in 1836. Norbert Rillieux, a man of color in
Louisiana, patented an evaporating pan by which the re-
fining of sugar was revolutionized. There is much evidence
that some of the inventions brought out by white persons
in the South prior to the Civil War were devices invented

by Negroes. The slave as such, according to an opinion of
Jeremiah S. Black, attorney-general of the United States in
1858, could not be granted a patent. The reason was that
the slave could neither contract with the government nor
assign his invention to his master. Confronting this problem, when Benjamin T. Montgomery, a slave of Jefferson
Davis, was on this ground denied a patent on an invention,
the President of the Confederate States secured the enactment of the law providing for patenting inventions of
slaves.[9]

In spite of these notable exceptions under this exploitation system, however, the Negro race became an element
with which the whites would not deal as man with man.
The whites were by law and public opinion **Negroes**
restrained from accepting Negroes as their **socially**
social equals. The miscegenation of Negro **proscribed.**
men and white women was penalized as a high crime, although there were always a few instances of such
association. Abdy, who toured the country from 1833 to
1834, doubted that such laws were enforced. "A Negro
man," said he, "was hanged not long ago for this crime at
New Orleans. The partner of his guilt—his master's
daughter—endeavored to save his life, by avowing that she
alone was to blame. She died shortly after his execution."

With the white man and the Negro woman, however, the
situation was different. A sister of President Madison once
said to the Reverend George Bourne, then a Presbyterian
minister in Virginia: "We Southern ladies are complimented with the name of wives; but we are only the mis-

[9] This law was:

And be it further enacted, That in case the original inventor or
discoverer of the art, machine or improvement for which a patent
is solicited is a slave, the master of such slave may take oath that
the said slave was the original; and on complying with the requisites
of the law shall receive a patent for said discovery or invention, and
have all the rights to which a patentee is entitled by law.

tresses of seraglios."[10]   But the masters of the female
slaves were not the only persons of such loose morals.
Many women of color were prostituted also
to the purposes of young white men and overseers. Goodell reports a well-authenticated
account of a respectable "Christian" lady of the South,
who kept a handsome mulatto female for the use of her genteel scn, as a method of deterring him, as she said, "from in-
discriminate and vulgar indulgences." Harriet Martineau
discovered a young white man who on visiting a southern
lady became insanely enamored of her intelligent quadroon
maid. He sought to purchase her, but because of her unusual worth the owner refused to sell the slave. The young
man persisted in trying to effect this purchase and finally
informed her owner that he could not live without this
attractive slave. Thereupon the white lady sold the woman
of color to satisfy the lust of her friend.

A weakness of the white man.

The Northern States were also showing an antagonistic
attitude toward miscegenation. This was especially true
of Pennsylvania. In 1820 a petition against the custom was presented to the legislature of Pennsylvania.
A mixed marriage was the cause of a riot at Columbia
in that State in 1834; and another had the same result in
the riot in Philadelphia in 1849. In 1838 members of the
Pennsylvania Constitutional Convention engaged in a
heated discussion of the custom. The agitation there,
however, was generally ineffective. Race admixture continued as is evidenced by the fact that one-fifth of the
Negroes in the State in 1800 were mulattoes and that in
1860 this proportion had increased to one-third. This had
been brought about in spite of the fact that public sentiment against Negroes in the North had so developed as to
afflict them with many of the evils from which they suffered in the South.

[10] *The Journal of Negro History*, Vol. III, p. 350.

Against the hardships of the system numerous slaves rebelled. So thoroughly had they become intimidated after
Nat Turner's fate that most of them did nothing to injure
their masters; but they endeavored to make their escape
into the woods, too often only to be brought **The runaway**
back after a few weeks' adventure. Offering **slave.**
in its advertisements some attractive reward, the news-

THE PURSUIT

papers quickly proclaimed the news of a runaway. White
men, assisted with firearms and bloodhounds trained to run
down fugitives, hunted them like game even in the North.
That section, struck by the inhuman methods to recapture
slaves, passed personal liberty laws to prevent the return of
the Negroes apprehended, as many of these were kidnapped
free persons taken under pretext of being runaways.[11]

[11] These Laws are collected in Hurd's *Law of Freedom and
Bondage.*

These laws, however, were nullified by the decisions of the federal courts and the Fugitive Slave Law of 1850. This undertook to impress into the service of slave-hunting men who were conscientiously opposed to the institution. The North was then the scene of the most disgraceful deeds. These aroused the consciences of the people and swelled the ranks of the abolition minority which at one time seemed to decline to meet premature death.

The efforts of the slaves to escape from bondage, however, were unusually successful in the Appalachian mountains, where there had been retained a healthy sentiment

Fugitives. against slavery. The mountaineers of North Carolina, Kentucky and Tennessee organized antislavery societies during the first quarter of the nineteenth century. When that movement became unpopular they generally supported the cause of colonization. This seemed a good solution of the immediate problem of the Negro; for the frontiersmen were not particularly attached to the unfortunate race. They believed that the institution of slavery was an economic evil of which the country should rid itself by a system of gradual emancipation as soon as possible. When, however, the conditions of the Negroes in the South became so intolerable that it was necessary to flee for larger liberty in the Northern States, they found it easy to make their way through this region where the farmers were not interested in the institution. It was of some help, too, that they could easily hide in the mountains and in the limestone regions which furnished comfortable caves. The promoters of the Underground Railroad, therefore, offered them a way of escape by extending their sys-

The Underground Railroad. tem southward through the mountains of these States so as to connect with the fugitives escaping thither. These lines led through Kentucky into Ohio, Indiana and Illinois, and connected with the Great Lakes. Along this route fugitives passed

into Canada, under the guidance of persons like the heroic
Josiah Henson, Harriett Tubman, and John Brown. [12]

A few slaves in the South, however, did not suffer sufficiently to want to escape.   Slaves in urban communities
were occasionally better
situated than other bond-
men.   Employed in the
trades and domestic serv-
ice affording close con-
tact with their masters,
they were economically
better off than **Town slaves.**
the free Ne-
groes whom they often
doomed to poverty by
crowding them out of the
various pursuits of labor.
There was scarcely any
industry in which slaves
did not engage, and in
most cases to the exclu-
sion or at the expense of
the poor whites as well as
of the free blacks. Some

Harriett Tubman

contractors owned their workmen just as masters owned the
Negroes on their plantations. Master mechanics less favorably circumstanced hired slaves. In a few cases slaves were
employed under the direction of an enterprising master mechanic who took contracts, managed the business, and reported to the master at certain periods. It was soon
learned, however, that a slave as such easily competed with
free Negroes and whites. It was, therefore, necessary for
the masters to grant such bondmen the larger freedom of

[12] W. H. Siebert, *Underground Railroad*, p. 166. See also *The
Journal of Negro History*, VII, 235-241 and 377-379.

profit-sharing or of hiring themselves to stimulate them to greater endeavor. This custom proved unsatisfactory to white mechanics. In several States, then, laws were passed to prevent the hiring of slaves to themselves. But this custom continued in spite of strenuous efforts to the contrary, as the enforcement of it would have materially restricted the use of slaves. Many slaves thus employed were cheated in the end by dishonest contractors, but others more fortunately situated contrived thereby to purchase their own freedom and that of their families. To do this many Negroes worked at night after finishing their tasks by day. But this privilege served as another reason for legislation against this custom. It would lead to an increase in the number of free Negroes who might promote servile insurrection.

In the city, too, it was possible for the Negroes to maintain among themselves certain social distinctions based upon their advantages of contact with the whites and the amount of culture they had taken over. Those employed **Social** in the higher pursuits of labor and as domes- **distinctions.** tic servants to the rich whites were enabled by the working-over of cast-off clothes and imitating their masters' language and airs, to lord it over the crude slaves of the fields. In culture the less fortunate Negroes were further separated from these urban free blacks than the latter were from the whites. In their social affairs house servants sometimes had much liberty and apparently experienced much joy. They so impressed travelers with their contentment in this situation that some concluded that the Negroes had no serious objection to their enslavement.

The South had finally succeeded in hedging in the Negro so that he might forever afterward do the will of **Slavery, the** his master. But this seemingly sane method **undoing of** of developing the South was what resulted in **the South.** its undoing. Since migration of slaveholders promoted a segregation of planters of the same class, moving under similar conditions and to the same section, it made reform almost an impossibility; and in preventing the immigration of white laborers into the slave States the system became so strongly intrenched that it had to be attacked from without. In the first place, in the effort to exploit black men it transformed white men into blood-thirsty beings. The system, moreover, promoted the formation of wasteful habits. It prevented the growth of towns and cities, it shut out industrialism, and it made the South dependent on the North or European nations for its manufactures. While the North was receiving an influx of free laborers the South was increasing unnecessarily its slave labor supply, indulging in unwise investments, and overstocking the markets with southern staple crops. In making labor undignified, moreover, it reduced the poor whites to poverty, caused a scarcity of money, cheapened land, and confined the South to one-crop farming at the expense of its undeveloped resources.

The economic interests of the two sections, therefore, began to differ widely during the thirties. When Missouri asked for admission to the Union, the struggle which ensued emphasized these differences. Prior to this pe- **Differing** riod slavery had well established itself in that **interests.** territory. When everything had been arranged and Congress was about to pass the bill providing for its admission, James Talmadge, a representative from New York, upset things by offering an amendment providing that slavery should not be allowed in that territory. This led to a fiery debate participated in by the stalwart defenders of the proslavery section of the country and by the Congressmen of the North, who, although at that time unprepared to advocate a general abolition of slavery, were convinced that it was an evil and desired to prohibit its expansion. It was pointed out by the antislavery element that a part of the State of Missouri lies farther north than the mouth of the

Ohio River, above which slavery was prohibited by the Ordinance of 1787 organizing the Northwest Territory.[13]

The main question was whether or not Congress had any right to limit a State coming into the Union. Decidedly it had, but it was necessary to argue the question. It was brought out that in the admission of the State of Louisiana Congress imposed certain conditions requiring that the State should use the English language as its official tongue, should guarantee the writ of habeas corpus and trial by jury, and should incorporate into its organic laws the fundamental principles of civil and religious liberty. They could have pointed out, too, that Ohio was required to comply with a number of requirements, among which was the use of certain of its lands in the Western Reserve and in the southeast.[14]

The antislavery group, moreover, contended that inasmuch as Congress is required by the Constitution to guarantee to each State a republican form of government it **Binding** was necessary to prohibit slavery because of its **a State.** incompatibility with that form of government. The proslavery party supported their cause on the ground that to impose a restriction on a State would place it on a basis of inequality rather than that of equality with other States. The privileges enjoyed by one State should be enjoyed by all. If one had the right to hold slaves, all should enjoy the same privilege as they had when all were admitted to the Union. It was contended, moreover, that powers not delegated to the United States Government

[13] There are discussions of the constitutional question growing out of slavery in Herman von Holst's *The Constitutional and Political History of the United States of America*, in John W. Burgess's *Middle Period* and his *Civil War and Reconstruction*, and in James Ford Rhodes' *History of the United States*, Chs. VI and VII. Burgess and Rhodes, however, are generally biased.

[14] Restrictions were also imposed later on California when it was provided that the duties on goods imported there should have to be fixed according to terms set forth in the amendment to the regular navy act.

nor prohibited to the States were reserved to the States. The question as to whether a State should hold slaves, therefore, was reserved to that commonwealth and Congress had no right to interfere therewith.

It was asserted also, as was admitted thereafter, that the restriction against slavery in the Ordinance of 1787 was not binding on those States of the territory that had been admitted to the Union, and that they could introduce slavery when they desired.[15] The The Ordinance of 1787. pro-slavery leaders believed that the expansion of slavery would be a benefit to the country rather than an evil. It would provide for an extension of the system; it would reduce the number held by each person and, therefore, would bring the slave into more direct and helpful contact with the master. The agitation was quieted for the time being by a compromise. This permitted Missouri to come into the Union as a slave State but prohibited the institution north of the parallel thirty-six thirty constituting the southern limit of Missouri.

Another important question came forward in the Missouri debate when the question had been all but settled, that is, when the State had framed a constitution in keeping with the instructions given in the enabling act, but had incorporated into this document a clause providing for the exclusion of free Negroes from that commonwealth. This provision was seriously attacked by the friends of justice. They argued that inasmuch as these Negroes were citizens of the United States, no State had a right to restrict their privileges, as such action would conflict with the Constitution of the United States, which guarantees to the citizens of each commonwealth all the privileges and immunities of citizens

The citizenship of Negroes.

[15] J. P. Dunn, *Indiana; A Redemption from Slavery*, pp. 218-260; N. D. Harris, *The History of Negro Servitude in Illinois*, Chs. III, IV and V; and B. A. Hinsdale, *Old Northwest*, pp. 351-358.

in every other commonwealth.   This drove home the real
truth which the country had not before realized, that there
was such a thing as citizenship of the United States in
contradistinction to citizenship in a State, and that the
citizenship of the United States is more than citizenship
of a State.   When a citizen, therefore, immigrated into and
settled in another State, he should not, according to the
Constitution, lose the right to be treated as a citizen of that
commonwealth.   When this involved the rights of the
Negro it was certainly startling to the representatives of
the South; and Missouri, for that reason, if for no other,
was less inclined than ever to change that provision of its
Constitution.   The matter was settled by a second compromise, to counteract the effect this clause might have.
This provided that nothing therein contained should be so
construed as to give the assent of Congress to any provision
in the Constitution of Missouri which contravened that
clause in the Constitution of the United States which declares that the citizens of each State shall be entitled to
all of the privileges and immunities of citizens in the several
States.

Slavery again showed its far-reaching effects.   During
the first three decades of the nineteenth century, the
South, in the natural order of things, became a section de-
Slavery and pendent solely on its peculiar institution, a
the tariff. district devoted entirely to agriculture and
almost solidly organized in defending such interests.   For
this reason the South developed into a mere plantation.
The North, on the other hand, in view of the shipping
industry, its commerce, and the manufacturing, which of
necessity grew during the War of 1812 and decidedly
expanded thereafter, developed a number of business and
industrial centers desirous of protecting their industries
by imposing certain duties on goods imported from
Europe.   This caused a shift in the positions of the leaders

of these two sections. Whereas, in 1816, John C. Calhoun
was an advocate of a protective tariff and Daniel Webster
was a free trader, in 1832 Webster was in favor of import duties and Calhoun had constructed a policy of free
trade. With the support of the West, desiring a protective
duty on its hemp and the like, the manufacturing districts
were able to secure the enactment of tariff-for-protection
measures in 1824, 1828 and 1832.[16]

Against the protective tariff the commonwealths of the
South began to argue that it was discriminatory and therefore unconstitutional, and that it imposed a tax upon one
section for the benefit of the other. Con- **Opposition to**
gress, as the South saw it, had no right to **the tariff.**
legislate in behalf of one section at the expense of the
other. So bitter did the South become because of this seeming imposition that in 1832 South Carolina undertook to
nullify the tariff law. South Carolina took the position
of Kentucky and Virginia in 1798, that a State had a right
to obey or to nullify a law passed by Congress, if, in its
judgment, it found out that that law was prejudicial to the
interests of the State concerned.

It was made clear, moreover, that South Carolina was
of the opinion that this country was not a Union but still
a Confederation loosely held together very much as the
States were under the Articles of Confedera- **A union or a**
tion. A State, therefore, as long as it chose **confederacy?**
to be bound by the terms of the Constitution could continue
to do so; but if at any time it felt that the union with the
other States was undesirable, it could of itself or in connection with a number of States constituting a majority
call a convention representing the same power by which the
Constitution was ratified and declare the severance of the
ties that bound them to the Union.

It was necessary, therefore, for the Union to take high

[16] See Calhoun's speech in the Appendix.

ground for its own self-preservation. Although Andrew Jackson, then President of the United States, did not hold any brief for the tariff himself, he could not countenance the act of nullification. He, therefore, threatened to use force should South Carolina refuse to obey the laws of Congress. This matter, like others threatening the foundation of the Union, was settled by a compromise brought forward by Henry Clay. It was enacted that the duties would remain as they were under the law of 1832, but by a gradual process would be diminished until they reached the rates acceptable to South Carolina.

Slavery brought out also another economic question in connection with internal improvements. It was difficult for a slaveholding section to expand as rapidly as the manufacturing and commercial parts of the country. In **Internal** this all but phenomenal growth of the **improvements.** North and West there was an urgent need for canals and roads to tap the resources of the interior. As the South in its slow development did not feel this need and thought that it would not generally profit by these improvements, it usually opposed them. The proslavery leaders held that the United States Government had no authority to make such improvements and the States had not the required funds. This opposition resulted from the observation that these improvements were unifying influences. They strengthened the Union at the expense of the South, which hoped to hold the axe of secession over the heads of the Unionists. They had a precedent for this in the Hartford Convention of 1815, when New Englanders threatened the country with secession because of their dissatisfaction with the trade restrictions imposed during the War of 1812.

CHAPTER XIV

THE FREE NEGRO

WHILE the fate of the slaves in the South was being determined, there was also a considerable number of free persons of color whose status was ever changing. Few people now realize the extent to which the free Negro figured in the population of this country prior to the Civil War.[1] Before slavery was reduced from a patriarchal establishment to

The status of the free Negro.

the mere business of exploiting men, a considerable number of Negroes had secured their freedom, and the fruits of the American Revolution, effective long thereafter in ameliorating their condition, gave an impetus to manumission. In some colonies Negroes were indentured servants before they were slaves, and became free upon the expiration of their term of service. The result was that there were in this country in 1790 as many as 59,557 free people of color, 35,000 of whom were living in the South. During the two decades from 1790 to 1810, the rate of increase of free Negroes exceeded that of the slaves, and the proportion of free Negroes in the black population increased accordingly from 7.9 per cent in 1790 to 13.5 per cent in 1810. After this date the tendency was in the other direction because of the reaction against the Negro, which brought about a restriction on manumissions.

[1] John H. Russell, *The Free Negro in Virginia, passim;* E. R. Turner, *The Negro in Pennsylvania;* F. U. Quillin, *The Color Line in Ohio, passim;* C. T. Hickok, *The Negro in Ohio, passim;* C. G. Woodson, *A Century of Negro Migration,* pp. 1-100; the *Journal of Negro History,* I, 1-68, 99-100, 203-242, 302-317, 361-376; II, 51-78, 164-185; III, 90-91, 196-197, 360-367, 435-441, and *Negro Population in the United States, 1790 to 1915.*

Between 1810 and 1840 the Negro population almost doubled, but the proportion of the free Negroes remained about the same. Because of further restriction on manu-

Slow increase. mission and the more secure foundation of galling slavery with rigid regulations to prevent the fugitives from escaping, this proportion of free Negroes in the black population decreased to 11.9 per cent by 1850 and to 11 per cent by 1860. While the Negro population as a whole doubled its percentage of increase, then, that of the free blacks declined. It became smaller in parts of the North and declined to one-fourth of the rate of increase between 1800 to 1810. In 1860 the rate of increase was about one per cent a year. It is worthy of note, however that there were 434,455 free Negroes in the United States in 1850 and 488,070 in 1860. At this latter date 83,942 of these were in Maryland, 58,042 in Virginia, 30,463 in North Carolina, 18,467 in Louisiana, 11,131 in the District of Columbia, 10,638 in Kentucky; in short, 250,787 in the whole South. About 50,000 of these had attained the independence of being heads of families by 1830, while a few thousand other free Negro families were reported among the white families as servants.[2]

This increase of free Negroes was largely a natural growth. There had been, of course, some additions by purchases of freedom and the acquisition of new territory.

Increase a natural growth. Only a few immigrated into this country, for merely 7,011 free Negroes enumerated in 1860 were born abroad. Some idea as to the extent that other factors figured in this may be obtained from the fact that 1,467 Negroes were manumitted in 1849 and 1,011 became fugitives. In 1859 there were 3,000 manumissions and 803 fugitives. The census of 1860 shows

[2] See Woodson's *Free Negro Heads of Families in the United States in 1830.*

that probably 20,000 manumissions were made during the decade between 1850 and 1860.

Negro Population, 1790 to 1860

Census Year	Total	Free Number	Per cent	Slave	Decennial Increase Number Free	Slave	Per cent Free	Slave
1860.....	4,441,830	488,070	11.0	3,953,760	53,575	749,447	12.3	23.4
1850.....	3,638,808	434,495	11.9	3,204,313	48,202	716,958	12.5	28.8
1840.....	2,873,648	386,293	13.4	2,487,355	66,694	478,312	20.9	23.8
1830.....	2,328,642	319,599	13.7	2,009,043	85,965	471,021	36.8	30.6
1820.....	1,771,656	233,634	13.2	1,538,022	47,188	346,660	25.3	29.1
1810.....	1,377,808	186,466	13.5	1,191,362	78,011	297,760	71.9	33.3
1800.....	1,002,037	108,435	10.8	893,602	48,908	195,921	82.2	28.1
1790.....	757,181	59,557	7.9	697,624	......	....	....	....

The statistics of the Negro population between 1790 and 1915 suggest as an explanation for this decrease that the free people of color were much older and therefore subject to a higher mortality rate; that they were Sex less normally distributed by sex and, there- distribution. fore, probably characterized by a marital condition less favorable to rapid natural increase. Among the Free Negroes at each of the five censuses, from 1820 to 1860, there were fewer males than females, whereas the distribution as to sex among the slaves remained about equally divided between the two. While this does not altogether account for the disparity, it doubtless had something to do with the situation; for the Negroes manumitted were, as a majority, men, and those who contrived to escape were largely of the same sex. Furthermore, masters controlled the slave supply so as to add what number they needed from whichever sex seemed deficient.

The customs and regulations restraining the slaves did not generally apply to the free people of color even when so provided by law. Some of them were closely connected with their masters, who gave them more consideration than that shown by many others who sold their The status of own flesh and blood. In spite of the law to the free Negroes. contrary, a few such benevolent masters maintained schools for the education of their mulatto children. When that became unpopular they were privately instructed or sent to the North for education. Charleston, South Carolina, affords a good example of the interest manifested in the free people of color by the sympathetic citizens. They winked at the efforts of the free blacks to educate their children in well-organized schools in defiance of the law. In the State of Louisiana, where many of these mixed breeds were found, their fathers sometimes sent them to Paris to avail themselves of the advantages of the best education of that time.

These free Negroes were not all on the same plane. In the course of time they experienced a development of social distinction which largly resembled that of the whites. There were freedmen in possession of a considerable amount of property, others who formed a lower class of mechanics and artisans, and finally those living with difficulty above pecuniary embarrassment. Among those in the large cities social lines were as strongly drawn as between the whites and the blacks, and the antipathy resulting therefrom was hardly less.

The well-to-do free Negroes were not merely persons with sufficient property to form an attachment to the community. Many of them owned slaves, who cultivated their **Progressive** large estates. Of 360 persons of color in **freedmen.** Charleston, 130 of them were assessed with taxes on 390 slaves in 1860. In some of these cases, as in that of Marie Louise Bitaud, a free woman of color in New Orleans, in 1832, these slaves were purchased for personal reasons or benevolent purposes, often to make their lot much easier. They were sometimes sold by sympathetic white persons to Negroes for a nominal sum on the condition that they be kindly treated. In 1830 there were reported to the United States Bureau of the Census 3777 Negro heads of families who owned slaves. Most of these

Negroes lived in Louisiana, Maryland, North Carolina, South Carolina and Virginia.[3]

Some of these instances are enlightening. A colored man in 1818 bought a sailmaker in Charleston. Richard Richardson sold a slave woman and child for $800 to Alexander Hunter, guardian of the Negro freeman, Louis Mirault of Savannah. Anthony Ordingsell, a free man of color, sold a slave woman in the same city in 1833. A Charleston Negro who purchased his wife for $700 sold her at a profit of $50 because she would not behave herself. To check this, laws restricting manumission, as in Virginia in 1806, were enacted to limit this benevolence of white men by imposing difficult conditions. Thereafter these freedmen were to be sent out of the State unless their former masters agreed to support them.

Some other Negroes of less distinction accomplished much to convince the world of the native ability of the Negroes to extricate themselves from peculiar situations and to make progress in spite of opposition. Samuel Martin, a benevolent slaveholder of color residing at Port Gibson, Mississippi, purchased *Undistinguished free Negroes.* his own freedom in 1829, and thereafter purchased two mulatto women with their four children, brought them to Cincinnati in 1844, and emancipated them. Another Negro named Creighton, living in Charleston, South Carolina, accumulated considerable wealth which he finally decided to devote to the colonization of the Negroes in Liberia. Offering his slaves the alternative of being liberated on the condition of accompanying him to Africa or of being sold as property, he disposed of his holdings. Only one of his slaves accepted the offer, but Creighton closed up his business in Charleston, purchased for the enterprise a schooner of his own, and set sail for Liberia in 1821.

[3] See Woodson's *Free Negro Owners of Slaves in the United States in 1830.*

Among the prosperous free Negroes in the South may be mentioned Jehu Jones, the proprietor of one of the most popular hotels in Charleston and owner of forty thousand

Wealthy persons of color.
dollars' worth of property. There lived Thomy Lafon in New Orleans, where he accumulated real estate to the amount of almost half a million dollars. In the same city was a woman of color owning a tavern and several slaves. A Negro in St. Paul's Parish, South Carolina, was said to have two hundred slaves, and a white wife and son-in-law, in 1857. In 1833 Solomon Humphries, a free Negro well known by men of all classes in Macon, Georgia, kept a grocery store there and had more credit than any other merchant in the town. He had accumulated about twenty thousand dollars' worth of property, including a number of slaves. Cyprian Ricard bought an estate in Iberville Parish, with ninety-one slaves, for about $225,000. Marie Metoyer, of Natchitoches Parish, possessed fifty slaves and an estate of more than 2,000 acres. Charles Roques of the same community left in 1848 forty-seven slaves. Martin Donato, of St. Landry, died in 1848, leaving a Negro wife and children possessed of 4,500 arpents of land, eighty-nine slaves and personal property worth $46,000.

These Negroes, however, were exceptions to the rule. Most well-to-do free Negroes in urban communities belonged to the artisan class, and there were more of them

Prosperous mechanics.
than one would think. In southern cities most of the work in the mechanic arts was done by the slaves. There was less discrimination in this field in the South than in the North. Contrasting the favorable conditions of southern Negroes with that of those in the North, a proslavery man referred to Charleston, South Carolina, as furnishing a good example of a center of unusual activity and rapid strides of thrifty free Negroes. Enjoying these unusual advantages, the Negroes of Charles-

ton early in the nineteenth century were ranked by some as economically and intellectually superior to any other group of such persons in the United States. A large portion of the leading mechanics, fashionable tailors, shoe manufacturers, and mantua-makers were free Negroes, who had "a consideration in the community far more than that enjoyed by any of the colored population in the northern cities."

What then was the situation in the North? The fugitive slave found it difficult. Most Negroes who became free as a result of manumission had been dependents so long that they lost their initiative. When thrown upon their own resources in the North where they had to make opportunities, they failed. In increasing the number of those seeking economic opportunities in the North, moreover, they so cheapened the labor as to make **Hardships in the North.** it difficult for the free Negroes already there to earn a livelihood. They were, therefore, branded by the writers of the time as the pariahs of society. There was, in fact, as much prejudice against the free Negroes in parts of the North as in the South. This feeling, however, resulted largely from the antipathy engendered by the competition of the Negroes with the large number of Germans and Scotch-Irish immigrating into this country a generation before the Civil War.

Some few Negroes facing these conditions returned South and reënslaved themselves rather than starve in the North. A larger number in the South, however, were enslaved against their wills for such petty of- **The return to the South.** fenses as theft and the like, which almost any poverty-stricken man would be liable to commit. They were ordinarily arrested as suspected fugitives, or for vagrancy and illegal residence, and finally sold for jail fees. As Negroes in these cases were not allowed to testify in their own behalf, the official arresting a free Negro generally preferred against him whatever charge best suited his convenience and disposed of the Negro accordingly. Eighty-nine were sold in Maryland under the act of 1858 justifying such reënslavement. Much of this repression was instituted for intimidation to keep the free Negroes down that they might never join with slaves in an insurrection.

How did the situation of the free Negro compare with that of the white man? In the first place, the freedman was not a citizen in any Southern State after **Restrictions.** 1834 and was degraded from that status in certain States in the North. In most States free persons of color had the right to own and alienate property with some limitations. They could even own and sell Negro slaves. Statutes and customs, however, prohibited them from owning whites as servants, and during the intense slavery agitation of the thirties this right of holding Negroes as slaves was gradually restricted to whites. This was due to the benevolent use made of it by certain Negroes, who purchased more than their wives and children. For fear of improper uses, too, free Negroes in the South were not allowed to own such property as firearms, dogs, fire locks, poisonous drugs and intoxicants. As they were prohibited from serving in the State militia, they would have no need for firearms. The Negro, moreover, had a weak title to property in himself. If the Negro's right to be free were questioned, the burden of proof lay on him.

In some cases, however, the free Negroes had a little chance in the courts. The freedmen had the remedy of *habeas corpus.* They could bring suit against persons **Some** doing them injury, and in the case of seeming **privileges.** injustice in a lower court they could appeal to a higher. When charged with crime the free Negro had the right to trial by jury and, after indictment, could give bond for his liberty. After Nat Turner's insurrection in 1831 the right of jury trial was restricted in several southern States to cases punishable by death. It must be remembered, however, that the Negro could not expect a fair trial; for, consistent with the unwritten primitive law of the white man in dealing with the blacks, judgment preceded proof. In the case of ordinary misdemeanors the lot of the free Negroes was no better than that of the slave. Corporal punishment in these cases was administered to the Negroes without stint, whereas a white man guilty of the same offense would be required to pay a fine. In most cases of felony the punishment for a white man and a free Negro was the same in the beginning, but the reaction brought on certain distinctions.

At times the free Negroes could go and come to suit themselves. During the ardent slavery agitation, however, it was necessary for them to exhibit their free papers when questioned. They were later restrained from moving from one State to another or even from one county **Egress and** to another without securing a permit. **regress.** Nearer the middle of the nineteenth century it was unlawful in some Southern States for a free Negro to return to the State after leaving. He might be spoiled by contact or education.

Although forcing the free Negroes to a low social status, the local government did not exempt them from its burdens. In Virginia, free Negroes were required to pay a poll tax of $1.50 in 1813 and $2.50 in 1815. In 1814, 5,547 free Negroes in that State paid $8,322 in taxes, and in 1863 they paid $13,065.22 in poll taxes. The Negroes in Baltimore paid $500 in school taxes in 1860, although their children could not attend the city schools. Most States inconsistently taxed the free Negroes in the same way.

Socially the Negro, whether slave or free under the economic régime, was an outcast. Prejudice based on color rather than on condition made him an object of oppro-

The Negro an outcast. brium in the nineteenth century, in contra- distinction to his condition a hundred years earlier. In the seventeenth century there followed mis- cegenation of the races. In the eighteenth century free Negroes still experienced some interbreeding and moved socially with the whites in certain parts. In the nineteenth century all social relations between the whites and the free Negroes became about the same as those of the former with the slaves.

No laws prevented the intermarriage of the free Negroes and Indians. Squaws accepted Negroes for husbands, and Indian men commonly had black wives. Extensive mis-

Interbreeding with the Indians. cegenation of these stocks was experienced in most States in the South. As these two races were in common undesirables among the whites, the one early manifested sympathy for the other. This was evidenced by the fact that in the massacre of 1622 in Virginia not an African was killed. In the raids of the Indians on the settlers of Louisiana, Negroes often acted in concert with them. Efforts had to be made to separate the Negroes from the Indians, when the former eagerly resorted to their reservations as places of refuge. In some cases the Negroes on these estates survived the Indians, who became extinct.

Free Negroes mingled more with the slaves, however, than with any other class. This was not the condition in the beginning. Some slaves disliked free Negroes because conditions had made the former apparently the inferiors of the latter. But in the course of time, when the free

Relations of free Negroes and slaves. Negroes dwindled in number and their chances for education and the accumulation of wealth grew less, the social distinctions be- tween them and the slaves diminished and they associated with and married among them. This became common in the nineteenth century. In fact, when the question of employment became serious, it was often advantageous for a free Negro to marry a slave wife. This attachment too often prevented a free Negro from being expelled from the State by the hostile laws when he had this all but permanent connection with the community. A master would not force him to leave for fear that he might induce his family to escape.

The accomplishment of this task of reducing the free people of color almost to the status of the slaves, however, was not easy. In the first place, so many persons of color had risen to positions of usefulness among **Exceptions** progressive people and had formed connec- **to the rule.** tions with them that an abrupt separation was both inexpedient and undesirable. Exceptions to the hard and fast rules of caste were often made to relieve the people of color. The miscegenation of the races in the South and especially in large cities like Charleston and New Orleans, moreover, had gone to the extent that from these centers eventually went, as they do now, a large number of quadroons and octoroons, who elsewhere crossed over to the white race. As the status of the Negroes remained fixed, however, while that of the poor whites changed, the close relations formerly existing between these classes gradually ceased.

The free Negro was in many respects a disturbing factor in the economic system. White laborers did not care to compete with them. The free Negro usually won in the contest, for the reason that his standard of **A disturbing** living was lower and he could work for less. **factor.** Moreover, being almost defenseless before a hostile public, he could be more easily cheated and was, therefore, to be preferred. According to testimony, however, they were of economic worth. Yet others called them idlers, criminals, vicious vagabonds, a vile excrescence and the like. These opinions may not be taken seriously when there are so many others to the contrary.

In the North the Negroes were likewise socially and, in **Successful** addition to this, economically proscribed. Yet **Negroes.** they usually succeeded in permanently establishing themselves wherever they had an opportunity.[4]

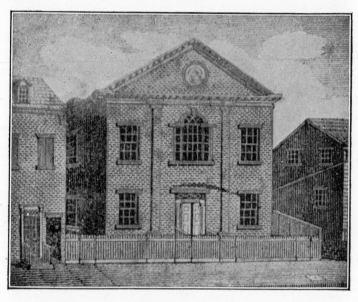

NEW YORK AFRICAN FREE SCHOOL, No. 2, built a century ago

Joseph C. Cassey and William Platt became enterprising lumber merchants in Western New York; Henry Topp came forward as a leading merchant tailor in Albany; and

[4] For other instances of free Negroes making economic progress, see William Wells Brown's *The Black Man*, M. R. Delaney's *The Condition of the Colored People of the United States*, Alexander Mott's *Biographical Sketches*, W. J. Simmons's *Men of Mark*, C. G. Woodson's *A Century of Negro Migration*, and *The Journal of Negro History*, under the caption *Undistinguished Negroes*.

Henry Scott of New York City founded and promoted for a number of years one of the most successful pickling establishments in that metropolis. Along with him arose Thomas Downing, a caterer, and Edward V. Clark, a prosperous jeweler. Other Negroes were building churches, establishing schools, and editing newspapers promoting the interests of the people of color.

In Pennsylvania, where Negroes were found in large numbers, more evidences of progress were noted. The Negroes of Philadelphia had taxable property to the amount of $350,000 in 1832, $359,626 worth **Evidences of** in 1837, and $400,000 worth in 1847. They **progress.** had established before emancipation more than a score of churches with which were connected more than a hundred benevolent societies and a number of schools. Five hundred of these Negroes were mechanics, and a considerable number ranked as business men. Among the latter were James Forten, a sail manufacturer, Joseph Casey, a broker, and Stephen Smith, a lumber merchant. William Goodrich of York was investing in railroad stock. Benjamin Richards of Pittsburgh was accumulating wealth in the butchering business, and Henry M. Collins of the same city was developing a real estate enterprise of considerable proportions.

Little progress in the education of the Negroes, however, was noted during these years. With the exception of some clandestine operations there were few schools for slaves and free Negroes in the South, after the fears resulting from the insurrectionary movement. Most of such schools were in towns and cities. Julian Troumontaine taught openly in Savannah until 1829 and clandestinely thereafter until 1844. The Union army in **Negro** 1864 discovered that a Mrs. Deveaux had been **schools.** secretly teaching Negroes there for thirty years. Such a school taught by a white woman was discovered in Norfolk in 1854. There was a private Negro school in New-berne about this time, and still another in Fayetteville, North Carolina. John Chavis was teaching whites in that State at this time. There was not much interference with secret Negro schools in Charleston, Wilmington, Norfolk, and Petersburg prior to the Civil War. Years before emancipation Simeon Beard conducted a Negro school in Charleston. In Baltimore, Louisville, and New Orleans there was no serious objection to private Negro educa-tion. In 1847 W. H. Gibson was teaching in a day and night school in Louisville. In New Orleans the education of the free people of color was regarded as necessary. In the North, too, especially in the cities most Negro communities had some of the facilities of education. Abolitionists, Quakers, and other sympathetic groups main-tained here and there a few Negro schools. When the idea of education at public expense became incorporated into the laws of Northern States some of them allotted a portion to the education of the Negroes in separate schools. In 1829, however, Ohio excluded Negroes from the benefits of public education and did not recede from this position until 1849. Indiana did the same in 1837 and reënforced the prohibition in 1853 by a provision that the names of Negro children should not be taken in the school enumera-tion and that the property of Negroes should not be taxed for school purposes.[5]

Outside of the large cities of the North, too, there were few Negro schools sufficiently developed to offer thorough instruction. The urban Negro schools began early in the

Schools in cities. century. There was a school for Negroes in the house of Primus Hall in Boston in 1798, and the city opened a primary school for Negroes in 1820. There were three such in Boston in 1828, one in Salem, one

---

[5] In Woodson's *Education of the Negro Prior to 1861,* this subject is treated in detail.

in New Haven, and one in Portland, Maine. Rhode Island legally provided for Negro schools in 1828 and Connecticut in 1830. The African Free Schools of the New York Manumission Society organized in 1787 developed considerably by 1810 and still more by 1814. The State Superintendent of Schools began to open special schools for Negroes in 1823. The State provided for them by law in 1841. The African Free Schools were taken over by the New York Public School Society in 1834 and organized as a system. With further public support, these schools became probably the best of their kind in the country. In Pennsylvania there were several private Negro schools supported by Quakers and sympathetic friends, but in 1818 some public aid was given to Negro schools in Columbia and Philadelphia. By the act of the legislature in 1834 a system of public schools thereby established offered the Negroes further help, but they were deprived of it until 1854. It was fortunate then that in 1839 Richard Humphreys left $10,000 to endow a school for the vocational education of Negroes. This became the Institute for Colored Youth. Removed to the present site, it is known as the Cheney School for Training Teachers. Lewis Woodson had a successful school in Pittsburgh in 1830, and it was not surpassed by any other there until Charles Avery gave for Negro education a fund of $300,000, from a part of which was established Avery College in that city in 1849.

In Cincinnati, Ohio, the Negroes had a school in 1820. They had a better one in 1834. In 1844 came the Rev. Hiram Gilmore, who established there a high school. In 1856 the Methodists established Wilberforce near Xenia. Negroes in the District of Columbia first studied privately with white friends, but in 1807 George Bell, Nicholas Franklin, and Moses Liverpool built the first Negro schoolhouse in the capital of the nation. No public support for such an institution could be obtained in a proslavery atmosphere.

Elsewhere, however, there was always some question about the public support of Negro education, even in the North where it had been provided. Men did not care to be **Caste in** taxed to educate the children of poor whites **schools** and Negroes. The first public schools for **opposed.** whites were not well provided for; and those of the Negroes were further neglected. The public was hardly able at that time to provide one efficient system for all. Negroes and their friends fighting for their freedom, then, attacked also caste in the public schools. They did not make much progress in this direction in the Middle States or the West. In Massachusetts, however, thanks to the agitation led by Wendell Phillips and Charles Sumner, caste in the schools was abolished in 1855.

CHAPTER XV

BLAZING THE WAY

The free Negroes, moreover, exhibited not only the power to take care of themselves in old communities, but blazed the way for progress of the race in new commonwealths and in all but forbidden fields. In the Northwest Territory, where many free Negroes from the South were colonized, their achievements were no less significant. Luke Mulber came to Steubenville, Ohio, in 1802, hired himself out to a carpenter for ten dollars a month during the summer, and went to school in the winter. At the expira- Instances of tion of three years he could do rough carpen- success. try work and had about mastered the fundamentals of education. With this as a foundation he rose to a position of usefulness among the people of his town. Becoming a contractor, he hired four journeymen and did such credit- able work that he was often called upon to do more than he could. David Jenkins, of Columbus, Ohio, was then a wealthy planter, glazier, and paperhanger. One Hill of Chillicothe was its leading tanner and currier.

In Cincinnati, where, as a group, the Negroes had their best opportunity, many made rapid strides forward. By 1840 the Negroes of this city had acquired $228,000 of real estate. One Negro was worth $6,000; another, who had purchased himself and family for $5,000 a Achievements few years prior to 1840, was worth $1,000. in Cincinnati. Another Negro paid $5,000 for himself and family and bought a home worth $800 to $1,000. A freedman who was a slave until he was twenty-four years of age, then had two lots worth $10,000, paid a tax of $40, and had 320 acres of land in Mercer County, Ohio. His estate altogether was worth about $12,000 or $15,000. A woman who was a slave until she was thirty then had property worth $2,000. She had also come into potential possession of two houses, on which a white lawyer had given her a mortgage to secure the payment of $2,000 borrowed from this

Emlen Institute.

A Secondary School in Mercer County, Ohio, admitting
Negroes in 1842

thrifty woman. Another Negro, who was on the auction block in 1832, had spent $2,600 purchasing himself and family. He had bought two brick houses, valued at $6,000, and 560 acres of land in Mercer County, Ohio, said to be worth $2,500.

Out of this group in Cincinnati came some very useful Negroes. Among them may be mentioned Robert Harlan, the horseman; A. V. Thompson, the tailor;
Statistics. J. Presley and Thomas Ball, contractors; and Samuel T. Wilcox, the merchant, who was worth $60,000

in 1859. There were among them two other successful
Negroes, Henry Boyd and Robert Gordon. Boyd was a
Kentucky freedman who helped to overcome the prejudice
in Cincinnati against Negro mechanics by inventing and
exploiting a corded bed. The demand for this bed was
extensive throughout the Ohio and Mississippi valleys.
He had a creditable manufacturing business in which he
employed twenty-five men.

Robert Gordon, the other Negro there, was doubtless a
more interesting character. He was born the slave of a
rich yachtsman in Richmond, Virginia. His master placed
him in charge of a coal yard. He managed it **A shrewd**
so faithfully that his owner gave him all of **business man.**
the slack resulting from the handling of the coal. Selling
this to local manufacturers, he thereby accumulated thousands of dollars in the course of time. He purchased himself in 1846; and, after inspecting several Negro settlements in the North, went into the coal business in Cincinnati. Having then about $15,000, Gordon made much
more progress in this coveted enterprise than his com-
petitors desired. They thereupon reduced the price of coal
so as to make it unprofitable for Gordon to continue in the
business. He was shrewd enough to fill all of his orders at
the white coal yards by making his purchases through mulattoes who could pass for white. Soon there followed a
general freezing on the Ohio River, which made it impossible
to bring coal to Cincinnati. Gordon then sold out his
supply at advanced prices. This so increased his wealth
that he was later in a position to invest extensively in
United States bonds during the Civil War and afterward
in real estate on Walnut Hills in Cincinnati.

This economic progress would have been greater had it
not been for race riots in communities in which free Negroes lived. On January 1, 1830, a mob drove eighty
Negroes from Portsmouth, Ohio; 1,200 Negroes left Cin-

cinnati for Canada as a result of the riot of 1829, and others lost life and property in the riots of 1836 and 1841.

Riots. The disastrous effects of this unsettled state were further aggravated by the Fugitive Slave Law of 1850. Many fugitives and their relatives residing in the free States moved immediately into Canada after the proclamation of this measure as the law of the land. Within thirty-six hours thereafter forty Negroes left Massachusetts for Canada. The Negro population of Columbia, Pennsylvania, decreased from 943 to 437. A **The fugitive** Negro settlement at Sandy Lake in the north- **slave law.** western part of that State was broken up altogether. Every member of a Negro Methodist Church, eighty-two in number, including the pastor, fled from a town in New York to Canada. The Negro churches of Buffalo lost many communicants. One in Rochester lost one hundred and twelve members and its pastor; and another in Detroit, eighty-four. Some Negroes stood their ground and gave battle. Such was the case of the Christiana tragedy in Lancaster County, Pennsylvania, where Edward Gorsuch was killed and his son wounded by free Negroes whom they tried to enslave.

Those Negroes who dared to remain in the free States to defy the slave catchers were not thereafter in a frame of mind to promote their economic welfare, so great was the **Personal** demand on their time for maintaining their **freedom** freedom. In fact, the main concern of many **a concern.** leaders among the free Negroes and their sympathizers was aiding fugitives to reach free soil. William Craft, escaping from Macon, Georgia, with his handsome quadroon wife who effected their escape by posing as his owner, caused unusual excitement in the North until this heroic dash for freedom ended with their flight to England. Then followed the arrest of Daniel as a fugitive in Buffalo, where the Federal commissioner remanded him to his claimant. Hamlet was captured by his pursuers in New York City while the arrest of Jerry   Seeking in Syracuse was stirring the whites and   fugitives. blacks throughout the North. Shadrach, claimed as a slave in Boston, was imprisoned but almost miraculously spirited away to Canada. Thomas Simms, arrested later, however, was returned to slavery. This was done to please those who feared the southern threats of secession if the Fugitive Slave Law was not enforced, and to satisfy Boston business men who did not care to lose their trade with the South. Then for a similar reason came the return of Anthony Burns, a Baptist clergyman, arrested at the instance of Charles F. Suttle of Virginia; but two hundred special policemen had to be sworn in to restrain

ELLEN CRAFT, a fugitive disguised as her master

citizens who considered the law an infringement upon personal liberty. The Dred Scott decision, denying that the Negroes were citizens and making slavery national and freedom sectional, was the climax of these invasions of human rights.

Thousands of fugitives, however, were never apprehended. They were generally well directed through the free States by the agents of the Underground Railroad conducted by Quakers and militant abolitionists. This was not any well-known route controlled by a well organized body. It was rather a number of Christian people scat-

The Underground Railroad. tered throughout the free States but united with their common purpose to promote the escape of slaves by clandestine methods in defiance of the mediæval laws of the United States. There were near the border important stations which were al-

WILLIAM STILL, an agent of the Underground Railroad

ways furnishing much excitement in the pursuit and capture. These stories have been related by William Still, in charge at Philadelphia, Levi Coffin, the station master at Cincinnati, and William Whipper, the moving spirit at Columbia, Pennsylvania.

Effective work was done in the Northwest Territory. Through this section extended numerous routes from Kentucky and Tennessee to Canada. Josiah Henson and Harriett Tubman used these routes in conducting fugitives to freedom. The career of the latter in this hazardous enterprise was

Harriett Tubman. unusually romantic. Born a slave in Maryland but endowed with too much love of freedom not to break the chains which held her, she became in the North the most venturesome worker in the employ of the Underground Railroad. When her co-workers had much fear as to her safety, she dared to go even into the very heart of the South. Once she returned to her old home in Maryland, where she met her master along the road, but easily contrived to prevent him from recognizing her. She did so much to aid the escape of fugitives and to rescue freedmen from slave hunters that the aggrieved owners offered for her capture a reward of $40,000. For these unusual exploits she became known as the ''Moses'' of her people.

After the first excitement caused by the execution of the Fugitive Slave Law, conditions became a little more favorable for the Negroes in the North. Forcing upon the country a radical proslavery policy which men formerly indifferent as to the issue could not accept, the southern leaders made friends for the Negroes in the North. The effort to impress the North into the service of recapturing fugitive blacks tended to raise up champions of individual liberty. The North had enacted personal liberty laws to counteract this slave-hunting, but these had failed. Sympathetic whites could not then go into the heart of the South to aid the

MYRTILLA MINER

blacks, but in the border States, and especially in cities like Baltimore and Washington, much was done for the improvement of Negroes through the many churches and schools established for their special benefit. Among many other workers promoting this cause was Myrtilla Miner, for years a teacher of girls of color in the District of Columbia and the founder of the first girls' school of methods in Washington.

In spite of all of their difficulties some of the northern

free Negroes attained national prominence.[1] Among those first to appear after the reaction was Dr. James McCune Smith. He was a distinguished graduate in medicine of the University of Glasgow and for years a practitioner in the **Prominent Negroes.** city of New York. Dr. Smith was a mixed breed of about equal proportions of Caucasian and African blood. In stature he was somewhat thick and

DR. JAMES McCUNE SMITH.

Dr. James McCune Smith

corpulent. He had a fine head with a broad and lofty brow, round, full face, firm mouth, and dazzling eyes. As an educated man given to writing, he was easily drawn into the discussion on the race question. His knowledge of history, science, and literature enabled him to treat the question in a scholarly way. He was also an eloquent speaker who always made himself clear and talked to the point.

In the field of writers there stood two other men as the first actual historians produced by the race. These were William C. Nell and William Wells Brown. There was **William C. Nell.** then so much talk about the Negroes that men wanted to know more about the achievements of the race. These writers supplied this need. Nell was a native of Boston, a man of medium height, slim, gen-

[1] These persons of color are given more honorable mention in Simmons's *Men of Mark*, in William Wells Brown's *The Black Man*, and in his *Rising Son*.

Blazing the Way

FREE NEGROES IN THE CRISIS

CHARLES L. REASON	WILLIAM WHIPPER
PHILLIP A. BELL	CHARLES B. RAY

teel figure, quick step, elastic movements, a thoughtful yet pleasant brow, and thin face. Chaste in his conversation and devoted to literature, he passed as a man of learning with the reputation of being a person of unimpeachable character. Nell wrote a book, entitled *Colored Patriots of the American Revolution*, a volume containing numerous facts of the history of the race. He wrote other books of less importance and collected data which made him the best informed man in this field during his time.

WILLIAM WELLS BROWN

William Wells Brown, the other writer, was born in Lexington, Kentucky, in 1816. His mother was a slave and his father a slaveholder. Serving in St. Louis in an office of Elijah P. Lovejoy before the editor was forced to go to Alton, Brown received his inspiration and start in education. He moved North, where he took an active part in the work of the Underground Railroad. From 1843 to 1849 he served as **William Wells Brown.** a lecturer of the American Antislavery Society. He then visited England and France. There he came into contact with such lovers of freedom as James Houghton, Richard Cobden, Victor Hugo, and M. De Tocqueville, as set forth in his *Three Years in Europe.* Brown then published *Clotelle: or the President's Daughter,* a narrative of slave life in the Southern States. He studied medicine during these years, but never practiced much. He was busily engaged in advancing the cause of freedom. He was a regular contributor to the *London Daily News, The Liberator, Frederick Douglass's Paper,* and *The National Antislavery Standard.* In 1854 Brown published *Sketches of Places and People Abroad.* His claims as an historian, however, are based on *The Black Man,* which appeared in 1863; *The Negro in the Rebellion,* published in 1866, and *The Rising Son,* brought out in 1882. Up to the time of George W. Williams, Brown had done more than any other writer to popularize Negro history.

The Negro also showed a tendency toward independent political action. He was not working through any of the leading political parties at that time, but nevertheless tried to change the attitude toward the Negro by influencing the thought of the nation. The first effort in this direction was by way of the printed page. By the end of the second generation of the nineteenth century there **Early Negro** were a considerable number of Negroes quali- **press.** fied to read as well as speak intelligently as had been the case of Negro preachers mentioned above. This literature was of a controversial sort, however, criticizing in the main the proslavery group and the American Colonization Society. In this case the Negro writers were trying to embody the sentiment expressed in the various resolutions of meetings of free Negroes held throughout the North to denounce the deportation program of the American Colonization Society. Among the persons thus expressing themselves honorable mention should be given to John B. Russwurm, Charles B. Ray, and Samuel Cornish. These were the pioneers in the development of the Negro press.

After completing his education at Bowdoin College, John B. Russwurm, the first Negro to receive a degree from a college in the United States, began in 1827 the publication of *Freedom's Journal*. This was the first **Freedom's Journal.** Negro newspaper published in this country. At the same time Russwurm edited another paper, entitled *The Rights of All*. The publication was a neatly printed and creditable organ presenting the program of the Negro in America. Russwurm later joined the colonizationists and went to Liberia where he creditably served as an educator and a governor of one of the provinces.

In 1837 there appeared another Negro newspaper entitled *The Weekly Advocate,* edited by Samuel E. Cornish and owned by Phillip A. Bell. The name of this paper was changed that same year to *The Colored American.* Like *Freedom's Journal,* its columns were filled with ex- **The Colored American.** cellently selected and original matter. It boldly advocated emancipation and the elevation of the Negroes to the status of citizens. In these efforts the editors had the coöperation of the distinguished physician and scholar, Dr. James McCune Smith. The papers continued equally as effective under a later editor, Charles Bennett Ray, then serving as a Presbyterian minister engaged in the Underground Railroad enterprise and the antislavery cause. Years later **Growth of the press.** there came *The Elevator,* ably edited at Albany by Stephen Myers: *The National Watchman,* conducted in similar fashion at Troy, New York, by William G. Allen and Henry Highland Garnett; *The People's Press,* edited by Thomas Hamilton and John Dias in New York; *The Mystery,* by Martin R. Delaney; *The Genius of Freedom,* by David Ruggles; *The Ram's Horn,* by Willis A. Hodges; *The Anglo-African,* by various editors, and *The North Star,* by Frederick Douglass. The name of the last mentioned was later changed to *Frederick Douglass's Paper.* Various other papers of shorter duration came and went in the battle of words incident to the

Blazing the Way

FREEDOM'S JOURNAL.

"RIGHTEOUSNESS EXALTETH A NATION."

SAMUEL E. CORNISH & JOHN B. RUSSWURM.
Editors & Proprietors.

NEW-YORK, FRIDAY, MARCH 30, 1827.

[Vol. I. No. 3.

MEMOIRS OF CAPT. PAUL CUFFEE.

(To be Continued.)

PEOPLE OF COLOUR.

(To be Continued.)

CURE FOR DRUNKENNESS.

A NEGRO NEWSPAPER EDITED A CENTURY AGO

antislavery and colonization agitation. Finally came *The Christian Recorder,* established in 1856 by Bishop Jabez Campbell. This is still in existence and boasts of being the oldest Negro newspaper in the United States.

The Negroes, however, began about 1830 to work through a national organization. This developed into an annual national convention. It was the most formidable effort made by the Negroes during that crisis. In reply to the suggestion that the Negroes emigrate under the protection of the American Colonization Society, a few bold thinkers **Negro annual** like Peter Williams, Peter Vogelsang, **conventions.** Thomas L. Jennings and Richard Allen, proposed a convention of the leaders of the Negroes in the United States. A preliminary meeting was held in Philadelphia on the 15th of September, 1830. Delegates from seven States were present. Richard Allen was made president; Dr. Belfast Burton of Philadelphia and Austin Steward of Rochester, vice-presidents; Junius C. Morrell of Philadelphia, secretary, and Robert Cowley of Maryland, assistant secretary. This led to the first actual convention of the people of color which was held at the Wesleyan Church in Philadelphia from the 6th to the 11th of June, 1831. At this time delegates from only five States were present. As Richard Allen, one of the prime movers, had by this time passed away, the control of the movement seemed to come into the hands of enterprising young men. There were present such rising characters as John Bowers of Philadelphia, Abraham D. Shadd of Delaware, William Duncan of Virginia, William Whipper of Philadelphia, and Thomas L. Jennings of New York. The convention made a favorable impression. It attracted some of the most distinguished men of the time. Among these were Benjamin Lundy, S. S. Jocelyn, Arthur Tappan and William Lloyd Garrison. By resolution the convention took the position that there should be a national meeting of the representatives of the free people of color, that the settlement of the Negroes in Canada be continued, that efforts be made to improve the "dissolute and intemperate condition" of the Negroes "and that the program of the American Colonization Society, in the wanton waste of slaves and property in carrying out its unconstitutional and un-Christianized policy be resisted."

The Negroes tended thereafter to meet in annual convention, often in Philadelphia, but sometimes in other cities of the North. With the exception of a few years for various reasons which cannot delay us here, these meetings were regularly held from 1830 until the Civil War. They were usually addressed by some of the most distinguished men of the race and by **Concerted action.** white men in sympathy with the cause. The convention annually sent out an address to the Negroes encouraging them to struggle upward and at the same time so to demean themselves toward their fellow men as to win the public favor. Memorials praying for the abolition of slavery and the improvement of the free people of color were annually sent to the State legislatures and to Congress. There were eight States represented at the meeting in 1832 with as many as thirty representatives. There were fifty-eight delegates present in 1833. In 1834 Henry Sipkins, a leader of prominence, was president. About forty delegates attended. By 1836 the movement had been substantially established by the increase of vital issues of the day like the Prudence Crandall affair in Canterbury, Connecticut, the agitation of the Lane Seminary in Cincinnati, and the expansion of slave territory. The convention, however, seemed to conflict with or to coincide with another for American Moral Reform, led by William Whipper. Associated with him were James Forten, Robert Purvis, Walter Proctor, John P. Burr, Jacob C. White, Joseph Cassey, Reuben Ruby, Samuel E. Cornish, and later John

F. Cook. State conventions like those held in Ohio, Massa-chusetts and Connecticut, New York and Canada claimed also the attention of the people. Into the foreground there were coming, too, other distinguished characters like Alexander Crummell, Martin R. Delany, William C. Nell,

and James Theodore Holly. Among them there stood out the most distinguished figure of all, Frederick Douglass.

There were at this time be-fore the American public a num-ber of other prominent Negroes ministering to other needs wher-ever necessary. There appeared Ira Aldridge, the successful Shakespearean actor: Edmonia Lewis, the sculptor; Edwin M. Bannister and William H. Simp-son, painters of promise; James M. Whitfield, George M.

ALEXANDER CRUMMELL

Horton, and Frances E. W. Harper, writers of popular verse;[2] Charles L. Reason, the educator called in 1849 to the chair of Mathematics and Belles Lettres of New York Central College; and George B. Vashon, a graduate of Oberlin, admitted to the bar in 1847. Vashon, however, devoted himself to education at New York Central College, where he distinguished himself in teaching the classics.

Some of the useful preachers were William P. Quinn, Alexander W. Wayman, Jabez Campbell, Daniel A. Payne, Peter Williams, William Douglas, Sampson White and **Prominent** M. C. Clayton, Alexander Crummell, and **ministers.** Henry Highland Garnett. Most of these clergymen, like the two last mentioned, rendered im-portant service in higher positions after the Civil War. Alexander Crummell, a man of unadulterated blood, at-

[2] White and Jackson, *Poetry by American Negroes*, 1-26.

tracted unusual attention. He happily combined with his commanding appearance and fluent speech a liberal education in the classics and theology obtained at Cambridge University, England. He made an impression by delivering in England in 1848 an address on the life and character of Thomas Clarkson. Crummell emigrated to Africa in 1852, but returned to this country in 1873 to engage in work in Washington.

One of the Negro students, because of whom the Canaan Academy in New Hampshire was closed, was Henry Highland Garnett, the son of a kidnaped African chief. He then sought education at the

HENRY HIGHLAND GARNETT

Oneida Institute under Beriah Green. He became a popular Presbyterian preacher and lecturer, but did not come into his own as a leader until he delivered to the Convention of Colored Americans at Buffalo, in 1843, his famous address on the Negro. Recognized widely thereafter as a man of influence on the platform, he went in 1850 to carry his message to England. From that point he proceeded to Jamaica to toil as a missionary. He served as a Presbyterian minister in Washington and New York City, and for a few years was the president of Avery College.

In these ranks unselfishly toiled David Ruggles, J. W. C. Pennington, Samuel R. Ward, and Josiah Henson. Ruggles was a man of African blood, medium size, gentle ad-

dress and polite language. He resided in the city of New
David York. There he became an eternal enemy
Ruggles. of slaveholders, bringing to that city servants,
whose escape to freedom Ruggles often effected by means

J. W. C. PENNINGTON

of the Underground Railroad. Deeply interested
in moral, social and political progress of the free
Negro in the North, Ruggles published for several
years *The Mirror of Liberty*, a quarterly magazine advocating the rights
of the Negroes. In this
work he exhibited unusual wit and logic in
hurling blows at his opponents, as is well evidenced
by his pamphlet, entitled
*David M. Rees, M.D.,
Used Up*. In this Ruggles exposed the fallacy
of the ardent colonizationists who had advocated the expatriation of the Negroes.

J. W. C. Pennington was born a slave in Maryland. He
J. W. C. was a man of common size, of unadulterated
Pennington. blood and of strongly marked African features. Slightly inclined to corpulency, he had an athletic
frame and a good constitution. He had no opportunities
for early education, but after his release from bondage he
so applied himself to the study of the languages, history,
literature and theology that he became a proficient preacher
in the Presbyterian denomination. He served as pastor of
a church in Hartford, Connecticut, where he won distinc-

tion as a preacher and a lecturer. He then made several trips to Europe to attend Congresses at Paris, Brussels and London. On these occasions he was invited to preach and speak before some of the most refined and aristocratic audiences of Europe. In recognition of his scholarship, the University of Heidelberg conferred upon him the degree of Doctor of Divinity.

Samuel R. Ward, thanks to aid received from Gerrit Smith, obtained a liberal education in the classics and in

SAMUEL R. WARD

theology. For several years he acceptably served a white congregation of the Presbyterian denomination at South Butler, New York. He was a black man, standing about six feet in height, distinguished by a strong voice, and energetic gestures. He shared with Frederick Douglass the honor of being one of the most Samuel R. popular ora- Ward. tors of his day. He directed his appeals to the understanding rather than to the imagination; but, says a contemporary, "So forcibly did they take possession of it that the heart yielded." Ideas formed the basis of his method. His greater strength lay in knowing that words and ideas are not inseparable. He never endeavored to be ornamental, although he was not inelegant. He was concise without being abrupt, clear and forcible without using extraordinary stress. Thus equipped for the deliverance of his great message, he preached or lectured in all the churches, halls and schoolhouses in Western and Central New York. His work extended to other parts of the North and to Jamaica and England.

Josiah Henson had neither the intellect nor the natural gifts of some of these men, but served as an example of the capability of the Negro. His experiences in slavery were so strange **Josiah** and peculiarly **Henson.** romantic that on hearing his story Mrs. Harriet Beecher Stowe reconstructed and embellished it so as to form the famous narrative known as *Uncle Tom's Cabin.* That he was the original Uncle Tom, however, has been disputed. Josiah Henson settled in Canada and then rendered service in promoting the escape of 118 Kentucky slaves by means of the Underground Railroad through Ohio and Indiana. He thereafter devoted himself to preaching and education among his people. Serving with him was Hiram Wilson, one of the founders of the British-American Manual Labor Institute. Henson engaged also in business in Canada, lectured throughout the North in behalf of the emancipation of the slaves, and finally visited England, where he was received by some of the leading men of that country and by Queen Victoria.

HARRIET BEECHER STOWE

CHAPTER XVI

COLONIZATION

In the proportion that slavery became an exploitation effort merely for the enrichment of the whites, the free Negroes who lived in the South became more and more undesirable in the eyes of the planters.[1] Debased to a lower status, the free Negroes naturally thought of making an effort to extricate themselves from these circumstances. They could not forget their former state when slavery was of a patriarchal order. During the first two or three decades of the nineteenth century, therefore, many Negroes gradually found their way to the North. They were first aided in the migration by masters philanthropically inclined, and especially by the Quakers. Seeing that their manumitted slaves had little chance for elevation in the midst of a slave society, some Quakers sold out their holdings in the South and moved to the Northwest Territory to establish them as freemen. On this free soil the Negroes soon faced other all but insurmountable obstacles. Then came with more force the thought of settlement in Africa.

From the earliest times there had been some interest in

The cause.

[1] The story of colonization is given in documentary form in *The African Repository,* the official organ of the American Colonization Society. The attack on colonization is presented in William Jay's *An Inquiry Into the Character and Tendency of the American Colonization Society.* See also J. H. B. Latrobe's *Liberia: Its Origin, Rise, Progress and Results;* John H. T. McPherson's *History of Liberia;* Frederick Starr's *Liberia; Description, History, Problems;* C. G. Woodson's *Century of Negro Migration,* Chapter IV; and *The Journal of Negro History,* Vol. I, 276-301, 318-338; II, 209-228; V, 437-447; VIII, 153-229.

Africa. It had been thought that the slave trade having its roots among the Africans themselves could be thoroughly exterminated only by Christianizing the Africans themselves. With this in view, the Rev. Samuel Hopkins **Early interest** of Newport, Rhode Island, proposed to Ezra **in Africa.** Stiles, later president of Yale, the sending of well-educated Negroes to Africa. Stiles seemed to think that an actual colony should be founded. Later we hear of two Negroes sailing as missionaries to Africa in 1774. The idea seems to be that of establishing a mission. Nothing definite followed because of the revolutionary upheaval which severed the economic and political connections between this country and Europe. But the idea remained in the mind of Hopkins. The idea sprang up, too, in the various antislavery societies which followed after the American Revolution. There was not at that time any clear-cut distinction between the colonizationists and the emancipationists.

From the very beginning of the antislavery movement there was an effort to provide for restoring the Africans to their native land. Such a scheme was developed by Quakers under the inspiration of George Keith as early as 1713 and was forever thereafter kept before the people throughout America. In the beginning this idea was that of those persons sympathizing with the Negroes and desiring to ameliorate their condition by emancipation. Such persons, however, were unable to think of incorporating them into their own society to live with the whites on a plane of equality.

The scheme was further advanced by Fothergill and Granville Sharp, and was given a new meaning by Anthony Benezet. Having much confidence in the intellectual **Promoters of** power of the Negroes, he felt that they might **colonization.** be colonized nearer to the white people. His proposal was that they should be settled on the western lands, which were ceded to the Congress of the Confederation. In this he was supported by a number of noted men of his time, chief among whom were Thomas Brannagan and Thomas Jefferson. During the Revolution, however, the manumissions of Negroes had led to the emancipation of a sufficiently large group of intelligent ones to justify the expectation that their liberation was not an experiment, should they be prepared by education and religious instruction. The number of Negroes receiving their freedom during this time did not render necessary an urgent agitation for colonization abroad.

At this time, moreover, opponents of the slave trade, like William Wilberforce, Thomas Clarkson, and Granville Sharp in England were actually promoting the settlement of Negroes in Sierra Leone on the west coast of Africa. The population of this colony was being increased by certain Negroes carried from the West Indies and from Canada. David George, a pioneer Baptist preacher in Georgia went by way of one of the West India Islands and Nova Scotia to Sierra Leone.

In the proportion as the Negroes showed evidence of plotting insurrections in protest against the ever-increasing encroachment of slavery the idea of colonization became more pronounced in the minds of the slaveholding class. It grew in the minds of free Negroes, more- **The colonization idea.** over, in the proportion as they were forced by law to leave the South for centers in the North. There was extensive correspondence on deportation between the Governor of Virginia and the President of the United States immediately after Gabriel Prosser's insurrection there in 1800. The governor was authorized by the legislature to take up the question of colonizing "persons obnoxious to the laws, or dangerous to the peace of society." Although the President of the United States could find no solution of the problem he addressed to Rufus King, then United States Ambassador to the Court of St. James, a communication suggesting asylum for such Negroes in Sierra Leone. Inasmuch as the infelicitous condition of Sierra Leone did not justify the importation of American Negroes, some of whom had already proved troublesome to that colony, the problem had to be otherwise solved. In 1805 the General Assembly of Virginia embodied another proposal in a resolution to the United States government praying that free persons of color and others emancipated thereafter be settled upon some portion of the Louisiana territory. But when in the westward movement of population thousands of whites rushed into the southwest, the idea of settling freedmen in such territory soon vanished from the American mind.

The acuteness of the Negro problem, however, revived speculation in other experiments for its speedy solution. Deportation seemed then more feasible than ever. Another stage in the transplantation of the free Negroes was therefore soon reached. Because of their being apparently a menace to slavery free Negroes were driven out of the South by legislation and public opinion either immediately or within a specified time. This forced into the North such a large number of free Negroes that there arose a strong protest from various communities. Some of them agitated prohibiting the immigration of Negroes into their commonwealths. Negroes were then coming into the North in larger numbers than could be easily absorbed; and coming, too, at the time when thousands of foreigners were immigrating into this country, they caused an intense race prejudice to develop against their group. From these two forces—that is, the effort to drive the Negroes from the South and the attempt to turn them away from the North —came a great impulse to the movement to colonize Negroes abroad. The condition of the free Negroes was such that it would seem that they should have been willing to go. They were proscribed by employers who preferred whites.

They were denied consideration in the courts when they appealed to them because of imposition by ill-designing persons. They were subject to the attacks of mobs spurred on to action by almost any petty offense committed by one of the free population of color.

The desire for the colonization of the Negroes abroad, therefore, became even more widespread. Foreigners then crowding the free blacks out of the industries in the North hoped to remove them from the field of com- **Projects** petition. Many slaveholders believed that the **abroad.** then ever-increasing important institution of slavery could be maintained only by removing from this country the most striking argument for its abolition, the free Negro. Colonization, therefore, received a new impetus. The movement was no longer a means of uplift for the Negro but rather a method of getting rid of an undesirable class that slavery might be thoroughly engrafted upon our country.

Up to this time, however, there had not been any unifying influence to give the movement the support adequate to its success. The various advocates of the deportation of the Negroes had done little more than to **No concerted** express their views. A few had set forth **action.** some very elaborate plans as to how the machinery for the transportation of the Negroes abroad could be easily worked out. Replying, in 1811, to Ann Mifflin, desiring an opinion on the matter of African colonization, Thomas Jefferson said that he considered it the most desirable measure which could be adopted for the gradual drawing off of the black population. "Nothing," thought he, "is more to be wished than that the United States should thus undertake to make such an establishment on the coast of Africa." Unwilling, however, to content himself with this mere discussion, Paul Cuffe, a New England Negro known to the high seas, transported and established thirty-eight Negroes on the west coast of Africa in 1815. This was the first actual effort at

Paul Cuffe.

colonization by Americans, and it served as an unusual stimulus to the movement. Cuffe recommended, however, that the region around the Cape of Good Hope he selected for colonization.[2]

PAUL CUFFE, the first actual colonizer

The colonization sentiment thereafter continued to grow. In the mountains of Tennessee and Kentucky, where the infiltration of slaves had made it impracticable for those emancipators in the mountains to continue to attack the institution, there developed a number of flourishing colonization societies which stimulated the movement. The Union Humane Society, an organization founded by Benjamin Lundy of Tennessee, had for one of its purposes the removal of Negroes beyond the pale of the white man. The same sentiment was expressed in Kentucky in its colonization society in 1812 and 1815. This

In the West.

body requested of Congress that some territory be "laid off as an asylum for all those Negroes and mulattoes who have been and who may thereafter be emancipated within the United States, and that such donations, allowances, encouragements, and assistance be afforded them as may be necessary for carrying them thither and settling them therein, and that they be under such regulations and government in all respects as your wisdom shall direct." The Virginia Assembly had taken up with the President of the United States, in 1800,

2 *Journal of Negro History*, VIII, 153-229.

the question of colonizing emancipated slaves and free Negroes. Encouraged by Charles Fenton Mercer, a slaveholder of colonization tendencies, the body passed a resolution in 1816 asking the American Government to find a place of asylum on the Northern Pacific coast on which to settle free Negroes and those afterwards emancipated in Virginia.

That very day a number of persons who for years had been thinking along this line met in Washington to effect a permanent organization. Among those present who had fostered the cause of colonization was Samuel J. Mills. While a student at Williams College he had become interested in this movement and, associating with others, had formed a missionary society to this end. Coming from Andover to Princeton to continue his preparation for the ministry, he became so interested in the work that he established at Parsippany a school to prepare Negroes for African colonization. Mills had likewise stirred up Robert Finley, a Presbyterian pastor, who **Organization.** had served as president of the University of Georgia and had been in touch with Paul Cuffe. Finley had called at Princeton, the first meeting held for the purpose of sending Christianized Negroes to Africa. There appeared, too, Hezekiah Niles, the editor of the famous *Niles Register,* Elijah J. Mills, a Congressman of Massachusetts, and Elisha B. Caldwell, clerk of the United States Supreme Court. Among the men who attended the first meeting were Henry Clay, the compromiser, Francis Scott Key, the author of the "Star Spangled Banner," John Randolph, a United States Senator from Virginia, Judge Bushrod Washington, a brother of George Washington, and Charles March, Congressman from Vermont. The first general conference of the colonizationists held in the home of Elisha B. Caldwell was devoted largely to prayer for the success of the enterprise. An address was delivered by

Henry Clay, who discussed the delicacy of the question and explained the purpose of the meeting and the condition on which he had attended. The principal address, however, was delivered by Elisha B. Caldwell. Various views were expressed indicating that although the members from the North had in mind the interests of the free Negroes, those from the South were primarily concerned with getting rid of this element to fortify slavery.

LOTT CARY

Bushrod Washington was chosen president, and the machinery was constructed for the extension of the work of the Society into all States. In the course of time, therefore, we hear of several States having colonization societies, and in some of them they were organized in ordinary towns. The purposes of these organizations varied according to the personnel of the management and the section of the country in which the Society was founded. The national organization established *The African Repository*, the organ of the Society and in that way made its declaration of its purpose to the whole world. Masters were not necessarily urged to free their slaves, but each community was called upon to take steps to provide for the transplantation to Africa of all slaves who might be liberated at the will of the masters concerned or purchased for this purpose.

Plans to extend colonization.

The latter was the case of Lott Cary, a Baptist preacher. In addition to rendering his denomination valuable service in Liberia, he served there creditably also as a public functionary of the country. The well-known promoter of colonization in later years was the successful lawyer and business man, John H. B. Latrobe. As secretary of the Maryland Colonization Society and finally President of the American Colonization Society, he did more than any other individual to advance this cause.

It was finally decided to expedite colonization in Africa. The United States Government was approached, and the matter received the attention of President Monroe, who submitted it to Congress. Upon his recommendation it was agreed to purchase in Africa certain territory lying near the Senegal River on the western coast. In making this purchase accordingly the country was designated as Liberia because it was to be the land of freedom. Its capital was called Monrovia in honor of James Monroe, the President of the United States under whom it was founded. The territory finally brought under control was an area of about 43,000 square miles between Sierra Leone and the French Ivory coast. The territory is cut into four unequal sections by the Cavalla, the St. John, St. Paul and Mano rivers. The natives there were of the Mandingo, the Vai, the Kpwessi, the Kru, the Grebo, the Bassa, the Buzi, and the Mano tribes.

The problem then was to produce in the United States a number of intelligent Negroes who might constitute a nucleus around which a government could be established in Liberia. As the colonizationists had learned from experience that it was necessary to begin with the youth, better institutions of learning for Negroes were established for this purpose. Occasionally one would hear of a southern

Preparation of colonizationists.

planter who freed his Negroes and sent them to eastern schools to undergo such education as would prepare them for higher life in their new home in Africa. Here we see that the blacks were encouraged to develop the power to work out their own salvation. It gave an impetus to the movement for more thorough education of the Negroes at the very time when the South was trying to restrict them

JOHN B. RUSSWURM.

JOHN B. RUSSWURM, first Negro to receive a degree from an American college

in such opportunities. Those Negroes to be sent out were to be trained in the manual arts, science, and literature, and in the higher professions. The Society, however, soon found itself in a dilemma of telling the people of this country that, because the free Negroes were a depraved class they could not be elevated in this country, while at the same time encouraging these Negroes and their friends to promote the education of the few to be deported that they might have that same mental development which the whites in this country considered necessary for citizenship.

The colonizationists soon found themselves facing other difficulties. The very people for whom Liberia was established arrayed themselves against it.[3] It was in vain that some contended that it was a philanthropic enterprise,

[3] L. R. Mehlinger, *The Attitude of the Free Negro Toward African Colonization* in *The Journal of Negro History*, Vol. 1, pp. 276-301.

since the meaning of colonization varied, on the one hand,
according to the use the slaveholding class hoped to make
of it, and on the other hand, according to the Difficulties of
intensity of the attacks directed against it. colonization
The abolitionists and the free people of color opposed the
Society because of the acquiescent attitude of colonizationists toward the persecution of the free blacks both in
the North and the South.

The inconsistency of the position of colonization was
logically exposed by William Lloyd Garrison in his
Thoughts on African Colonization. He showed how utterly
impossible it was to deport such a large number of persons. In this way Garrison anticipated Frederick Douglass, who summarized the situation saying that "individuals
emigrate but nations never." Garrison pointed, too, that
there was no more reason for thinking of the Negroes as
being natives of Africa and therefore deserving deportation to that continent than of thinking of the whites as
being natives of Great Britain. He could see no reason,
moreover, for persecuting the free Negroes to the extent
of making it so intolerable for them that they would have
to emigrate. He branded as a falsehood a statement that
the Negro population constituted a dangerous element.
He further charged with infidelity those who argued that
the racial situation could never be improved in this country
because of the inefficacy of Christianity in converting white
men to the principles of brotherhood. He said that the
Colonization Society was founded upon selfishness and that
it was antagonistic to instant emancipation. It apologized
to slaveholders, it recognized slaves as property, it ultimately aimed to drive out the blacks from this country, it
slandered the character of free Negroes, it declared the
elevation of the black people impossible in America while
claiming it was possible in Africa, and it tended finally to

misinform and dupe the whole nation into a scheme worked out in the interest of slaveholding.[4]

Almost before the colonization societies could be organized, therefore, the free people of color of Richmond, Virginia, thought it advisable to denounce the movement. They said that if they had to be colonized they preferred to be settled "in the remotest corner of the land of their nativity." They passed a resolution requesting Congress to grant them a portion of territory on the Missouri River. About the same time nearly three thousand free Negroes of Philadelphia took even higher ground. They claimed this country as their native land because their ancestors were the first successful **The protests** cultivators of its soil. They felt themselves **of Negroes.** entitled to participation in the blessing of the soil which their blood and sweat had moistened. Moreover, they were determined never to separate themselves from the slave population of this country as they were brothers by "ties of consanguinity, of suffering and of wrongs." In 1831 a Baltimore meeting of free Negroes denounced the American Colonization Society as being founded more upon selfish policy than in the true principles of beneficence and, therefore, as far as it regards the life-giving principles of its operations, it was not entitled to their confidence and should be viewed by them "with that caution and distrust which happiness demanded."

The free people of color in Boston inquired of those desiring to send them to Africa because they were natives of that land: "How can a man be born in two countries at **The feeling** the same time?" Referring also to the pro-**in Boston.** posal to stop the slave trade by the establishment of a colony on the western coast of that continent, they said: "We might as well believe that a watchman in the city of Boston would prevent thievery in New York;

---

[4] Garrison, *Thoughts on African Colonization.*

or that the customhouse there would prevent goods from being smuggled into any port in the United States.'' The Negroes of New York declared about the same time that the colonizationists were men of mistaken views, that their offer to colonize the oppressed free people was unjust, and illiberal, and tended to excite prejudice in the community. The free Negroes of Hartford, Connecticut, referred to the absurd idea of sending a nation of ignorant men to teach a nation of ignorant men. They asked, moreover, ''why should we leave this land so dearly bought by the blood, groans and tears of our fathers? This is our home; here let us live and here let us die.''

Some of the most distinguished men were effectively using the rostrum and press to impede the progress of the American Colonization Society. The best example of concerted action against the colonization

ROBERT PURVIS

movement, however, came from the annual convention of the free colored people, held first in Philadelphia in 1830 and afterward in that and other cities annually until the Civil War. The moving spirit of this enterprise was James Forten, **Support of distinguished men.** ably assisted by Robert Ray, James Cassey, Robert Purvis and James McCrummell. They early took the ground that they were unable to arrive at any other conclusion than that the doctrines which the society inculcated were ''suitable to those who hold religion in direct violation of the golden rule, and that the inevitable tendency of this doctrine was to strengthen the cruel prejudice of their enemies and retard their advancement in morals, literature and science—in short, to extinguish the last glimmer of hope and throw an impenetrable gloom over their former and more reasonable prospects.''

This feeling of antagonism of the free people of color manifested itself also in New York in 1848. W. S. Ball, **An incident** who had been sent to Liberia by the free **in New York.** people of Illinois, undertook to report there to a colonization meeting as to the lay of the land. In expressing himself as to the attractions and opportunities of that country he was interrupted by one Morrell. He approached the platform and addressed the meeting, saying that the question as to colonization and the Liberia humbug had been settled long ago. The audience was then disturbed with hisses and jeers, and finally with yells for a fight, until the room was thrown into pandemonium and the meeting broken up in disorder.

In 1852 there was held in Baltimore a pro-colonization meeting. After some sharp discussion, it was decided to examine the different localities for emigration, but preferably that of Liberia. Liberia became the bone of contention. **Colonization in** tion. Very few Negroes were willing to go **Baltimore.** to that country and a majority of the Negroes in Baltimore were opposed to colonization of any sort. As these delegates had come from various parts of Maryland and did not voice the sentiment of the people of Baltimore, they were hissed and jeered from an outside meeting. This developed almost into a mob, intimidating the delegates to the extent that they were not permitted to exercise that freedom of thought which the exigencies of the hour required. Another meeting of the Baltimore citizens denounced this assembly as unrepresentative and proceeded to proclaim the determination of the Baltimore people to oppose the policy of permanently attaching the free people of color to this country.

Colonization seemed destined, then, to have rough sailing.

Although the movement had the coöperation of an unusually large number of influential men both in the South
and in the North, it failed to carry out the **The failure**
desired object of taking the free Negroes over **of African**
to Africa. From 1820 to 1833 only 2,885 **colonization.**
Negroes were sent out by the Society. More than 2,700 of
this number were taken from the slave. States and about
two-thirds of these slaves manumitted on the condition of
their emigrating. Of the 7,836 sent out of the United States
by 1852, 2,720 were born free, 204 purchased their freedom, 3,868 were emancipated in view of removing them to
Liberia, and 1,044 were liberated Africans sent out by the
United States Government.

CHAPTER XVII

SCHEMES FOR DEPORTATION

IN the midst of the oppression of the free Negroes and the necessity for finding an immediate remedy, however, other schemes for colonization now came forward. There was proposed a colony of the Negroes in Texas, in 1833, prior to the time when the State became overrun with **Other** slaveholders. The opportunities of this country **schemes.** seemed to indicate that there was some reason for considering this plan feasible. But others thought that it would never suit Negroes on account of the fugitives there from Mexico and the presence of a superior race of people there already speaking a different language and having a different religion. There was some talk, too, of the transplanting of a number of Negroes to British Guiana. It was thought that because Santo Domingo had become an independent republic, it would prove to be an asylum for the free people of color in this country, as Jefferson a number of years before had predicted.[1]

This tendency towards the West Indies was promoted by the dearth of labor there resulting from the emancipation of the slaves. Thanks to the untiring efforts of Wilberforce and his co-workers, this was effected by 1833. The West Indies offered inducements to Negroes immigrating into these islands. Among these was Trinidad, which received a number of Negroes from Baltimore, Annapolis, and Philadelphia. Jamaica, with its many opportunities, placed her claims for these refugees and sent her agents

[1] C. G. Woodson, *A Century of Negro Migration*, pp. 67-80.

into this country to proclaim the beauties of her civilization and the opportunities of the land. So favorable did this scheme become that the colonizationists had to redouble their efforts to prevent an unusually **The danger of** large number of Negroes from going to Eng- **the exodus.** lish-speaking colonies. Living on a plane of equality with the whites and enjoying the rights of citizens, they would as freemen become too powerful factors in the hands of the British, should they again undertake to wage war against the United States.

WILLIAM WILBERFORCE, the anti-slavery leader in England

The most successful colonization, however, was a sort of migration at first proposed by Anthony Benezet, Thomas Brannagan and Thomas Jefferson. This was the migration to **Migration** distant lands **to Canada.** in America, especially to British America.[2] Canada had served as an asylum for slaves who had made their escape into that country, but during the period of the cruel oppression of their class free Negroes began to migrate there in large numbers. They secured land for farms, built homes, constructed churches, established schools and, in fact, covered a considerable portion of southern Ontario. In spite of the cold climate, the abolitionists and the free Negroes themselves usually considered it more practicable for Negroes to

[2] W. H. Siebert, *The Underground Railroad from Slavery to Freedom.*

settle there than to avail themselves of the opportunities offered by the American Colonization Society in Africa.

Nearer to the Civil War there were established in Canada a number of Negro communities and towns. They exhibited the evidences of civilization found in other parts. **Progress in Canada.** The Negroes themselves gave proof of what might be done, should their race as a whole be given the opportunity to make of itself what it would. They had learned to cultivate the soil, market their products, and engage in local manufactures. They were not only coming into contact with the commercial centers of the Northern United States but had begun to export and import from abroad. Out of these colonies in Canada emerged a number of intelligent Negroes who thereafter became factors in the progress of their race.

In the course of time, however, when the conditions of the free Negroes in Canada did not seem so inviting, a larger number of them began to think that colonization **Recrudescence of colonization.** elsewhere was a necessity, although few of them believed that they should go to Africa. To deal with this question there was organized in 1853 a national council of the leading Negroes, which attracted representatives from as many as twelve State conventions. So divided on this question had the Negroes become, however, that only those persons who believed in colonization somewhere were asked to attend. Among the persons thus interested were William Webb and Martin R. Delany, of Pittsburgh; Doctor J. Gould Bias and Franklin Turner, of Philadelphia; Augustus R. Green, of Allegheny, Pennsylvania; James M. Whitfield, of New York; William Lambert, of Michigan; Henry Bibb and James Theodore Holly, of Canada; and Henry M. Collins, of California.[3] Frederick Douglass, an uncompromising enemy to colonization, criticized this step as uncalled for, unwise, unfortu-

[3] *The Journal of Negro History*, V, 437-447.

nate, and premature. "A convention to consider the subject of emigration," said he, "when every delegate must declare himself in favor of it beforehand as a condition of taking his seat, is like the handle of the jug, all on one side." James M. Whitfield, the writer of verse, came to the defense of his co-workers, continuing a literary duel with Douglass for a number of weeks.

MARTIN R. DELANEY, an author, physician, and leader before the Civil War

The convention was accordingly held. In it there appeared three parties, one led by Martin R. Delany, who desired to go to the Niger Valley in Africa, another by James M. Whitfield, whose interests seemed to be in Central America, **Expeditions sent out.** and a third by Theodore Holly, who showed a preference for Haiti. The leaders of the respective parties were commissioned to go to these various countries to do what they could in carrying out their schemes. Holly went to Haiti and took up with the Minister of the Interior the question of admitting Negroes from the United States.

Before any results from these deliberations could be obtained there appeared evidence of considerable interest in emigration. This was especially true of Illinois and Indiana, from which commissioners **Interest in the West.** had been sent out to spy the land. This is evidenced, too, by the sentiment expressed by delegates attending the

Cleveland Convention in 1854. The next colonization convention was held at Chatham, Canada West, in 1856. One of the important features of this meeting was the hearing of the report of Holly, who had gone to Haiti the previous year. From this same meeting Martin R. Delany proceeded on his mission to the Niger Valley in Africa. There he concluded a treaty with eight African kings, offering inducements to Negroes to emigrate. In the meantime, James Redpath had gone to Haiti and accomplished some things that Holly failed to achieve. He was appointed Haitian Commissioner of Emigration in the United States, with Holly as his co-worker. They succeeded in sending to Haiti as many as two thousand emigrants in the first expedition in 1861; but owing to their unpreparedness and the unfavorable climate, not more than one-third of them remained.

Looking backward at the movement the laymen will doubtless consider the colonization effort a failure. The schemes for settlement of Negroes in Central and South America went awry. The settlements in Canada were apparently successful, but several of them were all but broken up immediately after the Civil War when so many of the Negroes returned to the United States to enjoy the benefits of Reconstruction. The bearing of the undertaking on the other efforts for the uplift of the Negro, however, makes it one of historical importance. Furthermore, there was one apparently successful effort at colonization. This was Liberia. It has endured as a republic down to the present time. As such its history becomes a unit in itself and should not long detain us here in our story.

Liberia.

Some few facts in the development of this country, however, require brief mention. The republic, as pointed out above, was the outgrowth of the American Colonization Society established in Washington, D. C., in 1816. In

THE MESURADO LAGOON

November of the following year that body sent out Samuel
J. Mills and Ebenezer Burgess to select a place for settlement. On their way they enjoyed in England the hospitality of the African Institution which was already
promoting the colony of Sierra Leone. They were thereby
introduced to certain persons in that colony that with their
coöperation the task of the American commissioners might
be facilitated. They selected Sherbro Island. On this
voyage Mills died and Burgess returned with a favorable
report. Nothing definite was done thereafter until 1819,
when the United States government in the effort to prevent
the smuggling and the sale of recaptured Africans by
slave traders appropriated $100,000. Samuel Bacon, of
the American Colonization Society, and John Bankson
were then sent to take eighty-eight emigrants to Sherbro
Island. Among them were Daniel Coker, who first elected
bishop of the A. M. E. Church, later resigned in favor
of Richard Allen. Disease and disaster followed in this
case, resulting in the death of most of the colonists and
in that of the agents themselves. The few persons who
remained repaired to Sierra Leone. In 1821 there went
out twenty-one other immigrants under the direction of
J. B. Winn and Ephraim Bacon. After tarrying some time
at Fourah Bay they decided upon a more hospitable site at
Cape Montserado. On account of the bad weather and
the fever which they could not easily withstand so many
of these colonists died that this expedition also proved a
failure. They had succeeded, however, in reaching the
present site of the capital of the republic.

That same year in November there came Eli Ayers as
agent of the Society and Captain Robert F. Stockton, of
the United States Navy. They were sent out to explore
the land. They examined the course as far as Mesurado
Bay and approached some of the native chiefs for a grant
of land. They succeeded in purchasing the mouth of the

Mesurado River and Cape Montserado and some portion of the back country. Most of the colonists were then removed from Fourah Bay, while some refused to go. **Early** They were eventually taken over by the Eng- **struggles.** lish. The pioneers then had some trouble with the English seamen and with the natives who desired to abrogate their treaty granting the land for settlement. Fortunately there appeared at the opportune moment Boatswain, a chief from the interior, who denounced the treachery of these natives and promised the colonists that they would be protected, and they were. The colony then made a permanent settlement at Cape Montserado. This was the actual beginning of the Liberian republic.

The troubles of the colony had just begun. The natives were hoping still to get back the territory which they had ceded, and the agent in charge became discouraged and left. Fortunately, again another Negro appeared upon the scene. This was Elijah Johnson, one of the colonists. He had come to Africa to stay and intended to fight it out on that soil. In this position he was warmly **Trouble** supported by Lott Cary, a Negro Baptist **multiplied.** preacher from Virginia, who arrived there about this time. Unfortunately Cary was killed in an explosion while preparing for the defense against the natives in 1828. He rendered the colony valuable service.

On August 18, 1822, however, there appeared another great leader who contributed much to the establishment of that colony. This man was Jehudi Ashmun from Vermont. He arrived with fifty-five immigrants. Although he had no intention of remaining, he decided to do so because of the exigencies of the hour. The rainy season and fever again did its fatal work and a large number of the colonists succumbed. Among these was the wife of Ashmun. He prepared, however, for the defense of the colony and met an attack of the natives with diminished forces.

Bringing a field piece into action, however, he succeeded in driving the enemies back. With help from a British vessel passing by, the colonists succeeded in withstanding a second attack, but it was only by diplomacy that they prevented the English from taking the colony in the name of the king of Great Britain. Further relief came from an American vessel arriving in 1822. Additional supplies were sent from the United States the following year. In 1823 Dr. Eli Ayers returned and took up the apportionment of land and the reorganization of the colony. Ashmun had fallen into discredit because of his efficient way of doing things, and wished to withdraw from the colony. But the colonists rallied to his support the following year and things moved on more prosperously.

The coming of R. R. Gurley in 1824 to look into the conditions marked another epoch in the history of the colony. To restore order there was established a constitution for the government of these settlements. There was to be an agent of the American Colonization Society in charge. Under him would serve all officers **Organization.** annually elected. There would be also a vice-agent, two councilors and two justices. The peace would be maintained by two constables and a defense unit of twelve privates, two corporals and one sergeant. Thereafter things became more encouraging, because the American Colonization Society sent out new immigrants and supplies twice a year after 1824. Fortunately there came, too, a more industrious and intelligent class of colonists.

The colony still had troubles. The slave traders disregarded the rights of the colonists. Ashmun had fearlessly attacked the slave traffic and for this reason had become unacceptable to some supporters of the Colonization Society. This trade flourished all around the Liberian settlements. After being worn out with the trials of this unusual undertaking, Ashmun himself retired to America in bad health and died in New Haven soon after arrival. This was a misfortune, for the colony needed Ashmun when much disturbed by the Dey-Gola War of 1832. But in spite of these difficulties the settlements still expanded. The colonization societies of the various States became active and sent out numerous settlers under their special protection. It was deemed necessary therefore to provide for a permanent government. By official request, Prof. Greenleaf, of Harvard, drew up a constitution for the "commonwealth." Under government set **Organization** forth in this constitution all except one of the **a necessity.** important settlements were gradually brought. These were Montserado, Grand Bassa, and Sinoe. The exception was the colony of Maryland. This was ruled by an independent government first by James Hall, a white man, and later by John B. Russwurm, until 1857. Because of trouble there at that time it was deemed expedient to come under the protection of the general government. The first governor of the combined settlement was a white man, Thomas H. Buchanan. He began his term of office in 1838. Buchanan, however, was the last white man to exercise such authority there.

In 1847 Liberia was forced by encroachments from the French and English to assume the position of independence. The United States Government failed to protect the colony from such encroachments, although it had repeatedly used the land as a dumping ground for "restored African captives" in the crudest **Independence** form, and thereby hampered the early prog- **declared.** ress of the country. A Constitutional Convention therefore was called in 1847. A declaration of independence was promulgated and the proper instrument of government was framed. This was modeled after the Constitution of the United States.

The first person elected president was a Negro who had

emigrated from Virginia to Liberia. This was Joseph Jenkins Roberts. He proved to be a sympathetic, energetic and efficient administrator. He served the country from 1848 to 1855. Under him independent Liberia had an encouraging beginning. The details of the administration of his successors, Stephen Allen Benson, David B. Warner and James S. Payne need not delay us here. England

MONROVIA

recognized the independence of Liberia in 1848, and France in 1852. Other European States did likewise soon thereafter; but because of the proslavery interests in control of the United States Government, this country did not grant Liberia such recognition until 1862.

As to the actual success of Liberia there can be no doubt. Instead of being evidence of the Negroes' failure in political organization the record of Liberia is evidence to the contrary. No colony which has endured has ever been beset with more difficulties than those which have afflicted Liberia. In the first place, the colony was established by ill-prepared emigrants. It was not a philanthropic experiment to show what the Negro could do. Some few members of the American Colonization Society had this idea, but they tended gradually to become a nonentity in the enterprise. The United States Government instead of endeavoring to make Liberia a member of the family of nations, used it as a dumping ground for recaptured Africans and for the settlement of poverty-stricken free Negroes removed from the Southern States to perpetuate slavery. In spite of all of these untoward circumstances, however, the first century of Liberia compares favorably with the first century of the Virginia colony. This first of the English colonies on the American continent did not penetrate the interior until 1716 when Governor Spottswood conducted his expedition to the West. The Virginia colony lagged behind in social and economic development; it did not believe in general education; and fifty years after its settlement Governor William Berkeley could "thank God that there were no free schools in the province." Liberia stood for education and social uplift and fought the slave trade which Americans diligently fostered. When we make due allowance for the fact that the Virginia colony antedated that of Liberia two centuries, we must think also of the infelicitous African climate, the foreign aggression, and the lack of help from without. Liberia, the land of the African, then, compares favorably with Virginia, the land of the Anglo-Saxon.

CHAPTER XVIII

ABOLITION

BECAUSE of the hard lot of the Negro, the opposition to slavery was fanned into such a flame during the thirties that the movement could no longer be properly designated **William Lloyd** antislavery. It was abolition, an effort to **Garrison.** effect the immediate emancipation of the slaves, since to hold them in bondage was contrary to the law of God.[1] Colonization was too slow in solving the problem. The most formidable leader of this radical reform was William Lloyd Garrison. He came forward with the argument that slavery was contrary to the natural rights of humanity, had bad effects upon the southern whites, and handicapped the whole Union, not only as an evil but as a sin.[2] Coming at a time when the world was again stirred by the agitation for the rights of man in Europe, this radical movement secured much more attention than it would have otherwise received. Men were then concerned with the better treatment of paupers, convicts, and the insane. They were directing their attention to special education for dependents and delinquents. Intemperance was becoming a serious problem. The rights of the laboring man were then claiming all but national attention, and women suffragists were taking front rank

[1] William McDonald, *Select Statutes*, 385-437; A. B. Hart, *Slavery and Abolition*, 152-295; his *History Told by Contemporaries*, IV, 24, 42, 72-143; William Jay, *Miscellaneous Writings;* W. P. and F. J. Garrison, *William Lloyd Garrison, passim;* F. L. Olmsted, *Back Country;* F. A. Kemble, *Georgian Plantation, passim;* D. R. Goodloe, *Southern Platform;* H. von Holst, *History of the United States,* III; J. B. McMaster, *History of the United States,* VI, 567-571.
[2] See Appendix for extract from the *Liberator*.

among the reformers. It was helpful to the Garrisonian movement, too, that new fields of opportunities were then opening in the North and West. With the growth of foreign trade, there arose a need for that sort of labor which the unskilled slave could not furnish. Appearing then at this time, Garrison could more easily arouse the

WM. LLOYD GARRISON

people of the whole country as to the inevitable doom of a slaveholding nation.

Basing his fight, therefore, on moral grounds and contending that slavery could not be defended, he evoked **Slavery a** the censure of the **moral evil.** proslavery people. They became just as radical and fiery in the defense of the institution as he was in attacking it. After having been forced out of Baltimore because of his antislavery

utterances he went to Boston and founded the *Liberator*.[3] The result was such a clash of words and a multitude of threats that it seemed likely that the South might secede. This feeling was further intensified by a number of uprisings among Negroes during the first three decades of the nineteenth century, culminating in Nat Turner's insurrection in Virginia in 1831. But intense as this excitement became, Garrison could not be hushed. His very words will give a better idea as to the earnestness of his purpose. He said, "I shall strenuously contend for the immediate enfranchisement of our slave population. I will be as uncompromising as justice on the subject—I am

[3] Almost any work on abolition deals largely with the career of William Lloyd Garrison, but the standard biography of the reformer is Wendell Phillips Garrison and Francis Jackson Garrison's *William Lloyd Garrison*, the story of his life told by his children.

not wrong, I will not equivocate, I will not retreat a single inch and *I will be heard.*"

The *Liberator* at that time, of course, could not have a very wide circulation, but it did find sufficient friends interested in the cause to maintain the publication. Garrison showed that he was by nature a journalist whose opportunity was unexcelled. He always succeeded in making his newspaper lively by conducting editorial combats and infuriating his antagonists. His work was made more effective by his impassioned oratory. "No banderillero," says a writer, "ever more skillfully planted his darts in the flanks of an enraged bull!" He had no mercy on slaveholders, accepted no excuses for their institution, and did not distinguish between those of the patriarchal order and those exploiting the slaves. Intensely interested in his cause, he breathed the very earnestness of his truths in everything that he said. Returning from one of his meetings he remarked: "The whole town has known of freedom. Every tongue is in motion. If an earthquake had occurred it could not have excited more consternation."

Garrison as a journalist.

LEWIS TAPPAN

To promote the cause effectively national organizations soon seemed a necessity. On October 29, 1833, therefore, there was issued by Arthur Tappan, Joshua Leavitt, and Elizur Wright, officers of the New York Antislavery Society, a call for antislavery representatives to meet in Philadelphia on the fourth of the following December. Sixty delegates appeared and adopted a constitution,[4] together with a declaration of sentiments, the original draft

[4] See Appendix for a copy of this constitution.

of which was drawn by William Lloyd Garrison. This organization for some years thereafter served as a clearing house for the expression of abolition sentiment; but because of differences arising in the ranks thereafter, it had to share the field with an American and Foreign Antislavery Society meeting the requirements of those who could not conform with the methods and procedure of the American Antislavery Society.

WENDELL PHILLIPS

Along with Garrison worked a number of radicals. There stood Wendell Phillips, a well-made, re- Wendell markably Phillips. graceful person of expressive countenance with a sort of fascination in the soft gaze of his eyes. He attracted attention wherever his beautiful musical voice was raised in behalf of the slave. Had he been interested in some other element than the Negro, he would to-day be known to history as the superior of Pitt, Sheridan, or Burke. Although having bright prospects for a future as a popular public man, he early chose the part of abolition. He could not respect the church which compromised on slavery; he gave up the practice of law because he could not swear to support a constitution legalizing slavery; and he refrained from voting because he could not participate in a proslavery government.

A number of others aligned themselves with these champions of liberty. There was the brilliant scholar, Edmund Quincy, not so eloquent as Wendell Phillips, but none

Other co-workers. the less staunch in his advocacy of freedom. There appeared also Francis Jackson, one of the first to stand by Garrison when the mob broke up his antislavery meeting in 1835. Maria Weston Chapman, another of this group, contributed much to the support of abolition by raising funds through the Antislavery Bazaar. Charles F. Hovey, the abolition merchant, gave large sums to support the cause. Eliza Lee Follen, a poet, sang of liberty and freedom. Sydney Howard Gay, the polished writer, boldly advocated instant emancipation. William J. Bowditch, a scholarly lawyer, used his talent to promote freedom. With sketches of intelligent Negroes, Lydia Maria Child gave the race a hearing in circles formerly closed. Thomas Garrett kept the same fires burning in proslavery Delaware.

Prominent in this group was Samuel May, Jr. For some years he served efficiently as the general agent of the Society. When the cause of abolition seemed helpless, May

Samuel May. abandoned a church paying him a lucrative salary that he might help to save the work; and ''to his perseverance, industry, gentlemanly manners and good sense,'' says an historian, ''the Society owed much of its success.'' Although simple and plain, he was an earnest speaker, showing such depth of thought that persons concerned with universal freedom learned to wait upon his words.

Samuel J. May, another abolitionist of almost the same name, was a philanthropist by nature. He sympathized with Garrison and assisted in the organization of the Society. He was one of the signers of Garrison's ''Declaration of Sentiments.'' This document presented the principles upon which the right of man to freedom is based and issued the call to all men to promote emancipation. May

Abolition

ANTISLAVERY APOSTLES

ABBY KELLY FOSTER   STEPHEN S. FOSTER
LUCY STONE   GEORGE THOMPSON

was one of the few who stood by Prudence Crandall in Canterbury, Connecticut, when by special enactment she was imprisoned because she dared to admit girls of color to her academy. He made his home a place of refuge for fugitive slaves and opened his church to any intelligent lecturer who carried the message of freedom.

To promote this cause a corps of workers were **Antislavery lecturers.** required to serve as lecturers in the field. These had to do the most difficult work of winning the public to the movement. Hissed and jeered by proslavery sympathizers, hurling upon them rotten eggs, sticks and stones, these agents unselfishly performed their task. Some neither asked nor received any compensation; others gave their time and paid their own expenses. Among these

PRUDENCE CRANDALL

lecturers who thus toiled was Abby Kelly Foster, the Joan of Arc of the antislavery movement. She was a slim but **Abby Kelly Foster.** well-proportioned and fine-looking woman of bright eyes, clear voice. She drew such lifelike pictures of the black woman in chains that one could not hear her without shedding tears. A logical, forceful speaker, successful with irony or argument and quick at repartee, Mrs. Foster usually convinced her audience or discomfited her opponents. Along with Mrs. Foster went her faithful husband, Stephen S. Foster. He was one of those who did not despise the cause in its day of small things. He labored incessantly to promote the work. But, because of his unusual zeal and honest method of "hewing to the line and the plummet" he became the most unpopular of the antislavery agents. Yet he always told the truth, did not overstate a question, and usually proved his point.

There were others scarcely less active. The eloquent Charles C. Burleigh, one of the most successful debaters championing the cause of the slave, would **Less active lecturers.** have been almost as effective as Wendell Phillips had he not spoken rather fast. Burleigh rendered the cause much aid as a lecturer and the editor of *The Pennsylvania Freeman.* Lucy Stone, an unprepossessing but pleasant woman of medium stature, round face, sparkling eyes, and with her hair cut short, became

LUNSFORD LANE, a native of North Carolina, who lectured in the North against slavery

with her abundance of enthusiasm one of the most active abolitionists. She moved the people by forceful arguments and pathetic appeals. Susan B. Anthony, later known to greater fame as an advocate of woman suffrage, stood out as an eloquent abolition speaker with few equals. Andrew T. Foss left his pulpit to devote all of his time to abolition. Sallie Hollie put so much Scripture and prayer into her appeals that few refused her a hearing. Oliver Johnson, the ready debater, accomplished writer and eloquent speaker, not only served on the platform but at times edited *The Herald of Freedom*, *The Antislavery Standard*, and *The Antislavery Bugle*. Henry C. Wright devoted the best years of his life to the cause. The Grimké sisters, daughters of a prominent citi-

LUCRETIA MOTT

zen in Charleston, South Carolina, left the South that, without interruption, they might bear witness against slavery. Charles B. Stebbins, the acute thinker and able speaker, also decidedly aided the movement. Nathaniel P. Rogers, with his penetrating mind, dealt hard blows at slavery through *The Herald of Freedom*. William Goodell and Theodore F. Weld exposed the institution by publishing works on slavery. James Miller McKim, a promoter of the Underground Railroad, was once the moving spirit of the Antislavery Society in Pennsylvania. There he was ably assisted by the untiring and eloquent Mary Grew.

Abolition was put on its feet in Pennsylvania, however, by Lucretia Mott.[5] She was a woman of faultless head, thoughtful countenance, beaming eyes, and full voice. Hesitant in speech at the beginning, she then easily grew

James and Lucretia Mott.   eloquent. Assisted by a husband giving his means and time to the work, Lucretia Mott stirred up the people. Abolitionist to the manner born, she endeavored to effect a proscription of the prod-

[5] A. D. Hallowell, *James and Lucretia Mott; Life and Letters.*

ucts of slave labor by discouraging the use of clothing and foods produced in the South. She carried with her, to sweeten her tea, sugar produced by free labor rather than run the risk of having to use that produced by slaves. A woman of culture and conversant with the conditions obtaining among the slaves, she attracted the attention of the indifferent observer and impressed upon his mind a new thought of the man far down. In her attack on slavery no abolitionist was more fearless, none more successful in presenting the cause.

Yet eloquent as was the appeal of white men in behalf of Charles L. the slave, Remond. the abolitionists soon realized that the Negro pleading his own cause could wield effective blows against slavery. The first Negro to be called to this service was Charles L. Remond. Until the rise of Frederick Douglass he was probably the ablest

CHARLES LENOX REMOND

representative of the Negro race. He was small of stature and of spare build. He was neat and genteel in appearance. He possessed a pleasing voice and early attained rank as an acceptable speaker. A free-born Negro himself, he felt more keenly the prejudice against his class than he did the persecution of the slaves. He confined his speeches largely to the desired change in the attitude of the whites toward the people of color. So proud was he of being a free man of color that he often boasted that he had not a drop of slave blood in his veins. He contributed to newspapers and magazines frequent letters and articles exhibiting clearness, force, and depth. It was said that no other man could put more real meaning in fewer words. Remond, thus equipped for his task, was employed by the Antislavery Society as a lecturer for about thirty years. In 1840 he attended the Convention of the World Antislavery Society in England, and re-

SOJOURNER TRUTH

mained abroad two years to lecture in Great Britain and Ireland. He made a very favorable impression.

Other Negroes were also successful. William Wells Brown thus served the Society from 1843 to 1849, and some years later also Lunsford Lane of North Carolina. Sojourner Truth, as a co-worker of the abolitionists, seemed to acquire miraculous power. Given to certain "mysterious communings" she could stir audiences with her heavy voice, quaint language and homely illustrations. But another Negro thus employed was more successful. He was not merely a Negro asking for the rights of freemen, but the intelligent, **Frederick Douglass.** emancipated slave going through the country as the embodiment of what the slave was and what he might become. He was then not only the thing discussed by the abolitionsts, but the union of the lecturer and his subject. Endowed, too, with philosophical insight and broader intellect than most men, he soon developed an effective oratory with which nature had enriched his gifts. This man was Frederick Douglass.[6]

Unlike Remond, Douglass had much originality and unadorned eloquence rather than a fine flow of language. When the country, therefore, had heard Frederick Douglass, Remond became a second-rate man. This soured the spirit of the latter; and he fell a victim to speaking disparagingly of his co-worker. But Remond was not the only anti-slavery orator to pale into insignificance on the approach of the "eloquent fugitive" from slavery in Maryland; for the people preferred to hear Douglass. And well might they desire to see and hear this man. He was tall and well made, with a fully-developed forehead. He was dignified in appearance, polished in his language, and gentlemanly in his manner.

The success of Douglass.

FREDERICK DOUGLASS

A contemporary said: "He is a man of lofty reason, natural and without pretension; always master of himself; brilliant in the art of exposing and abstracting." Another said: "In his very look, his gesture, his whole manner, there is so much of genuine,

[6] See Frederick Douglass' *Narrative of the Life of Frederick Douglass, as an American Slave,* and his *Life and Times of Frederick Douglass from 1817 to 1882.*

earnest eloquence, that you have no time for reflection. Now you are reminded of one rushing down some fearful steep, bidding you follow; now on some delightful stream, still beckoning you onward. In either case, no matter what your prepossessions or oppositions, you for the moment, at least, forget the justness or unjustness of the cause, and obey the summons, and loath, *if at all*, you return to your former post.''

CHAPTER XIX

FURTHER PROTEST

FOR economic reasons, too, abolition was gradually gaining ground in the western part of the country. There had always been much antislavery sentiment in the mountains of North Carolina, Tennessee, Kentucky, and Western Virginia. When the intolerable condition of **Abolition in** the Negroes in the South made it impossible **the West.** for the persons in that part of the country to do for the Negroes what they desired, they moved into the Northwest Territory where they could carry out their plans for the uplift of the blacks. Accordingly, there arose a number of antislavery societies in these mountains. Among the persons operating as the nucleus around which this sentiment developed were such men as Benjamin Lundy in Tennessee, James G. Birney in Kentucky, and Daniel R. Goodloe in North Carolina. Other ideas tended to influence the youth, too, as it happened in the case of the students in Maryville College in Tennessee. More than half of them had become antislavery by the year 1841. The same was true of Berea College in Kentucky, which developed from a group of students influenced largely by Cassius M. Clay, the antislavery editor, and John G. **In Kentucky.** Fee,[1] the abolition orator and founder of that institution. This school was established in 1855 to promote the principles of freedom. Its charter began with these words: "God hath made of one blood all nations that dwell upon the face of the earth."

[1] John G. Fee's *Antislavery Manual.*

As this sentiment tended to spread in the proportion that the antislavery leaders of the western slave States were forced to go North, there was made possible a better chance for abolition in centers where it had been considered dangerous. In Lane Theological Seminary in Cincinnati, the ardent discussion of slavery led to a sort of upheaval **Lane** resulting in a division of the students. Theo- **Seminary.** dore F. Weld, one of this group, actually espoused the cause of Garrison and undertook to translate into action his theories of Negro uplift by actually teaching colored children. As Lane Theological Seminary was then attended by a number of southern students, a separation of those who had thus become divided was necessary. When the trustees tried to prevent further discussion of slavery four-fifths of the students withdrew. Fifty-four asserted their right to a freedom of discussion of this important topic, and under leaders like Asa Mahan and John Morgan retired to the Western Reserve where they established Oberlin College.[2]

In that same section of Ohio, however, antislavery societies had already flourished under the leadership of Samuel Crothers, John Rankin, and Elizur Wright, later **The Western** a professor in the Western Reserve College. **Reserve.** These antislavery centers, too, were further strengthened by the coming of James G. Birney[3] from Kentucky, from which he had been driven because of his antislavery utterances. He first established in Cincinnati, Ohio, the *Philanthropist,* a newspaper which wielded great influence in preparing the minds of the people of this country for a fair discussion of slavery. Here his life was

[2] This is narrated in the *First Annual Report of the American Antislavery Society.*

[3] James G. Birney, *The American Churches, the Bulwarks of American Slavery;* and William Birney, *James G. Birney and His Times.*

Further Protest

SOUTHERN ABOLITIONISTS

BENJAMIN LUNDY   DANIEL R. GOODLOE

JAMES G. BIRNEY

JOHN G. FEE   CASSIUS M. CLAY

several times endangered and his press was twice broken up and destroyed.

Another group of abolitionists deserve honorable mention. These were reformers of a milder sort, who could neither tolerate radicalism nor approve the methods of some of the less ardent antislavery group. Among those taking this position was Dr. William Ellery Channing, a Unitarian minister of much fame in Boston and Newport. His appeal was **William E. Channing.** to the intellect rather than to the emotion. In presenting his case he wrote essays on slavery. He made a forceful argument as to evil of the institution, but suggested some remedy other than instant abolition. Along with Channing may be mentioned scores of writers like Frederika Bremer, Frances Kemble, Henry Wadsworth Longfellow, James Russell Lowell, and John G. Whittier.

GERRIT SMITH

There were abolitionists who, in addition to appearing on the platform, otherwise rendered the cause valuable service. Among these were Arthur and Lewis Tappan, successful merchants of New York. For years they had supported the cause of colonization but, seeing that it did not reach the root of the evil, abandoned that movement to promote abolition. More prominent than these was

Gerrit Smith of Peterboro, New York, a son of an ex-slaveholder. He, too, had at first restricted his efforts at uplifting the Negroes to what could be effected through the colonization society. Becoming more interested in the behalf of the Negroes and also developing in his mind anti-land monopolist tendencies, he devised the scheme of improving their condition by transplanting them from the city to small farms in the country. He, therefore, addressed a letter to Charles B. Ray, Dr. J. McCune Smith and Theodore S. Wright, prominent Negroes of New York City, to secure from them the names of Negroes whom he might thus colonize on **Gerrit Smith.** his lands in certain counties in southeastern New York. This list was accordingly given and the enterprise undertaken; but because of the infelicity of the soil and the lack of initiative on the part of the Negroes, it failed.

The more intense the abolition agitation grew, however, the more sectional the movement became. Backward as the institution of slavery seemed, the South became more and more attached to it and would not countenance any attack on it. Not only was the old-time abolitionist **The South** in danger there after 1840, but the ordinary **proslavery.** observer who suggested moral suasion held his social position by precarious tenure. Cassius M. Clay was driven out of Lexington, Kentucky, by proslavery citizens who could not tolerate the antislavery sentiments expressed in his *The True American.* Upon receiving some copies of the *Emancipator,* which he loaned to white friends while in Washington, Dr. Reuben Crandall of New York was arrested and imprisoned on the charge of inciting a riot among the slaves. After waiting trial eight months in jail, he was declared not guilty. An English traveling bookseller was whipped and driven out of Petersburg, Virginia, in 1832, because, not knowing the temper of the South, he dared to say at the time of the Nat Turner insurrection excitement that the blacks as men were entitled to their freedom and should be emancipated. Amos Dresser, a student of Lane Seminary and of Oberlin College, was whipped and expelled from the State of Tennessee because, while selling books in that State, he had a copy of the *Emancipator* wrapped around a Bible left in a Nashville hotel.

Abolition in the South, therefore, ceased to be openly agitated. The radicalism of Garrison tended to solidify the South against the struggle for free institutions. His advice to Negroes to educate their children, to build up **Abolition** their own trades, aid the fugitives, and to **quelled in** qualify as voters, stirred up the South; for **the South.** there it was believed that if both races were free, one would have to be driven out by the other or exterminated. Southerners caused alarm by the false rumor that the abolitionists advocated the amalgamation of the races. But Jay did not think that white men would have to select black wives, John Rankin disclaimed any such desire for miscegenation, and Channing thought we have no right to resist it and it is not unnatural. Other abolitionists frankly reminded slaveholders that they were largely responsible for the miscegenation which had already taken place.

Southerners were successful, too, in promoting their cause by raising the complaint of the circulation of incendiary publications. These portrayed by pictures, cuts and drawings, the cruelties of slavery to acquaint the bondmen with the awful state to which they were reduced. Because of the crass ignorance in which most Negroes were kept, however, these publications, as a rule, never reached them. With the exception of a few like Samuel Green, a free Negro, in Maryland, who was sent to the Maryland penitentiary for having in his home a copy of *Uncle Tom's Cabin,* there were not many instances of Negroes making use of these publications.

Moderate abolitionists in the South thereafter either abandoned their plan or coöperated with the colonizationists in seeking an opportunity for the national development of the Negro abroad. Radical aboli- **Martyrdom of** tionists either left for the North or re- **abolitionists.** mained in the South to entice Negroes to escape from their masters by way of the Underground Railroad. As this was a rather dangerous risk in the South where such action was heavily penalized, many of these persons almost suffered martyrdom in behalf of the fugitives. Jonathan Walker was branded with a hot iron for aiding the escape of a slave. In 1841 Thompson, Burr and Burke, abolitionists from Illinois, were sentenced to serve a term in the Missouri penitentiary for persuading slaves to escape from the town of Palmyra. In 1844 L. W. Paine, a Rhode Island machinist working in Georgia, was thus imprisoned six years for the same offense. In 1846 John L. Brown was condemned to be hanged for aiding fugitives, but the sentence was commuted to a whipping. Daniel Drayton, captain of a vessel upon which he permitted seventy-seven slaves to escape from their masters in the District of Columbia, lost his health while he was being almost starved there in confinement in an unsanitary prison cell. Another of these sympathizers, Delia Webster, a young lady from Vermont, teaching in Kentucky to find an opportunity for thus aiding fugitives, was sent to the penitentiary for two years. Calvin N. Fairbank, her accomplice, was sentenced to serve a term of fifteen years in the State prison. When pardoned by Governor John J. Crittenden, he immediately resumed his work in defiance of law and public opinion. In 1852 he was imprisoned the second time for fifteen years. He was not released until 1864, when the sympathetic Acting Governor Richard T. Jacobs, taking advantage of the absence of Governor Bramlette, pardoned Fairbank. Charles T. Torrey, a graduate of Yale and Andover Theological Seminary, went to Annapolis to report a slaveholders' convention. For this he was arrested and required to give bond for his good behavior. Some years later, upon being charged with having assisted a slave in escaping from his master, Torrey was convicted and imprisoned in a Maryland penitentiary, in which he died.

Exactly what the abolitionists accomplished is difficult to estimate. Some are of the opinion that the radicals did the cause of emancipation more harm than good. Few white men of that day felt that the slaves could be instantly emancipated. Most advocates of freedom had thought of gradual methods. The radical reformers who stirred up the whole country with the idea of immediate **Achievements of the abolitionists.** abolition set the conservatives against emancipation. The agitation itself, however, was hopeful. It showed that the country had developed a feeling of nationalism. A man living in Boston had begun to think that to some extent he was responsible for an evil obtaining in South Carolina. Leaders of thought were no longer content to leave it to the various States to decide for themselves whether or not an evil should be tolerated within their limits. Slavery had become so engrafted upon the country as to require national attention and national treatment. It resulted, therefore, in inciting a large number of antislavery people to greater activity and enabled the abolition societies to unify their efforts throughout the North by organizing and stimulating local bodies. All of these helped to make possible the destruction of slavery.

In the beginning their struggle was a hard one, but by 1836 they had gained considerable ground. In the first

Further Protest

WHITE MARTYRS IN THE CAUSE OF ABOLITION
DANIEL DRAYTON   L. W. PAINE
CALVIN FAIRBANK   CHARLES T. TORREY

place, the North did not take seriously the agitation for the abolition of slavery in a section closely connected with

Radical abolition. its financial and manufacturing centers. Others, who had no such interests, moreover, regarded the abolition agitation as a direct blow to the Union. The reformers attacked the provision in the Constitution for the continuance of slavery. Citizens in Southern States, considering these onslaughts as intended to disturb the peace in their commonwealths, declared that it furnished sufficient ground for withdrawal from the Union. In several of the Northern States, therefore, legislation was proposed to penalize as an offense against the peace of the State discussions "calculated to excite insurrection among the slaves." Some undertook to brand the efforts of the abolitionists as acts of sedition. As the abolitionists made good their right of free speech, however, they were not hampered much in the North by such laws.

As it was therefore necessary for the opponents of the abolitionists to express themselves in some other way, they resorted to mob violence. During the years from 1834 to 1836 about twenty-five or thirty efforts were made to break

Anti-abolition riots. up abolition meetings. There was an anti-abolition riot at Clinton Hall in New York in 1833. Then followed a number of riots, culminating in the destruction of the property of the abolitionists in 1834, when the same sort of violence broke out in Utica, New York. When George Thompson, the experienced spokesman of the abolitionists in England, came to this country to further the cause, and had himself advertised to speak in Boston, the so-called friends of the Union organized a mob; but Thompson, having had notice as to what they hoped to do, failed to appear. William Lloyd Garrison, who had the courage to attend, found himself in the midst of a riotous crowd whom the mayor, despite his efforts, could not control. When the mayor made known his inability to control the mob, the crowd ran Garrison down, put a rope around his body and pulled him through the streets of Boston. "The man," said an observer, "walked with head erect, flashing eyes, like a martyr going to the stake, full of faith and manly hope." To save his life, the mayor sent Garrison to the Charles Street jail, where with some difficulty he was rescued from the mob.

In Pennsylvania, in which the large city of Philadelphia offered many reasons for close commercial attachment to the South, the cause of abolition had much opposition, despite the healthy antislavery sentiment among the Quakers. The city of Philadelphia was being rapidly **Disorder in** filled up at this time with Germans and **Pennsylvania.** Scotch-Irish. With a covetous eye, they observed the prosperity of migrating freedmen. By a very little encouragement to the disorderly crowd, then, these business men could bring about a riot. This was easy, too, in a city so poorly policed. A mob disgraced the city in 1834 by beating a number of Negroes and damaging fifty-four houses. It was somewhat difficult thereafter to find a place for abolition meetings. Negro churches closed their doors to these agitators, not because they could not appreciate the impetus the abolitionists gave the cause of freedom, but, knowing that any building in which an abolition meeting was held might be burned, the Negroes had to exercise precaution. To solve this problem, the abolitionists constructed a building of their own, known as Pennsylvania Hall, but when it was noised abroad that Garrison and other abolitionists had addressed a meeting there, on May 16, 1838, there was formed a mob which broke open the doors, set fire to the building, and prevented the authorities from extinguishing the flames. Pittsburgh had such an outbreak the following year.

In the western part of the United States, where the

abolitionists were equally bold, the same sort of riotous condition obtained. In 1836 a mob, long since enraged because

Riots in the West. of the advocacy of abolition in the *Philanthropist*, edited by James G. Birney, destroyed his office and made desperate efforts to take his life. In Alton, Illinois, the place in which Elijah P. Lovejoy had sought refuge for his abolition efforts, when he had

SENATOR JOHN P. HALE

been forced to leave St. Louis for criticizing the burning of a Negro at the stake, the same violence broke out. After his press had been twice destroyed, his building was attacked by a mob on November 7, 1837. He returned their fire but, on waiting patiently on the outside for the exit of Lovejoy some time thereafter, the mob shot him dead. The jury appointed to inquire into the guilt of the offenders required only ten minutes to bring in a verdict of not guilty.

Instead of preventing the rise of abolition, as was expected, these efforts rather tended to increase the sentiment in the North against slavery. In some of the State legislatures there began to appear a number of antislavery mem-

Results of riots. bers, and very soon even in Congress. John P. Hale first took a stand against slavery in the Senate. In 1838 there came to Congress the downright abolitionist, Joshua R. Giddings of the Western Reserve.

William Slade of Vermont, an antislavery man, was sent to that body in 1840. There appeared, too, Thomas Morris, a United States Senator from Ohio, who rendered the cause much assistance. The abolitionists then had the opportunity to gain national recognition as a body primarily interested in elevating the moral life and atmosphere of the country. But they were far apart in their procedure. Their radical utterances denouncing the Constitution as a proslavery document, while others argued that it was antislavery did their cause unusual harm.

Salmon P. Chase insisted that the Constitution is an antislavery document, and made the institution a black forgery. Replying to the arguments of the proslavery element that slavery was maintained by the Federal Constitution, some others, although

Radical leaders increased.

not advocates of instant abolition, insisted that a higher law than the Constitution protested against the action of Congress in the premises. According to the law of human nature "no greater crime against human beings can be committed than to make them slaves." While Garrison, in 1835, called God to witness that the abolitionists were not hostile to the Constitution [4] of the United States, in 1843 he declared "that the compact which exists between the North and the South is a covenant with death and an agreement with Hell, involving both parties in atrocious criminality, and should be immediately annulled." There still remained milder abolitionists like William Jay and Channing, who disavowed the extreme theory. The cause of abolition, however, continued to suffer; for it had not only failed to interest a majority of the people in the North but had furnished sufficient radicalism upon which the proslavery spokesmen could stir up the country with threats of disunion and terrorize the gradual emancipationists in the South.

[4] See the appeal of a Southern matron in the Appendix.

CHAPTER XX

SLAVERY AND THE CONSTITUTION

DURING these years important constitutional questions grew out of the encroachment of slavery and its haughty pretension to national precedence. By 1830 the abolitionists had become unusually aggressive and were organizing **The right of** throughout the country to make a bold attack **petition.** on the institution. They were then presenting to the State legislatures and Congress various petitions asking, among other things, for the abolition of slavery in the District of Columbia. These petitions at first were received and then refused favorable consideration. In the course of time they had been more easily disposed of by merely being referred to a committee which permitted them to die a natural death. However, upon the occasion of a petition of John Quincy Adams, long known as the only spokesman in behalf of free speech in Congress, the House voted to refuse such petitioners a hearing. This implied that a reasonable portion of the citizens of the United **John Quincy** States were denied the right of petition guar- **Adams.** anteed by the Constitution of the United States.[1] Adams contended that these petitions must be received, heard, and referred to a committee; but when he insisted that there should be a report from the committee

[1] John W. Burgess, *Middle Period*, Chs. IV, X, XI, XIII, XVIII, XX; J. B. McMaster, *History of the United States*, VIII, pp. 473-521, 438-512; James Schouler, *History of the United States*, V, 389-433; T. C. Smith, *Parties and Slavery, passim;* James F. Rhodes, *History of the United States*, III, IV, V, VI; William McDonald, *Select Statutes*, I, 343, 365-372, 385-390, 397-454; II, 35-38, 42-43, 113; A. B. Hart, *American History Told by Contemporaries*, III, 574-655; IV, 122-192.

and a vote upon that report it looked too much like an insult from the antislavery party. He was, therefore, threatened with censure in the House in 1837.[2]

It is well to keep in mind, however, that Adams was not an antislavery man. His career had shown proslavery

JOHN QUINCY ADAMS, the champion of free speech

tendencies.[3] In the Senate in 1807, when the prohibition of the slave trade was **The record** brought be- **of Adams.** fore that body, he voted against the measure. As a member of the mission negotiating the treaty with Great Britain, by which the War of 1812 was closed, he demanded compensation for slaves who had been carried away from their masters by the British Army. During his incumbency as Secretary of State he was unfriendly to the proposal of Great Britain for a slave trade treaty in the interest of the Africans, and as President he manifested no particular interest in the bondmen. Throughout his struggle for the right of petition in Congress, therefore, he was interested, not in the work of abolitionists but in defending the right of the people of his section to free speech.

When the House, in 1835, tabled an antislavery petition presented by John Quincy Adams, Henry A. Wise of Virginia took occasion to remark: "Sir, slavery interwoven

[2] John W. Burgess, *The Middle Period;* A. B. Hart, *Slavery and Abolition;* and Herman von Holst, *Constitutional and Political History of the United States.*

[3] See the speech of John Quincy Adams quoted in the Appendix.

with our very political institution is guaranteed by our
Henry A.   Constitution, and its consequences must be
Wise.   borne by our northern brethren as resulting
from our system of government, and they cannot attack
the institution of slavery without attacking the institutions
of the country, our safety and welfare.'' In December of
that same year Slade of Vermont took occasion to remark
that as a constitutional right an abolition petition should
be printed, and that Congress had power to prohibit slavery
in the District of Columbia. He believed, moreover, that
the progress of abolition must be necessary to preserve the
balance of the situation or, rather, to restore it. When a
few days later two other such petitions were presented by
Morris of Ohio and Buchanan of Pennsylvania, John C.
Calhoun declared such a memorial ''a foul slander on
nearly one-half of the States of the Union,'' and urged
''that a stop be put to that agitation which had prevailed
in so large a section of the country and which, unless
checked, would endanger the extension of the Union.'' Congress did not grant the desire of John C. Calhoun, but did
vote to reject the prayer of the petition.

Southern members immediately thereafter secured a special ''gag rule'' that, without being either printed or referred, all petitions, memorials, resolutions, propositions
or papers relating in any way or to any extent whatever
''Gag Rule.''   to the subject of slavery or the abolition of
slavery should be laid upon the table and
that no further action whatever should be had thereon.
The proslavery advocates had taken the advanced position
that Congress could not legislate on slavery in the District
of Columbia and that the wishes of the slave States border-
ing on the District of Columbia took precedence over the
power of Congress to legislate for the District. Yet the
Constitution provides that Congress shall make no law
abridging the freedom of speech or the rights of the people

peaceably to assemble or to petition the government for the redress of grievances. Adams, therefore, held the resolution to be a direct violation of the Constitution of the United States and the rules of the House and of the rights of his constituents.

A new stage in the discussion of the right of petition in Congress was reached when, in 1837, there were presented resolutions from Vermont legislature praying that slavery be abolished in the District of Columbia. In **A petition** accordance with the Southern idea of State **from a State.** rights, no State could be questioned in presenting any petition to Congress, although citizens might be restrained therefrom. Driven to such an extremity then, Rhett of South Carolina summoned his Southern co-workers to a meeting to devise a plan for peaceably dissolving the Union. They finally agreed, however, to undertake the enactment of a law providing for a more successful "gag rule." This declared it "the solenm duty of the government to resist all attempts by one portion to use it as an instrument to attack the democratic institutions of another."

At this time Henry Clay and Daniel Webster, two of the weakest men in this country, were dodging the slavery question. Largely for political reasons, neither one of these compromisers had the moral courage to take a stand on the issue. Henry Clay, who declared that he **Webster and** was not a friend of slavery, preferring rather **Clay.** freedom for all men, nevertheless considered the petitions for the abolition of slavery "a great practical inconvenience and annoyance" from which he hoped the people in the North would desist. In 1830 Daniel Webster considered domestic slavery one of the greatest evils, both moral and political. In 1836 he felt that it was the duty of Congress to take care that the authority of this government be not brought to bear upon slavery by any indirect interference. He later announced that as to slavery he would do nothing to favor or encourage its further extension. Yet with regard to abolition he felt that it had taken such strong hold on the consciences of men that, if it were coerced into silence, he knew nothing, even in the Constitution or in the Union itself, which would not be endangered by the explosion which might follow. Hoping to become president, he later tended to become neutral, and bartered his birthright by an unsuccessful attempt to swallow the Fugitive Slave Law of 1850.

Growing bolder from year to year, the South during this period finally became sol-

Calhoun, the proslavery leader. idly organized under the leadership of John C. Calhoun. He had departed from his early position of nationalism to defend the institution of slavery. In 1836 he boldly declared that

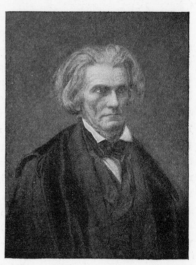

JOHN C. CALHOUN

"Congress has no legitimate jurisdiction over the subject of slavery either in the District of Columbia or elsewhere." [4] He believed that the abolitionists had no right to discuss slavery at all, that Congress should pass affirmative laws for the protection of slaveholders against abolition by mail, and that the Northern States should be prohibited from engaging in the agitation. He insisted that "the conflicting elements would burst the Union asunder, powerful as are the links that hold it together. Abolition and the Union

[4] See Appendix for J. R. Giddings's attack on this policy.

cannot co-exist; come what will, should it cost every drop of blood and every cent of property, we must defend ourselves."

Calhoun found for the South a safety valve in championing the desirable policy of expansion. The State of Texas, developed under direction of proslavery men led by Samuel Austin and Samuel Houston, be- **The Texas** came an independent slaveholding section de- **question.** siring annexation to the Union. This extension of our territory could not be easily defeated, although the purpose was to secure slave territory. Joshua R. Giddings, the first militant abolition member of Congress, however, showed in a speech attacking slavery, in 1841, exactly how the admission of Texas would increase the power of the South and affect the economic history of the whole country.[5]

JOSHUA R. GIDDINGS

Many constitutional difficulties were encountered, too, after some of the States had abolished slavery. The South continued to have trouble with fugitives escaping from its ports. It was always easy, moreover, for a few slaves **The return** to arrange with the Negro cooks and stewards **of fugitives.** on vessels to conceal them as cargo and deliver them to some agent of the Underground Railroad on arriving in the North. In 1837 the schooner *Susan*, sailing from Georgia,

---

[5] See Giddings's speech in the Appendix.

permitted a Negro stowaway to escape on reaching a port in Maine. The State of Georgia preferred charges against the officers of the ship and undertook to take them into custody, but the Governor of Maine refused to honor the requisition on the grounds that they had left Georgia before they were charged with the crime. Three sailors coming

WILLIAM H. SEWARD

into New York with the slave they helped to escape from Norfolk in 1839 were similarly protected by Governor William H. Seward. He despised the institution of slavery. This caused a prolonged controversy between the chief executives of the two States and the expression of much bitter feeling on both sides. Virginia finally passed a law requiring the inspection of all vessels bound for New York. Mississippi, taking up her cause, proposed "to unite with other States in any measure of resistance or redress."

Because of the disturbances resulting from the Negro insurrection in 1822, South Carolina passed certain "Negro Seamen Acts" requiring all Negroes on vessels to go to jail

Seamen Acts.

on arriving in port and to remain there until their vessels set sail again. These acts were earnestly protested against by Northern States and by England, because they interfered with the constant commercial intercourse between States. The measures were re-

FRIENDS OF THE FUGITIVES

JOHN NEEDLES
GRACE ANNE LEWIS

ABIGAIL GOODWIN
DANIEL GIBBONS

laxed with reference to England, but with respect to the Northern States they continued as law. Thinking that it would be advisable to make a test case of this legislation, antislavery members of the Massachusetts legislature sent Samuel Hoar to intercede in behalf of a Negro thus deprived of his rights in that State. Upon arrival Hoar was notified that his life was in danger for the reason that he was "an agent coming in not as a citizen of the United States but as an emissary of a foreign government hostile to the domestic institutions and with the sole purpose of subverting its internal policy."

The South undertook also to indict as criminals violating the laws of the States persons who, although they did not come within the limits of the States, had by way of mail **Defense of** or message incited insurrection or aided slaves **slavery.** to escape from their masters. William Lago, a free Negro, was thus indicted in Kentucky. The Supreme Court decided that the governor of the State had a moral right to surrender Lago, but that the Federal Government had no power to compel him to do so. Joseph P. Mahan, a Methodist minister of Brown County, Ohio, was indicted by a grand jury of Kentucky for having aided the escape of certain slaves. Upon receiving a requisition from the Governor of Kentucky, the Governor of Ohio issued a warrant for the arrest of the minister. Not long after, however, the Governor of Ohio became convinced that the warrant had been issued without authority because Mahan had never been in Kentucky. The grand jury of Tuscaloosa County thus indicted R. G. Williams of New York in 1835, and the chief executive called upon Governor Marcy of New York to surrender him. The requisition was refused for the reason that Marcy could not see how a man could be guilty of a crime in Alabama when he had never been there. Rewards were offered for abolitionists like Arthur Tappan, and the State of Georgia appropriated

Slavery and the Constitution

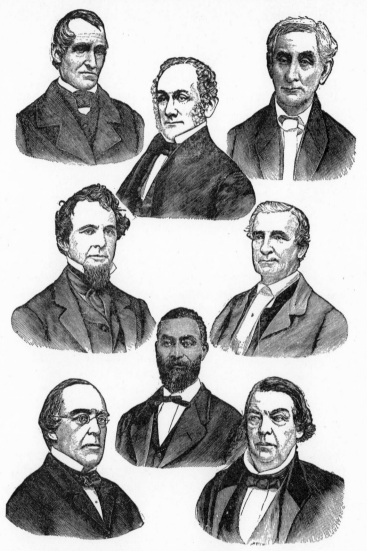

PROMOTERS OF THE UNDERGROUND RAILROAD

WILLIAM WRIGHT   E. F. PENNYPACKER

SAMUEL RHOADS

J. M. McKIM   JOHN HEMAN

JOHN HENRY HILL

WM. H. FURNISS   BARTHOLOMEW FUSSELL

$5,000 as a reward for William Lloyd Garrison, the editor of the *Liberator*.

This same assumption of authority in the defense of slavery extended also to the search of the mails for incen-

Searching the mails. diary matter sent out by the abolitionists. Because of the annoyance from which the South had long suffered, Calhoun introduced, in 1836, a bill providing that mail matter other than letters touching the subject of slavery should not be delivered in any State prohibiting the circulation of such matter. Congress, however, could not pass such a law, since many States had not prohibited the circulation of such matter. The matter was settled by a general search of the mails throughout the South, just as is done to-day in the time of war.

There arose also the question as to what effect on the status of the slave would his removal to a free State have and whether, according to the law of that State, it worked

Removal to a free State. his manumission. Would he be free on his return to the slave State from which he went? In Massachusetts slavery was forbidden for any cause, whereas in Missouri and Louisiana it was held that a freedman voluntarily returning to his master reverted to slavery. Indiana gave the master the right of transit with his slaves in that State. In Pennsylvania, however, it was not allowed. When John H. Wheeler of North Carolina passed through that State on his way to New York, from which he was to proceed to Nicaragua, Passmore Williamson informed Jane Johnson, the attendant servant, that she was free under the laws of that State, and the courts upheld that opinion.

During the darkest days of slavery many more fugitives escaped to the Northern States. In spite of sentiment to the contrary, however, masters hunted them down in the North and demanded of the local courts their return to slavery. State officers often refused to carry out these mandates, and certain Northern commonwealths passed personal liberty laws to impede these efforts by granting alleged fugitives a trial by jury. In Ver- **Personal** mont and New York local officials were de- **Liberty Laws.** prived of jurisdiction in such cases, and State attorneys were required to act as legal advisers for Negroes thus accused. Ohio, however, egged on by the mob cruelly treating free Negroes migrating from the South to that State, enacted in 1839 a Fugitive Slave Law more drastic than the Federal measure of 1793. Some excitement was caused in 1837, however, when a Kentucky slave, Matilda, who, without being asked any questions, entered the service of James G. Birney at Cincinnati, was claimed and surrendered as a fugitive. Despite the appeal to the Supreme Court by such valuable counsellors as Salmon P. Chase and William H. Seward, John Van Zandt was fined $1,200 in 1840 because he rescued one of nine slaves who had escaped to the other side of the Ohio River.

An epoch was reached in the execution of the Fugitive Slave Law, however, when Edward Prigg of Maryland undertook to return from Pennsylvania the fugitive Margaret Morgan. Because Prigg seized her **The Prigg** without first instituting proceedings in the **Case.** courts of the State, he was arrested for violating the Pennsylvania statute against kidnaping. Upon appealing to the United States Supreme Court, however, the opinion was given that the owner had a right to recover the slave, but that the act of 1793 could not be construed as making its execution an obligation of the State officials. Following this decision John Shaw of Boston refused not long thereafter to grant a writ of habeas corpus in ac- **The Latimer** cordance with the State personal liberty law **Case.** to remove Latimer, a fugitive, from custody of the Federal authorities. There followed such a storm of protest, however, such an array of abolitionists against the authorities thus administering the law, that an observer of the trend of the times could easily see that feeling was running too high to calm the people of the North. They were then openly resisting the execution of Federal law. The southern people bore it as a grievance, therefore, that by the application of personal liberty laws the enemies of their basic institution could deprive them of their property. They urged, therefore, the enactment of a more stringent measure which eventually culminated in the passage of the Fugitive Slave Law of 1850.

CHAPTER XXI

THE IRREPRESSIBLE CONFLICT

SLAVERY became more troublesome for the United States at home when it involved the country in entanglements abroad. As the British Government gradually emancipated its slaves in the colonies after 1833, there **International** was a tendency on the part of slaves and **entangle-** their sympathizers to seek refuge in those **ments.** parts when carried on the high seas. For years very little effort had been made to stop the numerous violations of the slave trade, despite the fact that European governments had repeatedly called upon the United States to unite with them to abolish this traffic in men. When the ship *Comet,* in 1831, carrying slaves, and bound for the United States, was wrecked at the Bahamas, they were brought ashore and set free on the ground that the British Government did not recognize slavery on the high seas. Similar instances occurred in the case of the *Encomium* in 1835, and the *Enterprise* and the *Hermosa* in 1840. The United States Government promptly demanded an indemnity, contending that the accidental presence of the vessels in **Slavery on** British waters did not interfere with the **the high seas.** relation of master and slave; but, doubtless for the reason that emancipation was not at that time completed in the West Indies, Great Britain granted the United States, in 1840, an indemnity of $115,000 for the slaves of the *Comet* and *Encomium.* Nothing was granted for the others. The only consolation our government received was to declare it a violation of international law for which no redress could be obtained.

There took place on the high seas, moreover, a number of mutinies of slaves which, the proslavery element believed, required intervention on the part of the United States. One of the most significant of these cases was that of the *Amistad*. There were on board the schooner fifty-four Negroes who were being carried coastwise from Havana to Neuvitas on the island of Cuba in 1839. Under the leadership of the African,

L'Amistad.

JOSEPH CINQUE

Joseph Cinque, the Negroes murdered the passengers and the crew with the exception of two Spaniards spared to steer the vessel toward freedom. After roaming on the high seas a few days, the vessel came ashore for water and provisions at Culloden Point on the east end of Long Island, and was espied and taken possession of a short while thereafter by Captain Gedney of the United States Navy. Joseph Cinque, the leader, undertook to escape, but finally yielded. The captives were then brought before the United States Circuit Court in Connecticut, presided over by Andrew T. Judson. As the proceedings lasted for some months, Cinque with some companions was turned over to certain abolition teachers, who so thoroughly grounded him in the fundamentals of education that he developed into a man of considerable intelligence and showed natural ability as an orator. The outcome of the case was that, although Van Buren was ready to remand them, the Supreme Court on appeal decided that the Negroes, being free when they left Havana, were violating no law in killing those trying to enslave them. They were therefore set free.

The mutiny of the slaves on the *Creole,* en route from Richmond to New Orleans, in 1841, gave rise to another Congressional inquiry in which the right of the United States to exercise authority over slaves on the high seas was questioned. The leader was Madison Washington. He had made his escape from slavery in Virginia to Canada, but on re- **The Creole Case.** turning to rescue his wife had been captured and started South for sale. The one hundred and thirty-four slaves overpowered the officers of the vessel, killed one, and directed the ship to the British port, Nassau. There they were held to await instruc-

CHARLES SUMNER, a fearless advocate of democracy

tions from the British Government. When proslavery men in Congress sought to have these Negroes returned to their masters on the ground that they were legally held at the time of their departure, Charles Sumner [1] insisted that the slaves became free when taken, by the voluntary action of their owners, beyond the jurisdiction of the slave States. On the other hand, Daniel Webster, then Secretary of State, contended that inasmuch as slaves were recognized as property by the Constitution of the United States, where slavery existed, their presence on the high seas did not

[1] See Appendix for Sumner's ideas.

effect a change in their status. The matter between Great Britain was drawn out into ten years of negotiations and was finally settled in 1853 by arbitration. It was provided that the British Government should pay an indemnity of $110,000 for having permitted these Negroes to go free.

To combat this view Joshua R. Giddings, an antislavery member of Congress, offered in connection with this case in 1842 resolutions to the effect that "slavery, being an abridgment of the natural rights of man, can exist only by force **Giddings'** or positive municipal law." [2]   Botts of Vir- **Resolutions.** ginia thereupon secured the adoption of a resolution to the effect that "this House holds the conduct of said member altogether unwarranted and unwarrantable, and deserving the severe condemnation of the people

[2] Giddings' resolutions were:

1. Resolved, That, prior to the adoption of our Federal Constitution each of the several States composing this Union exercised full and exclusive jurisdiction over the subject of slavery within its own territory, and possessed full power to continue or abolish it at pleasure.

2. *Resolved*, That, by adopting the Constitution, no part of the aforesaid powers were delegated to the Federal Government, but were reserved by and still pertain to each of the several States.

3. *Resolved*, That, by the 8th section of the 1st article of the Constitution, each of the several States surrendered to the Federal Government all jurisdiction over the subjects of commerce and navigation upon the high seas.

4. *Resolved*, That Slavery, being an abridgment of the natural right of man, can exist only by force of positive *municipal law*, and is necessarily confined to the territorial jurisdiction of the power creating it.

5. *Resolved*, That when a ship belonging to the citizens of any State enters upon the high seas, the persons on board cease to be subject to the slave laws of such State, and therefore, are governed in their relations to each other by, and are amenable to, the laws of the United States.

6. *Resolved*, That when the brig *Creole*, on her late passage for New Orleans, left the territorial jurisdiction of Virginia, the slave laws of that State ceased to have jurisdiction over the persons on board said brig, and such persons became amenable only to the laws of the United States.

7. *Resolved*, That the persons on board the said ship, in resuming their natural rights of personal liberty, violated no law of the United States, incurred no legal penalty and are justly liable to no punishment.

of his country and of this body in particular.'' Giddings
was, therefore, twice censured by the proslavery Congress. To show the attachment of his district to free institutions, however, he resigned and appealed to his constituents in the Western Reserve. They immediately returned him with a large majority.

The interpretation of the constitution brought other
problems. In the development of the proslavery policy
which dominated this country up to the Civil War, the
South actually forced the nation into a **The Wilmot**
struggle with Mexico to acquire territory for **Proviso.**
the extension of slavery. A rather serious question arose
when an act appropriating money for the purchase of territory from Mexico was blocked by David Wilmot's amendment providing that in the territory to be thus acquired
slavery should be forever prohibited. This amendment
caused much trouble years thereafter; for, introduced from
session to session, it became the nemesis of the proslavery
party in quest of new territory. The proviso evoked from
the proslavery advocates the claim that Congress had no

8. *Resolved,* That all attempts to regain possession of or to re-
enslave said persons are unauthorized by the Constitution or laws
of the United States, and are incompatible with our national honor.

9. *Resolved,* That all attempts to exert our national influence
in favor of the coastwise slave trade, or to place this nation in the
attitude of maintaining a "commerce in human beings," are sub-
versive of the rights and injurious to the feelings of the free States,
are unauthorized by the Constitution, and prejudicial to our national
character.

See *Text* of the resolutions in *House Journal,* 27th Cong., 2d Sess.;
for the resolution of censure, *ib.,* p. 580. For the discussions see the
Cong. Globe, or Benton's *Abridgement,* XIV. The diplomatic corre-
spondence regarding the *Creole* is in the *House Exec. Doc.* 2, 27th
Cong., 3d Sess., pp. 114-123, and *Senate Doc.,* 1, pp. 116-125. See
also von Holst's *United States,* II, 479-486; J. Q. Adams's *Memoirs,*
XI, 113-115; Wilson's *Rise and Fall of the Slave Power,* I, Chap. 31;
Benton's *Thirty Years' View,* II, Chap. 98.

The work of this statesman is treated in Byron R. Long's
Joshua R. Giddings, A Champion of Political Freedom and in
George W. Julian's *Life of Joshua R. Giddings.* See also J. B.
Moore's *International Arbitrations,* I, 417.

right to legislate on this question and that the question of slavery should be decided by those persons who would settle in the said territory.

About the year 1850, when the antislavery agitation was at its height and the various laws of interest to the many contending elements emerged in the form of the Omnibus Bill, several constitutional questions of importance were

The crisis of 1850.

raised. There came up the question of the admission of California, the paying of certain Texas claims, the organization of territory acquired from Mexico, the abolition of the slave trade in the District of Columbia, and the provision for a more effective fugitive slave law. The friends of slavery objected to having the State of California admitted without passing through the territorial probation period, and did not agree with Henry Clay, who contended that slavery in that State illegally existed. They believed that slavery existed everywhere unless it had been positively prohibited by law. Many northerners objected to paying claims incurred by the acquisition of slave territory and were not disposed to hurry up with the organization of slave States to be formed therefrom.[3] As to the prohibition of slavery in the District of Columbia, the southerners were still of the opinion that the Constitution had not given Congress any power to legislate regarding slavery. On the other hand, the friends of freedom were of the opinion that the proposed fugitive slave law, intended to impress into the service of slave-catching men who had no inclination to perform such a task, interfered with a man's rights as a citizen, and that it was unconstitutional because it did not guarantee the suspects any right of trial by jury and did not permit a fugitive to testify in his own behalf. In the midst of so many conflicting efforts to bring about a compromise between two militant sections, far-sighted men like William

[3] This is well expressed by Giddings's speech in the Appendix.

H. Seward [4] and Henry Ward Beecher saw no hope for peace in the Omnibus Bill, which emerged from the chaos of sectional claims.

A more interesting constitutional question arose some years later when out of the territory in the West it was proposed to organize Kansas and Nebraska without regard to slavery. Stephen A. Douglas, the champion of this movement, seemed to stultify himself in trying to harmonize his theory of squatter sovereignty with that of the free- dom of the **The Kansas- Nebraska question.** people in determining for themselves how the new commonwealth should come into the Union. How Douglas could make it possible for a man to take his slaves wherever he would and still hold them as goods and chat- tels, while at the same time the law would guar- antee to the people in a new commonwealth, when framing the Constitution, the right to decide for themselves whether or not the State should be free, was never satisfactorily ex- plained to the increasing number of antislavery men.

HENRY WARD BEECHER, a champion of freedom

The most formidable of all of these protagonists, how- ever, was not among the first to appear. He was a back- woodsman born in Kentucky and developed to manhood in Indiana and Illinois. As a rail-splitter he could under-

[4] See Appendix for Seward's *Higher Law*.

stand the hardships entailed upon those compelled to
engage in drudgery. When a young man he went on a
Lincoln on flatboat on a trading trip to New Orleans.
slavery. On the market square he saw human beings
auctioned off like cattle. Being deeply impressed with the
evil thereof, he said to himself that if he ever had a chance
to strike slavery he would strike it and would strike it
hard. Some years later, when Elijah Lovejoy was killed at
Alton, Illinois, by the proslavery leaders because of his
diatribes hurled at the bold defenders of that institution,
the legislature of the State passed a resolution which seemingly condoned that murder. Thereupon this representative joined with Daniel Stone in a protest to the effect that
"They believed that the institution of slavery is founded on
both injustice and bad policy." This man was Abraham
Lincoln.[5]

Against all temporizing and compromising efforts to placate the many proslavery advocates, Lincoln persistently
warned his fellow-countrymen. He early saw that by its
continuation of the policies of the proslavery party the
country had decided upon a fatal course of winking at a
terrible evil. "Under the operation of that policy," said
he, "that agitation has not only not ceased, but has constantly augmented. In my opinion it will not cease until a
crisis shall have been reached and passed. 'A house divided
against itself cannot stand.' I believe this government
cannot endure permanently half slave and half free. I do
not expect the Union to be dissolved—I do not expect the
house to fall—but I do expect it will cease to be divided.
It will become all one thing, or all the other. Either the
opponents of slavery will arrest the further spread of it,
and place it where the public mind shall rest in the belief
that it is in the course of ultimate extinction; or its advocates will push it forward till it shall become alike lawful

[5] See Lincoln's speech in the Appendix.

in all the States, old as well as new, North as well as South.''[6]   As a member of Congress he bore the same testimony in working for compensated and gradual emancipation especially in the District of Columbia.

The culmination of the proslavery discussion was the Dred Scott decision.   This was the case of a Negro who had been taken from the slave States into free terri- **The Dred Scott decision.**
tory a second time.   He then instituted proceed-
ings to obtain his freedom.   The case passed
through the local and higher courts and finally came before the Supreme Court of the United States.   It decided that at that time, when the Constitution of the United States was adopted, Negroes were not regarded as citizens of this country and they could not, therefore, sue as such in the United States courts.   That tribunal then had no jurisdiction in such a case and it was dismissed.   This was to say that the Negro, so far as the United States Government was concerned, had no rights that the white man should respect, and that although certain sections of the country were generally free by regulations to that effect, any part of the country might become slave, should persons owning Negroes choose to settle therein.   Slavery was therefore national, while freedom was sectional.

Against this interpretation of the Constitution to justify such encroachment upon the rights of the individual, the friends of freedom persistently protested.   William Henry Seward, then coming forward as the spokes- **Increasing opposition.**
man of those who dared to engage in the battle
for the right of citizens under the constitution, accepted the challenge in his *Impending Crisis* and *Irrepressible Conflict*.[7]   Salmon P. Chase and Charles Sumner, though not at first militant abolitionists, had reached the conclusion that slavery would have to yield ground to free soil, free

---

[6] Abraham Lincoln, *Speeches and Debates* (New York, 1907), p. 36.
[7] See Appendix for Seward's thought on the crisis.

speech and free men. The slavery debate then ceased to be a constitutional question and became largely political. The organization of the Republican party in 1854, and its all but successful campaign in 1856 with John C. Fremont on the platform of prohibiting the extension of slavery, made this **Slavery in** question the dominant thought of most for-**politics.** ward-looking men. Here we see the agitation for the rights of man connecting opportunely with modern economic movements to reduce slave labor to the point of a death struggle with free labor. Although aware of the fact that the civilized world had proscribed slavery, the South was willing to remain in a primitive state to retain it. The North was determined not to yield any more ground to an institution in which it had no interest and against which it had many reasons to be opposed.

Then followed the popularization of *Uncle Tom's Cabin.* This was a sentimental novel written by Harriet Beecher Stowe. As the wife of a professor in Lane Seminary in Cincinnati, a way-station to freedom just across the slave border, she had ample opportunity to learn the horrors of slavery. It was published in 1852, as a protest against the fugitive slave law, but did not do its work until a few years thereafter. Finding in this book the lofty feeling of a sensitive soul outraged by an iniquitous institution, the whole country was deeply moved. It even became so popular abroad that it had to be translated into many languages. It was a book which human beings could not easily read without having an impulse to do something for the destruction of slavery. The South, therefore, resented this picture of slavery, outlawed the book in that section, and attacked elsewhere all thinkers influenced by such sentiments. The book, however, became a factor in politics just before the Civil War and proved to be one of the disastrous blows to slavery.

Working effectively in another way, but not through

sentiment, was Hinton Rowan Helper in his work entitled
The Impending Crisis of the South. The importance of
this book may be understood by an appreciation of the
difficulty experienced in the House of Representatives in
the election of the speaker in 1859. A   The impending
member from Missouri introduced a reso-   crisis.
lution to bar from the speakership any one who had endorsed this book. It was not until the first of February
that this body could finally elect Pennington, a conservative
Republican of New Jersey. The doctrine set forth in this
treatise was a severe indictment of slavery by a non-slave-
holder of the South. It was at the same time an appeal to
effect a liberation from the leadership of slaveholders.
Its language seemed bitter, but it presented logically the
economic situation of the South as it really was. It alarmed
the slaveholding States. It could be easily seen that in a
country where there were only 225,000 persons who actually owned slaves or only one out of every five who had an
interest in slaves, if the non-slaveholding element combined
against the institution, it was doomed.

The Impending Crisis was the voice from the crushed
industrialism of the South. It had for a number of years
been plainly evident that industrialism could not develop
far in the South when that section with its unskilled slave
labor had to compete with the free labor of   Industrialism
the North. Some whites, not all of them of   in the South.
the poor class, deplored the comparative decline of the
South on a purely agricultural basis. Even those who
seemed to defend slavery could not fail to see the weakness
of that section, should it have to depend on agencies from
without to supply its needs other than agricultural. Certain white men in the South like J. B. O'Neal and Chancellor Harper of South Carolina had, therefore, advocated
for some years the repeal of southern laws prohibiting
Negro education, so that the Negroes might mentally de-

velop at least to the extent of being able to "read and cipher." Agricultural societies in the South, observing also how that section was running behind the North in both commerce and industry, took the same position. From such bodies there went to the legislatures memorials praying for some modification of these restrictive measures to improve the efficiency of Negro labor by mental development, and thus give the South a new chance in industry. Such a measure was introduced in North Carolina in 1855 and about the same time one all but passed both houses of the legislature of Georgia. There were also actual experiments in industry in the South. Some of the efforts were made to show that industrialism was compatibile with slavery, and others to show how poor whites properly encouraged could be used to develop industries in the South. The latter, however, sometimes assumed the phase of enterprises conducted by northern white men in the South to show the advantages of free labor. Eli Thayer made such an experiment at Ceredo, Virginia (now West Virginia), where he established a factory for matches and other such articles.

Then came the famous debates of Lincoln and Douglas, the division of the truncated Democratic party, the accession of northern liberals to the ranks of the Republicans, and the triumph of the Republican party in 1860. The southern States, believing that their last chance to maintain slavery in the Union had passed, thereupon seceded to establish a confederate government in keeping with their institutions. South Carolina took such action December 20, 1860, and before Lincoln had been inaugurated the following March all of the cotton States had followed her example. Was secession constitutional? James Buchanan, the weak executive then finishing his term as President, said that these commonwealths had no right to leave the Union, but

The last stand of the South.

he did not believe that he had any constitutional power to interfere with their going. This was the most critical period through which the Union had passed. Persons who had for some years observed the development of disintegrating forces doubted that the Union would weather the storm.

When the Federal Constitution was framed and adopted

1860

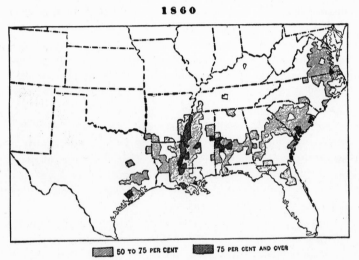

50 to 75 PER CENT   75 PER CENT AND OVER

THE DISTRIBUTION OF THE NEGRO POPULATION IN 1860
By permission of the United States Bureau of the Census

few persons were conscious of the fact that the foundation for a durable union of the States had been laid. The very language of the Constitution itself indicates **The nature of** that a consolidation of the States ratifying **the Union.** that agreement was not clear in the minds of the framers. In the course of time, however, the country developed into a Union. The majority of the States took the position that it could not be broken. Some States were in doubt as to whether a State could secede at the time of the agitation of the Alien and Sedition Laws which culminated in the high ground taken by Virginia and Kentucky in their threatening resolutions. More strength for the Union was evidenced when New England, because of its dissatisfaction with the conduct of the War of 1812, felt disposed to make an effort at secession. The Union sentiment was much more pronounced at the time of the nullification efforts of South Carolina in 1833. It indicated, as Benjamin F. Wade of Ohio boldly asserted, that there was little chance for a State to leave the Union of its own accord.[8]

BENJAMIN F. WADE, the defier of the Secessionists

In spite of this nationalistic attitude, however, the South had become so much attached to slavery and the North so far removed from it that this institution tended to force a conflict.

Threats of secession. To carry its point the South threatened the country with secession for three decades. Before the two participants in this contest lay the promising West. Each was making an effort to invade that domain to establish there States which would support their respective claims. As a free society expands much more rapidly than a slave community, the North easily outstripped the South. In seeking an advantage in the interest of free labor by preventing the expansion of slavery, the North forced the South to the radical position of undertaking secession. These threats were very much pronounced during the ardent slavery debates of

[8] See Appendix for Wade's speech.

1849 and 1850, and left certain sores which the all-com-prehending compromise of 1850 failed to heal. And when the agitation had seemingly been all but settled by these arrangements, the matter broke out anew in the effort to provide a government for Kansas and Nebraska and in the struggle there between the representatives of the North and South.

The bloodshed in Kansas was the beginning of the Civil War. Out of this stormy district John Brown came with a definite program for the liberation of the slaves and the establishment of a free republic in the South. In 1858, he made an excursion into slave-holding Missouri, which one historian refers to as ''a dress rehearsal for the final trag-edy.'' His original headquarters, where the scheme for servile insurrection was worked out, were at Chatham, Can-ada. He hoped to establish himself in the mountains of the South at some strategic point to which slaves might be attracted in sufficiently large numbers to defend themselves and maintain an independent government. He stopped first at Kennedy Farm, about 5 miles from Harpers Ferry. Proceeding from this point with only $2,000, about 200 rifles, and some pikes, he began his mission by taking pos-session of the arsenal at Harpers Ferry in October, 1859.

Intensely excited by this unexpected blow at slavery, the Virginia government and the United States authorities immediately dispatched troops to capture the invaders and to bring them to justice. John Brown and his followers made a desperate defense; but being overwhelmed, those who were not killed and did not succeed in escaping were captured and imprisoned. On December 2, 1859, John Brown was hanged. He faced his doom like a martyr. He said that he was sustained by the peace of God which passeth all understanding and the testimony of a good con-science that he had not lived altogether in vain. Believing that his death would do vastly more to advance the cause

of freedom than all he had done in life, he was willing to
die to seal his testimony for God and humanity with his
blood.

Although the slaves had not the opportunity to join
Brown, as he desired, five Negroes figured conspicuously in
this raid.   Among the ten killed were Lewis Sheridan
Leary, a free Negro native of Fayetteville, North Carolina,
and Dangerfield Newby, formerly a slave of Fauquier
County, Virginia, both at that time citizens of Oberlin,
Ohio.   Two of the seven hanged were John Anthony Cope-
land, a free man of color, born in Raleigh, North Carolina, but later transplanted to Oberlin for education, and
Shields Green, a fugitive from Charleston, South Carolina,
known as the protégé of Frederick Douglass.   One of the
five who escaped was Osborn Perry Anderson, a printer
born at Fallowfield, Pennsylvania.   He served with distinction in the Civil War and later wrote an account of the
venture entitled *A Voice from Harpers Ferry*.

This event was really the beginning of the Civil War.
It was not a disconnected act of an insane man, as some
persons of clouded vision contend.   Although John Brown
over-estimated the effect of his exploits, he did drive home
the fact that a number of people in the North had thought
so seriously of slavery as to endanger their lives in the
effort to exterminate the institution.   It made the country
realize that something would have to be done to bring the
matter to a conclusion, and the Civil War was the crown-
ing event of this long drawn out contest.   John Brown,
therefore, takes his place among the greatest martyrs of
the world.   His lofty purpose was vindicated by the success
of freedom's cause in the almost immediate emancipation
of the freedmen.

CHAPTER XXII

THE NEGRO IN THE CIVIL WAR

WHEN the war broke out, Lincoln, hoping to curry favor at home, openly declared that it was not his purpose to interfere with the institutions of the South. He meant, of course, that he had no desire to attack slavery in those commonwealths in which it existed. The South, on the other hand, was anxious to win favor abroad. Knowing how it would harm its cause in foreign countries to have it said that it had undertaken a war to promote slavery, the Confederacy declared its position one of self-defense to maintain its right to govern itself and to preserve its own peculiar institutions. Negroes, therefore, were not to be freed; and, to be sure, were not to take a part in the war. It was considered a struggle between white men. This does not mean, however, that Abraham Lincoln had lost sight of the fact that he had been elected by a party opposed to the extension of slavery, nor that he ceased to put forth efforts, whenever possible, to check the institution as he had formerly declared. After the war had been well begun and it was evident that such efforts as the peace convention could not succeed, Lincoln took up with the Border States the question of setting the example of freeing the Negroes by a process of gradual emancipation.[1]

[1] J. K. Hosmer, *The Appeal to Arms* and his *Outcome of the Civil War;* J. W. Burgess, *Civil War and the Constitution;* James Ford Rhodes, *History of the United States,* Vol. III; J. B. McMaster, *History of the United States,* Vol. VIII, p. 473; James Schouler, *History of the United States,* VI, 1861-1865, *passim;* William Wells

ABRAHAM LINCOLN

Before the war had proceeded very far, however, the Negroes came up for serious consideration because of the many problems which developed out of the peculiar situation in which they were. In the first place, **The Negro** there were in the North free Negroes who, **involved.** knowing that the success of the South meant the perpetuation of slavery, were anxious to do their share in defeating the purposes of the Confederate States. There were in the North, moreover, white men who were of the opinion that free Negroes should share a part of the burden entailed by waging the Civil War. Furthermore, as soon as the invading Union armies crossed the Mason and Dixon line into the South, disturbing the plantation system and driving the masters away from their homes, the Negroes were left behind to constitute a problem for the army. There arose the question as to what was the status of such Negroes. Nominally they were slaves; actually they were free: but there was no law to settle the question. A few slaves who had been taken over by the Union armies from persons in rebellion against the United States, were confiscated by virtue of the legislation providing for this disposition of such property of the Confederates. Yet there were Negroes who did not wait for the invading armies. When their masters had gone to the front to defend the South, they left their homes and made their way to the Union camps.[2]

The first effort to deal with such slaves was made by General Butler at Fortress Monroe in 1861. **Butler's** Such slaves as escaped into his camp in flight **contrabands.** from their masters, he accepted as contraband of war on the grounds that they had been employed in assisting the

Brown, *The Rising Son*, 341-381; George W. Williams, *History of Negro Troops in the War of the Rebellion, passim;* William Mac-Donald, *Select Statutes of United States History*, 34-39; and A. B. Hart, *American History Told by Contemporaries*, IV, 181-458.

2 The best authority on the Civil War is James Ford Rhodes. See his *History of the United States from the Compromise of 1850 to the Final Restoration of Home Rule in the South;* Volumes I-IV.

Confederate armies and could be confiscated in the same
sense that one would take over other supplies of the
Confederates. Much discussion was aroused by the action
of General Butler, and there was doubt as to whether or not
it would be supported by the President. This plan, however, was followed by General Wood, Butler's successor,

NEGROES IN THE SERVICE OF THE CONFEDERATES

and by General Banks when he was operating in New Orleans. General Halleck, while fighting in the West, at first
excluded slaves from the camps, as did also General Dix in
Virginia. Some generals, like General McCook and General Johnson, permitted slave hunters to come into their
lines and reclaim their fugitive slaves. Later, however,
General Halleck seems to have receded from his early position. General Grant refused to give permits to those seeking to recapture the Negroes who had escaped from their
former masters. He used the blacks at such labor as the

building of roads and fortifications, very much as they were
first used by General Butler. This anticipated a policy
which was later followed by the United States Army.[3]

In the course of time, however, the national government
saw the necessity of treating the Negro ques- **The Negro**
tion more seriously. It was evident that if **question**
the South continued to use the Negro slaves **serious.**
in building fortifications and roads and bridges and, in

U. S. GRANT

fact, to do practically all
of the labor required in
the army, it was incum-
bent upon the Union
armies operating in the
South to do likewise. Lincoln, therefore, soon ac-
cepted the policy of using
the slaves in this capacity.
He receded from his for-
mer position of thinking
that, should the slaves be
given any encouragement
to leave their homes they
might start a servile in-
surrection, and in pro-
moting such he would
weaken himself in his
hold on the North.

At first these Negroes did not find their life a pleasant
one. They were suddenly thrown among strange men from
the North, who had never had much dealing with such
Negroes and whose first impression of them **The Negro in**
was not favorable. Arriving among these **the camps.**
soldiers, naked, hungry, and often diseased—moreover,

[3] G. W. Williams, *History of the Negro Troops in the War of the
Rebellion, passim;* William Wells Brown, *The Rising Son;* and John
Eaton, *Grant, Lincoln, and the Freedmen.*

lacking the initiative to provide for themselves what the average freeman was expected to do, these wanderers presented a piteous spectacle which baffled the skill of the army. The refugees were finally organized under directions sent out from headquarters of the army, and placed in charge of a superintendent having under him sufficient assistants to relieve most of the cases of distress and to make some use of the able-bodied Negroes.

Most of these refugees were sent to Washington, Alexandria, Fortress Monroe, Hampton, Craney Island, Yorktown, Suffolk, Portsmouth, Port Royal, South Carolina, and certain camps of the West near Memphis. At one time, in the camp at Arlington, just across from Washington, there were as many as 30,000 Negroes. This number increased to almost 100,000 in the various camps near Washington, in the proportion that the war advanced and the territory of the Confederates became overrun by the invading Union armies.[4] It was easy to find employment for those in camps near cities. Some of them were put to work on deserted plantations. Others were incorporated into the army as teamsters, mechanics, and common laborers. Sojourner Truth, who served the Union army as a messenger and a spy, rendered valuable service in these camps by teaching the refugees cleanliness and habits of industry.

It was arranged also to send a number of these Negroes from the congested districts in the loyal States as fast as opportunities for their employment presented themselves. Those found near cities and manufacturing points, where **Fugitives** there was a demand for labor, were employed, **sent North.** in some cases, to do work in which white men sent to the war had been engaged. A good many passed

---

[4] For more extensive treatment, see John Eaton, *Grant, Lincoln and the Freedmen;* E. L. Pierce's *The Freedmen of Port Royal, South Carolina;* G. W. Williams's *The History of Negro Troops,* 90-98; E. H. Botume's *First Days Amongst the Contrabands,* and *The Atlantic Monthly,* XII, 308.

through Cairo, Illinois, into the West, and some others were sent through York, Columbia, Harrisburg, and Philadelphia to points in the North. This, however, did not continue to a very great extent, for the reason that there was some apprehension that the North might be overcrowded by such freedmen. Several schemes were set forth to deport this population. When this number was still further increased by the thousands of Negroes emancipated in the District of Columbia in 1862, Abraham Lincoln himself thought to get rid of these freedmen by colonizing them in foreign parts.

To carry out this plan as he desired, he sent a special message to Congress to show the necessity for Congressional action in the way of an appropriation to finance such an enterprise. Thinking that certain nations could be induced to accept Negro emigrants from this country, the Secretary of State opened correspondence with various countries having colonies settled partly by Negroes. He thus brought the matter before Great Britain, Denmark, France, Sweden and all of the South American countries. In the beginning it became evident that only two countries, Liberia and Haiti, each of which were settled by Negroes, were willing to admit these refugees. But the Negroes themselves, because of their prejudice against Liberia and the unsuccessful effort at colonization in Haiti, did not care to emigrate to those countries. Favorable replies, however, finally came from the Island of Vache, a part of Haiti. The government immediately planned to send a colony to that settlement by virtue of an appropriation made by Congress. Bernard Koch approached the government and induced the authorities to make with him a contract for the transportation of Negroes to this island.

At the same time Koch connected himself with certain business men in New York. In return for commercial advantages to be gained there, they agreed also to finance the enterprise. When this double dealing was discovered the United States Government severed connection with Koch.

The double dealing of Koch. The capitalists, however, still determined to conduct this enterprise, engaged the services of Koch as governor. Accordingly a number of Negroes were sent to this island in the year 1862; but owing to the unfavorable conditions and their lack of initiative, unusual suffering ensued. It was necessary for the Government, because of the many complaints received therefrom, to send a special investigator to report on the situation. Finally, on account of his unfavorable report, the Government dispatched a transport to bring the emigrants back to the United States.

James Watson Webb, United States Minister to Brazil, proposed that the freedmen be colonized in that country. To emphasize the feasibility of this project he submitted to Lincoln and Seward various arguments. Brazilian Negroes were decreasing, labor was scarce in that country, the free Negroes would make progress there since Brazil allowed an open door to all honors and had social equality. A treaty with Brazil was suggested; but, thinking that the slavery question was too acute for such a far-reaching plan, the administration declined to undertake it.[5]

Lincoln, however, remained fundamentally antislavery in spite of the failure of the colonization schemes, although he religiously adhered to his gradual emancipation plans. He would not permit the abolition sentiment of the country to force upon him the policy of instant emancipation. As there were in the field generals availing themselves of every opportunity to weaken the slave power much vigilance had to be exercised to avoid extreme measures which might embarrass the Federal Government. Taking the advanced position that the slaves should be free, Fremont issued a decree abolishing slavery in Missouri. It was necessary for

5 *Journal of Negro History*, XI, 35-49.

Lincoln to say to him on September 2, 1861: "I think there is great danger that the closing paragraph, in relation to the confiscation of property and the liberating of slaves of traitorous owners, will alarm our southern Union friends and turn them against us; perhaps ruin our rather fair prospect for Kentucky. Allow me, therefore, to ask that you will, as of your own motion, modify that paragraph so as to conform to the first and fourth sections of the act of Congress, entitled *An Act to Confiscate Property used for Insurrectionary Purposes.*"

The following May, Lincoln had to deal similarly with Major-General Hunter, then stationed at Port Royal, South Carolina. This commander had issued a declaration to the effect that the commonwealths within his jurisdiction, having deliberately declared themselves no longer under the protection of the United States of America and having taken up arms against the United States, it became a military necessity to declare martial law; and as slavery and martial law were incompatible in a free country, the persons of these States held to service were declared free. Lincoln then issued a proclamation declaring that neither General Hunter nor any other commander or person had been authorized by the government of the United States to take such action and that the supposed proclamation in question, whether genuine or false, was altogether void so far as respects such a declaration. He considered it sufficient at that time to rely upon his proposed plan for the gradual abolition of slavery on the compensation basis recently accepted by Congress.

Writing Hunter again on the eleventh of the same month, Lincoln said: "The particular clause, however, in relation to the confiscation of property and the liberation of slaves appeared to me to be objectionable in its nonconformity to the act of Congress passed the 6th of last August upon the same subjects; and hence I wrote you, expressing my wish that that clause should be modified accordingly. Your answer, just received, expresses the preference on your part that I should make an open order for the modification, which I very cheerfully do. It is, therefore, ordered that the said clause of such proclamation be so modified, held, and construed as to conform to, and not to transcend, the provisions on the same subject contained in the act of Congress, entitled *An Act to Confiscate Property used for Insurrectionary Purposes.*"

It was growing more and more apparent, however, that the Negro would have to be treated as a citizen of the United States. In the army he had demonstrated his ca-

A convincing pacity as a man. He had shown that he could
record. become industrious, that he was thrifty, and that he would serve unselfishly. Where he had an opportunity to toil upward he succeeded. It was, therefore, recommended by a number of men, and among them General Grant himself, that certain Negroes be so equipped and trained that they might be employed not only as teamsters and mechanics and the like, but as soldiers. This change of policy was necessary not merely for sentimental reasons but because the North, in its effort to subjugate the haughty South, had found those warriors too well trained and too spirited to be easily conquered. In most of the important engagements the South had won. Farragut had captured New Orleans, Thomas and Grant had won a few victories in the West, and the *Monitor* had held its own with the *Merrimac* in defending the nation's cause, but the Union army had been twice ingloriously defeated at Manassas, and McClellan had lost in his Peninsular campaign and had thrown away his advantages gained at Antietam. As the army was unsuccessful under Burnside at Fredericksburg, and under Hooker at Chancellorsville, the North, growing tired of the war, was becoming fertile ground for seeds of a second secession sown by copperheads secretly

planning to establish another republic in the Northwest. It was deemed advisable, therefore, to bring the Negro into the army that he might help to save the Union. By this time, too, the Federal Government had reached the position

That on the first day of January, in the year of our Lord, one thousand eight hundred and sixty-three, all persons held as slaves. within any state, or designated part of a State, the people whereof shall then be in rebellion against the United States; shall be then, thenceforward, and forever free; and the executive government *including the military and naval authority thereof* *ment of the United States, will, during the war* ~~~~ *and maintain the freedom of cognize. such persons,* ~~~~ *and will do no act or acts to repress such persons, or any of them, in any efforts they may. make for their actual freedom.*

FACSIMILE OF THE ORIGINAL DRAFT OF THE EMANCIPATION
PROCLAMATION

that slavery, the root of most of the evils of the country and the actual cause of the war, would have to be exterminated. Congress passed sweeping confiscation acts by virtue of which the armies could take over slaves; and, in 1862, Lincoln came

The Emancipation Proclamation.

forward with the Emancipation Proclamation, declaring that after the first of January in 1863 all slaves in those parts of the country where the people might remain in rebellion against the United States, should be declared free.

Northern men like General DePeyster, General Thomas W. Sherman, General Hunter, Governor Yates of Illinois, Henry Wilson, and Charles Sumner, had been emphatic in urging the United States Government to arm the Negroes to weaken the South. And well might the United States Army take this action, for the seceders had not only made use of the Negroes as laborers, but in Tennessee and Louisiana had actually organized free Negroes for military service in the Confederate Army. Yet, although the confis-**The arming of Negroes.** cation acts and other legislation justified the employment of Negroes, Lincoln hesitated to carry out these provisions. In 1862, however, General David Hunter, commanding in South Carolina, issued an order for recruiting a Negro regiment, which in a few months was in the field. This caused much dissatisfaction among the Unionists, who did not feel that Negroes should be called on to fight the battles of a free republic. An effort was made to embarrass General Hunter, but he emerged from the investigation without being reversed, although he did not have the support of Lincoln. General J. W. Phelps, under General B. F. Butler in Louisiana, undertook to carry out Hunter's policy, but his superior was then willing to use the Negroes as laborers only.

Certain leaders in the North, however, were becoming a little more aggressive in their demand for the employment of Negroes as soldiers. On August 4, 1862, Governor Sprague of Rhode Island urged Negro citizens to enlist, and that same month Butler himself appealed to the free people of color of Louisiana to come to the defense of the Union. The next month a regiment of Negroes marched forth to war as the "First Regiment

of Louisiana Native Guards,'' soon changed to the ''First
Regiment Infantry Corps d'Afrique.'' There was later organized the ''First Regiment Louisiana Heavy Artillery.''
Other Negro regiments soon followed, and before the end of
1862 four Negro regiments had been brought into the
military service of the United States.   Then came the

ROBERT GOULD SHAW LEADING THE FIFTY-FOURTH MASSACHUSETTS
REGIMENT

''Kansas Colored Volunteers'' early in 1863.   When the
Emancipation Proclamation had been signed Lincoln officially authorized the raising of Negro troops.   Then followed the famous Fifty-fourth and Fifty-fifth Massachusetts and so many other troops that there was established in
Washington a special bureau for handling affairs respecting these units.   Before the end of the war they aggregated 178,975.

In keeping with the custom which was all but followed during the World War, the Negro troops were commanded almost altogether by white officers. There was some doubt that the Negro would make a good soldier; and, of course, **The use of** the Negro officer was then almost impossible. **Negro troops.** Massachusetts, however, commissioned ten Negro officers, Kansas three, and the military authorities a considerable number in Louisiana. Negroes held altogether about seventy-five commissions in the army during the Civil War. Among these officers were Lieutenant Colonel William N. Reed of the First North Carolina, a man well educated in Germany. He made a gallant charge with his regiment at the battle of Olustee, Florida, where he was mortally wounded. In the Kansas corps there were Captain H. Ford Douglass, First Lieutenant W. D. Matthews and Second Lieutenant Patrick A. Minor. In the U. S. C. T. One Hundred and Fourth Regiment, there were Major Martin R. Delany and Captain O. S. B. Wall of Company K. Dr. Alexander T. Augusta, who was surgeon of the U. S. C. T. Seventh Regiment, was finally breveted with Lieutenant-Colonel. Dr. John V. DeGrasse was assistant surgeon of the U. S. C. T. Thirty-fifth Regiment. Charles B. Purvis, Alpheus Tucker, John Rapier, William Ellis, Anderson R. Abbott and William Powell were hospital surgeons at Washington, D. C.

One might inquire, too, as to exactly what was the status of the Negro troops. In the first place, they were not treated as the equals of white men. There was objection to giving them the same compensation offered the whites. **The status of** In the matter of bounties there was a dis- **the Negro** crimination against Negro soldiers who were **soldiers.** slaves on April 19, 1861. This caused dissatisfaction among the Negro troops, whose families thereby seriously suffered. Sergeant William Walker was shot by order of court martial because he had his company stack arms before the captain's tent for the reason that the Government had failed to comply with its contract. The Fifty-fourth and Fifty-fifth of Massachusetts refused to receive their pay until it had been made equal to that of the whites. Negro troops, moreover, were often used by white troops for fatigue duty. Because of this notorious discrimination many of these soldiers became restive, sullen and even insubordinate.

Col. Thomas W. Higginson, a commander of Negro troops

Yet, these Negroes distinguished themselves as soldiers. Men under whom these troops fought in battle were loud in praise of their gallantry and martyrdom. Negroes served in almost all parts of the South. They engaged in the perilous South **Valuable service.** Edisto Expedition to burn a bridge above Walton Bluff to aid General Sherman, and participated in the action at Honey Hill. Speaking of their behavior in the expedition to Dobey River in Georgia, General Rufus Saxton said that they fought with most determined bravery. Surgeon Seth Rogers, operating in South Carolina, said that braver men never lived. Colonel T. W. Higginson himself believed that "it would have been madness to attempt with the bravest white troops what he successfully accomplished with the black." Even in the failure to carry Fort Wagner, a point necessary for the capture of Charleston, the Negro troops bore the severest tests of valor. They sacrificed themselves along with their gallant leader, Colonel Robert Gould Shaw, who in this charge fell mortally wounded.

In the Mississippi Valley they fought still more bravely. Negro troops made six such desperate charges on a fort at Port Hudson that a reporter said that the deeds of heroism

Bravery in the West. performed by these black men were such as the proudest white men might emulate. General Banks said in referring to their behavior: "It gives me great pleasure to report that they answered every expectation. Their conduct was heroic; no troops could be more determined or more daring." Other troops from Louisiana showed themselves equally brave at Milliken's Bend. Reporting this battle, Captain Matthew M. Miller said: "So they fought and died, defending the cause that we revere. They met death coolly, bravely; nor rashly did they expose themselves, but all were steady and obedient to orders." And so went others to death in the massacre at Fort Pillow in Tennessee. There the Confederates, in keeping with their bold declaration not to give quarter to the slaves striking for their own freedom, slaughtered them as men kill beasts.

In the Department of the Potomac the Negro maintained there his reputation as a soldier. Under General Wild, at Fort Powhatan in 1864, the Negro soldiers bravely held

Bravery along the Potomac. their ground against the heavy onslaught of Fitzhugh Lee's brilliant soldiers, who were badly worsted in the conflict. When General Grant was endeavoring to reduce Petersburg, a brigade of Hinck's Negro division brilliantly dashed forward and cleared a line of rifle-pits and carried a redoubt ahead. They did valiant work of the same order at South Mountain and died bravely in carrying the fortified positions of the Confederates at New Market Heights and nearer to Petersburg. In the dash along the James and in the pursuit of Lee's weakened forces, the Negroes under arms maintained their bearing as brave men and came out of the Civil War as heroes.

In the course of the Civil War many constitutional questions arose. Chief among these was the suspension of the writ of habeas corpus in the cases of certain copperheads or "pacifists" in the North, who arrayed themselves against the United States Government and at one time even threatened the country with an additional secession. The Constitution provided for the suspension of the writ in times of great danger, but it is not clear whether the framers of the Constitution contemplated that this power should be exercised by the President of the United States. Furthermore, those who asserted that the writ could be suspended under certain conditions did not concede the right of the President to suspend it in sections where the courts were open and where the armies were not in operation. The most important case of this kind was that of Milligan in 1864. By operation of the courts the plaintiff undertook to secure his liberty through a writ of habeas corpus and the President of the United States interfered.

Constitutional questions.

BISHOP DANIEL A. PAYNE, an Educator and Churchman active during the Civil War

There arose also other questions. The Government, it was charged, was unduly taxing the people to support an administration waging war to coerce certain States, interfering with the freedom of the press, enforcing conscription acts, compelling men to fight

Taxation.

against their will, and finally promoting by action of Congress gradual emancipation in certain border States and the abolition of slavery in the District of Columbia. Whether Congress could constitutionally legislate respecting slavery was still a question, but the Civil War gradually brought the country to a realization that Congress, representing the people of the United States, had adequate power in the premises. Because of vesting the President with dictatorial power to wage the war effectively, however, there came from certain sources a bitter antagonism which led to the organization of a party of opposition advocating the "Union as it was and the Constitution as it is."

The most important constitutional matter coming up during the Civil War was that of the Emancipation Proclamation itself. Lincoln had for some time wondered whether or not he had such authority. He long hesitated **The emancipation problem.** to issue this mandate declaring free all the Negroes in the districts then in rebellion against the United States. Fremont, Hunter and Butler, in charge of Union armies, had undertaken to do this, but had to be restrained. One of the members of Lincoln's cabinet was of the opinion that he had no such power and that such a step would doubtless do more harm than good. In the end, however, just after a number of encouraging Union victories, the Emancipation Proclamation was issued and had its desired effect; but to become legal it had to be fortified by the Thirteenth Amendment. It declared that neither slavery nor involuntary servitude, except as a punishment for crime, should exist within the United States. This was passed in Congress and ratified by the States by December 18, 1865. Few persons have since questioned the Thirteenth Amendment, although peonage still exists in parts of the United States. However, the Fourteenth and Fifteenth which followed there-

upon have since given rise to all sorts of constitutional questions involving the rights of the Negroes and of others.

The reasons for these different attitudes on constitutional matters cannot be readily understood now by the
layman. We are so far removed from that time that we
cannot easily appreciate the underlying reasons for the
positions which statesmen of that day took. Negroes of
to-day, for example, severely criticize Abraham Lincoln
for his inaction and hesitancy in matters re-   **Lincoln and**
specting the emancipation and recognition of   **the Negro.**
the race; and they, therefore, laugh at the idea of recording him in history as the "Great Emancipator." Lincoln
often expressed his contempt for abolitionists like Sumner
and Stevens. They worried him by urging the instant
liberation of the "d——d niggers." He repeatedly said
that he would save the Union with slavery or that he
would save it without slavery. His chief purpose was to
save the Union. Lincoln countermanded the emancipating
orders of Butler, Fremont and Hunter. Lincoln could
not easily come to the position of immediate emancipation.
He had thought only of gradual and compensated emancipation to be completed by the year 1900.

With respect to Negroes after they became free, moreover, he was not very liberal. He did not care to have
Negro soldiers in the Union Army, and when finally all
but forced by circumstances to admit them, he did not
desire to grant them the same pay and the same treatment accorded white soldiers. He believed, moreover, that
Negroes, if liberated, should be colonized abroad, inasmuch
as they could not hope to remain in this country and
become socially and politically equal to white men. His
attitude was made clear in 1862, when after the liberation
of the Negroes in the District of Columbia, he summoned
certain of their group to urge them to emigrate. "And,
why," said he, "should the people of your race be colo-

nized and where? Why should they leave this country? You and we are different races. We have between us a broader difference than exists between almost any other two races. Whether it is right or wrong I need not discuss, but this physical difference is a great disadvantage to us both, as I think. Your race suffer very greatly, many of them, by living among us, while ours suffer from your presence. In a word we suffer on each side. If this is admitted, it affords a reason why we should be separated.''

Lincoln, however, should not be unsympathetically condemned as the Negro's enemy who sought to exterminate slavery merely because it was an economic handicap to the white man. It must be remembered that Lincoln was not elected on an abolition platform. His party had merely repudiated the Dred Scott decision and opposed the ex-

Lincoln sympathetically considered. tension of slavery. Lincoln, himself, had borne eloquent testimony against mob rule, lynching and slavery throughout his career. In Congress he had worked for gradual and compensated emancipation, and he had kept this plan before the slave States as the best solution of their problem. To say that he would save the Union with or without slavery does not necessarily show a lack of interest in emancipation. No one will hardly think that emancipation would have had much of a chance if the Union had been lost. It succeeded with the Union saved. In his hesitancy as to emancipation and the arming of the Negroes there may be evidence of statesmanship rather than lack of interest in freedom and democracy. As he often well said, the main thing was to win the war. Everything depended upon that. Had Lincoln immediately declared the Negroes free and turned them armed upon their masters he would have lost the war. Many of the people in the border slave States who were kindly disposed to the Union, were nevertheless proslavery. A considerable number of the people in the free States, moreover, especially the "Copperheads" in the Northwest, objected to the "coercion" of the South. They would have risen in protest against anything resembling a servile insurrection. The war was not an effort to free slaves. Lincoln, as President of the United States, could not carry out his own personal plans. In a situation like this an executive must fail if he undertakes a reform so far ahead of the time that his very coworkers cannot be depended upon to carry out his policies. The abolitionists were a small minority. Men had to be gradually brought around to thinking that immediate emancipation would be the proper solution of the problem. There was much fear that such a radical step would lead to inter-racial war. For this reason Lincoln and others connected deportation with emancipation. As the experiment had not been made, the large majority of Americans of Lincoln's day believed that the two races could not dwell together on the basis of social and political equality. A militant minority of the descendants of these Americans do not believe it now. The abolitionists themselves were not united on this point. Lincoln, moreover, gradually grew unto the full stature of democracy. Observing finally that the Negroes would remain permanently in this country, he urged upon the States in process of reconstruction to make some provision for the education of the freedmen, and suggested that the right of franchise be extended to those who were intelligent and owned property. Whatever Lincoln did was what he thought best for all concerned. He was not prejudiced against any race in the sense that men are to-day. Frederick Douglass said that Lincoln was the first white man he ever met who did not say or do something to make him feel that he belonged to a different race.

CHAPTER XXIII

RECONSTRUCTION

RECONSTRUCTION began in the schoolhouses not in the State houses, as uninformed persons often say. Misguided men of that day did not know it. Having the idea that voting and holding office are privileges for oppressing the **Actual recon-** weak rather than opportunities for serving **struction.** humanity, they have emphasized unduly the part played by messages of governors, the proceedings of conventions, and the measures of legislatures. The missionary teacher was at work in the South long before it was known how the war would end. As the Union armies gradually invaded that area the soldiers opened schools for Negroes. Regular teachers came from relief societies and the Freedmen's Bureau. These enlightened a fair percentage of the Negroes by 1870. The illiteracy of the Negroes was reduced to 79.9 by that time. When about this time these freedmen had a chance to participate in the rehabilitation of State governments in the South, they gave that section the first free public school system, the first democratic education it ever had. This was the real reconstruction and the only thing which will bring the South out of its present medieval state. Some of these days there will arise in the South a white man fair-minded enough to propose the building of a monument to these Negroes who were so far ahead of their exploiters.

The first substantial support for education in the South came from philanthropists. Following up the good work done by the Union soldiers in teaching Negroes coming within their reach during the Civil War, these philanthropists sent the best blood of the North as missionary teachers. They gave their lives as a sacrifice for the enlightenment of the Negro. **Reconstructing agencies.** The unselfish teachers engaged by the Bureau of Refugees, Freedmen and Abandoned Lands, established March 3, 1865, were early in the field. They had paved the way for the expansion of the work. For example, as early as 1861, Lewis Tappan, the Treasurer of the American Missionary Association, learned by communication with General Butler, in charge at Fortress Monroe, that education was the immediate need of the freedmen. He, therefore, sent C. L. Lockwood to establish at Hampton the first day-school for the freedmen. The first teacher of this

GEN. O. O. HOWARD, head of the Freedmen's Bureau and founder of Howard University

school was Mrs. Mary S. Peak, an educated free woman of color. Other such schools followed at Norfolk, Newport News, and at Hilton Head and Beaufort, South Carolina. In the West, the Rev. John Eaton was giving some attention to the education of the freedmen in the camps. There were 83 of these missionary teachers in 1863 and 250 in 1864. Many of them were preachers.[1]

These Christian workers, however, cared not so much about proselyting as they did about education. This was

[1] *Journal of Negro History*, VIII, 1-40; IX, 322-345; XI, 379-415.

the greatest need of the freedmen. The Baptists and Methodists, who had considerable communicants among the Negroes prior to the Civil War, took the lead in this move-

The first schools. ment. They opened at strategic points schools which they believed would become centers of culture for the whole race. The Baptists established Shaw University at Raleigh in 1865; Roger Williams at Nashville, and Morehouse at Atlanta, in 1867; Leland at New Orleans in 1869 and Benedict at Columbia in 1871. The Freewill Baptists founded Storer College at Harpers Ferry in 1867. The Methodists, who were no less active, established Walden at Nashville in 1865, Rust at Holly Springs in 1866, Morgan at Baltimore in 1867, Haven Academy at Waynesboro in 1868, Claflin at Orangeburg in 1869, and Clark at Atlanta in 1870. The Presbyterians, who could not compete with the Baptists and Methodists in proselyting Negroes, restricted their efforts to a few small schools and to the establishment of Biddle at Charlotte in 1867. They promoted also the work begun at Lincoln University in Pennsylvania, established as Ashmun Institute in 1854. The Episcopal Church established some small institutions: St. Augustine at Raleigh in 1867, and the Bishop Payne Divinity School in Petersburg, in 1878.

Another factor was equally effective in this uplift of the freedmen. This was the American Missionary Association. These earnest workers established Avery Institute at Charleston, Ballard Normal School at Macon, and Washburn at Beaufort, North Carolina, in 1865. They founded,

The American Missionary Association. too, Trinity at Athens, Alabama, Gregory at Wilmington, North Carolina, and Fisk at Nashville in 1866. Then came Talladega in Alabama, Emerson at Mobile, Storrs at Atlanta, and Beach at Savannah in 1867. Next appeared Hampton Institute in Virginia, Knox at Athens, and Burrell at Selma, now at Florence, and Ely Normal in Louisville in 1868.

Straight University opened at New Orleans, Tougaloo in Mississippi, Le Moyne in Memphis, and Lincoln at Marion, Alabama, in 1869. Dorchester Academy began at McIntosh, and the Albany Normal in Georgia in 1870. The Congregationalists, moreover, figured with the Freedmen's Bureau in the establishment of Howard University. This institution was chartered by the United States Government in 1867 with provisions for the education of all persons regardless of race.

GEN. SAMUEL C. ARMSTRONG
A Friend in War and Peace

Some other less effective forces were at work during this **Missionary** period ac- **educators.** complishing here and there results seemingly unimportant but in the end productive of much good. In 1862 Miss Towne and Miss Murray, members of the Society of Friends, established the Penn School on St. Helena Island, South Carolina. Cornelia Hancock, a Philadelphia woman of the same sect, founded the Laing School at Mount Pleasant, near Charleston, South Carolina. Martha Schofield, another Friend of Pennsylvania, opened at Aiken in 1868 the Schofield Industrial School. In 1864 Alida Clark, supported by Friends in Indiana, engaged in relief work among Negro orphans in Helena, Arkansas, and in 1866 established near that city what is now known as Southland College. The Reformed Presbyterians maintained a school at Natchez between 1864 and 1866, and in 1874 established Knox Academy at Selma, Alabama. The United Presbyterians opened a sort of clandestine school in Nashville in 1863, and in 1875 established Knoxville College as a center for a group of schools for Negroes in Eastern Tennessee, Virginia, North Carolina, and Northern Alabama. Franklinton Christian College, maintained by the American Christian Convention, was opened in 1878 and

TEACHING THE FREEDMEN

chartered in 1890. Stillman Institute was established by the southern Presbyterians at Tuscaloosa in 1876. Paine College was founded at Augusta for the Colored Methodists in 1884. Lane came later.

The Freedmen's Bureau and the relief agencies were chiefly effective in educational work between 1865 and **Agencies in** 1870. During the first year of the war, the **this field.** Bureau itself reported the establishment of 4,239 schools with 9,307 teachers and 247,333 students in the various States. These schools were free and tended to emphasize the necessity for democratic education at public expense. When these schools closed as a result of the withdrawal of Federal support in 1870, they had probably brought under instruction ten or fifteen per cent of the Negro children. In 1870 twenty-one per cent of the Negroes were literate largely as a result of these efforts. The work of the Freedmen's Bureau was turned over then to various agencies, mainly to the American Missionary Association. This body had been organized some years earlier, prior to the Civil War as an interdenominational effort, but in 1881 it came under the control of the Congregational Church.

The other agencies participating in this effort were the Pennsylvania Freedmen's Relief Association, the Tract Society, Pennsylvania Friends Freedmen's Relief Association, the Old School Presbyterian Mission, the Reformed Presbyterian Mission, the New England Freedmen's Aid Committee, the New England Freedmen's Aid Society, the New England Freedmen's Mission, the Washington Christian Union, the Universalists of Maine, the New York Freedmen's Relief Association, the Hartford Relief Society, and the National Freedmen's Relief Association of the District of Columbia. Along with these forces should be mentioned the liberal elements of the South, represented by Haygood, Curry, Ruffner, Northern, and Vance, who urged upon the people the importance of enlightening the freedmen. High upon the roll of honor should be inscribed such immortal apostles to the lowly as Myrtilla Miner in the District of Columbia,[2] Corey at Virginia Union, Packard and Giles at Spelman, Cravath at Fisk, Ware at Atlanta, Armstrong at Hampton, Graves at Morehouse, and Tupper at Shaw. They left the comforts of a modern home and went into a benighted land to face social ostracism, persecution, and sometimes death, in spending their lives in the uplift of the Negro. These men and women

[2] *Journal of Negro History,* V, 448-457.

gave the world a new meaning of what their Great Teacher had in mind when he said: "Greater love hath no man than this, that a man lay down his life for his friends."

The Negro church was equally effective in working out reconstruction in the South. In fact, what has been said above with respect to the extensive work undertaken by the schools is also a sketch of the operations of the church. Christian work-ers learned in the be-ginning of this effort that the exten-sive proselyting and thor-ough Christianization of the Negroes would be im-possible until the schools could do their work of en-lightening the freedmen. The whole educational movement then may be properly styled as a work of missionary teachers in-spired and largely sup-ported by the church.

Reconstruction through the church.

RICHARD DeBAPTISTE

Most of the first teachers sent to the Negroes were persons who taught during the week and preached on Sunday. Schoolhouses were churches, and churches were school-houses. However, this was not a revival of anything like the church combined with the state. Denominations forgot their sectarian differences and unselfishly coöperated in the general uplift of the Negro.

The further development of the Negro churches as such after the war, however, was also a factor in reconstruction in the South. The church went forward under distinguished ministers like Bishop Daniel A. Payne and James Poindexter in Ohio, Rufus L. Perry in New York, and Richard DeBaptiste in Illinois. In the South where the majority of the freedmen were found, the Negro church had its real opportunity. Thousands of them had been communicants segregated in the pews of white churches or ministered unto at different hours or in separate buildings. With the spirit of freedom, these Negroes went out to establish a religious system of their own. Under the leadership of Bishop W. H. Miles and Bishop R. H. Vanderhorst, the Colored Methodist Episcopal Church began its eventful career in 1870. Later this work was decidedly stimulated by Bishop L. H. Holsey. After the removal of the restrictions which handicapped independent religious efforts there prior to emancipation, the work of the

W. H. MILES

African Methodist Episcopal Church was extended rapidly through the South by Bishops A. W. Wayman, R. H. Cain, H. M. Turner, and W. B. Derrick. The African Methodist Episcopal Zion Church invaded the same field with unusual success, especially the State of North Carolina, where it was efficiently aided by Bishops J. W. Hood and J. J. Clinton. The Negro membership of the Methodist Episcopal Church, maintaining its connection with the North, went also into this field of a waiting harvest and accomplished much in the enlightenment of the freedmen. The Baptists at the same time were blazing the way through such men as Henry Williams, James Holmes, Walter H. Brooks, and Richard Wells in Virginia; through J. J. Worlds, George W. Lee, and E. M. Brawley in North Carolina; J. P. Brockenton and J. J. Durham in South Carolina; W. J. White in Georgia; and W. R. Pettiford in Alabama.[3]

The political reconstruction, however, attracted the attention of the whole country. As **Lincoln's reconstruction.** soon as the Union armies began to occupy a considerable portion of the territory of the so-called seceded States, there was some thought about the rehabilitation of these commonwealths.[4] As to the exact position of these commonwealths which had undertaken to withdraw

J. W. Hood

from the Union, there was a wide difference of opinion. Lincoln himself was of the impression that a State could not get out of the Union. "Once in the Union, forever in the Union," was his theory. Lincoln therefore issued,

[3] These facts are given in detail in Woodson's *History of the Negro Church.* See also *The Journal of Negro History,* IX, 346-364; and XI, 425-458.

[4] There are no scientific studies of the nation-wide reconstruction in which the Negroes took a part. W. L. Fleming, James F. Rhodes, W. A. Dunning and J. W. Burgess have written works in this field, but they are biased and inadequate. Almost a score of other so-called scientific studies of Reconstruction in the various States have

on December 8, 1863, a proclamation setting forth a plan for the reconstruction of these commonwealths. He proclaimed full pardon to the people in the Confederate States with the restoration of all rights of property except as to slaves if they should take and subscribe to an oath of allegiance to the United States Government and thenceforward keep and maintain this oath inviolate. He made exception of those who had served in the civil or diplomatic service of the Confederate Government or in judicial stations, of those who had served in the army or navy with rank above colonel, or who had abandoned Congress to aid the rebellion, resigned commissions in the army, or cruelly treated Negroes or white persons in charge of them.

Lincoln further proclaimed that whenever in any of these States there should be loyal persons to the number of not less than one-tenth of the votes cast in such States at the Presidential election of the year 1860, each having taken this oath and not having violated it and being a qualified voter by the election law of the State existing prior to the secession, the commonwealth should establish a State government. This government should be democratic, should be recognized as the true government of the State, and should receive the benefits of the constitutional provision which declares that the United States shall guarantee to every State in this Union a republican form of government. The ten per cent basis.

Lincoln also proclaimed that any helpful provision which these commonwealths thus restored might adopt in relation to the freed people within their limits would not be objected

been made, but these merely try to make a case for the white man's side of the question as to whether the reduction of the Negro to serfdom was just. John R. Lynch in his *Facts of Reconstruction,* and W. E. B. DuBois in his *Reconstruction, and Its Benefits* (in the *American Historical Review,* XV, No. 4) have undertaken to point out these defects. Some other views of John R. Lynch are given in the *Journal of Negro History,* II, 345-368; III, 139-157; V, 420-436.

to by the President. He wanted the States to recognize and declare their permanent freedom, and provide for their education by way of some temporary arrangement

Interest in the freedmen. which might be consistent with their condition as a laboring, landless and homeless class. The President was of the opinion that the name of the State, the boundary, subdivisions, constitution, and the

JAMES POINDEXTER

former code of laws should be maintained, subject only to the modification made necessary by the conditions elsewhere stated in the proclamation. He did not object to other measures, not contravening the conditions of the proclamation, if deemed expedient by those framing the new State government.

Upon this basis Lincoln undertook the reconstruction of the States of Louisiana, Arkansas, and Tennessee prior to the close of the Civil War as soon as loyal men to the number of one-tenth of the voters exercising suffrage in the presidential election of 1860 were

States reorganized. found in those commonwealths. Believing that Lincoln's position in this case was sound, Andrew Johnson, his successor, undertook to carry out this policy. When the cessation of arms finally came, several of the rebellious commonwealths, thinking that the States as such could never be destroyed, proceeded to organize similar governments. The rebellious States complied with the conditions of repudiating the Confederate debts, declared allegiance to the Union, and ratified the Thirteenth Amendment. Thinking, therefore, that they would be immediately admitted to the Union with the rights and privileges formerly enjoyed by the Southern States, they elected representatives and senators to sit in Congress. This, however, was not acceptable to the statesmen then in control of affairs, and the right of such persons to serve as representatives of these commonwealths was questioned.

They found in Congress men led by Charles Sumner and Thaddeus Stevens. These men were of the opinion that inasmuch as the Southern States had rebelled and had failed to maintain their cause, they were then subject to the same treatment as any other people in a conquered territory. This, to be sure, conflicted with certain other views, as it admitted that secession had been temporarily successful, and conflicted with the administrative plans of Lincoln and Johnson. They held that secession was merely an unsuccessful effort and that the States were still in the Union. Shellabarger contended that secession was a nullity. Although disloyalists could not assume control of the territory in which secession existed, it nevertheless worked a loss of the status of a member of the Union. The citizens remaining therein were, therefore, exclusively subjected to the jurisdiction of the United States Government. This was endorsed by Sumner, Fessenden and Wilson, and became, in fact, the theory of the reconstructionists in Congress. This meant antagonism to the administration and led to the long differences of opinion between that body and Johnson, which finally culminated in the impeachment of the President.

Various theories.

There came also to the national capital various reports which further convinced the gentlemen in charge of affairs in Congress that the South was unwilling to grant the

Negro the right to enjoy the fruits of the victory of the
Civil War. The freedmen were being oppressed almost to
The unwill-   the extent of being enslaved. Disorder fol-
ing South.   lowed. Native whites undertook to "manage" or "control" the freedmen as they were handled when
slaves. If the freedmen objected, they were beaten or
killed. Referring to South Carolina an authority said:
"The pecuniary value which the individual Negro formerly
represented having disappeared, the maiming and killing
of them seemed to be looked upon by many as one of those
venial offenses which must be forgiven to the outraged
feelings of a wronged and robbed people." "E. H.
Johnson, a Virginia clergyman, killed a Negro soldier in
1865." According to the *Richmond Enquirer* on November 3, 1866, "J. C. Johnston, a law student of Lexington
charged with killing a freedman, was acquitted." For a
trivial reason one Queensbury, a planter in Louisa County,
killed a Negro in his employ. Because of slight mis-
understandings, R. N. Eastham of Rappahannock, and
Washington Alsworth of Lunenburg killed Negroes in their
service. On November 24, 1866, the *Enquirer* reported that
Dr. James Watson, "one of the most respectable gentlemen
of Rockbridge county," killed a Negro for driving into his
vehicle. These criminals were not punished.[5]

A bloody race-riot broke out in Memphis in the spring of
1866. In the following July a more serious conflict took
place in New Orleans when freedmen on the way to a political meeting clashed with native whites. Going into the hall
to which they were proceeding they found themselves surrounded by their pursuers aided by the police. Forty
Negroes were killed and about a hundred were wounded.
Twelve of the whites were killed and a few were wounded.

The first official reports on conditions in the South were
brought in by General Grant and Carl Schurz. The former

[5] *Journal of Negro History*, XI, 325.

contended that the Southerners were in the main willing
to accept the changes effected by the Civil War, and the
latter that the rebellious commonwealths were not loyal
and intended to reënslave the Negroes. Some of these
States were enacting black codes providing for apprenticeship, penalizing the vagrancy of Negroes, and interfering
with the civil rights of the freedmen. Many of the blacks,
having wandered about or flocked to the towns where they
too often were reduced to poverty and subject to tempta-
tions and vicious influences, tended to retrograde rather
than advance. The vagrancy laws, therefore, generally
provided for fines, corporal punishment, indenturing for a
certain period of service, and in a few cases required that
every Negro should be attached to some employer.

Some of these measures will bear detailed treatment
here. Virginia, for example, empowered officers to bring
the vagrant before a justice of peace. If condemned as
such, he was to be hired out for a period not   **Vagrancy
exceeding three months. If during this time   Acts.**
the vagrant absconded without cause, he would be penalized
by adding another month, or the employer could shackle the
vagrant with ball and chain to prevent such an escape.
Such a fugitive might be placed in the public service of the
county, or he might be imprisoned and fed on bread and
water. Five classes of persons were defined as vagrants.
These included "all persons who shall unlawfully return
into any county or corporation whence they have been
legally removed"; "all persons who, not having where-
with to maintain themselves and their families, live idly
and without employment, and refuse to work for the usual
and common wages given to other laborers in the like work
in the place where they then are"; "all persons who shall
refuse to perform the work which shall be allotted to them
by the overseers of the poor as aforesaid"; "all persons
going from door to door, or placing themselves in the

streets, highways or other roads, to beg alms, and all other persons wandering abroad and begging, unless disabled or incapable of labor''; and ''all persons who shall come from any place without this commonwealth to any place within it, and shall be found loitering and residing therein, and shall follow no labor, trade, occupation or business, and have no visible means of subsistence, and can give no reasonable account of themselves or their business in such places.''

In South Carolina orphan children of color were subjected to compulsory apprenticeship like that provided for a servant under contract. Practically all Negroes were compelled to enter the service of some planter. They had to sign an indenture of service and be bound thereby. Servants should rise at dawn in the morning, feed, water and care for the animals on the farm, do the usual and needful work about the premises, prepare their meals for the day, if required by the master, and begin the farm work or some other task by sunrise. All losses of implements and supplies not caused by the act of the master would be deducted from the wages of the servants and also the cost of food and other necessaries in cases of sickness necessitating absence from work. No person of color should pursue or practice the art, trade or business of an artisan or shopkeeper, or any other trade without a license from the Judge of the District Court. Vagrancy was defined very much as in the case of Virginia. Such offenders might be sentenced to imprisonment and hard labor. One or both should be fixed by the verdict not exceeding twelve months. The defendant, if thus sentenced, might be hired for such wages as could be obtained for his service to any owner or lessee of a farm, or might be hired for labor on the streets, roads or public buildings. The person receiving such a vagrant should have all the rights and remedies for enforcing good conduct and diligence at

labor. No person of color should immigrate into the State
unless within twenty days he could give bond for his good
behavior.

Aggravating the situation still more, Mississippi provided in its black code, "that if any apprentice shall leave
the employment of his or her master or mistress, said master or mistress may pursue and recapture said apprentice,
and bring him or her before any justice of peace of the
county, whose duty it shall be to remand said apprentice
to the service of his or her master or mistress; and in the
event of a refusal on the part of said apprentice so to return, then said justice shall commit said apprentice to the
jail of said county."

For the improvement of the social conditions of the
Negroes, these codes provided also for the marriage of
the freedmen according to law and vested the children of
the former unions during slavery with the right of inheritance of the property of their parents. The Negroes
were also granted the right to own property and that of
suing and being sued in the courts. They could give
testimony in cases in which only Negroes were concerned.
They could not serve on a jury or in the militia; and, of
course, could neither vote nor hold office. Their right of
locomotion was restricted in that they were forbidden
to assemble under certain circumstances. Furthermore,
there had set in a general intimidation of Negroes.

Assured that the situation was deplorable, Congress
passed the Civil Rights Bill in 1865 to secure to Negroes
the full enjoyment of social and civil privileges. The
body then proceeded to draft the Fourteenth Amendment as a condition of readmission of a seceded State to
the Union. The aim was to prevent any State from making
or enforcing a law which would encroach upon the privileges or immunities of citizens of the United States, deprive them of life, liberty or property without due process

of law, or withhold from any one within its jurisdiction the equal protection of the law. It guaranteed to all persons the enjoyment of the privileges and immunities of citizens without regard to race, color, or previous condition of servitude. Congress also deemed it necessary at this juncture to bring the South under military rule. Then came the establishment of military districts into which the unreconstructed States were organized for the rule of the army. In 1870 came the Fifteenth Amendment declaring that the right to vote shall not be denied on account of race, color or previous condition of servitude. In this way the South, by taking a radical position in its unwise application of its power to deal with persons over whom it would have been given more control, brought upon itself a military rule from which it would not have suffered if it had been disposed to treat the freedmen humanely.

The official reports led also to the extension of the work of what is known as the Freedmen's Bureau, the commission established for the protection and the assistance of the freedmen. Several times some such idea had been expressed in both houses of Congress. On March 3, 1865, therefore, Congress established in the War Department "a bureau of refugees, freedmen and abandoned lands." This action was taken after hearing numerous suggestions as to how the Government should control and manage the freedmen coming within the lines of the Union Army. The The Freed- actual work of this bureau, however, followed after the Civil War. In their struggle with President Andrew Johnson, the reconstructionists in Congress sought to increase these powers of the Federal Government, although this had been done in a measure passed in 1865. A bill to this effect, however, was proposed in 1866. The measure was debated long and carefully by both houses. Some doubted the necessity for such a grant of additional military power in the time of peace. The

Reconstruction

SOME FACTORS IN THE RECONSTRUCTION
WILLIAM P. FESSENDEN   SAMUEL SHELLABARGER
CARL SCHURZ
FREDERICK T. FRELINGHUYSEN   THADDEUS STEVENS

measure to give the department additional powers was vetoed by President Johnson. In presenting his reasons he so antagonized the leaders in Congress as to widen the irreparable breach between the executive and legislative departments. This bill, with certain objectionable features removed, was later passed over the President's veto, but it had to be amended.

The act provided for the appointment of a commissioner with a number of assistants under the administration of the President to care for the freedmen in the districts in rebellion or controlled by the Union Army. Primarily the Freedmen's Bureau was intended to aid refugees and freedmen by supplying them with provisions and by taking up abandoned lands in the South. These were to be distributed in parcels of not more than forty acres each. On account of misrepresentations many Negroes expected from this quarter forty acres of land and a mule for each of the landless freedmen. This prospective charity tended to produce vagrancy and shiftlessness among people indulged as dependent children. The Freedmen's Bureau was vested with the power to build schoolhouses and asylums for the Negroes, and it was proposed to give it unusual power in its jurisdiction over all civil and criminal cases where equality in civil rights and in the application of justice was denied on account of race, color, or previous condition of servitude. With this unusual power vested in machinery coming from without the State and intended to benefit persons recently enslaved, the Freedmen's Bureau became a source of much irritation to the whites of the South. Grant thought that the officers of the Freedmen's Bureau were a useless set of men and recommended that the work be placed in charge of army officers. For a number of years the Freedmen's Bureau was directed by General O. O. Howard, who founded Howard University with sums appropriated to the use of the Freedmen's Bureau.

When Congress finally decided to ignore Johnson's reconstruction schemes, a committee was appointed to work out a more acceptable plan. After some deliberation these gentlemen returned with a majority and a minority report. The majority report, representing the views of the Unionists, was to the effect that the attempted secession of eleven States had re- **Congressional reconstruction.** sulted in the loss of their status and in their becoming disorganized communities, but that although the State governments in the same had been destroyed, the commonwealths had not escaped the obligations of the Constitution and the authority of the United States Government. The minority report, representing the secessionist theory, was that a State could never be anything less than a State, regardless of what its deeds may be, and each was, therefore, entitled to the same powers, rights and privileges under the Constitution as those given any other State. It is needless to say that under these circumstances the minority report had little weight.

Congress thereupon proceeded in accordance with the views of the majority to work out a plan for the control of the disorganized States. In spite of the President's opposition and his vetoes, it was decided to divide the seceded States into five military districts, to each of which the President would assign an army officer **Military districts.** of not lower rank than a brigadier general, with a sufficient force to enable him to carry out the laws of the Union. The commanders were to govern these districts by martial law as far as in their judgments the reign of order and the preservation of public peace might demand. No sentence of death, however, could be carried out without the approval of the President. To escape from this military government, a rebellious State had to accept universal manhood suffrage of all male citizens of twenty-one years of age without regard to color, race or previous condition of servitude. At a special election the State might provide for the framing of a State constitution through delegates to be chosen among persons who were not disqualified by participation in the rebellion. There would have to be a ratification of this constitution by a majority of the voters as designated by the same law of suffrage for the delegates of the convention. These States, moreover, would have to ratify the Fourteenth Amendment. This new measure of freedom provided that no State should abridge the privileges or immunities of citizens of the United States, nor should any State deprive any person of life, liberty, or property, without due process of law, nor deny to any person within its jurisdiction the equal protection of the laws. The South had refused to ratify this amendment.

JOHN M. LANGSTON

Some of the States immediately availed themselves of this opportunity to be relieved of the military régime, for there was among them a natural antagonism to such a rule. Hoping to find a better solution of the problem by adopting the policy of watchful waiting, however, other States, Virginia, Georgia and Texas, refused to take advantage of this opportunity. The citizens of these States found out that the military government was more acceptable than the governments so quickly organized in some of the other Southern States. They decided then for the time being to obey the dictum of the army. In the course of time there was an enlargement of the white minority by the extension of the terms of granting pardon to those who had participated in the rebellion. As there was already a larger percentage of

Different courses followed.

white persons than Negroes in these three States, when the time did come for them to organize State governments, there soon developed a majority opposed to liberal reconstruction. The other States in the South, from 1868 to about 1872, became subjected to what is commonly known as "Negro carpet-bag rule."

To call this Negro rule, however, is very much of a mistake. As a matter of fact, most of the local offices in these commonwealths were held by the white men, and those Negroes who did attain some of the **Not a Negro regime.** higher offices were usually about as competent as the average whites thereto elected. Only twenty-three Negroes served in Congress from 1868 to 1895. The Negroes had political equality in the Southern States only a few years, and with some exceptions their tenure in Congress was very short. Hiram R. Revels of Mississippi completed an unexpired term in the Senate, and B. K. Bruce served there six years. John M. Langston, the Negro member from Virginia, served in the House one term. From North Carolina there were sent to the House of Representatives John A. Hyman for one term and James E. O'Hara, H. P. Cheatham and George H. White for two terms each. Jefferson F. Long represented a district of Georgia a part of a term. Josiah T. Walls of Florida served in the House two terms. Alabama elected to Congress Jere Haralson, Benjamin S. Turner and James T. Rapier, who served one term each. Louisiana sent Charles

John R. Lynch, a member of Congress

SOME NEGRO CONGRESSMEN

ROBERT B. ELLIOTT   JOSIAH T. WALLS
ROBERT C. DELARGE   RICHARD H. CAIN

E. Nash for one term, and Mississippi John R. Lynch for two. South Carolina had the largest number of Negro representatives in the House. Joseph H. Rainey of that Commonwealth sat in Congress five terms; Richard H. Cain, two; Robert C. DeLarge, one; Alonzo J. Ransier, one; Robert B. Elliott, two; Robert Smalls, five; Thomas E.

Miller, one; and Geo. W. Murray, two. J. W. Menard, of Louisiana, was not recognized. At one time all the Representatives of South Carolina were Negroes.

The charge that all Negro officers were illiterate, ignorant of the science of government, cannot be sustained. In the first place the education of the Negro by Union soldiers in the South began in spots as early as 1861. Many of the Negro leaders who had been educated in the North or abroad returned to the South after the war. Negro illiteracy

H. R. REVELS, U. S. Senator from Mississippi

had been reduced to 79.9 by 1870, just about the time the freedmen were actually participating in the reconstruction. The masses of Negroes did not take a part in the government in the beginning of the reconstruction.

It is true that many of them were not prepared to vote, and decidedly disqualified for the positions which they held. In some of the legislatures, as in Louisiana and South Carolina, more than half of the Negro **Negroes** members could scarcely read or write. They, **capable.** therefore, had to vote according to emotions or the dictates of the demagogues. This, of course, has been true of legislatures composed entirely of whites. In the local and State administrative offices, however, where there were frequent chances for corruption, very few ignorant Negroes ever served.

Some of the Negro officeholders had undergone consider-**Literacy of** able training and had experienced sufficient **voters and** mental development to be able to discharge **officers.** their duties with honor. Hiram R. Revels spent two years in a Quaker seminary and was later instructed at Knox College. B. K. Bruce was educated at Oberlin College. Jere Haralson learned enough to teach. R. H. Cain studied at Wilberforce. James T. Rapier was well educated in a Catholic school in Canada. Benjamin Turner clandestinely received a fair education in Alabama. James E. O'Hara obtained a secondary education. According to Frederick

B. K. BRUCE, U. S. Senator from Mississippi

Douglass, Robert Brown Elliott, educated at Eton College, England, had no peer in his race except Samuel R. Ward. John M. Langston, after finishing both the college and theological courses at Oberlin, practiced law in Ohio. John R. Lynch, as evidenced by his addresses and writings, was well educated by his dint of energy, although he had only a common school training. Most Negroes who sat in Congress during the eighties and nineties, moreover, had more formal education than Warren G. Harding, once President of the United States.[6]

Other Negro officeholders, furthermore, were liberally trained. Richard T. Greener, a reconstruction officeholder in South Carolina, was the first Negro graduate of Harvard College. F. L. Cardozo, another functionary in the same State, was educated at the University of Glasgow, Scotland. E. D. Bassett, who distinguished himself as an educator and as Minister to Haiti, studied the classics, mathematics and general literature at Yale after being graduated at the Birmingham Academy and the Connecticut State Normal School. P. B. S. Pinchback admirably united common sense with his fundamental e d u c a t i o n obtained largely at Gilmore's High School in Cincinnati, Ohio, prior to the war.

JOSEPH H. RAINEY, a member of Congress

Most of the local, State and Federal offices, however, were held not by Negroes but by southern white men, and by others who came from the North and profited by the prostration of the South. They were in many respects selfish men, but not always utterly lacking in principle. The northern whites, of course, had little sympathy for the South. They depended for their constituency upon the Negroes, who could not be expected to placate the ex-slaveholders. Being adventurers and interested in their own affairs, the carpet-baggers became unusually corrupt in certain States. They administered af-

White men in control.

[6] *Journal of Negro History*, VII, 127-171.

fairs not for the benefit of the body politic but for their own personal aggrandizement. Yet although Negroes were implicated in these offenses, few of them materially profited by this procedure. Most Negro officers who served in the South came out of office with an honorable record.

JAMES T. RAPIER, a member of Congress

Such was the case with J. T. White, Commissioner of Public Works and Internal Improvements in Arkansas; M. W. Gibbs, City Judge in Little Rock; J. C. Corbin, State Superintendent of Schools in the same State; Jonathan C. Gibbs, a Dartmouth graduate elected the first Superintendent of Public Instruction in Florida; F. L. Cardozo, State Treasurer of South Carolina; T. Morris Chester, Brigadier General in charge of the State Guards of Louisiana, and P. B. S. Pinchback, Lieutenant and Acting Governor of Louisiana. Others who held office elsewhere lived up to the same record. Chief among these may be mentioned Frederick Douglass, who served in the District of Columbia as Marshal and Recorder of Deeds and abroad as Minister to Haiti.

CHAPTER XXIV

POLITICAL RECONSTRUCTION UNDONE

WHETHER or not the Negro was capable, whether he was honest, however, had little to do with the southern white man's attitude toward the Negro officeholders. To produce evidence that the Negroes lacked these essentials, the whites well knew, would help them to justify themselves to the world for using such harsh measures to over- Prejudice a throw the new régime. But the Negro was factor. unacceptable merely because he was black, because he had not enjoyed the distinction of wringing his bread from the sweat of another's brow. Government, as the Southern man saw it, should be based on an aristocratic exploitation of the man far down. As the slaveholders had for centuries enjoyed this exclusive privilege, they could not but bear it grievously that it had been suddenly taken away.

Wherever they could, the native whites instituted government by investigation to expose all shortcomings of Negro officials. The general charge was that Corruption they were corrupt. The very persons who explained. complained of the corruption in the Negro carpet-bag governments and who effected the reorganization of the State governments in the South when the Negroes were overthrown, however, became just as corrupt as the governing class under the preceding régime. In almost every restored State government in the South, and especially in

Mississippi, the white officers in control of the funds defaulted. These persons who had been so long out of office came back so eager to get the most out of them that they filled their own pockets from the coffers of the public. No exposure followed.

In contradistinction to this rule of stealing from the public treasury, there stood out Dubuclet, the Negro who served as Treasurer of the State of Louisiana. When the government of that State was taken from the reconstructionists by the restored aristocrats, he had still two years to serve. He was investigated with a view to finding out some act of misuse of the public funds that he might be impeached and thrown

Excellent record of Dubuclet.

BISHOP L. H. HOLSEY, a factor in Reconstruction through the Church

out of office. The committee, of which E. D. White, later Chief Justice of the United States Supreme Court, was chairman, reported after much deliberation that his funds had been honestly handled and that there were no grounds on which proceedings against him could be instituted. In these investigations the political purpose was clear. For example, the Negro treasurer of South Carolina was declared a criminal for diverting funds appropriated for a definite purpose, although no theft was shown. The white treasury of "Conservative" Virginia during the reconstruction repeatedly thus diverted the money appropriated to education, but no white person thought of him as a criminal.

The gravest charge against the Negroes seemed to grow out of the unwritten law that the "superior" white race should not be ruled by its "inferiors." That there should be unusual friction in communities where persons, who a few years prior to their elevation to citizenship had served as goods and chattels, should excite little sur- **Haughtiness.** prise. The South could not appreciate a Negro in uniform or in office. But true students of history know that the Negroes were not especially anxious to put themselves forward. While there were a good many among them seeking to be placed where they could not serve, the majority of the blacks were anxious to secure the coöperation of the best whites. But the former slave-holders refused to coöperate. They believed that the Negroes should have no part in the government at all. They hoped that they could in some way effect the complete elimination of the Negro from politics, as they have done in recent years. The result, therefore, was that the Negroes were compelled in the beginning to support for office white men who had never been tried and who had in some cases given evidence of dishonest purposes.

The argument against this, however, is that the Negroes should not have been enfranchised and that the government should have been organized among the loyal whites. To this it may be replied that there were **Enfranchise-** few loyal whites, and many of those who **ment question.** pretended that they were and undertook to organize governments, proved to be just as oppressive as they ever had been. In fact, they undertook to reëstablish slavery. Had there been a close coöperation among the best whites in the South and a gradual incorporation of the intelligent freedmen into the electorate, many of the mistakes made would have been obviated; and the recent steps backward towards peonage, segregation and lynching might not have been made.

Another trouble, too, was the fear of a social upheaval. It seemed to be more probable at that time than ever before in the history of this country. The prejudice of a large number of persons of that day was based on caste rather than on color. A few white men who had long **Fear of a so-** looked with wishful eyes upon Negro **cial upheaval.** women prior to the war and could associate with them only clandestinely married such women after emancipation. A few white women having long since known of the relations of white men and Negro women, dared to

W. R. Pettiford
A Reconstructionist in the Church

break over the social barrier to marry Negro men. For this change of attitude there were various reasons. Just after emancipation the Negroes were looked upon as the "coming people." Thousands of persons were working for their uplift through the church and school. They could vote and hold office. More industrious, too, than the poor whites, the freedmen often became the more progressive element in the community. Prosperous Negro men, therefore, sometimes seemed more attractive to white women than males of their own race. Consequently a number of intermarriages followed in the various Southern States. Against this admixture, however, the press of the conservative whites persistently inveighed, but it continued in some places clandestinely a generation after emancipation.

The whites seriously objected to the granting of civic privileges to Negroes also on the ground that this would ultimately lead to miscegenation. Interpreting the liberal reconstruction constitutions and the Federal Civil Rights Law as granting mixed schools and an **Social** open door to inns, hotels and public places **privileges.** of amusement, moreover, Negroes endeavored to avail themselves of these opportunities. The whites as a majority bitterly opposed any such democratization of our institutions. Almost before the public schools could be established Southerners who had never been enthusiastic about education at public expense began to oppose the system because a few interpreted the Federal Civil Rights Law to mean the coeducation of the races. They believed that it was better to have no education at all than to have the two races attending the same school. The public schools were finally made separate, and custom and public opinion generally kept the races apart in social matters until specific laws of the restored reactionaries to this effect could be placed on the statute books.[1]

The attack on the policies of the carpet-bag governments, moreover, had the desired effect among the poor and ignorant whites. Reared under the degrading influences of slavery, they could not tolerate the blacks as citizens. The Negroes thereafter were **Ku Klux Klan.** harassed and harried by disturbing elements of anarchy, out of which soon emerged an oath-bound order called the Ku Klux Klan established to terrorize the Negroes with lawlessness and violence. The Ku Klux Klan started in Tennessee in 1865. It did its work of intimidation here and there largely by clandestine methods. In the early seventies the order proceeded to its task in bolder fashion and drew into action other lawless combinations which helped to spread terror and dismay among the Negroes. Negroes and their friends could not make a case against

[1] For a discussion of this social upheaval see *The Journal of Negro History*, IX, 249-251; and XI, 294-309.

these agents of disorder, because only native whites of proslavery sentiment could join. Proceeding at night, too,

A hooded order. in hooded white attire shaped and decorated in scarecrow fashion, they easily terrified ignorant Negroes.

Congress, therefore, deemed it necessary to pass a series of repressive measures, known as "force bills," to protect the Negroes in the enjoyment of the civil and political rights. The President was authorized to suppress insurrection in the Southern States where and when local authorities were powerless and to suspend the writ of habeas corpus. The jurisdiction of the Federal courts was so extended as to take cognizance of cases in which Negroes complained of being deprived of their rights. This legislation also contemplated the use of Federal troops to secure fair election in these States. While these measures offered temporary relief they caused such deep resentment in the South, especially among those whites who were endeavoring to suppress mob violence, that the South tended to become a smoldering volcano awaiting an opportunity for eruption.

Some of the clashes became almost as serious as the battles of the Civil War. The United States Government appointed a committee in 1870 to investigate these opera-

Inter-racial clashes. tions. The committee went throughout the reconstructed territory, sitting in various cities to take evidence. The report which the committee made consists of many volumes. The facts set forth therein show that the situation was alarming. At the same time the report shows how difficult it was to obtain evidence there because of the organized opposition of the native whites and the determination to dispatch unceremoniously any one who disclosed their operations. Men were killed at their post of duty, innocent persons were shot down in cold blood, and groups of Negroes were massacred.

The most cruel of these massacres was that which took place at Hamburg, South Carolina, in 1876. This was a sequel of the solid native white party organization which was then taking shape in the State. This was the election year of 1876, when by such methods the native whites won the day in South Carolina. The leaders of the movement had passed the word to get rid of the new **The Hamburg** régime even if it had to be done by foul **Massacre.** means. To do this they had to dispose of the Negro militia. This state guard which, under the reconstruction laws, admitted Negroes, worked the exclusion of the whites in South Carolina. Because of caste the native whites would not join. The very uniform on Negroes enraged them as a red flag does a bull. This made the fight on the militia a bloody one in South Carolina.

At Hamburg the outbreak developed in this way. Thomas Butler and Henry Getzen interfered with the drill of the local Negro militia on a back street in Hamburg on July 4, 1876. On the following day the plot was further developed by preferring against these Negroes in the local court of a Negro justice of the peace the charge of blocking the streets. By postponement for various excuses the matter was prolonged until the following Saturday. Under the direction of General M. C. Butler, of Confederate fame, the agents of disorder had then had time to organize their forces and assemble them. Hundreds of armed white men began to reach the town. The trial was ordered by Butler. After some hesitation the Negro justice of the peace appeared upon the scene. Butler then called on the Negro militiamen to apologize for the offense of blocking the streets and to surrender their arms. This they refused to do. Butler then went to Augusta, Georgia, and cannon and other munitions soon followed. The Negroes, seeing that they were outnumbered and surrounded, asked Butler whether he would protect the people if the guardsmen gave up their arms. Butler, however, gave no definite assurance. The Negroes then inquired as to whether it would be acceptable to Butler if they shipped the arms to the Governor of the State. To this he replied: "D—— the Governor." The Negroes then repaired to the armory to protect themselves, but the native whites had already begun firing. When the Negroes heard of the cannon brought from Augusta they tried to escape from the town. Two of the guardsmen had then been killed. The native whites captured twenty-seven others. Five of these were shot down in cold blood after they had surrendered. James Cook, the Negro chief of police of the town, was murdered in like manner. Commenting on this in an exaggerating fashion characteristic of pagan civilization, the *Sumter True Southron* said: "As usual in all these outbreaks the whites behaved with calmness and moderation. But we solemnly warn the colored people that these things occur too often. The white people of this State do not intend to be ridden over by ignorant and foolish Negroes who lead these riots. We may not be able to carry the State at the ballot box, but when it comes to a trial of the cartridge box we do not entertain any doubt of the result. The whites seek no contest with the colored people, but the latter must behave themselves and submit to the laws which they have made, and to office-holders whom they or their friends have placed in power."

The dénouement came from President Rutherford B. Hayes in the withdrawal of the troops to the support of whom he probably owed his doubtful election. Reconstruc-

The withdrawal of troops. tionists defeated by fraud and intimidation in South Carolina asked for troops to sustain them in office. Hayes said: "In my opinion there does not now exist in that State such domestic violence as is contemplated by the Constitution as the ground upon which the military power of the National Government

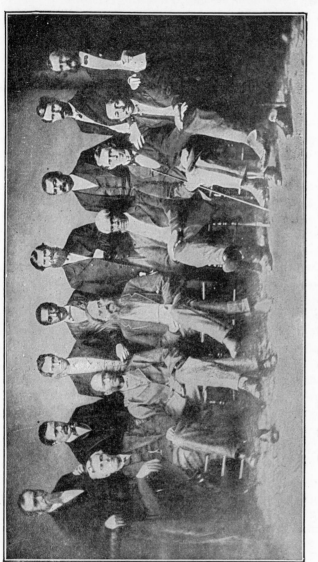

The New Freedom, the first mixed jury in the District of Columbia

may be invoked for the defense of the State, but these are settled by such orderly and peaceable methods as may be provided by the Constitution and laws of the State. I feel assured that no resort to violence is contemplated in any quarter, but that, on the contrary, the disputes in question are to be settled solely by such peaceful remedies as the Constitution and the laws of the State provide.''

The withdrawal of the national troops from the South gave much relief to the whites in that section. It pleased a majority of the Northern citizens, who, despite the efforts of the Southerners to break up the Union, could not support the policy of forever afflicting them with martial law. The Negroes and their sympathizers, however, have always considered this the most unstatesman-like act any President has committed since the war. They contend that by a corrupt bargain for the South Carolina electoral vote Hayes immediately restored to power the unreconstructed element. Because of the color and former condition of the freedmen, these reactionaries have segregated, disfranchised and lynched Negroes to the extent that the United States can now be criticized for not complying with that clause of the Constitution guaranteeing every State a republican form of government. These troops should have undoubtedly been withdrawn by gradual process, in the proportion that the districts thus relieved exhibited evidence of the ability to protect all citizens in the enjoyment of their rights and privileges.

The closing chapter of political reconstruction is its undoing. The reactionaries reclaimed the State governments from the liberal functionaries. Not only were they determined to assume exclusive control of things, but to prevent the Negroes from further participation in politics the restored caste later enacted measures which eliminated most Negroes from the electorate. This has been done on the grounds that they

The undoing of the reconstruction.

could not read and write, did not own property of a fixed value, or were not descendants of persons who had voted prior to 1866. The method last mentioned has been referred to as the "grandfather clause" because it permitted all white persons to vote if their grandfathers had formerly exercised that privilege. Mississippi set the example in 1890 by passing a law disfranchising the Negroes, South Carolina followed in her footsteps in 1895, and Louisiana added the "grandfather clause" in 1898. Other restrictive suffrage measures reaching the same end were enacted by North Carolina in 1900, by Virginia and Alabama in 1901, by Georgia in 1907, and by Oklahoma in 1910. All of these laws hedged around the Fifteenth Amendment which provides that the right to vote shall not be denied or abridged by the United States or by any State on account of race, color, or previous condition of servitude.

The reactionaries further curtailed the privileges of Negroes, moreover, by segregation laws dealing first with railway accommodations and then with schools and places of amusement. This was made possible by a number of reactionary decisions of the United States Supreme Court by which the Civil Rights Act of 1875 has been finally nullified. The first of these decisions was that of 1869 in the case of *Hall* v. *De Cuir*. In this case this tribunal set aside as unconstitutional a law of Louisiana enacted in 1869 to prevent discrimination against Negroes on railroads. The Supreme Court was of the opinion that this particular law interfered with the regulation of interstate commerce; but it has not yet felt this way about laws enacted since that time to provide for the separation of the races. Its decision in the case of *Plessy* v. *Ferguson* upheld such State measures as valid. The Fourteenth Amendment provides that no State shall make or enforce any law which shall abridge the privileges or immunities of citizens of the United States; nor shall any State deprive any person

THREE SURVIVORS OF THE RECONSTRUCTION

M. W. GIBBS   P. B. S. PINCHBACK   JAMES LEWIS

M. W. Gibbs was municipal judge in Arkansas. P. B. S. Pinch-back was elected lieutenant governor of Louisiana, served a short period as acting governor, was elected United States senator, but was not seated. James Lewis was for some years the collector of New Orleans' port.

of life, liberty, or property, without due process of law, nor deny to any person within its jurisdiction the equal protection of the laws. According to these decisions, this serves merely as a restriction on the States rather than on individuals, and it does not deprive the States of the police power exercised in forcing the Negro into the ghetto.

The chief reason given for thus abandoning the Negroes to their fate was that the State governments which they had assisted in establishing had become too corrupt for honest people to support. If rumors and misrepresentations be taken as facts, such a conclusion might easily be reached. However, investigation has shown **Corruption general.** that the Negro carpet-bag governments were just as clean as the governments of other States at that time and as clean as that of the United States itself. If those of the South were too corrupt to be sustained we had ample reason for abandoning government altogether. Never had the country heard of such malfeasance as that implied in the scandalous transactions of the "Tweed Ring," the "Credit Moblier," the "Whisky Ring," and the "Star Route Frauds." The country had gone mad with economic development. Railroads were being built here and there, sometimes in unprofitable fields, only to bring ruin to their promoters. Enterprises without capital were being financed at the expense of the people. Connected in one way or another with these corrupt machines were some of the most distinguished men in our history. Men prominent in life permitted themselves to be drawn into these "get-rich-quick" schemes with the understanding that they would use their influence to build and operate them out of the public treasury. The reconstructed States suffered from the same sort of corruption; but the actual corruption in the South was grossly exaggerated for political purposes.

The wave of fraud in the South, furthermore, had passed before reconstruction was undone. For example, in South

Carolina, the most maligned of the reconstructed States, Governor Chamberlain had actually cleaned up every department of the State. He gave the commonwealth the

Fraud at end. most respectable administration it has ever had. According to the native whites themselves, Chamberlain broke the backbone of the "Ring" and "restored decent government." He corrected the abuse of the pardoning power, appointed competent and honest men to office, rejected fraudulent claims, refunded the State debt, reduced taxes, and diminished the expenses of the State enough to save $1,719,488 in two years. *The Greenville Enterprise and Mountaineer,* therefore, said in 1875: "If Governor Chamberlain continues in the course he has so far pursued, and we have faith that he will do so, he will place his name high on the roll of great men, who have adorned the history of South Carolina. The honest citizens of the State will have reason to rejoice that he came from New England to take part in our public affairs."

Whatever may be said about the corruption in the reconstructed States, moreover, should not leave any stigma attached to the Negroes. They were participants in the rehabilitation of these commonwealths, but not the actual powers in control. At no time did the Negroes have con-

Negroes exonerated. trol of the whole government of one of these States. With the exception of South Carolina and Mississippi, moreover, the Negroes never even controlled a legislative, judicial, or executive department of these States. White men who came into the South after the Civil War and the native whites of the section coöperating with them kept the control of things during the reconstruction. This situation was aptly presented by a writer in the *Nation* in reference to South Carolina when he said that "in the distribution of its spoils, the poor African gets the gilt and plush, the porcelain spittoons, the barbaric upholstery, while the astuter Caucasian clings to the solider and more durable advantages."

In a broader sense, however, we cannot speak of reconstruction as having been undone. The far-reaching reforms set going by this upheaval can never be over- **Reconstruction** come. The reconstructionists accomplished **a success.** definite results which will continue to bear fruit as long as political and social institutions exist in this country. In overthrowing the proslavery aristocratic régime these reformers democratized the governments of the new South by establishing free manhood suffrage and apportioning representation o n t h e basis of population rather than on interests. To enlighten the poor whites as well as the Negroes the reconstructionists provided for the first public school system the South ever had. Finally, the reconstructionists instituted a social reform in abolishing such relics of barbarism as the whip-

W. J. SIMMONS

A Reconstructionist in Education

ping post, the branding iron, and the stocks. "By forty odd years," says Louis F. Post in reference to South Carolina, "those Negroes forestalled Lloyd George with his proposal for old age pensions; by nearly four they preceded Henry George in apprehending the deadly import of land monopoly." In fact, so acceptable were the new constitutions providing for these reforms that they were not

"Reform Reconstruction Members of the First South Carolina Legislature after Emancipation and Enfranchisement of All Citizens"

altered for one or two generations after the overthrow of
the reconstructionists, and then largely to eliminate the
Negro from politics. The fundamental principles of social
justice proclaimed in the reconstruction constitutions still
remain. It is true enough that the Negro was thrown out
of office, driven to the ghetto and denied education, but the
very forces which the enfranchised freedmen set going are
now gradually having such effect on the whites that they
are beginning to understand how they handicap themselves
by trying to keep the Negro down.

CHAPTER XXV

FINDING A WAY OF ESCAPE

THE abridgment of the Negroes' rights came as a calamity. For a generation following the restoration of the reactionaries to power, the Negroes were in a state of confusion; and they could not extricate themselves from their difficulties.[1] There then ensued a most cruel persecution of the blacks by the degraded and impecunious poor whites. Although assured that under the circumstances the Negroes could not soon regain their political rights, certain criminal communities found special delight in killing and lynching Negroes on account of offenses for which a white man would hardly be accused, if the complainant happened to be black. By the art of psychological appeal to the race prejudice of the masses the leading newspapers easily succeeded in convincing the public that the general cause of these lynchings was criminal assault; but statistics show that ordinary misdemeanors of Negroes were the excuses for three out of every four of these lynchings.

The untoward condition.

The extent to which the country has been disgraced by

---

[1] George W. Williams, *History of the Negro Race*, II, 375-380; C. G. Woodson, *A Century of Negro Migration*, chs. VII and VIII; *The Atlantic Monthly*, XLIV, page 222 *et seq.; The Vicksburg Commercial*, May 6, 1919; *The Nation*, XXVIII, 242, 386; *The American Journal of Social Science*, XI, 1-35; *Public Opinion*, XVIII, 370 *et seq.; The American Law Review*, XL, 29, 52, 205, 227, 381, 547, 590, 695, 758, 865, 905; *Reports of Committees of the Senate of the United States for the First and Second Sessions of the Forty-sixth Congress, 1879-1880*, pp. iii-xiii.

the institution of lynching may be more easily estimated by a few statistics. According to General Sheridan, 3,500 persons were killed in the South during the first decade after emancipation; 1,884 were killed and wounded in 1868, and probably 1,200 between 1868 and 1875. Most of these massacres occurred in the disturbed area of Louisiana. Following that period the number of Negroes annually lynched in the whole country aggregated between fifty and a hundred, and the whole number for the reconstruction and readjustment periods not less than 2,500. As the Negroes were no longer valuables attached to owners, as horses or cattle, there was little to restrain the degraded class from murdering them in communities where few white men had any conception of the blacks as persons entitled to life, liberty, and the pursuit of happiness.

Lynching.

The economic situation in the South in the meantime became critical. The poor whites, who were unwilling to labor themselves, so disturbed the Negroes that their employment was precarious. The ex-slaveholders, moreover, imposed upon the Negroes willing to work. The Negroes were the only dependable laboring class in the South, and too many were trying to live on the fruits of Negro labor. Whether aware or not of being duped, the Negroes had to seek employment by the whites, as they had no capital to operate farms and factories independently. Some of those who, during the happiest days of reconstruction, succeeded in acquiring property, saw it thereafter seized on the plea of delinquent taxes and transferred to the master class to satisfy fraudulent claims.

The economic situation.

The land in the South, moreover, remained mainly in large tracts held by planters. Except in the case of poverty, they never desired to dispose of it; and even if they had been thus inclined, the Negroes, under the existing régime, could not quickly earn sufficient money to purchase holdings. There was then no chance for the Negroes to develop at once into a desirable class of farmers. They then became mainly a wage-earning element dependent on the will of their employers. As few of the Negroes could read and write, they were cheated in signing contracts and had to suffer the consequent privations aggravated by cruelty, if they unduly complained.

Land tenure.

Except in the sugar district, the wage system of the South early failed to give satisfaction. The planters then made the experiment of working on shares, but had to abandon this because the employer was not always able to advance the Negro tenant supplies pending the growth of the crop, and some insisted that the Negro was too indifferent and lazy to make the partnership desirable. It was then decided to resort to the renting system, which became the accepted tenure in the cotton district. While this system apparently threw the tenant on his own responsibility, it frequently made him the victim of his own ignorance and the rapacity of his landlord. As the Negroes could do no better, they had to pay such high rent that they hardly derived from their labor adequate returns to support their families.

Wage system tried.

Rent system.

The worst feature of the rent plan was its iniquitous concomitant, the credit system. Having no capital to begin with, a Negro tenant became dependent on his landlord for advance of supplies of tools, food and clothing during the year, secured by a lien on the crop. As these new tenants had had only a few years of freedom to learn business methods, they became a prey to dishonest men. Through their stores and banks they extorted from the Negroes practically all of their earnings

The credit system.

before the end of the year. A few honest planters desired to protect the Negroes by supplying them at reasonable prices; but, subject to usury themselves, their efforts availed little. It was necessary then for the Negro tenant to begin the year with three mortgages, covering all he owned, his labor for the coming year, and all he expected to acquire during that twelvemonth. According to an observer of the time, he paid "one-third of his product for the use of the land; he paid an exorbitant fee for recording the contract, by which he paid his pound of flesh; he was charged two or three times as much as he ought to pay for ginning his cotton; and, finally, he turned over his crop to be eaten up in commissions, if any was still left to him."

Various means of escape from these conditions were therefore considered. Believing that a reconstructed Republican Party would again interfere in southern affairs to relieve the freedmen, some Negroes looked forward to a change in politics. Others had the idea that religion would be the solution of the problem. They insisted that the calamities of the race resulted as an affliction with which they had been visited because of their wandering away from God. He would right their wrongs as soon as they heeded His pleading voice.

Remedies proposed.

The unrest, however, first found a safety valve in the exodus of the Negroes. During the seventies a considerable number of them moved from North Carolina to Indiana. Because of the pivotal political situation in that State their hasty migration gave rise to the accusation that they were being brought thither for the purpose of carrying doubtful States for the Republican Party. A Congressional investigation proved that these charges were absurd. The larger number of the Negroes who were induced to migrate during this period went not to Indiana but to Kansas, because of its known attitude towards the black man as evidenced by its willingness to bleed in behalf of freedom.

This movement was organized. It was promoted by two men who were not widely known as race leaders but attained distinction as the organizers of one of the most disturbing migrations ever effected among Negroes. They were Henry Adams of Louisiana and Benjamin or "Pap" Singleton of Tennessee. Seeing that the Negroes had almost lost the fruits of their emancipation and that there was little hope that their situation would be greatly improved, they had organized a committee which they later increased by the hundreds. They circulated information as to the intolerable oppression of the blacks and the opportunities in the West for relief. In this way, according to these promoters, they interested 100,000 or 200,000 Negroes, although not more than one-fourth or one-fifth of this number actually went West.

The exodus to the West.

This unusual movement of the Negroes threatened the South with economic ruin. The thinking class saw that the section was soon to lose the economic foundation of its prosperity, and that if something were not speedily done the land would doubtless become a waste place in the wilderness. Meetings, therefore, were called among the whites and the blacks to induce the latter to remain where they were. The most important meeting of this kind was that held at Vicksburg, Mississippi, on May 6, 1879. There were assembled the representatives of the best of both races seeking to reach some conclusion as how to deal with the situation. Frank expressions as to the causes of the grievances were made on both sides, and most persons concerned were willing to make such sacrifices of personal feeling and opinion as to remedy the evils of which the Negroes complained.

Alarm among the planters.

Unwilling to rely upon moral suasion, however, the whites resorted to force to stop the exodus. They denied the Negroes transportation and imprisoned them on false

charges. But Negroes to the number of many thousands
The resort   continued their way West despite this opposi-
to force.   tion—despite even the discouragement of their
greatest leader, Frederick Douglass. He advised them to
the contrary, believing that it would be better for the
blacks to remain in the South where they would have suffi-

R. T. GREENER

cient numbers to wield political
power. The promoters of the
movement were fortunate in
having the support of Richard
T. Greener and John M. Langston. Having sufficient foresight to see that the United
States Government would not
soon interfere in behalf of the
Negroes in the South, these men
advised them to flee from political oppression to a free country.
They considered it a hopeful
sign that the blacks had passed through that stage of
development of appealing to philanthropy into that of
appealing to themselves.

This rapid migration was soon checked, but the Negroes
gradually found their way into the West, into the Southwest
and into the industrial centers of the Appalachian Moun-
The migration tains. The masses of the Negroes, however,
checked.   became settled in the South in a condition not
much better than their former state; for the planters forgot
their promises of better treatment just as soon as the exodus
ceased. The economic adjustment after the Civil War,
culminating in the resumption of specie payments in 1879,
moreover, brightened somewhat the dark age through
which the South was passing. During the eighties and
nineties, however, the masses of Negroes could do little more
than eke out an existence. Following this period some

of them prospered sufficiently to appreciate the difference between free and slave labor. The income of the average Negro even then, however, was very small. The most fortunate Negro tenants or farmers did not generally come to the end of the year with more than they needed to keep them while producing their crop during the next. The rural wage earner did well to receive for his toil, from sunrise to sunset, twenty-five or forty cents a day, including board restricted to half a gallon of meal and half a pound of fat bacon. Mechanics believed that they were highly favored when they earned from seventy-five cents to a dollar and a half a day.

In the midst of such circumstances the Negroes could not establish homes and educate their children. It was of much assistance to the Negroes in the

J. C. PRICE

South, however, that the North raised considerable money and sent some of its best citizens to found institutions for the enlightenment of the freedmen. This **Education** philanthropic scheme presupposed that educa- **tried.** tion in the classical field was the urgent need of Negroes, in that it was essential to a proper understanding of the problems of government, and that when this was supplied the masses thus enlightened would have an advantage by which they could triumph over all opposition. Heeding this call to avail themselves of such opportunities, Negroes not only crowded such institutions as Howard,

Fisk, Lincoln, Morehouse, and Atlanta, but began to establish higher institutions of their own. Out of these schools came not many scholars, but enthusiastic teachers devoted to the enlightenment of their people, a large number

KELLY MILLER

of race-leading preachers proclaiming religion as the solution of the problem, many well informed orators, like J. C. Price and William Pickens, and educating controversialists, like Kelly Miller and W. E. B. DuBois. Under different conditions these men, no doubt, would have been historians, scientists, or mathematicians, but their race was passing through the ordeal of kith and kin democracy. Their talent had to be impressed into the service of exposing the folly of the reactionaries promoting the return to medieval civilization in proscribing the citizenship of the Negroes.

The majority of the Negroes in the South finally became **Resignation** settled to conditions as they were, endeavor-**to fate.** ing to make the most of an undesirable situation; but Negroes who had experienced mental development and had had their hearts fired with the desire to enjoy the rights so eloquently set forth by their uncompromising leaders, contrived to escape from their political and civic humiliation. To these Negroes of talent it seemed that the South would never be a decent place to live in;

for even the North was then turning a deaf ear to the pleadings of their spokesmen sent thither to portray to the children of the Negroes' former friends exactly how the fruits of their victory for human rights had been so quickly permitted to perish from the earth. After the reconstruction period the North was too busy in developing its industries and had established too close relations with the South to think of severing these ties. The prevailing opinion was that the South should be permitted to deal with the Negroes as it felt disposed.

As the South, in this position of renewed supremacy, became increasingly intolerant of the talented freedmen, many of them left. To this the whites offered no objection whatever. The exodus of the intelligent Negroes was much desired by the southerners. Every one migrating diminished the chances of the Negro for mental development, a thing which most southerners believed spoils the Negro. It has been the policy of most Anglo-Saxon nations to keep in ignorance the exploited races, that in their ignorant state the one group may be arrayed against the other to prevent them from reaching the point of self-assertion. In keeping with that same policy southerners would not only discourage but would have little dealing with the talented Negroes; and in making desire father to the thought, insisted that there were no intelligent Negroes. Well might some sections reasonably reach this conclusion as to the mental development of the Negroes, if it is to be judged by the amount of money spent for their education. In its backward state the South could not afford large appropriations for education; but in most of the districts the Negro public schools were almost a mockery. With the exception of the State industrial schools almost no provision at all was made for the higher education of the Negro after the undoing of reconstruction. Elementary schools were generally neglected

Cruelty of the restored South.

and secondary schools hardly existed at public expense. The per capita expenditure for educating the Negro child was about one-fourth of that for the white.

In the effort to get away from the South there was a renewal of the colonization scheme under the leadership of
Colonization again. Bishop H. M. Turner. With the encouragement of Senator Morgan, of Alabama, it seemed that the plan might prove feasible. After the reactionaries had well completed the task of depriving the Negroes of their rights, Morgan believed that they should then go to a foreign land to develop independently a nation of their own. Some thought again of Africa as the place of refuge, but the memory of the antebellum struggle of the free Negroes to defeat that enterprise made that continent too frightening to attract many. In the early nineties a few Negroes emigrated to Mapimi, Mexico, from which, after some hardships, they returned to their homes in Georgia and Alabama. Resorting to Africa then, 197 Negroes sailed from Savannah, Georgia, for Liberia in 1895. The expedition to Liberia was not as unsuccessful as that to Mexico, but in carrying out their plan the deportationists soon discovered that it is impossible to expatriate a whole race. Liberia at that time, moreover, was not doing well. Under President Edward James Roye, the country made the all but fatal mistake of borrowing £100,000 from the British. The transaction was

BISHOP H. M. TURNER, a fearless spokesman for his people

handled in such a manner that Liberia lost rather than gained by this supposed aid. Gloom and depression then hovered over Liberia for years to come.

Many of the talented Negroes who had been conspicuous in politics, thereafter decided to yield to the white man's control, and devoted themselves to the accumulation of wealth. But, as hell is never full and the eyes of man are never satisfied, the mere domina- **Terrorism.** tion did not meet all of the requirements of the degraded class of whites. Slavery had made them brutal. They had been accustomed to drive, to mutilate, to kill Negroes, and such traits could not be easily removed. The reign of terror, ostensibly initiated to overthrow the carpet-bag governments by means of the Ku Klux Klan, continued, and it became a special delight for the poor whites to humiliate and persecute the Negroes who had acquired education and accumulated some wealth. The effort was to make the Negro realize that he lives in a white man's country in which law for the Negro is the will of the white man with whom he meets. The Negroes had to undergo punishment for presuming to assume the reins of government during the reconstruction. They had to be convinced that this country will never permit another such revolution. Further legislation to restrict suffrage inalterably to the whites, to deprive Negroes of the right to serve in the State militia, to segregate them in public conveyances, and to exclude them from places of entertainment, soon followed as a necessity for maintaining white supremacy, so precarious has its tenure at times seemed.

At the same time the laboring Negroes not only saw themselves overwhelmed by a rent and credit system which would not pass away, but lost further ground in the new form of slavery called peonage. This once had legal sanction in Alabama, Florida, Georgia, **Peonage.** Mississippi, North Carolina, and South Carolina. It was a sort of involuntary servitude by which the laborer is considered bound to serve his master until a debt he has contracted is paid. The origin of this was in a custom in Mexico, and the opportunity lay in the poverty of the Negroes who had to borrow from the whites. In working to pay these debts they must still borrow to live. As the white man was the bookkeeper and his statement of account was law in the courts, it was the former master's prerogative to say how much the peon owed, to determine exactly when he should leave his service, or whether he should ever leave it.

Peons during these years were recruited from the chain gang. In collusion with courts arranging with the police **Peonage and** to arrest a required number of Negroes to **the courts.** secure the desired amount in fees and fines, innocent Negroes were commonly apprehended. When fined in court they had to agree to enter the service of some white man who would pay their fines for the opportunity to reduce them to involuntary servitude. A brief account from one of these peonage districts is sufficient to illustrate this point. Passing along the street where a Negro was employed by a white man, a sympathetic observer noticed that his employer frequently kicked and cuffed the Negro when he was not working satisfactorily. "Why do you stand this? Why do you not have this man arrested for assault?" inquired the observer. "That is just the trouble now," responded the Negro. "I complained to the court when another white man beat me, and the judge imposed upon me a fine which I could not pay, so I have to work it out in the service of this man who paid it to have the opportunity to force me to work for him." Inasmuch as some Negroes died of starvation and exposure in unhealthy quarters while others were actually killed, the fate of the chain gang peon might have been the lesser of two evils. The Supreme Court of the United States undertook to put an end to peonage in 1911 by declaring the Alabama law unconstitutional. But in the many districts, where there is no healthy public opinion to the contrary or where the employer is a law unto himself, peonage has continued in spite of the feeble effort of the Federal Government to eradicate the evil.

These increasing encroachments convinced many thinking Negroes that they should no longer endure such humiliation. They could not adequately educate their children at public expense, although taxed to support the public schools; they enjoyed little security **Negroes going North.** in the possession of property, and dared not defend their families from insult. Their first thought, then, was to go North. For more than a century the North, despite its lack of hospitality for the Negroes, had remained in their minds as a place of refuge. From time immemorial Negroes had gone to that section, and sometimes in considerable numbers. During the nineties and the first decade of the present century these numbers decidedly increased and brought nearer home to the North the so-called race problem.

There went first the dethroned politicians who, when failing to secure employment in Washington, endeavored to solve the problem by migration. A few Negroes well established in business, moreover, closed up **Politicians leaving the South.** their affairs and moved out. The educated Negroes—especially the Negro college graduates who were imbued with the principles of justice set forth by Pickens, Trotter and DuBois—had too much appreciation for freedom to remain longer where they were politically and socially proscribed. A few professional men, who under the undesirable conditions were reduced to want, also made their escape. Intelligent laborers who knew that they were not receiving the proper returns from their labor tired also of the ordeal and went in due time to try life in other parts. In fact, this slow but steady migration was a gradual drawing off from the South of the most advanced classes, those best qualified to lead the race more rapidly toward achievement. In its backward state, however, the South could not appreciate this loss, so willing has it been to pay the high cost of race prejudice.

The undesirable feature of this migration was that it was mainly to the cities. The hostility of the trades unions to the Negroes was already a handicap rendering **The rush to** their presence in large northern cities a **cities.** problem. The increase of numbers resulting from this new influx aggravated the situation. It was further aggravated in the course of time when, because of the increasing popularity of the North, many Negroes "just happened" to go. Some went on excursions to Columbus, Indianapolis, Chicago, Cleveland, and the like, and never returned South. In the North, moreover, educated Negroes had to follow drudgery. Not many could practice professions or work at skilled labor as they could in the South. Hoping that at some time the fates would bring it to pass that they would secure an economic foundation in the North, they were, then, willing to pay this price for social and political rights. The attainment of the economic objective, notwithstanding some encouraging events, however, has been a battle against well-established precedents in the effort to maintain the supremacy of the laboring whites. They feel that they should not be compelled to compete with Negroes. In labor, as in other things, they contend, the sphere of great remuneration must be restricted to the white man, and drudgery to the Negro.

Some systematic efforts were made to break down the barriers of these trades unions. White men, like Eugene V. Debs, high in the councils of these bodies, attacked this medieval attitude of the white laborers, but to no avail.

As Negroes in the North and West, therefore, were pitted against the trades unions, they engendered much feeling between the races by allying themselves with the capitalists to serve as strikebreakers. **Trades unions.** In this case, however, the trades unions themselves were to be blamed. The only time the Negroes could work under such circumstances was when the whites were striking, and it is not surprising that some of them easily yielded then to the temptation. In those unions in which the Negroes were recognized, they stood with their white co-workers in every instance of making a reasonable demand of their employers. Some of these unions, however, accepted Negroes merely as a subterfuge to prevent them from engaging in strikebreaking. When the Negroes appealed for work, identifying themselves as members of the union in control, they were turned away with the explanation that no vacancies existed, while at the same time white men were gladly received.

As a rule, therefore, the Negroes migrating to the North had to do menial service. It was pathetic for the traveler to see Negroes, once well established in a business in the South, reduced to service as porters to earn **In menial** a living in the North. The Negroes were so **service.** scattered in the North that they did not supply the opportunity for mutual help. Since the whites were not willing to concede economic opportunity, the northern Negroes were, so to speak, isolated in the midst of a medieval civilization founded on the caste of color. While the migrating Negroes of intelligence hid their lights under a bushel in the North, the illiterate Negroes in the South, in need of their assistance in education and enterprise, too often fell into the hands of the harpies and **Results in** sharks. Many of these white impostors had **the South.** the assistance of unscrupulous Negroes in plundering these unfortunates.

There came forward then a Negro with a new idea. He said to his race: "Cast down your buckets where you are." In other words, the Negroes must work out their salvation in the South. He was a native of Virginia. He had

Booker T. Washington's idea.

been trained at Hampton and under adverse circumstances had founded a school in Alabama, which afforded him the opportunity to study the Negroes in all their aspects. Seeing that the need of the Negro was a foundation in things economic, he came forward with the bold advocacy of industrial education of the Negroes "in those arts and crafts in which they are now employed and in which they must exhibit greater efficiency if they are to compete with the white men." The world had heard this before from Pestalozzi, Owen, Douglass and Armstrong, but never before had an educator so expounded this doctrine as to move the millions. This man was Booker T. Washington.

BOOKER T. WASHINGTON

The celebrated pronunciamento of Washington was well set forth in his address at the Atlanta Exposition in 1895.

The Atlanta address.

His educational theory and practice have not since ceased to be a universal topic. He insisted that since the Negroes had to toil they should be taught to toil skillfully. He did not openly attack higher education for Negroes, but insisted that in getting an education they should be sure to get some of that which they can use. In other words, the only education worth while is that which reacts on one's life in his peculiar situation. A youth, then, should not be educated away from his environment, but trained to lay a foundation for the future in his present situation, out of which he may emerge into something above and beyond his beginnings.

Washington's plan was received by the white people in the South as a safe means by which they could promote Negro education along lines different from those followed in the education of the white man. They desired to make education mean one thing for the whites and another for the Negroes. The North was at first divided on the question. The sympathetic class felt that such a **Washington's** policy would reduce the Negroes as a whole to **plan accepted.** a class of laborers and thus bar them from the higher walks of life through which the race must come to recognition and prominence. The wealthy class of whites in the North took the position that there was much wisdom in Washington's policy. With the encouragement which they have given his industrial program, with the millions with which they have endowed Tuskegee and Hampton, and with the support given the many other schools established on that basis, they brought most northern people around to their way of thinking in less than a generation.

With exception of a small minority, the Negroes, however, regarded this policy as a surrender to the oppressors who desired to reduce the whole race to menial service, and they proceeded militantly to attack Washington. They branded him with the opprobrium of a traitor **Opposition to** to his people. In the course of time, however, **Washington.** the South, following the advice and example of Washington, reconstructed its educational system for Negroes and began to supply these schools with faculties recommended by men interested in industrial education and too often by Washington himself. The South thus gradually elevated to leadership many Negroes who, in standing for industrial education, largely increased the support of Washington among his people. When, moreover, his influence as an educator extended into all ramifications of life, even into politics, to the extent that he dictated the rise and fall of

W. E. B. DuBois

all Negroes occupying positions subject to the will of the whites, that constituency was so generally increased that before he died there were few Negroes who dared criticize him in public or let it be known that they were not in sympathy with his work.

Against this policy, however, there always stood forth some Negroes who would not yield ground. The most outspoken among these were W. M. Trotter and W. E. B. DuBois. These men have had the idea that the first efforts to secure recognition for the Negro must come through agitation for higher education and political equality. What they de- **Trotter and** mand for the Negro is the same opportunity, **DuBois.** the same treatment, generally given the white man. To accept anything less means treachery. Feeling that Washington's position was a compromise on these things, they persistently denounced him from the rostrum and through the press in spite of the great personal sacrifices which they thereby suffered. DuBois lost the support of white friends who cannot understand why all Negroes do not think alike, and Trotter suffered unusual humiliation because he undertook by unlawful means to break up one of Washington's meetings in Boston.

This agitation has exhibited evidences of unusual vitality. It has given rise to widely circulated organs which stand for equal rights a n d equal opportunities—in short, for a square deal for all men regardless of race, color or previous condition of servitude. One of these, *The Crisis*, is now a self-supporting popular magazine with a circulation of almost 100,000. It is the organ of the National Association for the Advancement of Colored People, a movement launched by the remnant of the aboli-

OSWALD GARRISON VILLARD

tionists in connection with the militant Negroes. Among its makers are William English Walling, a popular author; Charles Edward Russell, a most liberal journalist; Mary W. Ovington, the indefatigable worker; W. E. B. DuBois, the radical thinker; Oswald Garrison Villard, the grandson of William Lloyd Garrison; Moorfield Storey, one of the most prominent members of the American Bar; Joel E. Spingarn, a scholar of national reputation; Jane Addams, the social reformer; and A. H. Grimké, a fearless advocate of equality for all. While at times the Association and its promoters may have gone rather far in blaming Washington for his silence, it has nevertheless kept before the Negroes the ideal which they must attain if they are to count as a significant factor in this country.

Washington's long silence as to the rights of the Negro, however, did not necessarily mean that he was in favor of the oppression of the race. He was aware of the fact that **An unjust** the mere agitation for political rights at that **criticism.** time could not be of much benefit to the race, and that their economic improvement, a thing fundamental in real progress, could easily be promoted without incurring

the disapproval of the discordant elements in the South. He may be justly criticized for permitting himself to be drawn into certain entanglements in which he of necessity had to make some blunders. As an educator, however, he stands out as the greatest of all Americans, the only man in the Western Hemisphere who has succeeded in effecting a revolution in education. A few centuries h e n c e, when this country becomes sufficiently civi-

MOORFIELD STOREY, President of the National Association for the Advancement of Colored People

lized to stand the truth about the Negro, history will record that Booker T. Washington, in trying to elevate his oppressed people, so admirably connected education with the practical things of life that he effected such a reform in the education of the world as to place himself in the class with Pestalozzi, Froebel and Herbart. Seeing that the white people have realized that industrial education is not only a good thing for the Negro but a blessing to the white man, the Negroes as a whole have little to say now against his educational policy. The whites have accordingly proceeded to spend millions of dollars for buildings and equipment to secure these advantages to their youth. Washington's advocacy of industrial education, moreover, in spite of all that has been said, was not a death blow to higher education for the Negro. That movement has lived in spite of opposition. Washington himself frequently stated that industrial education, as he emphasized it, was for the masses of the people who had to toil. Knowing that the race had to have men to lead it onward, he did not object to higher education. To-day Hampton and Tuskegee, the exponents of this idea, are offering college courses and may soon be reorganized as universities.

CHAPTER XXVI

ACHIEVEMENTS IN FREEDOM

DURING these stormy years most Negroes had all sorts of advice. They were told how they might emerge from the muddle of controversy about the best solution of their prob-

An era of progress. lems; but they did not all spend their time in academic discussion. Building upon the foundation that they made before the Civil War, the Negroes soon developed into one of the most constructive elements in our economic system.[1] The census of 1910 shows that although the Negroes constituted about thirty per cent of the population of the South, more than half of the agricultural laborers of that section were Negroes. In the main, moreover, the Negroes were useful citizens, showing little tendency to become peddlers, agents, and impostors who make their living robbing the people. On the corners of the streets in some cities there might be found a few Negroes who were not disposed to work for a living, but these constituted a small fraction of one per cent of the Negro population of the United States.

The census reports will help us further to determine what the Negroes in this country had been doing. In 1910, 5,192,535, or 71 per cent, of the 7,317,922 Negroes between

[1] The statistics bearing on the progress of the Negro are found in the *United States Census Reports*. Other valuable facts may be obtained from Monroe N. Work's *Negro Year Book* and the files of *The Crisis*. There is also Mr. Henry E. Baker's informing article on *The Negro in the Field of Invention* (in the *Journal of Negro History*, II, 21-36). Dr. Thomas J. Jones's *Negro Education* in two volumes throws light on what has been going on in that field during the last half century.

the ages of ten years and over were engaged in agriculture, forestry and animal husbandry. In the number employed in agriculture were included 893,370 farmers, **Occupations** planters and overseers; 218,972 were owners, **of Negroes.** 672,964 tenants, and 1,434 managers. Owners free of debt possessed 8,835,857 acres, owners having mortgaged farms had 4,011,491, and part owners, 2,844,188. There were 12,876,308 acres operated by cash tenants, 13,691,494 by share tenants, and 349,779 by managers. This area of 42,279,510 acres will appear more significant when one realizes that it is as large as New England, or Belgium and Holland combined.

The field in which most Negroes had been employed is agriculture, and next to that domestic and personal service. While in most of the unskilled occupations the Negroes constituted a larger percentage than their per- **Unskilled** centage of the entire population, the increas- **labor.** ing number of skilled laborers had reduced the percentage of unskilled laborers from a very high mark to about seventy per cent. The standard of the unskilled laborer, moreover, had been raised, peonage had been gradually giving way to a system of wages, and the intelligence of the workmen had been increased. Negro laborers had become so dependable that, despite the large influx of immigrants, they had been able to withstand the competition. So much improvement in the unskilled Negro laborer had been made during the previous generation that his increasing efficiency had rendered difficult the distinction between the skilled and unskilled laborer.

Other statistics as to the number of Negroes employed at skilled labor will further emphasize this point. According to the census of 1910 there were among the males, 12,401 brick and stone masons, 9,727 black- **Skilled** smiths, 8,035 glaziers, painters and varnishers, **labor.** 6,175 plasterers, 5,188 locomotive firemen, 4,802 stationary

A Negro Country Seat, the home of Scott Bond

engineers, 3,296 machinists and millwrights, 2,304 coopers, 2,285 plumbers, and gas and steam fitters, 2,156 molders, and 4,652 tailors. At the same time there were among the females, 38,148 dressmakers and seamstresses, 8,267 operators in cigar and tobacco factories, and 6,163 employed in general manufacturing.

Building upon these achievements in labor, the Negroes had towered higher and higher in the professions. In 1910 one Negro out of every 146 was engaged in some professional pursuit, whereas one white person in **Negroes in** every 51 was thus engaged. The proportion **professions.** of clergymen among Negroes exceeded that among the whites, but in the other cases the whites showed the excess of the ratio of population to professional workers. While it appears that professions among Negroes were still undermanned, a decided increase in this direction had been noted during the past generation. It meant a great deal to be able after forty-five years of freedom to produce 29,485 teachers, 5,606 musicians and teachers of music, 3,077 physicians and surgeons, 478 dentists, 798 lawyers, 123 chemists, 329 artists, sculptors and teachers of art, 247 authors, editors and reporters, 59 architects, and 237 civil engineers. That in half a century they had achieved enough in the professions to bring them within the range of comparison with the whites is striking evidence of the ability of the Negro to meet the test of competition.

This growing usefulness of the Negro in the new fields had made a corresponding reduction in the numbers of those disposed to waste their time. The criminal class of the Negroes in America, therefore, had decidedly improved, despite the reports to the **Less crime.** contrary. These false alarms were based largely on unwarranted charges growing out of the convict lease system and the imposition of unjust fines for ordinary misdemeanors and such petty offenses as vagrancy. The attitude of the Negroes themselves toward maintaining the peace was well reflected in their efforts to better conditions by establishing law and order leagues working in cooperation with the local governments. To further this cause the Negroes once had the coöperation of Southern white men who, believing in justice for all, had tried to

THE RESIDENCE OF MADAME C. J. WALKER

improve rather than exterminate the Negro. These citizens were endeavoring to understand the causes of crimes of the whites against Negroes, as well as crimes of the latter. Both races, too, were much aided by the abolition of the liquor traffic.

The actual forces which have in general effected the improvement in the Negro race, however, have been strictly Negro organizations themselves. Chief among these were the Negro churches, social welfare agencies, and schools.

Achievements In Freedom

PROMINENT CHURCHMEN OF THEIR TIME

BISHOP G. C. CLEMENT   BISHOP R. A. CARTER

BISHOP R. E. JONES   BISHOP B. F. LEE

In 1906 the Negroes of white denominations had 6,210 churches with 514,571 communicants, 5,330 Sunday schools, **Churches as factors.** 293,292 scholars, and property worth $12,107,-655. The independent Negro denominations had 33,220 churches with 3,789,898 communicants, 30,999 Sunday schools, 1,452,095 scholars, and property valued at $45,191,422. These churches were in the main Baptist and Methodist. The latter comprised four distinct groups, known as the African Methodist Episcopal Church, the African Methodist Episcopal Zion Church, the Colored Methodist Episcopal Church, and the Negro membership of the Methodist Episcopal Church. But the Baptists, until the schism of 1916, had only one national organization. This exercised loose supervision over the whole denomination. Although smaller in numbers, however, these various Methodist churches succeeded in accomplishing much by their well-constructed organizations through their forty-three well-informed bishops and enterprising general officers. The work of other denominations, like the Episcopalians, the Presbyterians, Congregationalists and the Catholics, became very effective also in Negro uplift wherever they secured a following.

Coöperating with these, labored the 3,077 physicians, surgeons, and dentists, preachers of health, supplementing the work of the ministers of the gospel. They were able to **Physicians.** direct the attention of entire communities to the necessity of observing the laws of health and of making the community a decent place to live in. These well-trained Negroes thereby decidedly supplemented the serious work of the Anti-Tuberculosis League and the American Hygiene Association, and extended the operations of the annual school conferences held at Atlanta University, Hampton, and Tuskegee. So much good was so readily accomplished by the staff of workers lecturing to the soldiers in the camps on social hygiene that national bodies promoting health later paid more attention to the problems of Negroes. As a result of this persistent struggle against ignorance, poverty and negligence, the mortality rate among Negroes has decreased and much improvement has been noted in their physique.

To do for the race some of the things which the church had not accomplished, social welfare work was undertaken among Negroes decades ago. The first colored Young Men's Christian Association was organized in Washington, D. C., in 1853 by Anthony Bowen, a man of color; the second in Charleston, South Carolina, in 1866; and the third in New York City in 1867. **Work of the Y. M. C. A.** The first colored Student Association was organized at Howard University in 1869. E. V. C. Eato, of the New York City Branch, attended the Montreal Convention in 1867 as the first Negro delegate thus to serve. In 1876 George D. Brown, ex-Confederate soldier, was appointed to supervise the Negro branches of the Young Men's Christian Association throughout the country. In 1888, however, the lamented William A. Hunton, a man of color, who had served as general secretary of the Negro Young Men's Christian Association of Norfolk, Virginia, was appointed to succeed Brown. Thereafter the work was placed altogether under the supervision of Negro secretaries.

The work was widely extended with some difficulty. It was given much needed impetus by the accession to the ranks of enterprising secretaries laboring in many cities and in most Negro schools of the South. Interesting here and there the many persons who were against the movement because of its discrimination as **The growth.** to race, these gentlemen gradually worked their way into the very hearts of indifferent communities. Now in almost all of the large cities where Negroes are found in considerable numbers, business and professional men of both races, thanks to the noble example set by the large donations of Julius Rosenwald, have united to establish for Negroes branches of the Young Men's Christian Association. In these they enjoy a comradeship and temporary homelike life which the transient of color could not theretofore find in those cities. Recently an effort has been made to provide for young women in these centers the same facilities. The success of the useful branches of the Young Women's Christian Association already established in New York, Washington, Louisville and St. Louis, has been sufficient encouragement to the authorities in charge to provide elsewhere similar facilities for women of color.

As a result of the work of these agencies the home life of the Negroes has been decidedly improved. Every Negro, of course, has not heeded the advice of his friends, and the **Improvements in homes.** fact that some have lagged behind while others have gone forward makes it no longer possible to speak of all Negroes as belonging to two classes. Before the Civil War Negroes were referred to as slaves and worthless free persons of color. Negro homes now show the same difference in standards as found among the whites. The majority of Negroes have advanced beyond the point of being satisfied with a one-roomed hut conspicuous by its lack of ordinary comforts. They are buying land and building houses of several rooms. An effort is made to decorate the walls and supply the home with adequate furniture. Negro children attending school read the latest books, newspapers and magazines. Where the evidence of such progress is not manifest it is possible in most cases to show that, because of economic conditions, the Negroes concerned have been too much handicapped by poverty to improve their situation as they would like. Recent improvements in their economic situation, however, have made these conditions exceptions to the rule.

For the remaking of Negroes most credit must be given to the schools at work among them. The teacher has made

the school, the school has figured largely in the making of
the home, and the home has produced a new   **The efforts**
civilization. Yet, despite the efforts of kindly   **of schools.**
disposed educators like Ruffner, Curry, and Dillard, the
facilities for education offered Negroes in the public schools
of the South have been unusually meager, hardly extending beyond that of teaching them to read and write. But

there have been offered
in schools maintained in
the South by Northern
philanthropy opportuni-
ties for so much en-
lightenment that teachers
going out from these in-
stitutions have come to
their people like missionaries inspired to preach a
new gospel to the lowly.
Lincoln and Wilberforce
Universities set a high
standard for the educa-
tion of the Negroes prior
to the Civil War. How-
ard University, under

JULIUS ROSENWALD

its distinguished founder, General O. O. Howard, undertook to equip for leadership a number of youths of color
to toil for the enlightenment of their people in higher
pursuits. This was the first Negro university. A large
number of other philanthropists having the same ideals
as the founders of these institutions, established schools
like Fiske, Atlanta, Tougaloo, Talladega,   **Industrial**
Morehouse, Livingstone, Knoxville, Lane, and   **schools.**
Straight. Then came Hampton, Tuskegee and the like, to
direct attention primarily to the education of the masses in
things fundamental so as to enable the youth to begin with

life where he is and to make of it what his opportunities will permit.

Meeting thus in a way almost every need for Negro education, offering facilities for training of all sorts, the Negro schools have been very successful. They owe much to the impetus given them by such philanthropists as William H. Baldwin, Jr., Robert C. Ogden, H. H. Rogers, John D. Rockefeller, Andrew Carnegie, and Julius Rosenwald through their liberal contributions

Aid from philanthropists.

ANDREW CARNEGIE. The donor of $600,000 to Tuskegee. The first philanthropist to set the example of giving large sums of money for the elevation and development of the Negro race.

to the establishment and the development of various institutions. Negro education may at times have been ill-directed, in that persons, without giving due consideration to their capacity and opportunities, have wasted time undertaking to master things to which they were not adapted and which they would never have to do; but the readjustment has worked out in such a way that Negroes, like the whites, now have opportunities to equip themselves for whatever they feel disposed to do. In action they have exhibited the same mental endowment found among the ranks of all other races.

The good work of these institutions has been effective in putting the race on its feet, so to speak, in enabling the Negro to do for himself what the thousands of sympathetic and benevolent whites of the missionary spirit had to do

JOHN D. ROCKEFELLER AND HIS SON. Through appropriations of the General Education Board and the Laura Spelman Rockefeller Memorial large sums have come from these philanthropists to agencies engaged in the uplift and the education of the Negro.

Copyright by Underwood & Underwood.

for the helpless freedmen immediately after the Civil War. Out of these schools have come thousands of Negroes of **Trained leadership.** scholarly tendencies. In devoting their time and means to the study of educational problems and school administration, they have equipped themselves for leadership in education in the South. It has for some time been a matter of much regret that white persons

R. R. MOTON, the Principal of Tuskegee

in charge of schools in the South, maintained by philanthropy, have failed to recognize this ability of the Negro and still adhere to the policy of restricting them to subordinate positions. Negroes have borne it grievously that they have had to contend with white persons who feel that whenever a Negro is given a position of responsibility he needs careful watching or supervision by some wise white man that it may be done in keeping with an established policy.

The Negroes have not only learned lessons in religion, **Progress in business.** education and health, but have shown unusual progress in the business world. They have accumulated so much property in the rural districts that they constitute a desirable class of small farmers. In the cities in which recently there has taken place the concentration of large numbers of Negroes, enterprising men of color are gradually taking over business formerly monopolized by whites. Near a Negro church you will find an undertaker of color. In almost any Negro urban community one sees a successful real estate dealer, a reliable contractor, an insurance office, and sometimes a bank. So popular has it become for Negroes to deal with their own people that white men owning business in Negro sections have learned to employ considerable Negro help.

The Negro in business, however, is not a new thing. The point to be noted here is the unusual progress of the race in this field during recent years. It is more Unusual than encouraging, moreover, to observe how achievements. easily the Negroes have learned the lesson of pooling their efforts in larger enterprises. To promote the economic progress of the race, Negroes have been wise enough to organize several efficient agencies. The first of these to attain importance was the National Business League founded by Dr. Booker T. Washington. There are also the National Negro Bankers' Association, the National Association of Funeral Directors, and the National Negro Retail Merchants' Association. Negro fraternal organizations, although established for social purposes, have taken on a business aspect in recent years in providing for the purchase of property and the insurance of the lives of their members. In some parts of the South the Negroes use no other insurance. The managers of this work constitute in reality an industrial insurance company. The Negroes have about sixty banks and fifteen insurance companies, four of which are regular old line life insurance companies. In 1910, 3,208 Negroes were employed in banking and brokerage, 2,604 in insurance, and 1,095 in real estate.

Among these captains of industry thus pressing forward should be mentioned John R. Hawkins, financial secretary of the A. M. E. Church and president of the Prudential Bank of Washington; Samuel W. Rutherford, Captains of secretary of the National Benefit Association industry. of the same city; Isaiah T. Montgomery, the capitalist of Mound Bayou, Mississippi; John Merrick, founder of the North Carolina Mutual and Provident Association; C. C. Spaulding, now the promoter of these same interests; Mrs.

FACTORS IN THE ECONOMIC PROGRESS OF THE NEGRO

MRS. A. E. MALONE   JOHN MERRICK
HEMAN E. PERRY   SAMUEL W. RUTHERFORD

A. E. Malone, the rich manufacturer of the Poro products in St. Louis; Anthony Overton, president of the Victory Life Insurance Company of Chicago; W. G. Pearson, a business man of Durham; and the late Madame C. J. Walker, the manufacturer of toilet articles, out of which she accumulated more than a million dollars' worth of property. The Negroes in the United States now own property worth more than a billion dollars.

In the midst of the busy bustle and the economic development of the United States since the Civil War the Negro has not only demonstrated his ability to accumulate a portion of the world's goods, but by his inventive genius has contributed much toward the economic **Inventive** progress of the country. As to exactly how **genius.** many Negroes have appeared in the field of invention we are still in doubt. The United States Patent Office has not in all cases kept a record as to the race of the applicants. While in many instances the racial connection has been easily determined, an investigation has shown that many inventors of color have not disclosed facts to this effect because the value of the invention might thereby be depreciated. By correspondence with patent attorneys and the inventors themselves it has been established as a fact that there are in the United States Patent Office a record of 1,500 inventions made by Negroes. This number, no doubt, is only a fraction of those which have been actually assigned to persons of color.

Some of these inventions have been remarkable. Probably the most significant one of them is that of a machine for lasting shoes invented by Jan E. Matzeliger, a Negro born in Dutch Guiana in 1852. Early in his **Matzeliger.** youth Matzeliger came to this country and served as an apprentice at the cobbler's trade in Philadelphia and in Lynn, Massachusetts. Undergoing unusual hardships which undermined his health, Matzeliger applied his brain to working out a labor-saving device by which his trade might be relieved from drudgery. He invented, therefore, a lasting machine which adjusted the shoe, arranged the leather over the sole, and drove in the nails. Matzeliger died in 1889, in his thirty-seventh year, before he could realize the value of his invention. The patent was bought by Sydney W. Winslow. Upon the advantages derived from this machine he established the well-known United Shoe Machinery Company, which absorbed over forty smaller corporations. This company is operated now with a capital stock of more than $20,000,000, employing 5,000 operators in factories covering more than twenty acres of ground. Within the twenty years from the time of its incorporation its product increased from $220,000 to $242,631,000 and the shoes exported increased from 1,000,000 to 11,000,000. As a result the cost of shoes decreased 50 per cent, the wages of the operators decidedly increased, the working hours diminished, and laboring conditions improved.

Some other inventions of Negroes of less consequence were of much value and deserve mention. J. H. Dickinson and S. L. Dickinson, both of New Jersey, have been granted **Valuable inventions.** a dozen patents for mechanical appliances used in player piano machinery. W. B. Purvis of Philadelphia has accumulated much wealth by his inventions of machinery for making paper bags, most of which have been sold to the Union Paper Bag Company of New York. A. B. Albert, a native of Louisiana, invented a cotton-picking machine a few years later. Charles V. Richey of Washington, D. C., invented and patented several devices for registering calls and detecting the unauthorized use of the telephone. Shelby J. Davidson invented a mechanical tabulator or adding machine; Robert A. Pelham, a pasting machine; and Andrew F. Hilyer,

J. E. MATZELIGER
LASTING MACHINE

No. 274,207.

PATENTED MAR. 20, 1883

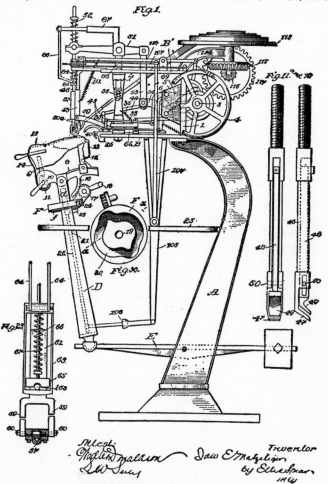

Fig 1.

AN ILLUSTRATION SHOWING THE MODELS MADE BY MATZELIGER TO ILLUSTRATE
HIS INVENTIONS IN SHOE MACHINES.

two hot-air register attachments. Benjamin F. Jackson of Massachusetts invented a heat apparatus, a gas burner, an electrotypers' furnace, a steam boiler, a trolley wheel controller, a tank signal, and a hydrocarbon burner system. Frank J. Ferrell of New York obtained about a dozen patents for improvements in valves for steam engines. George W. Murray, a former member of Congress from South Carolina, patented eight inventions of agricultural implements. Henry Kreamer of New York made seven different inventions in steam traps. William Douglass of Arkansas secured six patents for inventions of harvesting machinery. James Doyle of Pittsburgh devised the automatic serving system so as to dispense with the use of waiters in cafés.

Fred J. Lowden, known to fame as one of the Fisk Jubilee Singers, patented in 1893 a fastener for the meeting rails **Useful** of sashes, and a key fastener the following **appliances.** year. J. L. Pickering of Haiti, James Smith of California, W. G. Madison of Iowa, and H. E. Hooter of Missouri, have been granted patents for inventions in airships. No less significant, moreover, was the patent, in 1897, of Andrew J. Beard, of Alabama, for an automatic car-coupling device, sold to a New York car company for more than $50,000. William H. Johnson of Texas invented a successful device for overcoming dead center in motion, one for a compound engine, and another for a water boiler. While keeping a hotel in Boston, Joseph Lee patented three inventions for kneading dough. Brinay Smart of Tennessee invented a number of reverse valve gears. J. W. Benton of Kentucky invented a derrick for hoisting heavy weights. John T. Parker invented screws for tobacco presses with which he established a thriving business as the Ripley Foundry and Machine Company of Ripley, Ohio.

The most useful inventor with a career extending into the twentieth century, however, was Granville T. Woods.

He doubtless surpassed most men in his field in the number and the variety of his devices. He began Granville T. in Cincinnati, Ohio, in 1889, where he ob- Woods. tained his first patent on a steam boiler furnace. Then came an amusement machine apparatus in 1889, an incubator in 1900, and electrical air brakes in 1902, 1903, and

1905. He then directed his attention to telegraphy, producing several patents for transmitting messages between moving trains, and also a number of transmitters. He thereafter invented fifteen appliances having to do with electrical railways and a number of others for electrical control and distribu-

GRANVILLE T. WOODS

tion. To further his interests he organized the Woods Electrical Company, which took over by assignment all of his early patents. As in the course of time, however, he found a better market for his devices with the more prosperous corporations in the United States, the records of the patent office show the assignment of a large number of his inventions to the General Electric Company of New York, the Westinghouse Air Brake Company of Pennsylvania, the American Bell Telephone Company of Boston, and the American Engineering Company of New York. During this period of his larger usefulness he had the coöperation of his brother, Lyates Woods, who himself invented a number of such appliances of considerable commercial value.

Another inventor of consequence was Elijah J. McCoy. He was unique in that he was the first man Elijah J. to direct attention to the need for facilitating McCoy. the lubrication of machinery. His first invention was patented in 1872 as a lubricating cup. From that day his fame as an inventor of this useful appliance went throughout this country and abroad. In responding to the need for still further improvements in this work, he patented about fifty different inventions having to do with the lubricating of machinery. His lubricating cup became of general use on the leading railroads in the United States and abroad and on the vessels on the high seas. In his work, however, Mr. McCoy was not restricted to lubricating machinery. He patented a variety of devices for other purposes, and he was long active in the production of other mechanical appliances in demand in the industrial world.

The achievements of the Negroes in this field become much worthier of mention when one takes into consideration the hard problems of the inventor of color. In this **Difficulties of the inventor.** country it has not been a very easy matter for white men with ample protection of the law to secure to themselves by patents the full enjoyment of the fruits of their own labor. The achievements of Eli Whitney and Robert Fulton are cases in evidence. Henry A. Bowman, a Negro inventor of Worcester, Massachusetts, therefore, found himself facing the same difficulty. After he had established a thriving business on the basis of his invention of a new method of making flags, he discovered that a New York firm was outstripping him by using his invention. As he was unable to hire competent attorneys to protect his interests, he was soon compelled to abandon his business. The experience of E. A. Robinson of Chicago is another case in evidence. He invented a number of devices, such as the casting composite for car wheels, a trolley wheel, a railway switch and a rail. His patents, however, were infringed upon by two large corporations, the American Car and Foundry Company and the Chicago City Railway Company. To restrain these corporations from appropriating his property to their use, he instituted proceedings in the local courts and finally in the Supreme Court of the United States; but he was unable to have his patent protected.

Exhibiting this same sort of genius ever manifesting itself despite difficulties, Negroes have shown in other fields evidences of unusual attainment. In music the world has seen the lowly life and higher aspirations of The Negro the Negro in J. W. and F. W. Work, Will in music. Marion Cook, Nathaniel Dett, and Harry Burleigh, who have followed in the footsteps of Samuel Coleridge Taylor. In sculpture the race has been well represented by Meta Vaux Warrick Fuller, who won fame by her first work in clay in the Philadelphia School of Industrial Art. She studied in Paris, where she attracted the attention of the great sculptor, Rodin. In 1893 she exhibited the highly prized model of art, *The Wretched,* her masterpiece. She has since added some other works, *The Dancing Girl, The Wrestlers,* and *Carrying the Dead Body.* In the same field has also appeared Mrs. May Howard Jackson, whose works have elicited honorable mention in many circles. E. M. Bannister, William A. Harper, and William E. Scott have attracted considerable attention by their paintings.

The most distinguished Negro in the field of art, however, is Henry O. Tanner. With the white artist, Sargent, Tanner represents the best America has produced in painting. He had little encouragement in this Henry O. field, but early attracted attention by *The* Tanner. *Bagpipe Lesson,* portraying a workman sitting on a wheelbarrow observing the efforts of a youth on a musical instrument. Lacking in this country the atmosphere conducive to the development of the best in man, Tanner went to the city of Paris in 1891. There, under the instruction of Jean Paul Laurens and Benjamin Constant, he mastered the principles of art. In contact there with men in his own sphere, he has developed into one of the greatest artists of his time.

His first painting of value was exhibited in 1894. The following year he completed *The Young Sabot Maker;* but it was not until 1896 that, with the encouragement given him by the great artist Gérôme, Tanner won recognition as a painter. In 1897, however, his *Raising of Lazarus* attracted so much attention far and wide that thereafter

H. O. TANNER'S *Christ and Nicodemus*

there was little doubt in the circles of art as to the greatness of this man. This picture was awarded the gold medal by the French government and placed in the Louvre. In 1898 he presented to the public *The Annunciation* at the Academy of Fine Arts in Philadelphia, where it elicited favorable comment. His *Judas,* presented to the public in 1899, was bought by the Carnegie Institute of Pittsburgh. That same year *Nicodemus,* awarded the Walter Lippincott prize of $300, was purchased by the Pennsylvania Academy of Fine Arts. For his *Daniel in the Lions' Den* he was awarded second class medals at the Universal Exposition in Paris in 1900, at the Pan-American Exposition in 1901, and at the St. Louis Exposition in 1904. In 1906 his *The Disciples at Emmaus* was awarded the second gold medal and purchased by the French government. That same year his *The Disciples at the Tomb* was declared the best painting at the annual exhibition of art in Chicago and was awarded the N. W. Harris prize of $300. In 1908 appeared *The Wise and Foolish Virgins*, which was characterized as a masterpiece of a sincere artist.

As a painter, Mr. Tanner has directed his attention largely to religious and lowly life, as evidenced by the names of his paintings. He no doubt owes this attitude to the fact that he is the son of a bishop of the African Methodist Episcopal Church, and early in life was encouraged to apply himself to theology. As an artist his productions have a reverent atmosphere, and his pictures are clean-cut and luminous. In his paintings there are subtle power, purity of line, and thorough charm, with sentiment prevailing over technique. While the shades are luminous, the coloring is neither heavy nor muddy. "He always brings out of all his work," says one, "an admirable dramatic sentiment given full value and fully expressed."

In the field of literature the Negroes are sometimes considered as beginners, but much progress in this field is evident. Kelly Miller, W. E. B. DuBois and William Pickens have done well in controversial literature. George W. Williams, John W. Cromwell and **In literature.** Booker T. Washington have made contributions to history. Following in the wake of Jupiter Hammon, Phyllis Wheatley and Frances E. W. Harper, writers of interesting verse, Paul Laurence Dunbar came before the public in the early nineties as a man endowed with the unusual gift of interpreting the lowly life of the Negro. As an elevator boy in a hotel, writing a few lines in dialect, he himself did not realize his poetic genius. Succeeding, however, in having a few of these published in daily papers and magazines, he attracted attention. It was not long before William Dean Howells, a contemporary, became interested in his works and proclaimed him to the world as a poet worthy of the **The rise** consideration given Whittier, Lowell and **of Dunbar.** Longfellow. Dunbar had fortunately reached that unusual stage in the development of a belated people

PAUL LAURENCE DUNBAR

of having his education react upon his environment. He saw the Negro as he is, saw something beneath the surface of his mere brogue, in fact, saw a philosophy for which the world wanted an interpretation. This interpretation came in his first book, *Oak and Ivy,* and was still better exhibited in his second w o r k, *Majors and Minors,* appearing in 1895. Very soon then we hear such comments on him as that coming from Richard Watson Gilder, saying that Dunbar is the first black man to feel the life of the Negro esthetically and to express it lyrically.

Dunbar made an attempt at novel writing, in the production of his *The Uncalled.* This was a character study upon which fortunately his reputation as a literary man does not rest, for it does not come up to the standard of his verse. Unstinted praise awaited him upon his publication of *Lyrics of Lowly Life, Folks from Dixie, Lyrics of the Hearth-side, Poems of Cabin and Field, The Strength of Gideon, The Love of Landry, The Fanatics, The Sport of the Gods, Lyrics of Love and Laughter* and *Candle Lighting Time.* Some of the popular poems in this collection which are worthy of special mention are *When Malindy Sings, When the Co'n Pone's Hot, The Party* and *The Poet and his Song.*

His success as a literary man was due to his originality. There had appeared from time to time scores of whites and blacks who had undertaken to write verse in Negro dialect; but Dunbar was the first to put into it such thought and make of it such a portraiture of the feeling and the aspirations of the Negroes as to give his work the stamp of originality. While he was always humorous, his poetry showed deep pathos and sympathy. With no problems to solve and no peculiar type to represent, he went into the Negro life, saw it as it was, and emerged portraying it with living characters exhibiting the elasticity, spirit, tone, and naturalness in the life about him.

In life he was respected and known throughout this country and abroad. In 1897 he visited England, where because of his fame as a poet he was received with marked honor. Upon returning to this country his literary engagements became such that he could devote himself entirely to work in his field. His health early began to decline, however, and he died at the age of thirty-four at his home in Dayton, Ohio. Thanks to the interest of sympathetic persons of both races, this home is now maintained as a monument to remain as a museum in honor of the poet, Paul Laurence Dunbar.

Since the days of Dunbar a number of other Negro writers of prominence have considerably interested the public. Among these should be mentioned Angelina W.

Grimké, a woman of poetic insight; Benjamin Brawley, an author of many interests; Jessie R. Fauset, a writer of varying purpose; Georgia Douglas Johnson,

Other writers. whose interesting poems have recently appeared as *The Heart of a Woman;* Leslie Pinkney Hill, distinguished by his *Wings of Oppression;* Joseph Seaman Cotter, known to the public through his poems contributed to various magazines and his collection entitled the *Band of Gideon;* and James Weldon Johnson, whose invaluable works are collected in the volume, *Fifty Years and Other Poems.* These authors are at their best in writing poems which have no bearing on the life of the Negro. In this field they have exhibited evidences of the thought, feeling and imagination found in the best literature. In taking up Negro life, however, they have not reached the standard of Dunbar. Their difficulty has been that because of suffering from social proscription in the white man's world they have faced their task with a problem to solve; and, unlike Paul Laurence Dunbar, who went into life and merely portrayed what he saw, they prejudice their readers against them by a premature introduction to an unpleasant atmosphere. The younger writers like Langston Hughes, Countée Cullen, Jean Toomer, and Rudolph Fisher, have a different approach, and are producing some of the best contemporary literature. Honorable mention belongs here to Walter White, whose novels, *Fire in the Flint* and *Flight,* have attracted much attention.

One of the most remarkable writers of Negro blood since Dunbar is William Stanley Braithwaite. As a writer he is not a Negro. Although realizing the fact that the race has obstacles to surmount, that it is in a great

Braithwaite. struggle, and that the battle is being hard fought, Mr. Braithwaite, by his literary production and criticism, has won much consideration for the Negroes, not by singing of their woes, but by demonstrating that the

Negro intellect is capable of the same achievements as that of the whites. Because of his poems, his annual publication, the *Anthology of Magazine Verse*, and his numerous literary criticisms appearing from time to time in the leading publications of this country, Mr. Braithwaite, although a man of African blood, is accepted as one of the foremost literary critics of our day.

CHAPTER XXVII

IN THE COURT OF THE GENTILES

IN spite of these achievements, however, most white men were still reluctant to concede the right of the Negro to enjoy the full measure of citizenship. His rise to a position **Citizenship** of usefulness in the North often brought him **begrudged.** into competition with white men who selfishly endeavored to proscribe him in the economic sphere, and most Southern spokesmen boldly proclaimed that any effort on the part of the Negro to improve his social and civil status would not be countenanced in that section. The Negro was to be tolerated there only in recognized inferiority. It was in vain, then, that Negroes pointed to their economic progress, intellectual development, contribution to art, and preservation of the Christian religion.

Stating the matter much more frankly, some white men openly asserted that the Negro thrives too rapidly. They observed that he is more anxious than the poor white citizen to educate his children. To prevent the enlightenment of the Negro, then, public education must be discouraged, although it might be beneficial to the poor whites. They noted with some regret, too, that Negroes acquire land more readily than the poor whites and do not willingly alienate it. To prevent the Negroes from outstripping their unprofitable neighbors, therefore, the former must be further handicapped.

This desire for concerted action against the Negro, however, had resulted somewhat from an increasing feeling that the Negro, being socially inferior to the white man, is a menace to his civilization. From the point of view of most of these whites, it mattered not what the Negro had accomplished, he is nevertheless inherently inferior to the most despicable white man on earth, and any attempt to change his status must be visited with condign punishment inflicted by "law." While the race, they believed, will some day become extinct, the whites could not await that solution of the problem. There must not, therefore, be any contact with the Negro except that of master with servant.

The Negro called a menace

This feeling had been intensified by the work of pseudo-scientists who endeavored to prove that Negroes are carriers of social diseases. As a matter of fact, however, history shows that these evils originated among whites and were never known among Negroes until thus contaminated by Caucasians. These diseases once worked ravages among Negroes because time had not then established in them the immunity found in the whites who have so long been accustomed thereto. Education, moreover, the very thing which has proved to be the significant factor in removing man from the grasp of social diseases, these same whites denied the Negroes. Further support to this bias came from unscientific reports circulated by prejudiced authors like Edgar G. Murphy, Thomas Dixon, Thomas Nelson Page, A. H. Stone, E. B. Reuter, and Ulrich B. Phillips. They undertook to prove the inefficiency of Negro labor and other such fallacies by uprooting the contention of science that one race cannot be inherently inferior to another.[1]

The influence of biased writers.

[1] For this point of view see E. G. Murphy's *Problems of the Present South;* Thomas Dixon's *Clansman;* Thomas Nelson Page's *In Ole Virginia, Red Rock,* and *The Negro; The Southerner's Problem;* A. H. Stone's *Studies in the Race Problem;* U. B. Phillips's *Plantation and Frontier, Documentary History of American Industrial Society, American Negro Slavery,* his lectures and reviews of books, and E. B. Reuter's *The Mulatto in the United States.*

NEGROES OF CREATIVE GENIUS

MRS. G. D. JOHNSON   ROLAND HAYES
EGBERT AUSTIN WILLIAMS   CHARLES S. GILPIN

To preclude the possibility of changing the Negro's situation, then, by overcoming the obstacles already thrown across his path, others had to be added under the guise of the "mutually beneficial system of segregation." The Negroes had already been de **Segregation.** spoiled of their pro rata share of public school funds, ingeniously disfranchised, and denied the democratic use of public utilities; but now it must be made utterly impossible for them to profit by any good which may accrue to the benefit of the white community. Negroes, therefore, were deprived of the right to frequent public places of amusement, to move into city blocks where white people were in the majority, to purchase farm land in sections restricted to white ownership, or to serve with whites in civil service.

The more desirable districts must be reserved to whites, some argued, because lazy Negroes attached such a stigma to labor that the white men will not work among them at certain occupations. The Negroes, they fur **The argument** ther contended, have a low standard of liv **for social** ing; their wants are easily supplied. Yet **distinctions.** the facts prove that proportionately Negroes have excelled white men in the establishment of homes and in the purchase of land. The census of 1920 showed that 218,612 Negroes had bought land. This land increased from about 6,000,000 acres in 1880 to 13,948,512 in 1920. In addition to this large number of owners of farms there were 705,070 Negro tenants cultivating an acreage of 27,077,582,[2] worth together with buildings $1,676,315,864.

Statements as to the laziness of Negroes, however, are fraught with downright prevarication. It requires only a trip of forty-eight hours through the South to prove that

[2] These figures were a little higher in 1910. As a result of the migration the Negro farm owners decreased from 218,978 to 218,612 in 1920. These figures are for Negro farmers, not for colored farmers among whom are included Japanese, Chinese, Indians and the like.

the Negroes constitute the working class in that section. As the race makes progress, however, a large number **Biased** of Negroes become economically independent **statements.** of the white people not only to the extent of employing themselves, but to that of requiring the assistance of other Negroes. Under different circumstances these would enter the service of whites. Inasmuch as so many whites have never learned to work and instead have made their living exploiting Negroes, they now bear it grievously that the Negroes available for this purpose are comparatively diminishing.

Persons who have advocated residential segregation have tried to disguise their real feeling by advancing other arguments. Business men have said that the presence of **The Negro** Negroes in a white community depreciates the **and property** property. If they have in mind the "color- **values.** phobia" which seizes white residents when a Negro becomes their neighbor and the race prejudice which impels them to dispose of their property quickly below cost; or if they take into consideration the abandoned condition in which the local government generally leaves a Negro residential section, this contention is right. But it is not the Negro causing the depreciation. This fault lies at the door of the whites. The value of property, moreover, is determined by its income, and history has shown that as soon as Negroes move into a section formerly occupied by whites, the landlord receives from such property a larger income than before. The rent is often increased from 15% to 30%.

While custom, city ordinance, and acts of legislatures accomplished the purpose of segregation in various parts, **Temples of** in the State of Oklahoma this movement as- **injustice.** sumed the form of open robbery in collusion with courts of the commonwealth. Negroes, who had freely interbred with Indians there, came into the possession of valuable oil lands by special federal legislation guaranteeing the inheritance of persons having even an infusion of Indian blood. To deprive their Negro offspring of their property the courts appointed white men as guardians of such Negroes under age. To extend this guardianship the courts often declared such wards irresponsible or of unsound mind. These guardians received a percentage of the income from the valuable oil properties, but this was not sufficient. Often in collusion with the purchaser they disposed of the properties altogether on the condition that the guardian should share in the fortunes made from oil found on the lands sold.

In this movement for the social degradation of the Negro, moreover, the majority of the church finally joined. Having in the preachment of men like Lyman Abbott, justification for segregation in the "court of **Doughfaced** the gentiles," the "Christians" of the me- **"Christians."** dieval type could more boldly proclaim the injustice of forcing their members to break bread with devotees whom the god of race hate has not made their social equals. Churches in which Negroes had worshiped with whites from time immemorial contrived to organize their Negro membership as separate bodies. These were usually provided for by a make-shift inadequate system of religious institutions. Bishops, moreover, soon tired of the ministrations entailed by their communicants of color. There arose, then, a clamor not only for complete separation of the races in the edifices, but for a separate church administration throughout the whole system.

This, however, would cause as many problems as it would solve. White men were reluctant to serve Negroes in their special groups. Yet it was considered **Hypocrisy** "impracticable" to exalt Negroes to positions **supreme.** of trust in the mixed churches. Furthermore, while many churchmen disliked contact with Negroes, they believed that it would be a mistake thus to abandon the control of Negro religious thought as the Southern churches did after the Civil War. This mingled feeling, too, blocked the movement for the unification of the Methodist churches. Some of the Northern Methodists stood out for at least as much recognition under the proposed system as this connection has hitherto given the Negro, but the Methodist Episcopal Church, South, would accept communicants of color only on the basis of adherents to be tolerated as undeveloped children.

Social agencies undertaking the work which the church never performs faced the same problem. The Young Men's Christian Association and the Young Women's Christian Association had for years maintained separate branches of their work for Negroes in the South. For a long time after the Civil War race prejudice was not sufficiently rampant to exclude the few Negroes in the North from the occasional use of these conveniences. But race hate would not down, and in those centers, too, Negroes were socially proscribed when their numbers increased as a result of the migration. This problem was worked out by the compromise of constructing in urban centers separate buildings for the accommodation of men and women of African blood. These establishments have been very useful as hospices for transients; but their branches have had difficulty in finding a definite function among Negroes whose situation, made unlike that of the whites by law and custom, requires social uplift effort different from that applied to persons otherwise circumstanced. The Negroes in charge of the branches of these agencies, however, are not responsible for this situation, since they have never been left to their initiative in working among Negroes.[3]

The compromise of social agencies.

Some believed with Senator J. B. Foraker that this segre-

[3]*Journal of Negro History*, IX, 127-138.

gation rage was stimulated by Theodore Roosevelt's dishonorable dismissal of the Negro soldiers charged with raiding Brownsville, Texas, in 1906. Eloquent defenders of Roosevelt, however, assert that he did so much for the social and civic
Policies of Roosevelt and Taft.
recognition of the race in dining with Booker T. Washington and in forcing upon the Senate and the Southerners the appointment of Dr. William D. Crum as collector of the port of Charleston, that such a motive could not have thus actuated him. But there is little doubt that this accentuation of caste was decidedly aided by the policy of William H. Taft. In his inaugural address he announced that he would not appoint Negroes to office where they were not wanted by the whites. Interpreted broadly, this finally would mean that, with the increasing prejudice against the race, no Negroes at all could secure appointments to civil positions of usefulness. Taft thereby abetted segregation.

Wishing to secure universal approval of this reactionary program, legislators from the unprogressive districts of the country endeavored to enact special laws for further segregation of the races in all ramifications of
life. The courses of study in State schools were further changed, and threats were made
Efforts for further segregation.
to cut off the appropriations of Negro institutions of learning altogether. These legislators advocated also the prohibition of persons of African blood from immigrating into and becoming citizens of this country, and the exclusion of Negroes from employment in certain capacities desirable for white men. Florida and Kentucky enacted laws making it a crime for a white person to teach a Negro.

Where there were no special laws or ordinances providing for segregation, the end was reached another way. Negroes purchasing homes in desirable white residential districts were often warned not to
Riots rampant.
move into them. If they did they were often terrorized

The Negro In Our History

Co-workers in Various Causes

George E. Haynes   E. K. Jones
C. W. Chesnutt   W. S. Braithwaite

by having their homes stoned or bombed from day to day as in the cases of Kansas City, Baltimore, Philadelphia, and Chicago. In fact, this organized effort of the whites to prevent the expansion of the Negro residential districts was an important cause of the race riots in Newbern, Tulsa, East St. Louis, Chester, Knoxville, Washington and Chicago. In these cases the mob acted in, the absence of the "law." Many assert, moreover, that in some of these instances the Negro section was burned primarily to force them into less desirable quarters that the property of Negroes might be used for the extension of the business districts. Some Negroes were thus deprived of their property thereafter by s p e c i a l ordinances requiring rebuilding on such expensive plans as to force the homeless to sell out and establish themselves in the suburbs of the cities.

DR. L. K. WILLIAMS, a prominent factor in socializing the Church

The worst of all in this perplexing situation was that men who formerly had been counted upon to speak for the Negroes advised them to accept the situation philosophically. Few white men encouraged Negroes to criticize adversely anything which members of the **Non-resist-** haughty race might inflict upon persons of **ance advised.** color. Negroes were told that it is unwise to infuriate a lion when you have your head in his mouth. Charles F.

Dole, voicing the sentiments of the majority of whites, said: "Don't antagonize, don't be bitter; say the conciliatory thing; make friends and do not repel them; insist on and emphasize the cheerful and good, and dwell as little as possible on wrong and evil."

This advice could not be followed, as Dr. DuBois well said, when Negroes were denied education; driven out of the Church of Christ; excluded from hotels, theaters and public places; labeled like dogs in traveling; refused decent employment; forced to the lowest wage scale; compelled to pay the highest rent for the poorest homes; prohibited from buying property in decent neighborhoods; ridiculed in the press, on the platform, and on the stage; disfranchised; taxed without representation; d e n i e d the right to choose their friends or to be chosen by them; deprived by custom and law of protection for their women; robbed of justice in the courts; and lynched with impunity.

CLAUDE McKAY

Negroes had recourse to "law," but without much avail. Many in cities in the North appealed to State civil rights acts which protected the individual against discrimination in the use of such places as theaters, hotels, railroads, steamboats and the like; but the biased courts usually evaded the issue by some sort of fallacious reasoning, or merely allowed nominal damages. The Civil Rights Act which forbade such discrimination had long since been declared unconstitutional so far as it undertook to forbid citizens of States to do these things. The rest of the act was nullified by a decision of the United States Supreme Court in 1913. A Negro woman sued a steamship company under this statute because she was denied equal accommodations with white passengers solely on the ground of color. She was not traveling within a State, but on the high seas from a port in one State to a port in another. This decision was reached by misapplying the well-established rule of construction that when an act has been passed which must stand or fall together, because the legislature would evidently not pass it at all unless it could pass it as a whole, then, if one part was beyond the power of the legislature and must fall, the rest must fall with it. The court held that "if Congress had known that it could not forbid the citizens of the various States from discriminating against each other on the ground of color, it would not have attempted thus to restrict the citizens of Territories, or other people subject in this respect to the control of Congress." No candid thinker, well read in Civil War history, will agree with the court, that, even if Congress had known that it could not enact such a measure which would bind the citizens of States, it would not have made it extend so far as it could by applying it to the citizens of districts subject to the direct legislation of Congress. In this case, then, the Supreme Court of the United States was merely giving its sanction to caste.

An unconstitutional decision.

In several other decisions more favorable to democracy there was offered a little hope that this high tribunal might some day ally itself altogether with justice and truth. One of these decisions was that covering three cases testing the validity of State laws imposing the literacy qualifica-

The "grandfather clause" unconstitutional.

tion for voters but exempting from its operation those persons whose grandfathers could vote prior to 1866, which was before the Negroes had been granted this privilege. In 1915 the Supreme Court decided that while the literacy test was legal and not subject to revision, it was so closely connected with the grandfather clause that both were unconstitutional. The standard of voting set by these measures, this tribunal held, was in substance but a revitalization of conditions which, when they prevailed in the past, had been destroyed by the self-operative force of the Thirteenth Amendment.

The decision in 1917 as to the validity of ordinances of various cities endeavoring to segregate Negroes in residential districts, was also favorable. It had been argued **Residential segregation outlawed.** that such measures preserve the purity of the races, maintain the public peace, and prevent the depreciation of property. The court conceded the seriousness of the situation, and admitted the right of a State to make race distinction on the basis of equal accommodations, but it could not go so far as to sanction the deprivation of Negroes of such rights altogether. It held, then, that a law to prevent the selling of property to a person of color is not a legitimate exercise of the police power of the State, and is in direct violation of the fundamental law enacted in the Fourteenth Amendment of the Constitution preventing State interference with property rights except by due process of law.

Another of these decisions was that in the case in which Negroes legally protested against the law of Oklahoma **A favorable opinion.** which deprived them of the rights guaranteed inter-State passengers using common carriers. Giving the opinion of the court in 1914, Justice Charles E. Hughes upheld the validity of separate coach laws applying to passengers within a State, but contended that so much of the Oklahoma act as permitted carriers to provide sleeping cars, dining cars, and chair cars exclusively for whites and provide no similar accommodations for Negroes, denies the latter the equal protection of the laws guaranteed by the Fourteenth Amendment of the Federal Constitution.

During these years, moreover, the Negroes did not remain inactive. They felt powerless but they would not despair.

BISHOP JOHN HURST, distinguished by valuable services for freedom within and without the Church

It was just this plight **Propaganda organizations.** of the Negro that brought into existence the National Association for the Advancement of Colored People. It sprang from whites and blacks who believed that some good can be accomplished by publicity, by agitation, and by memorializing the State Legislatures and Congress for a redress of these grievances.[4] These evils were well set forth also in 1911 in a memorial by the National Independent Political Rights League at its meeting in Boston. This body drafted a petition for the enforcement of the Constitution. It prayed Congress to stop disfranchisement and peonage, to pass a Federal "Anti-Jim Crow" law for inter-State passengers, to give Federal aid to education, to enact a national anti-lynching bill, and to reinstate the soldiers discharged for connection with the Brownsville riot in 1906.

[4] *Journal of Negro History*, IX, 107-116.

Forced by the logic of Negro agitators attacking these evils, some white men justified this medievalism on the ground that the leaders of the Negroes themselves have advocated the separation of the races in things civic and

Misrepresentation of the Negro's attitude.
social. If they had in mind those Negroes, who to curry favor in using white persons to reach an end have pretended that they accept their point of view, there may be a bit of truth in such a statement. Too often, moreover, when a Negro complained of the hardships of travel, or of the denial of the ease and comforts provided for the public, the personnel responsible for these injustices referred to Booker T. Washington as the outstanding Negro whose career and teachings support segregation. As a matter of fact, however, neither Washington nor any other self-respecting Negro has ever countenanced segregation.

Booker T. Washington, on the contrary, was one of the worst enemies of segregation. Believing in the helpful contact of the races, he associated with the best white people, dined with President Roosevelt, and feasted among the

Booker T. Washingon opposed to segregation.
crowned heads of Europe. In an article of his in the *New Republic* in 1915, he forcibly characterized segregation as unjust because it invites unjust measures. He believed that it would not be productive of any good, "because practically every thoughtful Negro resents its injustice and doubts its sincerity." "Any race adjustment based on injustice," said he, "finally defeats itself. The Civil War is the best illustration of what results where it is attempted to make wrong right or seem to be right. It is inconsistent," he contended; "the Negro is segregated from his white neighbor, but white business men are not prevented from doing business in Negro neighborhoods. There has been no case of segregation of Negroes in the United States that has not widened the breach between the two races. Wherever a

form of segregation exists, it will be found that it has been administered in such a way as to embitter the Negro and harm more or less the moral fiber of the white man. That the Negro does not express this constant sense of wrong is no proof that he does not feel it.''

Segregation thus at its worst left the Negroes in a morbid state of mind with a feeling of despair mingled with revenge. Because their former friends were weakening under the stigma of loving the race, the Negroes thought seriously of turning to their enemies. They were all but convinced that the attitude of the Southern white man toward the Negro is due in a measure to the attachment of the Negro to the ideals of the Northerner, whom the Southerner still hates. With a change in the political affiliations of the Negro, moreover, many politicians proclaimed there would dawn a new day for the race in the South. This accounts for the large Negro vote given Woodrow Wilson for the presidency in 1912, especially since he promised such Negroes that if elected he would see that they received justice abundantly.

Negroes in a quandry.

W. M. Trotter, a fearless opponent of segregation

Never were constituents more disappointed. The very functionaries whom they had elected manifested more enmity than ever. With the sanction of Wilson, Negroes were eliminated from all of the higher positions in the government and segregated in the civil service. Some **Disappointed by Wilson.** check to segregation was effected by the numerous memorials coming from indignation meetings of the Negroes throughout the country. These protests were fostered in the main by the National Association for the Advancement of Colored People through its various branches, and by the National Equal Rights League, of which Monroe Trotter is the moving spirit. Trotter secured an interview with Wilson to protest against the injustice of segregation in the government service; but the President, whose attitude toward the Negro was practically that of Jefferson Davis, suddenly took umbrage at the serious tone in which Trotter fearlessly criticized the policy and abruptly terminated the conference.

In the meantime, moreover, the voice of former white friends of the Negro could not be heard except as expressed in occasional editorials and resolutions suggested by Negroes who persistently kept the offense before the **Apathy of the public.** country. On the other hand, the whole country generally heard with conviction the misrepresentation of the race and found some delight in seeing the *Birth of a Nation,* the dramatization of Thomas Dixon's *Clansman.* This exaggerated the part played by the Negro during Reconstruction and idealized the aristocracy which instituted a régime of blood to reëstablish its rule. After all, the reactionaries had brought it to pass that a large number of citizens had begun to think that this is a white man's country and if the Negro remains here he must be content with an inferior status.

Segregation, moreover, was extended abroad wherever the United States Government controlled or wherever its white citizens had influence. It has been decided by the United States Supreme Court that the Constitution does not necessarily follow the flag, but it cannot be denied that the caste of color does. The intervention of the United States in the war of Cuba with Spain, the **Segregation** consequent acquisition of territory from the **carried** latter, the construction of the Panama Canal, **abroad.** the conquest of helpless Haiti, and the purchase of the Virgin Islands by the United States, all opened promising fields for the extension of our Caucasian autocracy into the West Indies, where persons of color had formerly been treated as members of the human family. Citizens of the United States have established the rule of the white man in Cuba; they have carried segregation into the Canal Zones; they have subjected the Haitians to the will of descendants of slave drivers; and they have deprived the natives of the Virgin Islands of the opportunities for development enjoyed under the control of Denmark. Because of the protests of Negroes against the dishonorable conquest and occupation of Haiti by the United States, President Harding thought that he would placate some of them in 1922 by appointing a commission headed by W. T. B. Williams to report on the situation in that island. For a similar purpose President Coolidge sent to the Virgin Islands in 1924 a commission headed by George H. Woodson. The other members of the commission were W. H. C. Brown, C. E. Mitchell and J. S. Coage. So far, however, there has not been observed any decided change in the condition of these natives as a result of these investigations.

Hitherto Liberia has been spared from these iniquities, but the encroachment of ill-designing foreigners has invited the segregating Americans. Under James S. Payne, President in 1876, the country did not rapidly recover. In the administration of Anthony W. Gardiner, however, the hope for the republic seemed to be practically lost. England and France were slicing away the territory of Liberia. Because certain natives maltreated some shipwrecked Germans, their country's warships bombarded Nana Kru and forced the payment of damages. The colony had become involved in troubles with England and Germany. Its numerous debts could not be paid. The French and English, therefore, were endeavoring to take over the country. This sort of situation continued through the administrations of Hilary R. W. Johnson, Joseph James Cheeseman, William D. Coleman and Arthur Barclay from 1884 to 1896. To secure further relief the Government authorized in 1906 another British loan of £100,000 through the Liberian Development Company. The understanding was that a stipulated sum of this money would be used to meet the pressing obligations while the other was for the development of the country. It soon appeared, however, that this scheme backed by Sir Harry H. Johnston was another effort to defraud the Liberian Government and encroach upon its territory. It was fortunately avoided by the Government of the United States. Upon hearing of the untoward condition of Liberia, the Taft administration sent to that country in 1909 a commission of inquiry of the following persons: Roland P. Faulkner, George Sale, and Emmet J. Scott. This commission made definite recommendations to eradicate the evils affecting Liberia. The United States, they said, should aid Liberia in settling its boundary disputes, in refunding its debt, in reforming its finances and in organizing a defense force. Some opportunity for aggression appeared in the recommendation that the United States should establish and maintain a research station in Liberia and should reopen the question of establishing there a coaling station. The commission, however, did not provide any means, although it forestalled the theft projected by the Liberian Development Company. Colonel Charles Young was sent twice to Liberia to reorganize its military force in keeping with one of the recommendations, but lost his life in Lagos in the midst of hardships in 1921.

The Republic of Liberia then turned to the United States Government for a loan of $5,000,000. Charles D. B. King, inaugurated President in 1920, spent some time thereafter in this country in the interest of this loan. Such a loan was finally proposed in Congress, but the measure provided for the expenditure of this money almost altogether by Americans. This left little possibility for the republic to profit thereby. It was fortunate, then, that the country did not finally receive such expensive aid.

CHAPTER XXVIII

THE TENDER MERCIES OF THE WICKED

As the second decade of the century found President Taft officially advocating the elimination of the Negro from politics in the South and his successor upholding racial segregation in the government service, the majority of the **Taft and** Northern people easily acquiesced in the **Wilson.** policy of abandoning the Negro to whatever lot his enemies might grant him. By this time the immigration of unsympathetic Europeans had gone to such an extent and the third generation was so far removed from the social upheaval of the Civil War that the Negro and his problems tended to pass from the public mind in the North. Elihu Root did warn the South in one of his speeches in the Senate not to go so far in the oppression of the Negro as to invite again the interference of the North; but most statesmen, while deprecating the awful plight in which the Negro was, expressed the belief that the North would never again champion such a cause.

The country, however, registered no striking protest against the appointment of various Negroes whom President Taft placed in positions of trust outside of the South. **Few Negroes** His most important appointment was that of **in office.** William H. Lewis, an Amherst and Harvard man, who had distinguished himself as a member of the Massachusetts Legislature and as an Assistant United States District Attorney in Boston. Lewis was made an Assistant Attorney General of the United States under George Wickersham, who fearlessly defended him when the Southern members of the American Bar Association endeavored

494

to exclude him from that body on account of his color. In making this particular appointment, however, Taft did not show any more courage than Woodrow Wilson. Upon the recommendation of his Attorney General James C. McReynolds, he renominated Judge Robert H. Terrell for the municipal bench in the District of Columbia and kept his

OFFICEHOLDERS BECAUSE OF MERIT

WILLIAM H. LEWIS   ROBERT H. TERRELL

name before the Senate until he was confirmed despite the efforts of the reactionaries to the contrary.

Such loyaty to a Negro, however, was exceptional. The chief interest manifested in the race during these years was the effort of philanthropists to support the "optimistic, constructive, educational program" of Tuskegee and Hampton, **The optimistic program popular.** where they said the training of the Negroes was "rightly directed." The South accepted this educational policy, hoping to make of the Negro a sort of super-servant. But, as Ray Stannard Baker said, the very system itself turned out instead independent, upstanding, intelligent men and women who acquired property and thus came into sharper competition with whites. A man's mental power may develop just as easily in studying chemistry to improve the soil as in learning languages to appreciate the classics. During that generation, therefore, Negroes in spite of themselves developed in the direction of agitative organization under leaders who controlled or influenced the press.

This development more than anything else accounts for the return of the Negro to politics in certain States. The old line politicians, who figured conspicuously in Republican conventions, corralled the Negroes and delivered more than a million votes merely for such positions as Recorder of Deeds in the District of Columbia and Register of the Treasury, lost their influence. Negroes began to clamor not for office, but for issues. They desired to know what candidates had done, or would pledge themselves to do for equality and justice regardless of race or color. Most Negroes finally realized that the party of Lincoln and Grant went down with them into their graves. In the Border States and in the North, therefore, it became difficult to determine beforehand how the Negro would vote. Recognizing this wise use of power by Negro voters, citizens have elected meritorious men of color to the State Legislatures in Massachusetts, New York, Missouri, New Jersey, Pennsylvania, West Virginia, Ohio, Indiana, and Illinois. Voters have also chosen deserving Negroes to represent them in the municipal councils in New York City, Baltimore, and Chicago. The unusual migration of Negro voters to the North in recent years, moreover, has brought home to the public

The Negro in politics again.

the possibility of electing Negroes to Congress in certain urban centers of the North.

On the other hand, many Negroes of foresight saw little hope in the unsatisfactory results obtained in politics. They looked to constructive agencies by which political affiliations are determined and controlled. The Negro, they believed, will gain little in **The constructive program.** this sphere unless his claims for social and civic recognition are supported by economic achievement. Therefore, whereas the talented Negroes just after the Civil War took up politics, teaching, or preaching, and the next generation of their group directed its efforts toward mechanical pursuits and practical professions, the educated Negroes of the third generation went into business. This change took place so rapidly that the schools, churches, and social agencies of the race were left largely in the hands of Negroes who had not the initiative to succeed in commercial pursuits. Once it had been considered exceptional to find a Negro succeeding in business, but after this change of objective one observed in every large urban community of Negroes a considerable number rising to commanding positions in the economic development of the race. The Negro had learned that his chief hope is to develop from within and he was carrying out this program.

Some of the most encouraging signs for a brighter day for the Negro, however, came from without and, strange to say, from the South, from the enlightened, thinking men and women of the South. These workers were not politicians themselves and had little or no concern **The awakening of the South.** with the movement to restore the political power of the Negro. These were educated persons of vision, students of history and government sufficiently informed to realize that the repression of the Negro was merely developing an evil which in the future would react most unfavorably on the white man himself. They knew, according to history, that in all cases of oppression, the oppressor loses his moral sense and pristine vigor in the long run while developing against himself entwining social, economic, and political forces which eventually work his own destruction. Let us come together, then, they said, and do something to constrain both races to work out their destiny in harmony and brotherly love. In short, having particularly the interests of the white man at heart, these leaders of the new thought in the South had begun to appreciate the force of Booker T. Washington's wisdom when he said: "I will let no man drag me down so low as to make me hate him."

This very movement was an open confession that customary methods of violence had failed. The South, the reformers observed, was handicapping itself by impoverishing the Negro and preventing his mental and moral **Unrest among** development. The Negroes decreased their **Negroes.** illiteracy of persons over 10 years of age from 79.9 per cent in 1870 to 22.9 per cent in 1920, but most of this progress was above the Lower South. Negroes were, therefore, in a state of unrest; and as long as this continued there could be no security in any effort for economic amelioration dependent upon him as a stable factor. The farming sections were rapidly losing Negro labor as a result of their flocking to the cities of the South in quest of a larger return for their labor and better educational facilities, offered in the main by Northern philanthropy. The Negroes found it impossible to accumulate much on the worn-out soil; and, being generally unable to buy land, they held it tempora- **Beginnings** rily only on terms of a stringent land lease **of the** which deprived them of practically all of their **migration.** earnings. This was especially true when most of such Negro farmers in addition to these inconveniences had to bear that of paying usurious rates of interest and had to endure brutal treatment if they succeeded in maintaining themselves independently of the whites. These Negroes, moreover, were not remaining in the Southern cities. For a number of years the talented tenth of the Negroes in the South had lost large numbers to the North, and the laboring element gradually found its way to the same centers.

JOHN R. HAWKINS, a business man, an educator, and a factor in the Church

Those who had refused to treat the Negro as a man were then having trouble **The failure of intimidation.** in using him merely as an instrument. Gradually it had become evident that you cannot settle a question by satisfying only one of the parties concerned, that nothing is settled until it is settled right. For the first time in the history of the South the thinking class began to believe that the country had been actually befuddled by politicians like Ben Tilman, Hoke Smith, Cole Blease, and James K. Vardaman. For generations they had ridden into office on the worn-out issue of "Down with the Negro."

Among a few of the educated aristocracy of the South the effort became largely publicity. After **Southern Sociological Congress.** much academic discussion the proposals for racial coöperation took form under the Southern Sociological Congress founded by Mrs. Anne Russell Cole and inaugurated at Nashville in 1912 by Governor

Ben W. Hooper of Tennessee. All of the persons presenting themselves did not have the same ideas as to how racial harmony could best be promoted. They differed as to what should or should not be done for the Negro. It was noteworthy, too, that the Congress appointed a Committee on Race Problems, among the members of which were such workers among the Negroes as Miss Belle H. Bennett, Bishop W. P. Thirkield, Miss Grace Bigelow House, Dr. J. D. Hammond, Dr. H. B. Frissell and Dr. George W. Hubbard. At this first meeting of the Congress, too, there was formed what is known as the University Commission on Race Questions consisting of representative educators of ten Southern State Universities. Negroes were permitted to join the Sociological Congress, and at the second annual meeting five of them were invited as speakers. But the body did not grant the Negroes any significant share in the administration of the society, and in choosing its Negro speakers the management carefully selected those leaders who have always been known to be conservative. This policy caused the impatient element of Negroes to question the movement and to doubt its sincerity.

This Southern coöperative movement, however, was not organized to solve the race problem. Its program was "to study and improve social, civic and economic conditions in the South, to make the South better by promoting brotherhood and to enlist the entire South in a crusade of social

Efforts to improve conditions.

health and righteousness." To do all of these things the leaders of the movement realized that the coöperation of all races was necessary and for the first time in the history of the South a group of high-minded white men said to the Negroes: "Come and let us reason together." "The Negro," said they, "is the weakest link in our civilization and our welfare is indissolubly bound up with his."

The Southern leaders of thought, moreover, felt that while they could not accomplish everything at once, they might do much good in directing attention to a few urgent needs. As far as these gentlemen went in the direction of helping the Negro was to attack mob violence and request the extension of educational opportunities for the race. *The appeal to the college man.* Appealing to college trained men to influence public opinion in favor of these things, they did some good in convincing the better element of the South that the lynching of Negroes brutalizes the white man and that the mentally undeveloped laborer is an economic handicap to the nation.

Endeavoring not to alienate the rabid white man, however, the leaders of the movement lost the confidence of many Negroes when they proclaimed their belief in the integrity of races and emphasized for the Negro only that sort of education which is "rightly directed." It did not help matters to hear one of the workers say: "Agencies controlled by ideals in accord with the spirit of the South should be provided for *Difficulties in facing the issue.* training Negro ministers, teachers, and supervisors of schools." And it did not seem encouraging to have so many insist that before much could be done for the education of the Negro, more facilities would have to be provided for the mental development of the poor whites. Yet, there resulted a somewhat increasing respect for the Negro, a wider interest in industrial education, and a bold attack on the strongholds of lynching, all of which began to become effective by 1915.

This Southern coöperative movement, like its successor, the interracial effort, too, did not succeed in getting definite results. This may be accounted for by the lack of confidence in the movement, the stupendous task undertaken, and the failure to *Definite results wanting.* secure adequate funds to finance the work. Educated

Negroes severely criticised the University Commission because it was undertaking to solve the race problem without officially coöperating with the race by taking on their staff representatives of Negro schools. In connection with the Phelps-Stokes Fund, however, the Commission made a step forward in the actual study of the Negro. It established at the universities of Virginia and Georgia fellowships of $1,250 each supporting white graduate students desiring to exploit this field. Scholars, however, have not looked favorably upon the all but undergraduate type of dissertations produced by these students. The *New York Evening Post,* moreover, expressed the thought of many in saying: "While some of the educated colored people will feel like endowing scholarships elsewhere for the scientific study of the white man and of his failure to adjust himself to American civilization by lynching from Coatesville to the Gulf and his persistent nullification of the Constitution with regard to suffrage, the experts will agree that these gifts are usefully bestowed."

Such an effort as that of these few advanced Southern thinkers, however, could not immediately succeed. Unfortunately, too many of the so-called friends of the Negro had then surrendered to the reactionaries. Few white men then contributed anything to the support of propaganda in behalf of the rights of the Negroes. A Negro known to be

The Negro battling by himself. anxious to break down social barriers or to have the rights of his race respected made as little headway in raising funds in one section of the country as in another. In most cases of financial aid to institutions it had to be known beforehand that the management was safely conservative or that some white man would supervise the expenditure of the funds contributed. The Negro, according to this idea, must be carefully guarded and directed from without. You cannot leave a Negro to his own initiative, for you do not know what he

will do. He may run amuck and advocate social equality
or demand for his race the privileges of democracy when
he should restrict himself to public health, economic improvement, and industrial education.

The use made of the Phelps-Stokes Fund strikingly illus-
trates how "friends of the Negroes" often serve them.
This factor in the life of the Negro resulted from the bequest of $900,000 by Miss Caroline Phelps-   **Misdirected**
Stokes in 1909. The income from this fund   **philanthropy.**
was to be used for the improvement of tenement houses in
the city of New York, for the relief of poor families there,
"for the education of the Negro both in Africa, and in the
United States, North American Indians, and needy and
deserving white students." Almost immediately after con-
forming to the provisions for the execution of this will, the
trustees offered the United States Bureau of Education the
coöperation of this foundation in studying the private
and higher schools for Negroes. The offer was accepted by
Commissioner Claxton. Upon the recommendation of Dr.
Hollis B. Frissell, and despite the protest of Dr. Booker T.
Washington, Thomas Jesse Jones was chosen to make this
study. He had the assistance of Ocea Taylor, Thomas
Jackson Woofter, and Walter B. Hill, all of whom had not
been adequately trained in methods of scientific investigation.

Their report made in 1917, then, pertained largely to
such matters as attendance, number of teachers, income,
value of property, organization, and methods of administration. A standard which Americans and Europeans
have spent centuries reaching was agreed upon as the test
for Negro schools in operation for less than fifty years.
Those which did not measure up accordingly were pronounced uunworthy of support. Partiality was shown to
those schools for Negroes directed or controlled by white
persons.

It was proper for these investigators to expose and thereby close up many institutions which were mismanaged or used as a means for imposing upon the public;

Negro initiative discouraged. but this report worked a gross injustice to those schools founded and supported by enterprising Negroes themselves. Thomas Jesse Jones did not find much virtue in this type of school. Some of such institutions are still unable to employ adequate teachers, or purchase necessary equipment; but they are living monuments to the initiative of these pioneers. Many useful Negroes of to-day would not have received any education at all, had it not been for these very institutions. Their students did not always thoroughly learn mathematics or science; but seeing men of their own race in action, they received that better boon, the inspiration to achieve in spite of difficulties. As Jones's idea of uplifting the Negroes does not get beyond that of the benevolent tutelage of children to be developed as useful instruments for the whites, there would be no need for such initiative in Negroes. Jones would have Negro schools and social uplift agencies brought under direct control of the whites or placed in charge of Negroes whom white men can use.

By persons who know little about the Negro this report of Thomas Jesse Jones has been evaluated as one of the most important achievements in the history of Negro uplift. A little examination of the situation, however, shows that this report redounded not to the good of the Negro but to the aggrandizement of the man who made it. The

An unusual liability. work favorably impressed many philanthropists, who, having little time to study the Negro institutions in which they were interested, welcomed this biased investigator as their guide in contributing to Negro education. Booker T. Washington had often spoken for the race, but now they had some one better qualified, a white man to serve as the almoner of the despised group.

After working out the salvation of the Negro on this wise in America, moreover, he appointed himself as redeemer of the heathen in Africa through the control of its missions. This last step was a direful calamity in the life of the Negro, for Jones is too narrow-minded to understand that all of the wants of the race cannot be supplied by agencies of one sort, and the program for its uplift cannot be worked out by one man.

A careful investigation of the methods of Jones, moreover, has revealed startling facts. He has proscribed the many Negroes who criticise his policies, and he has conducted a general campaign among philan- **A bureau of** thropists to prevent their giving to institu- **espionage.** tions in which such Negroes are working. Furthermore, he may be personally interested in an agency, but if he happens to have a misunderstanding with its Negro administrative officer, he will insidiously lie in wait for every opportunity to destroy the work to wreak vengeance upon the person in charge. And worst of all, he never fights in the open, or permits his victim to know that he is doomed to slaughter. He proceeds always by indirection, writing letters of misrepresentation and holding conferences by which he influences persons against those whom he seeks to destroy. His efforts, then, have gradually degenerated into those of a bureau of espionage directed by a destructively vindictive man. He is detested by the majority of thinking Negroes. Among them his name is mentioned only to be condemned.

The Slater and Jeanes Funds, both of which are under the direction of Dr. James H. Dillard, have been more wisely used. The first of these was created by a bequest of $1,000,000 as a trust fund in March, 1882, by John F. Slater of Norwich, Connecticut, for the purpose "of uplifting the lately emancipated population of the Southern States and their posterity." The income from this fund was once used for the support of public and private schools, which had proper standards of efficiency and maintained normal and industrial departments. In the course of time, however, one of its chief concerns became the education of **County Train-** Negro rural teachers in a system of County **ing Schools.** Training Schools. These are supported in part by this fund on the condition that the local school district contribute its pro rata share and accept these institutions as a part of the public school system. There are now more than two hundred of these schools with more than a thousand teachers. The General Education Board has generously aided the work by annually contributing sums designated for building and equipment. The amount received from this foundation approximates twice the income from this fund.

The other agency known as the Rural School Fund, Anna T. Jeanes Foundation, was established in 1907 to carry out the terms of a bequest of $1,000,000 by the lady whose **Helping** name it bears. Her aim was to help "the **the rural** small rural schools." The trustees, therefore, **schools.** decided to apply the income of this fund to country schools by employing teachers trained in the handicrafts, each to serve several schools in a supervising capacity. They work under the direction of the county superintendents and endeavor to help and encourage the rural teachers. They introduce into the small country schools simple home industries, give talks and lessons on sanitation and cleanliness, promote the improvement of the school houses and the grounds, and organize clubs for the betterment of the community.

The system has so expanded that there are now employed 269 Supervising Teachers paid partly by the counties and partly by this fund. According to the last report, these workers visited regularly 7,872 country schools, making in all 35,822 visits, and raised for the purpose of school

Educators in Charge of Land Grant Colleges

improvement $338,882. Among these teachers have appeared workers like Miss Virginia E. Randolph in Virginia, who deserves honorable mention as the first Jeanes teacher to carry the work over the whole county. The success of the work throughout the South is due to the efficient State Agents connected with the State Departments of Education and to the indefatigable efforts of Mr. B. C. Caldwell and Dr. W. T. B. Williams, who have been Dr. Dillard's assistants.

This increase in the efficiency of Negro rural schools made possible the development of the Negro college separate and distinct from secondary work. This became the tendency at Shaw, Wiley, Claflin, Morehouse, Spelman, **The development of the Negro college.** Straight, Tougaloo, Talladega, Fisk, and Atlanta. It facilitated also the expansion of the work of industrial schools. Tuskegee, under Dr. R. R. Moton, for example, considerably raised the standard of its secondary academic work and began to do accredited college work in teacher training, agriculture, and business practice. During the administration of Dr. James E. Gregg, Hampton not only enriched its secondary course, but established a college department offering degrees in education and agriculture. Through these improved schools, too, it was possible to do so much more than formerly to improve the farming methods, the health, and the home building of the Negro peasantry.

The initiative of the Negro as evidenced by the support which the race has given higher institutions, however, is one of the outstanding facts in the recent history of the race. While most philanthropists refused to aid such institutions on the ground that higher education **Self-help in higher education.** for the Negro is purely experimental, the Negroes themselves sacrificed luxuries and comforts to maintain these centers that their ambitious youth might sit at the feet of Gamaliel. The amount which

The Tender Mercies of the Wicked

EDUCATORS OTHERWISE INTERESTED

MORDECAI W. JOHNSON
JOHN HOPE

W. G. PEARSON
JAMES E. SHEPARD

they thus contributed to higher institutions far exceeds the $2,000,000 which they raised for rural schools.   Dr. C. H. Parrish continued to stimulate the growth of Simmons University in Louisville, and Dr. Robert C. Woods made the Virginia Theological Seminary and College the outstanding institution for the training of Negro Baptist ministers.   The well-organized forces of the Methodists steadily promoted the development of Wilberforce, Edward Waters, Morris Brown, Livingstone, and Lane.

CHAPTER XXIX

THE NEGRO IN THE WORLD WAR

WHILE the Negroes were suffering from persecution in the South and economic proscription in the North, the world plunged almost unexpectedly into a universal struggle which materially affected the interests of **A factor** the blacks.[1] The heir-presumptive to the **in the war.** Austro-Hungarian throne was shot at Serajevo June 28, 1914. Blaming the Serbs for this crime, the Austrian government sent Serbia an ultimatum demanding that the offenders be brought to trial by a tribunal in which Austria should be represented. Serbia refused to yield to these demands and was supported by Russia in this position; but feeling that if such an act passed without punishment, it would soon be impossible for the crowned heads of Europe to maintain their empires, Germany upheld Austria. England, France, and Italy recommended that the matter be adjusted by arbitration; but Germany, contending that mobilization of the Russian army was in reality a declaration of war against her, declared war on Russia the first of August and on France two days later. England sympathized with France, to which she was attached by various ties, and accordingly entered the war against Germany. When Germany showed such disregard of her treaty obli-

[1] The history of the World War has not yet been written. There have appeared several subscription volumes for the purpose of making money rather than to publish the whole truth, and they have been extensively sold. As to the rôle of the Negro in this drama there is but scant reliable information. Emmett J. Scott has written a popular account of the achievements of the Negroes in this struggle, but it is hoped that this may soon be followed by a scientific treatise.

gations as to invade Belgium, a neutral country, she lost
the sympathy of most European and American countries,
most of which finally joined the allies to curb the power of
the Hohenzollerns.

The United States deeply sympathized with the struggle
against autocracy, but did not deem the interference with
our commerce and even the sinking of our neutral ships
sufficient cause for intervention. This coun-
Prosperity. try, then, entered at once upon an unprece-
dented period of commercial prosperity in becoming the
source of supply for almost everything needed by the numerous nations involved in the war. Industries, formerly
in a struggling state, received an unusual impetus; new
enterprises sprang up in a day; and persons once living
merely above want multiplied their wealth by fortunate investments. The aggressions of Germany upon our commerce, resulting in the death of our citizens upon ships
destroyed on the high seas, became so numerous, however,
that thousands of Americans, led by Theodore Roosevelt,
insisted upon a declaration of war against Germany. But
our trade with the Allies was so lucrative that it was difficult to convert a majority of the people of the country to
the belief that it would be better for us to disturb the era
of commercial prosperity to go to war for the mere principle that Germany wronged us in trying to break up our
lawful commerce with the belligerents in Europe.

This continued prosperity brought on a new day for the
laboring man and consequently a period of economic advancement for the Negro. The million of immigrants an-
A new day nually reaching our shores were cut off from
for labor. this country by the war. Labor in the United
States, then, soon proved to be inadequate to supply the
demand. Wages in the industrial centers of the North and
West were increased to attract white men; but a sufficient
number of them could not be found in this country, so

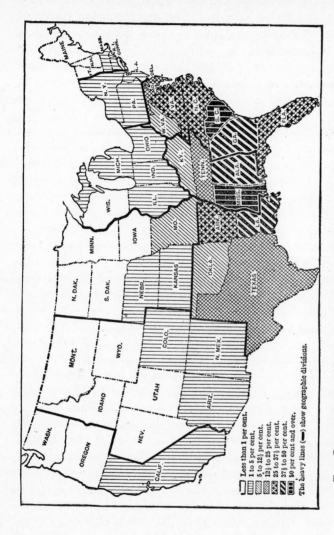

The Percentage of Negroes in the Population of the United States in 1920

great was the demand in the industrial centers, the plants, and cantonments, making preparations for war. Departing then from the time-honored custom in the North, the needy employers began to bid for Negro labor of the South. All **Negro labor** Negroes who came seeking unskilled labor **in demand.** were hired, and occasionally skilled workmen of color found employment. But the Negroes of the South were not merely invited; they were sent for. Those who first ventured North to find employment wrote back for their friends; and when this method failed to supply the demand, labor agents were sent for that purpose wherever they could find men. The Mississippi Valley, for several reasons, proved to be the most favorable section. Throughout this section conditions had at times become unsettled on account of the periodical inundations of the Mississippi; and the Negroes in those lowlands, usually the greatest sufferers, welcomed the opportunity to go to a safer and more congenial part. Throughout the Gulf States, however, where the boll weevil had for years made depredations on the cotton crop, Negroes were also inclined to move out to a section in which their economic progress might be assured. In short, the call from the North came at the time the Negroes were ready and willing to go.

It may seem a little strange that Negroes who had for years complained of intolerable persecution in the South never made any strenuous efforts to leave until offered **Economic** economic advantages in the North. Such a **advantages** course was inevitable, however; for, intoler- **in the North.** able as conditions were in the South, the Negro had to live somewhere and he could not do so in the North. There the monopoly of labor maintained by trades unions stood in the way. In this more recent movement, instead of making his way to the North where among unfriendly people he would have to eke out an existence as a menial, he was invited to come to these industrial centers where friends and employment awaited him. History, moreover, does not show that large numbers of persons have migrated because of persecution. If not assured of an equally good economic foundation elsewhere, the majority of those persecuted have decided in the final analysis to bear the ills they have rather than fly to those they know not of.

The oppression of the Negroes in the South, however, was also a cause of the exodus, though not the dominant one. When men from afar came to tell the Negroes of a way of escape to a peaceful and law-abiding **Oppression,** place, they were received as spies returning **a cause.** from the inspection of a promised land. While the many migrated with the hope of amassing fabulous sums, they all sighed with relief at the thought that they could at last go to a country where they could educate their children, protect their families from insult, and enjoy the fruits of their labor. They had pleasant recollections of the days when Negroes wielded political power, and the dream of again coming into their own was a strong motive impelling many to leave the South. Negro leaders primarily interested in securing to the race the full enjoyment of its rights rejoiced that they were going North, while the conservative, sycophantic, toady classes advised them to remain in the service of their employers in the South.

In the North the Negroes readily entered upon the full enjoyment of many privileges denied them in the South. Here and there, however, they were brought into close competition with the radical white laboring ele- **Troubles in** ment. At Chester, Youngstown, and East St. **the North.** Louis they precipitated riots in trying to get rid of Negro labor. At East St. Louis in July, 1917, Negroes long harassed by this element finally became the object of onslaughts by the whites. They were overcome by the mob, which was supported by the silence of the militia sent to maintain order. They permitted individuals to take their guns to drive the Negroes into their congested quarters, where they massacred and burned 125. The administration of justice in this Northern State seemed no better than that in the South; for although the whites were the aggressors in

A RESULT OF THE MIGRATION. A NEGRO TEACHER WITH PUPILS OF BOTH RACES

the riot, the court inflicted more punishment on the Negroes than on the whites. One Negro was sentenced to life imprisonment but later acquitted. Ten other Negroes were to serve fourteen years, whereas four white men were imprisoned for from fourteen to fifteen years, five for five years, eleven for less than one year; eighteen were fined, and seventeen acquitted.

These outbreaks, of course, justified the predictions of Southern employers that the Negroes would not be welcomed in the North and encouraged certain seriously thinking Negroes in believing that the prosperity of the Negro in the industrial centers was merely **Differing** temporary. It was said that the trades **reflections.** unions, when strengthened by the immigrants from Europe after the war, would eventually force the Negroes out of employment after having severed the ties which bound them to the South. Other Negroes had little fear from the immigrants. Believing that the depopulation of Europe during this war would render a large immigration from that quarter an impossibility, others urged the Negroes to continue their coming North in spite of all conflicts and difficulties. They rejoiced that they were then migrating in such numbers as to be mutually helpful and to wield economic and political power.

Knowing that the South was losing the only sort of labor it can use in its exploiting system, employers of that section considered the exodus a calamity. They, therefore, took steps to impede and if possible to stop the **The exodus** movement. Moral suasion was first used. **a calamity.** Negroes were told of the horrors of the North and especially of the hard winters. When letters to Negroes from friends who were easily braving these hardships reached the South, another sort of argument was necessary. Labor agents were first handicapped by requiring a high license. By special ordinances, they were then prohibited from inducing Negroes to leave, and finally they were driven out of the South. As the mail proved to be almost as good an avenue for reaching the prospective migrant, those seeking to prevent the exodus found their efforts still futile. Negroes going North were then driven from the railway stations, taken from trains, and imprisoned on false charges to delay or prevent their departure from southern cities. But the Negroes continued to go North. The movement was not checked until after the intervention of the United States in the war. The administration spent so much money in the South while hurrying the preparation for war that wages so rapidly increased and work became so general that it was unnecessary for the Negroes to go North to improve their economic condition.

The final intervention of the United States in the World War marked another epoch in the history of the Negro in this country. In the first place few people in America **The interven-** were anxious to go to the front, although a **tion of the** majority of our citizens felt that the Hohen-**United States.** zollern autocracy should be destroyed. Men had to be converted to the war. German spies had long been abroad in this country, and millions, because of their German descent, felt bitter toward the United States for going to the aid of the Allies. There was then much apprehension as to the attitude of the Negroes. Throughout this country they had been treated as pariahs, unprepared for the full measure of that democracy for which Woodrow Wilson desired to fight in Europe that the world might be a decent place to live in. As a matter of fact German spies **German spies.** did approach Negroes, and a few of them expressed themselves as being in sympathy with Germany. A still larger number boldly advocated making this country a decent place for the Negroes before taking Negroes to Europe to secure to the oppressed there privileges which the blacks could not enjoy at home.

In thinking that the Negro would prove disloyal to the United States, however, the white man showed that he did not understand the race. The Negroes of this country **The Negroes** love their native soil and will readily die, if **loyal.** necessary, to defend it. However, they do not love the reactionaries, who during the last sixty years of their control of the Federal Government have failed to live up to their oath to carry out the Constitution of the United States, which guarantees to the Negroes the enjoyment of every right, immunity, and privilege, found in the most liberal democracy on earth. The Negroes have continued to be loyal to their country, with the hope that the degraded elements in control may become sufficiently civilized to abandon medieval methods for government based on liberty, equality, and fraternity. As the principle is worth fighting for, and as the struggle for it must not be hopeless in view of the interest occasionally shown in the man far down, the Negroes would not permit their dispositions to sour; they forgot their wrongs and offered themselves to fight the battles of humanity.

The reactionary class, however, although ready to brand the Negroes with suspicion and to prosecute them for disloyalty, urged the government not to recruit Negroes. The Negroes, according to the whites of this attitude, constituted an inferior class which should not participate in the struggle of white men. **Reactionaries against Negroes.** Many Southerners who, in their faulty judgment, "have solved forever" the race problem by depriving Negroes of social, political and civic rights, moreover, considered it alarming to train them in the arts of war; for men who have waded through blood to victory are not easily intimidated into subjection to the insult and outrage legalized in the backward districts. The efforts of the reactionaries were futile, however, and the Negroes were drawn into the army in much larger numbers than they should have been. Although constituting one-tenth of the population, the Negro element furnished thirteen per cent of the soldiers called to the colors. At the same time the European nations had not sufficient prejudice to hesitate as did Americans in deciding the question of employing Negro troops. There were 280,000 Senegalese who had helped to repel the Germans on the Ourcq and the Marne, 30,000 Congolese, and about 20,000 from the British West Indies, who also did their part in saving France from autocracy.

When the American Negro was finally decided upon as

desirable for the army, the same reactionaries in control of the Federal Government endeavored to restrict them in the

Restriction in the service required. service. Negroes had to register under methods of discrimination, that they might not be confused with the whites. No provision in the beginning was made for training Negro officers, and southern congressmen urged that all Negroes be confined to stevedore regiments to labor under white commissioned and non-commissioned officers. Fearing that this would be done, Negro leaders protested. They charged the War Department with conscripting Negroes for labor. The Secretary of War, of course, assured them that nothing of the sort was planned when it was actually being done.

To the Service of Supply regiments most Negro draftees were sent. Not less than three-fourths of the 200,000 of the Negroes sent to France were reduced to laborers. It resulted that one-tenth of the population of the nation was compelled by a country fighting for democracy abroad, to

In the Service of Supply. supply three-fourths of the labor of the expeditionary force. They were commanded, moreover, largely by illiterate, prejudiced white men, and finally all but enslaved in the Service of Supply divisions abroad by unsympathetic whites, the majority of whom were Southerners on the order of slave drivers. These Negroes were subjected to unnecessary rigor; they were assigned unusually hard tasks; they were given inadequate recreation, while white soldiers in the same camp were exempted from these hardships. Abusive language, kicks and cuffs and injurious blows were the order of the day in dealing with the Negroes impressed into this branch of service. As there were in these camps no Negroes in touch with the outside world except the Young Men's Christian Association secretaries, and the slave-driving officers succeeded in displacing some of these, there was no one to

whom these Negroes could take a complaint. The Bureau
of Negro Economics directed by George E. Haynes in the
Department of Labor was very busy with various plans
during the war; but these efforts did not continue long
enough to effect much of a change in the status of the
Negro laborers in civil life, and the Bureau was not required to deal with those in the army.

These Negroes, however, accepted their lot as good soldiers. Loyal to the cause of humanity, they faced humiliation, hardships and insult without murmur. But the universal opinion is that the Negro stevedore, in
spite of all he had to endure, was the best
laborer in the war and that without this efficient service the Allies could not have been supplied with
food and munitions rapidly enough to save them from ex-
haustion. These men were stationed at the English and
French ports and at depots like that at Givres. Millions
of American wealth handled by 25,000 men there passed
through enormous masses of warehouses with 140 miles of
interior railroad lines for the handling of freight. They
unloaded the transports, prepared the vehicles to convey
the supplies to the interior, and built depots for storing
them. When the way to the expeditionary force lay
through woods and over hills, the labor battalions built
roads from the port of entry to the front. Moreover, they
buried the dead, salvaged war material, and detonated ex-
plosives scattered over France by the enemy.

The Negroes were diplomatically told that they would be
drafted to fight in the ranks as other men. The War Department, however, was not at first sure that the army
could make use of the Negro as an officer. This situation
offered little hope to the thousands of well-educated Negroes, who in the army would be serving under inferior
whites. Therefore, the students and a few members of the
faculty of Howard University instituted a nation-wide

campaign for a training camp in which Negroes of certain educational qualifications should have the opportunity to

The demand for Negro officers. qualify as officers in the national service. As this movement soon had the support of all Negro schools of consequence and was promoted, too, by many white and black citizens, the War Department was forced to take the matter under advisement. After some hesitation the administration decided to

establish at Fort Des Moines a camp for the training of colored officers. There was, however, much apprehension as to how the experiment would work out and still more as to whether the United States Government would actually commission a large number of Negro officers. Six hundred and seventy-five of the twelve hundred accepted at the camp, however, were commissioned in October, 1917, and the country saw going hither

COL. CHARLES YOUNG
The highest ranking Negro graduate of West Point

and thither the largest number of Negroes who had ever worn the stripes and bars.

The Negro officer, however, had already been proscribed. The administration had granted the Negro this recognition to secure the support of the Negroes for the war, but the

Proscription of the Negro officer. Negro officer was not desired in the army, and the personnel in control did not intend to keep him there. Colonel Young was soon retired because of high blood pressure from which he did not dreadfully suffer until in a time of rapid promotion it seemed likely that he would advance high enough to command too many white men and disturb race superiority in the United States. Then followed in the cantonments the campaign to discredit and force the Negro officer out of the army. Through the Secretary of War, Emmett J. Scott was able to counteract some of these efforts made within the limits of the United States.

This attack, however. finally centered on the Negro officer in action in France. as it was a little difficult to do here some things which could be effected abroad before the War Department could intervene. In the Fighting the 92nd Division, in which most of the Negroes Negro officer trained at Fort Des Moines served, the Negro in France. officer suffered unusually. The division was placed in command of an incompetent man, General Ballou. Surrounded by officials prejudiced against the Negro, he became unduly influenced thereby and shaped his policy accordingly. He showed very little judgment in trying to force his division to accept race discrimination, and still less in criticizing Negro officers in the presence of their subordinates. He said that they were failures before they had been tested. Wherever Negro officers were stationed, morover, a systematic effort was made to get rid of them by bringing them as early as possible before efficiency boards to find excuses for their retirement or assignment to labor battalions. In regiments where there were all Negroes the same end was reached. This happened in the case of the New York Fifteenth, from which Colonel Hayward, the white commander, secured the transfer of all Negro officers after retiring a few for inefficiency. The staff could then contend that as additional officers thereafter were necessary and other Negro officers could not be supplied, the regiment would have to take on white officers altogether,

Many superior officers openly asked that white officers be sent to their regiments regardless of the question of efficiency.

To carry out this purpose grave complaints were filed against the Negro officers. They were often charged with cowardice, although the Negro soldier was by the same man praised for his bravery. Such was the experience of four officers of the 368th Regiment. Having received the orders first to advance and then to withdraw, they obeyed both and withdrew to their former positions. As a matter of fact, these troops had not been prepared for this attack. They were without maps, without hand grenades, and without adequate ammunition, and wholly without artillery support. The "high command," as evidenced by orders, had no intention of sending these troops "over the top" in the first phase of this offensive, but had reserved for them the duty of combat liaison unit between the Seventy-seventh Division on the right and the French Chasseurs à Pieds on the left. Contrary to orders, however, these troops thus ill equipped were sent "over the top at zero hour." Major Merrill, a white officer supposed to be leading them, was nowhere to be found during the engagement. Two companies of the Second Battalion became disorganized on account of confusion in orders and Major Max A. Elser, the battalion commander, was not near enough to the front to be communicated with. He had gone well to the rear as soon as the fire became intense. Major Elser later made charges of inefficiency against four of the officers of this battalion, and regardless of his dishonorable conduct under fire he was later promoted to the rank of Lieutenant Colonel. An investigation by Newton D. Baker, the Secretary of War, showed that the Negro officers were not to be blamed and he exonerated them. He took occasion to laud these and other Negro officers and soldiers for their valor and patriotism.

In keeping with the policy of eliminating Negro officers

The New York Fifteenth in the World War

from the army, Colonel Allan J. Greer addressed a letter
to Senator K. D. McKellar, in violation of a law which, in
a country believing in justice, would subject him to court
martial. Pointing out the so-called weakness in the Negro
officer, he said: "Now that a reorganization of the army
A step be-   is in prospect . . . I think I ought to bring
yond bounds.   a matter to your attention that is of vital
importance, not only from a military point of view but
from that which all Southerners have. I refer to the question of Negro officers and Negro troops.

"The record of the division," said he, "is one which
will probably never be given full publicity, but the bare
facts are about as follows: We came to France in June,
we were given seven weeks in the training area instead of
the four weeks in training area as usually allotted, then
went to a quiet sector of the front. From there we went
to Argonne, and in the offensive starting there on September 26, had one regiment in the line, attached to the 38th
French Corps. They failed there in all their missions, laid
down and sneaked to the rear, until they were withdrawn.
Thirty of the officers of this regiment alone were reported
either for cowardice or failure to prevent their men from
retreating, and this against very little opposition. The
French and our white field officers did all that could possibly have been done; but the troops were impossible."

While these white officers of superior rank were persistently trying to weed out the Negro officers on the
Praised by   grounds of their inefficiency, the French, with
the French.   whom some of the Negro officers and troops
were fortunately brigaded, had nothing but words of praise
for their gallant leadership. Among the French officers of
consequence who thus complimented them was the unbiased
leader, General Goybet. In fact, the French officers, easily
observing that the trouble with the Negro officer and his
American superior was merely a question of color, often

interfered to save many a Negro officer from humiliation and from dishonorable discharge from the army. That there was no truth in the reports as to the general inefficiency of the Negro officer is evidenced by the fact that the 370th (the 8th Illinois), which was officered throughout by Negroes, rendered such gallant service that it received more citations and croix de guerre than any other American regiment in France. And many wondered how it could be possible for a Negro to be such a good soldier and have no possibility for leadership.

It is true that some Negro officers were inefficient; and so were many whites, thousands of whom could not stand the ordeal. It is true also that it does not make for the morale of the army to criticize, abuse and **The criticism** humiliate an officer in the presence of his men. **unjust.** If the white officers could not by army regulations be forced to respect the Negro officers, how could the Negro soldiers be expected to do so? Yet it is not true that the Negro soldiers in France did not respect and follow their Negro officers. Unusually proud of the honor conferred upon men of their race, they rather treated them with every mark of respect. The Negro officers were not lowered in the estimation of the Negro soldiers by the whiff and scorn of the white officers higher in the ranks, for the same dart of prejudice hurled at the Negro officer was also directed against Negro soldiers. They were all in common to be socially proscribed in France by Americans while fighting to make the world safe for democracy.

A few cases in evidence will be interesting. Certain colored troops were ordered to sail on the battle ship *Virginia,* but after going aboard, the officer in charge had these troops removed on the ground that no **Insult.** colored troops had ever traveled on board a United States battleship. Where under ordinary circumstances it would have been sometimes necessary for officers of both races to eat together, special arrangements were made so as to have the whites report to certain quarters while the blacks went elsewhere.   In most of these cases the blacks had inferior accommodations.   Planning for a reception of General Pershing at one of the forwarding camps, General Logan ordered that all troops except Negroes should be under arms.   Negro troops not at work were to be in their quarters or in their tents.

Every effort was made to separate the Negro soldiers from the French people.   General Ervin, desiring to reduce the Negro soldier to the status of undesirables, issued **Prejudice in** among other regulations in his order *Number* **the army.** *40*, a proclamation that Negroes should not associate with French women.   The order, of course, was not obeyed, but an effort was made to enforce it even in the case of Negro officers.   Some Negro officers who were in school at Vannes accepted the invitation to attend certain entertainments given for charity as Franco-American dances requiring an admission fee.   Upon hearing of this, General Horn prohibited their attendance by ordering that no officer of the 167th Brigade should be permitted to attend a dance where a fee was charged, although the white officers at this same school, but belonging to other brigades, could attend.

To extend systematically the operation of race prejudice throughout France the Americans had issued, August 7, 1918, through a French mission from General Pershing's **A bold** headquarters, certain *Secret Information con-* **slander.** *cerning Black American Troops.* The Americans proclaimed that it was important for French officers in command of black Americans to have an idea as to the status of the race in the United States. The Negroes were branded as a menace of degeneracy which could be escaped only by an impassable gulf established between the two races. This was an urgent need then because of the tendency of the blacks to commit the loathsome crime of assault, as they said the Negroes had already been doing in France. The French were, therefore, cautioned not to treat the Negroes with familiarity and indulgence, which are matters of grievous concern to Americans and an affront to their national policy. The Americans, it continued, were afraid that the blacks might thereby be inspired with undesirable aspirations. It was carefully explained that although the black man is a citizen of the United States, he is regarded by the whites as an inferior with, whom relations of business and service only are possible; and that the black is noted for his want of intelligence, lack of discretion, and lack of civic and professional conscience. The French Army then was advised to prevent intimacy between French officers and black officers, not to eat with

Major Joel E. Spingarn, an enemy of prejudice in the army

them nor shake hands nor seek to talk or meet with them outside of the requirements of military service. They were asked also not to commend too highly the black American troops in the presence of white Americans. Although it was all right to recognize the good qualities and service of black Americans, it should be done in moderate terms strictly in keeping with the truth. The French were urged also to restrain the native cantonment population from spoiling the Negroes, as white Americans become greatly incensed at any deep expression of intimacy between white women and black men.

From accessible evidence it is clear that if some of the American soldiers had struggled as hard to defeat the Germans as they did to implant race prejudice in France, the army would have been much nearer the Rhine when the armistice was signed. They failed, however, to bring the French around to their way of seeing liberty; and the Negroes, in appreciation for the democracy of France as they saw it and felt it, willingly sacrificed their lives to save this beautifully humane people. Whether in Champagne, in the Argonne Forest or at Metz, it was the history of the Negro repeating itself—unflinching stand before a brutal enemy, eagerness to engage in the conflict, and noble, daring endurance in the heat of the battle. Many **The Negro as a fighter.** a white soldier, many a white officer, returned with the testimony that they were braver than any white man that ever lived. They fought the enemy from behind and in the front and still came out the victor. But they were not merely victors. A score of them, like Roberts and Johnson of the New York Fifteenth, returned as heroes decorated by France for their bravery in action and their glorious triumph over Germans by whom they were greatly outnumbered.

Thinking that the record of the Negro in France might be taken as a reason for enlarging his measure of democracy for which he fought, the Negro-hating element in the **The welcome home.** army, navy, and civilian life organized to prevent this even before the close of the war. They tried so to intimidate the Negroes on their return home that they might remain content to continue in a position of recognized inferiority. The temper of editorials appearing in reactionary newspapers indicated a hostile reception for Negro soldiers returning from the war, and soon Southerners openly declared that demands for equality would be firmly met with opposition typical of the Ku Klux Klan. The Negro soldiers returning to the South, therefore, were objects of contempt. The very uniform on a Negro was to the Southerner like a red rag thrown in the face of a bull. Negro soldiers clamoring for equality

FIRST SEPARATE BATTALION OF THE DISTRICT OF COLUMBIA, receiving the Croix de Guerre in France

and justice were beaten, shot down, and lynched, to terrorize the whole black population. They were not guilty of the violation of any law, but the South considers it advisable to lynch a few Negroes even when it is known that they are innocent; for it generally results in intimidating others who might otherwise insist that they be treated as men.

This post-war down-with-the-Negro propaganda spread from the South into some points in the North, and finally reached Washington, the capital of the nation, itself. Dur-

ing the second decade of the century Washington was
southernized by an influx of public functionaries and civil
Race war in service employees hypocritically parading as
Washington. promoters of democracy but inalterably attached to the caste of color. Because of exaggerated reports that Negroes had assaulted white women and the
rumor that the wife of a marine had been thus attacked
there appeared in the streets of Washington on the 19th of
July, 1919, a number of soldiers, sailors, and marines, who
proceeded to the southwest section of Washington where
they beat several innocent Negroes. On Sunday, the following day, these whites on leave from the United States
Army and Navy, supported by civilians, had effected a
better organization to carry out their purposes. They
formed at Pennsylvania Avenue and Seventh Street a mob
which took over the city from the Capitol to the White
House. Negroes were pulled from vehicles and street cars
and beaten into unconsciousness. One was thus taken possession of by the mob and beaten unmercifully right in
front of the White House. The President must have heard
his groans, but failed to utter a word of protest. Other
Negroes were shot and left to die on the streets.

Going along Pennsylvania Avenue that night the author
himself walked into the midst of the mob at the intersection
of Eighth Street and Pennsylvania Avenue. Before he
realized where he was, there resounded shots all around
A lynching in him. A large mob swept down Pennsylvania
Washington. Avenue pursuing a Negro yelling for mercy.
Another mob at the debouchment of Eighth Street had
caught a Negro whom they conveniently adjusted for execution and shot while the author, walking as briskly as possible to escape the same fate himself, heard the harassing
groans of the Negro. To be sure that their murderous task
was well done a leader yelled to the executioners, "Did you
get him?" The reply was, "Yes, we got him."

The events of the following day, however, showed that
this mob had misjudged the Washington Negroes. They
made extensive preparation for the retaliatory onslaught of
the whites. Weapons were bought, houses were barricaded,
and high-powered automobiles were armored for touring
the city late in the night. The augmented police force and
the 300 provost guards supplied with rifles and machine
guns did not deter the Negroes. When attacked by the
white mob they easily stood their ground. They took the
offensive when the white mob attempted to invade Negro
quarters, although Thomas Armistead, charging in defense
of the Negroes, fell mortally wounded. Whereas the whites
wounded about 300 Negroes the Sunday night when they
were not expecting the attack, the casualty list of Monday
night showed two Negroes and four whites killed and a
much larger number of whites than Negroes wounded.

A riot almost of the same order broke out in Chicago a
few weeks later. In that city the large migration of Negroes to its industrial plants and the invasion of desirable
residential districts by these newcomers incensed the whites
to the point of precipitating a race war. The trouble
started there by an interracial clash at a bathing beach,
but there had already been much bombing of recently purchased Negro homes on the best streets. The Negroes, however, showed by the number of whites killed the same tendency of the Washington Negro to retaliate when attacked
by cowards. The Negro helped to save democracy abroad,
but he must fight to enjoy it at home.

CHAPTER XXX

THE NEGRO AND SOCIAL JUSTICE

DURING the last quarter of a century the Negro has had some ground for hope in the forces which bid fair to bring about a social readjustment involving the leveling of society **Impending** if not the elevation of the underman to rule **crisis.** over his hitherto so-called superiors.[1] All elements of our population during this period have been subject to change by these evolutionary movements at work among the masses. The laboring man is no longer a servile employee of serf-like tendencies, but a radical member of a dissatisfied group, demanding a proper division of the returns from his labor. He is made more potential in this position by a recent propaganda to the effect that, so far as the laboring man is concerned, political affiliation means little, since all parties have been under the influence of aristocratic leaders. Taking advantage of the ignorance of their constituents, they have been able to rule this country for the benefit of those that *have* rather than in the interest of those that *have not*. In conformity then with the cycles of government borne out by history, this country has passed through the stage of aristocracy to that of the white man's democracy and bids fair to be revolutionized in the near future by the rule of the mob represented by so-called organized labor. In other words, the country has

[1] This study may be further extended by reading W. E. B. DuBois's *The Soul of Black Folk*, his *The Negro*, William Pickens's *The New Negro*, Kelly Miller's *Race Adjustment, Out of the House of Bondage* and *Appeal to Reason*, Alain Locke's *The New Negro*. *The Atlanta University Studies* and the *Occasional Papers of the American Negro Academy* are helpful. The files of *The Crisis, The Messenger, The Crusader, The Boston Guardian, The Chicago Defender* and *The New York Age* should be consulted.

developed from aristocracy to frontier democracy, from
frontier democracy to progressivism and from progressivism almost to socialism.

This has been all but true even in the South where this
social upheaval has expressed itself politically in the rise
of the poor white man. During the days of slavery the
South and, to some extent, the whole country, **The rise of**
continued under the domination of aristo- **the poor**
cratic slaveholders. The poor whites, driven **whites.**
to the uplands and the mountains where slavery was unprofitable, never accumulated sufficient wealth to attain
political recognition enjoyed by those living near the coast.
There followed, therefore, a long train of serious clashes,
urgent debates, charges, and counter-charges coming from
discordant elements among the mountain whites requiring
an equalization of political power. When, however, after
1850 and especially after the Civil War there resulted an
extension of the franchise, making it universal free manhood suffrage, the poor whites did not long delay in realizing the power given them through the ballot. Under the
leadership then of men like James K. Varda- **Radical**
man, Benjamin Tillman, and Cole Blease, these **leaders.**
uplanders have come into their own. Lacking that sympathy for the Negroes found among the ex-slaveholders,
these poor whites, in getting control of the southern governments, however, have effected sufficient changes to deprive
the blacks of their civil and political rights and even of
some economic opportunities. Giving so much attention to
the perpetuation of caste, then, the molders of public opinion in the South have not permitted the radically democratic movements to invade that section. There it was
discovered that it would be impossible to live up to the
principles set forth without giving the Negroes a larger
share of social and political privileges. In the North, where
a smaller number of Negroes have been found, there has

not been any serious handicap to such movements. So far
The situation as the Single Taxers, the Socialists, and the
in the North. *Bolsheviki* are concerned, the Negro may
share at their table the same blessings vouchsafed to others.
The rank and file of the people, however, have hesitated

to recognize the Negro.
Leaders in the North are
still trying to decide how
large a share of social
Conservatism justice, how
of the Negro. much of the
world-wide democracy,
the Negro should enjoy.

The Negro, however,
has been loath to drift
into anarchy. His claim
f o r social justice is
rightly based on his work
as a conservative and
constructive force in the
country. Although the
present-day encroach-
ment on the part of the
degraded class of whites
has forced many Negroes
to take up arms in self-

JAMES WELDON JOHNSON, Secretary
of the National Association for the
Advancement of Colored People

defense, as in Houston, Washington, and Chicago, in
Elaine, Arkansas, Knoxville, Tennessee, and Tulsa, Oklahoma, the blacks have not and do not desire to become
radical. Increasing persecution, however, is gradually
forcing Negroes on the defensive into the ranks of the
Socialists and Radicals. Negro preachers, editors, and
teachers, who have for years pleaded at the bar of public
opinion for the recognition of the Negro as a man, now
find themselves unconsciously allied with the most radical

forces in the United States. This, of course, if not arrested by a more sympathetic consideration of the Negro's
rights, may increase the ranks of the malcontents to the
extent of effecting a general upheaval in this country.

It is well to note that there no longer exists a frontier
with all of its opportunities for free arable land. In the
midst of so many changes there the frontiersmen passed
so rapidly through the various stages of the civilization of
the backwoods, the farm, the town and the city that in a
generation they became thoroughly Americanized. Since
1890 we have been confronted with the aftermath of the
frontier—the increase of restlessness, pessimism and revolutionary sentiment, aggravated by the presence of un-
Americanized foreigners who, no longer able to go West,
must remain in our large cities to wage war against the
capitalists whom they now consider the source of all their
evils.

Labor and capital now face each other in the cities in
a restricted area, and each has to combine to protect its
interests. The combination of capital was **The conflict
in cities.** impossible when land was abundant and individualism was strong. To protect the weak we are now
reduced to a new sort of radicalism. This differs from that
of the European Socialists in that while the latter are trying to build a democracy out of the remains of monarchical
life, our malcontents are resorting to various political experiments to hold on to the ideals of the frontier which
have been shattered by the concentration of the population
in cities. There has followed, therefore, such assimilation
of the black and white people to urban conditions as to
mark an epoch in the making of our civilization. It means
a revolution not only in industry but in politics, society,
and life itself. The rural society has been destroyed by
commercialism, which has transformed the majority of the
American people into commercial beings. As more than

half of the people of the United States now live in urban communities of over 5,000 inhabitants, the problems of this country to-morrow will be the problems of the city. As the

MARY WHITE OVINGTON, Chairman of the Board of Directors of the National Association for the Advancement of Colored People

cities are now in control of the most radical elements in the United States, it is only a matter of time before the national policy will be dominated by radical thought. Men disposed to hold on to the best in republican government should think seriously of the danger of driving by persecution into the ranks of this unrestrained element the Negroes, who constitute the most conservative and the most constructive stock in America.

With the migration of a large number of Negroes to Northern cities, however, there have been tendencies indicating that wherever Negroes are numerous enough to impress themselves upon the community, disturbing race prejudice develops. We hear, therefore, of the agitation for separate schools in Philadelphia, Pittsburgh, Columbus, Indianapolis, and Chicago.

Race conflict.

There is also a desire among certain whites, not necessarily to segregate the Negroes by special ordinances to that effect, but by a common understanding to restrict them to certain parts of the cities where they may not come into such close contact with the so-called superior whites. Race

prejudice in these parts then has become much more
volcanic at times than it is in certain sections of the South,
as was evidenced by the recent riots at Chester, Pennsylvania, Youngstown, Ohio, East St. Louis, and Chicago.
Although it does not appear that any part of the North
has developed into what may be properly styled a criminal
community, as in the case of the regions like that around
Tyler, Texas, it has shown possibilities in that direction.

The greatest difficulty of all which the Negroes have
had in the North has been the problem of earning a
living. When the North had few Negroes on its hands it
was an unusually pleasant experience for **The·economic**
a Negro to go to that section and spend **problem.**
his money without restriction. He enjoyed all of the
social privileges usually denied the Negroes in the
South. But until recently it had always been extremely
difficult for the same persons of color permitted to worship in a white church or to attend a white school, to
earn a living among these same sympathetic persons. It
is only since 1916, when Negroes went North in such
large numbers as to enable employers to hire enough
of them to take over the entire operation of plants, that
they have easily succeeded in finding employment.

This difficulty has seemed a problem impossible of solution. The reason is that back of the protests against the
employment of Negroes in higher pursuits have been the
trades unions. They wield such power that
in the economic world their will has been **Trades unions.**
law. Several years ago the American Federation of Labor
declared that its purpose was for the organization of all
working people without regard to class, race, religion, or
politics; that many organizations affiliated with the
American Federation of Labor had within their membership Negro workmen with all other workers of trades;
and that the American Federation of Labor had made and

was making every effort within its power for the organization of these workmen. This, however, was largely diplomacy; but a change of attitude was evident as early as 1910 when the national council of the American Federation of Labor unanimously passed a resolution inviting persons of all races to join. The body gave instructions for making a special effort to organize Negroes, in 1913. It required the dearth of labor during the World War, however, to give the Negroes such a basis for economic freedom in the North as to secure actual consideration from the trades unions. Seeing that Negroes had to be employed and that they would be worth so much more to the trades unions than the latter would be to the Negroes, the American Federation of Labor feebly expressed a desire for the organization of Negro laborers as units of the various trades unions.

Dr. F. J. Grimké, a preacher of the New Democracy

In carrying out this program, however, the American Federation of Labor was taking high ground. In fact, it found itself far in advance of the sentiment favorable to the Negro in the rank and file of the local trades unions themselves. There was a tendency nomi-
The position of the unions. nally to admit the Negroes to the union when it was found that their competition was such as to necessitate their admission. By certain excuses and

evasion thereafter, however, the employers would take white men in preference to the Negroes, although the latter might be members of the union. During the migration, however, the American Federation of Labor had to take another stand. At the annual meeting of the American Federation in 1916, therefore, it was reported that the Negroes who were then being brought North were to fill the places of union men demanding better conditions; and it was, therefore, felt necessary to take steps to organize these Negroes who were coming in rather large numbers to be checked by strikes and riots.

The following year, the American Federation of Labor, after giving more attention than ever to the situation of labor conditions among the blacks, found itself **Attention** somewhat handicapped. This was due to the **given** fact that not only was there an antipathy of **Negroes.** the Negro toward labor unions, but they were not informed as to their operations and their benefits. It was, therefore, urged that a Negro organizer be appointed to extend the work of these trades unions among them. Many of the delegates assembled thought it advisable to suggest that at the peace table closing up the World War the American people should endeavor to influence the nations participating in this conference to agree upon a plan of turning over the continent of Africa or certain parts thereof to the African race and those descendants of the same residing in this country.

At the meeting of the American Federation of Labor in Atlantic City in 1919, there was reached the decision to admit Negroes indiscriminately into the various trades unions, to grant them the same privileges as **The American** the whites. Proclaiming thus so boldly the **Federation of** abolition of race distinction in the labor **Labor in 1919.** organizations, the American Federation of Labor has at least laid the foundation for the economic advancement of the blacks. This declaration, however, must be accepted merely as a basis upon which the Negro may take his stand for the economic struggle before him. Broad as the decision may seem, this, like any other law or constitution, must be carried out by persons who, if not sympathetically disposed, may give this decision such an interpretation as to make it mean nothing. Liberal as the American Federation of Labor may now be, moreover, the Negroes have before them a struggle. To enjoy economic freedom they must still bring about such changes in the laws and constitutions of the labor locals as to permit the carrying out of the purpose of the national body. As the matter now stands, then, the victory has been won in the national council, but the battle is yet to be waged in the locals.

A number of Negroes, not content with the efforts for their economic advancement made from without, have endeavored to remedy their own evils through agencies either established by Negroes or by white persons closely **Efforts among Negroes.** coöperating with them. One of the factors in effecting the proper distribution of labor during the World War and in securing for them justice in many communities where they would have otherwise been imposed upon, was the National League on Urban Conditions among Negroes. This is an organization with forty-one branches dealing with the Negro laboring, dependent, and delinquent classes in the various large cities. The Negroes organized also in New York a Negro labor union largely intended to find employment for Negroes rather than to secure an increase in their wages. In the Southwest, there was organized the Inter-State Association of Negro Trainmen of America, intended to perfect the union of all unorganized railway employees of color. During the World War there were several such organizations following in the wake of this. Recently an effort has been made to effect the organization of a national body which will be for the Negroes just what the American Federation of Labor has been for the whites.[2]

The Negroes have sought justice, too, not by trying to force themselves socially on the whites, but by certain im-

A. H. GRIMKÉ, "A Defender of his People"

improvements in the situations in which they now are. One of their attacks is **A just** directed **complaint.** against the poor railroad accommodations in the separate cars and stations assigned Negroes in the South. They complain also of the inadequate school facilities. They contend that it is poor logic to insist that the Negroes must be denied certain privileges because of their undeveloped state and at the same time be refused those opportunities for improvement necessary to make themselves worthy of those privileges which they are denied. They have insisted that certain recreational facilities be given the Negroes in the interest of their contentment and health. These are essential to the maintenance of that physical strength necessary to efficient labor. They have wisely contended also that if the white man is the superior of the two, the black must be brought into sufficiently close contact with the white to learn by his example. Segregation will tend to keep one part of a community backward while the other is hopelessly struggling to go forward.

[2] *Journal of Negro History*, IX, 117-127.

In spite of this, however, the South has spoken out more boldly than ever for a more radical segregation of the race. The motive here is to prevent miscegenation. Southern leaders believe that if you permit Negroes to be elevated to positions of importance, it will be only a matter of a few generations before they will be sufficiently attractive to white persons to promote the intermarriage of the races. Inalterably attached to their own ideal and believing in their superiority as the chosen people of God in line of succession with the Jews, the whites have insisted upon all sorts of social and political proscription, in fact, every measure necessary to discourage the recrudescence of the miscegenation of the races. There has been, therefore, among those Southerners who have endeavored to fall in line with the radical democratic and social movement, a tendency to accept the program so far as it does not include the Negroes. As a natural consequence, then, they have brought around to their way of thinking a large number of Southern men who have gradually gained control of the Northern press. These are idealizing the institutions of the South and pitying that section because of being handicapped by the presence of the Negro. They are demanding for the freedman exemption from unusual cruelties and persecution only, while ignoring the clamor for recognition as a real citizen of the United States.

Radical reaction.

To justify this position there have come forward a number of writers disguised as scientific investigators to prove by psychology and ethnology that the Negro is a sort of inferior being. They disregard the contention of the world's best scientists that no race is essentially inferior to any other race and that differences in civilization have resulted from varying opportunities and environments. Loath to give up this theory of superiority, however, they have devised various schemes to

Biased investigators.

make a case for the natural superiority of the white man.
Among these methods have been the collection of data intended to show that the Negro is naturally a criminal.
Some have made psychological measurements of various
types of humanity with a view to proving that the Negro
is mentally weaker than other peoples. Others are busy
writing history of the countries outside of Africa to prove
that the Negroes in Africa are inferior to races without.

A passing remark as to these methods may be worth
while. In almost all of the investigations as to the crime
of the Negroes the evidence is *ex parte*. No man should
be condemned as a criminal merely on the Unscientific
testimony of his enemies. In the matter of conclusions.
criminal statistics of the Negro the evidence is always
questionable, for the white man is the sole judge. He
makes the arrest, determines the guilt of the Negro, and
applies the penalty. Just as during the days of slavery
prejudiced masters spoke of the crimes of their slaves
and branded free Negroes as pariahs of society, so now we
hear the same concerning the Negroes. In other words, all
of this evidence is from those persons who, making desire
the father of thought, have issued statements without
evidence to support them. Such so-called statistics of the
whites adversely critical of the Negroes, against whom
they are intensely prejudiced and to whom they have
denied the rights and privileges of men, are worthless in
seeking the truth.

In making some of the psychological measurements the
experiments have been very interesting. One man found
in a white school a Negro who showed more mental capacity than any other member of the institu- Measurements
tion. To explain this away in keeping with used.
his theory that the Negro is inferior, he contended that the
Negro far off in the North among the white people by himself was better selected than the whites. In another case,

in which the purpose of the experiment was to prove that the Negro was inferior both to the Indian and white man, it was discovered that the Negro stood between the Indian and the white man. Adhering to the contention that the Negro was still inferior even to the Indian, the biased writer attributed the Negro's superior mental capacity to his closer contact with the white man. Such a little is known of the Negro race as a whole, however, that these conclusions must pass as facetious. Because the whites of modern times succeeded in finding in Africa slaves for exploitation at the time when the country was torn to pieces by wars of migrating hordes, they have concluded that these weak captives in war, whom they enslaved and debased, must be taken as a sample of what the Negro is capable of. Yet if the Negroes of this country are to serve as an indication of the capabilities of the race, it is both unscientific and unjust to expect the Negroes to pass through two hundred and fifty years of slavery and in three generations achieve as much as the whites have during many centuries. If they could do such a thing instead of thereby showing that they are equal to the whites, they would demonstrate their superiority.

To disabuse the public mind of this slander proceeding from ill-designing investigators, C. G. Woodson organized the Association for the Study of Negro Life and History The study of   in Chicago in 1915, hoping to save and pub-
the Negro.   lish the records of the Negro, that the race may not become a negligible factor in the thought of the world. The work of this Association is to collect sociological and historical data, to publish books on Negro life and history, to promote studies in this field through schools and clubs with a view to bringing about harmony between the races by interpreting the one to the other. The supporters of the movement have been well known philanthropists like Moorfield Storey, Julius Rosenwald and

John D. Rockefeller, Jr.; writers like Roland G. Usher, John M. Mecklin, Justice W. R. Riddell, Jerome Dowd, J. Franklin Jameson, and Charles S. Johnson; and publicists like Frederick L. Hoffman, Talcott Williams, and Oswald Garrison Villard. For many years the Association has published *The Journal of Negro History*, a quarterly

scientific magazine which now circulates throughout the civilized world as a valuable help to students and investigators. It has published also scientific works bearing on all phases of the Negro.

A new note in the progress of the Negro has been sounded in the appeals of the churches and the civic organizations in behalf of a square deal for the Negro. As the murder of Negroes has led to the murder of white men, many citizens [3] have begun to cry out for a halt all along the line. Citizens of both races have been appointed by mayors, governors and the like to effect an agreement by which both races may live together for the greatest good of the greatest number. An effort also has been made to bridle the radical press. By playing up in bright headlines the crimes of Negroes and suppressing the similar crimes of whites, this agency has inflamed the public mind against the Negroes as a natural criminal class. Nevertheless, a new day is dawning.

CARTER GODWIN WOODSON

[3] See Lincoln's speech in lynching in the Appendix.

CHAPTER XXXI

COURAGEOUS EFFORTS

SELF-HELP among Negroes, however, has become significant. In the first place, it has made impracticable the program of those bodies accustomed to meet for the mere academic discussion of the race problem. Their efforts were fortunately superseded to some extent by agencies designed to translate beautiful theories into action. Mere talk did not suffice when the Ku Klux Klan was terrorizing the country by exciting the poor white Protestants against the Catholics, the Negroes, and the Jews. The public had winked at the sporadic outburst of mob violence in backward communities, but unusual horror struck the public mind on seeing the agents of anarchy effecting a national organization. Once more in the history of this country some white men dared to say that the continued infringement upon the rights of the Negro will eventually mean the loss of the privileges of citizenship by white men. The churches which formerly winked at the lynching of Negroes by criminals whom they too often welcomed among them to pray and preach, began to work out plans for interracial cooperation.

Ku Klux Klan again in the saddle.

These efforts have recently taken the form of local, State and national bureaus primarily organized to find a basis on which the sane leaders of the two races may meet as citizens of a common country and dispassionately solve their problems. These workers at last have seen from experience that the perpetuation of race hate only complicates the problem of readjustment and that if any improvement

Interracial cooperation versus racial antagonism.

548

Courageous Efforts

Representative Women

MARY CHURCH TERRELL   MARY TALBERT
MARY M. BETHUNE   NANNIE H. BURROUGHS

of the situation is possible, it must come from allaying antagonisms and promoting toleration. The Negroes have been told not to expect everything they want, and white men have been entreated to cultivate a more tolerant spirit and more generous sympathy, to emphasize the best rather than the worst features of interracial relations, and to secure greater publicity for those views which are based on reason rather than on prejudice. These agencies set to work in the South to reshape public opinion, and in a short while the number of the local interracial committees exceeded a thousand.

This work has finally been given a national aspect through Secretaries W. W. Alexander and Dr. George E. Haynes of the Interracial Commission of the Federal Council of the Churches of Christ in America. A large share of the success, however, has been due to the stimulus given the cause by men and women of both races. The whites have been represented in this work by persons of the type of Mrs. Luke Johnson, Mrs. L. H. Hammond, Miss Belle H. Bennett, Dr. Plato T. Durham, Dr. M. Ashby Jones, and Dr. C. B. Wilmer. The case of the Negro has been ably stated in such councils by spokesmen like E. K. Jones, James Bond, C. S. Johnson, J. R. E. Lee, and by these useful women: Mrs. Booker T. Washington, Mrs Charlotte Hawkins Brown, Mrs. Mary McLeod Bethune, Mrs. Mary Church Terrell, Mrs. Mary B. Talbert, and Miss Nannie H. Burroughs.

Fearless workers.

To say that these achievements in racial adjustment have been due altogether to the personnel of these agencies, however, would be putting effect for cause. Such a claim would do injustice to the Negro pulpit and press, and especially to the National Association for the Advancement of Colored People. By publicity and agitation directed by Dr. DuBois. this society did much to stimulate the South

National Association for the Advancement of Colored People.

to action by making it feel ashamed of itself. Much credit
is due especially to James Weldon Johnson, the statesman-
like secretary of this organization, for the indefatigable
manner in which he has labored to unite the Negroes in
this movement and the success with which he has urged
State Legislatures to pass laws proscribing mob violence.
How he influenced Congress to the extent of forcing it to
do as much as take notice of the Anti-Lynching Bill was
in itself an achievement, great as is the credit due its
sponsor, Mr. L. C. Dyer.

It meant a great deal for reform for the country to
learn and to be repeatedly reminded that from 1885 to
1918 there were 3,224 persons lynched in the United States,
that 702 of these were white persons and 2,522 Negroes,
or 21.8 per cent whites and 78.2 per cent **Lynching**
Negroes. It was alarming to intelligent per- **exposed.**
sons in the sections concerned to observe from the scientific treatments that these lynchings were restricted in
the main to the Lower South with the occurrence of a
diminishing number in the Upper South, and that the
number in the South as a whole reached 2,834. The public,
too, was not permitted to forget the Atlanta massacre of
1906 repeated in bloody fashion in East St. Louis, Elaine,
Washington, and Chicago, during the upheaval of the
World War.

A large share of the praise for these favorable developments belongs to the Negro press. Without the aid of
the Negro newspaper this program of publishing to the
world the grievances of the Negro could not have been
carried out. Yet when one thinks of the ridi- **The Negro**
cule formerly evoked on the mention of a **press.**
Negro newspaper, one has to wonder how this agency has
been so effective in the development of the race. The
Negro press as such has contrived to exist from time immemorial. In recent years one has appreciated the influence

of such weeklies as the *Cleveland Gazette, Philadelphia Tribune, Richmond Planet, New York Age, The Freeman, The Guardian, The Dallas Express,* and *The Atlanta Independent.* Most of these papers, however, moved along in an uninteresting way without showing signs of any more growth than some which came and went prior to the emancipation of the race. The World War, however, taught the Negro newspaper how to conduct a ''drive,'' how to popularize an idea. Upon applying these methods, many of these weeklies like the *St. Louis Argus,* the *Pittsburgh Courier,* the *Norfolk Journal and Guide,* the *Baltimore Afro-American,* the *Messenger,* and the *Crisis,* found themselves with an increasing list of subscribers, additional advertisements, and correlated business which assured them a promising future.

The Negro newspaper had its opportunity in restricting itself largely to matters in which Negroes are interested, **Influence of** but which find no place in the white press. **the Negro** The Negro gets publicity among whites only **newspaper.** for the crimes committed by the race. Seeing this opportunity, the Negro press displayed race wrongs, race protest, race progress, and race aspiration. During the period from 1916 to 1920, the Negro press had much to say about migration. In fact, the Negro newspaper was one of the causes of the migration; and, in turn, the development of the Negro newspaper into a more effective force in Negro life resulted from the migration.

In no case was this more strikingly exemplified than in the rise of the *Chicago Defender.* This publication was started in 1905 by Robert S. Abbott, an all but penniless Hampton graduate. He began on the small scale of issuing the publication as copies of handbills, which he himself distributed. Abbott at once learned the value of glaring headlines featuring the sensational to attract the average man, while at the same time he filled his paper with strong editorials in defense of his race. The paper developed unexpectedly. During the migration of 1916-1918, the *Chicago Defender* became a sort of "Bible" to the Negro seeking to escape from his lot in the South. Exploiting this demand for enlightenment, Mr. Abbott attracted an efficient editorial staff, built an up-to-date printing plant, expanded the circulation beyond 200,000 and made this one of the most influential weeklies in the world.

ROBERT S. ABBOTT

The increasing power of the Negro press, moreover, has tended to solidify large num- **Achievements of the Negro editor.** bers of Negroes in the effort to extricate themselves from their present difficulties. It has not yet meant unification, but the race does not have to reach this end to carry out far-reaching schemes. The Negroes of to-day are far from thinking all alike. Public opinion among them is rapidly developing. They have not the attitude which they had just after the Civil War. The Negro leader denounced as a radical a generation ago is now branded a sycophantic conservative. A few impatient Negroes follow the fortunes of the National Equal Rights League. The majority of thinking Negroes have long believed in the sanity and feasibility of the program of the National Association for the Advancement of Colored People. These two movements, however, now seem lukewarm to the more socialistic element of the race. The discontented natives from the West Indies augmented by some ambitious Negroes of this country attach themselves to the fortunes of the Back-to-Africa movement headed by Marcus Garvey.

To most men Garvey's idea of transplanting Negroes to Africa seems insanely Utopian. In spite of his fraudulent

The Back-to-Africa movement. methods, unsound economics and unwise politics, however, Garvey has made himself one of the noted characters of his time. He has attracted a larger personal following than any Negro in the Western Hemisphere. His incarceration for misuse of the mails merely made him a hero. He is finding further support among Negroes, an unexpected thing which some have tried to account for in the ignorance of his followers. Garvey's power, however, has been due to his frank facing of the issue. Most Negro reform agencies do not do this. Believing that two separate and distinct races can live together in harmony, they are undertaking the impossible in trying to break down the social and civil barriers without promoting miscegenation. Garvey knows enough history to understand that as long as one race is white and the other black there will always be a race problem. The races must either amalgamate or separate. Garvey advocates the latter as the line of least resistance. While the deportation to Africa has proved impracticable, many contend that the emigration of a few Negro captains of industry to that land of undeveloped resources will mean much more to the Negro than the distant protest of those who from afar decry the white man's exploitation of the natives.

The Garvey movement has made a more successful appeal to the multitudes than the Pan-African idea advanced by Dr. DuBois. The latter hopes to "establish some common

The Pan-African idea. meeting ground and unity of thought among the Negro people" of the whole world through biennial meetings of the Pan-African Congress.

This body began operation in 1917 and found limited support among talented Negroes in the United States, the West Indies, and Europe. No definite program has been promulgated except that of keeping alive an idea, holding to the ideal of establishing a continuity of action toward unity and coöperation in the solution of the universal Negro problem. To use the words of the *Crisis:* "The problems of the American Negro must be thought of and settled only with continual reference to the problems of the West Indian Negroes, the problems of the French Negroes and the English Negroes, and above all, the problems of the African Negroes. This is the thought back of the Pan-African movement in all of its various manifestations."

As few white men expect any solution of the Negro problem and only a small number of any race can understand such an idealistic movement, the Pan-African Congress is generally referred to as visionary. The case But the movement goes on. At the meeting of Africans held in London in 1922 thirteen countries stated. and six of the commonwealths of the United States had representatives. From the resolutions of this meeting one may grasp an idea of the objectives of these reformers. They asked for peoples of African descent a voice in their own government, access to the land and its sources, trial by juries of their peers under established forms of law, free elementary education for all, broad training in modern industrial technique, and higher training for selected talent. They demanded, moreover, the development of Africa for the benefit of Africans rather than for the profit of Europeans, the abolition of the slave trade and of the liquor traffic, the organization of commerce and industry so as to make the main objects of capital and labor the welfare of the many rather than the enriching of the few. World disarmament and the abolition of war, they urged; but failing this, as long as white folk bear arms against black folk, these memorialists demand the right of blacks to bear arms in their own defense.

Kelly Miller sees little virtue in the hazy schemes for world-wide reform in behalf of the Negro. This race has too long looked to others; it must now look to itself. The

Uniting all agencies of the race. Negro in this country cannot be indifferent to the fate of the race as a world unity, but he must first show his competency to deal with his own domestic problems before he can assume leadership and direction of the millions of his blood now dispersed over the face of the globe. Miller has, therefore, projected an all-comprehending race conference known as the Negro Sanhedrin. This body differs from other such agencies in that, instead of burdening the race with another organization, it is to serve as a harmonizing medium to reduce these fractional agencies to a common denominator. He is endeavoring to make the Sanhedrin a clearing house through which can be pooled all interests which they hold in common. It is to be not so much an organization as an influence, a union of organizations which can speak with the consent and authority of them all.

On the other hand, some of Kelly Miller's best friends brand his scheme as more visionary than that of the Pan-African idea or the Back-to-Africa movement. They point out the impracticability of thus uniting all of the agencies working among Negroes. Self-interest, they say, will prevent the union of any large number of organizations, and if thus brought together, they cannot proceed far without differing so widely as to make impossible the construction or execution of any definite program. Already various race leaders have begun to array themselves against the movement. It has actually failed.

All of these reformers, of course, cannot be right. Somebody must be wrong. It is essential to the makeup of a reformer, moreover, that he think himself right and everybody else wrong. Although one may not agree with their ideas and methods, however, he must give them credit for continuing a hard fight. This becomes more evident when one takes into consideration the number of Negroes who acquiesce in the program of racial distinc-

TWO NEW FACTORS IN BUSINESS

C. C. SPAULDING   ANTHONY OVERTON

tions. Many innocent Negroes advocate separate playgrounds, separate schools, and the like to provide for themselves and their children employment which **The profits of** would not be available in the case of keeping **segregation.** these institutions open to all races. They are at the same time fighting segregation elsewhere, because they are inconvenienced or do not profit thereby. They show very little judgment in failing to understand that if they once yield the principle of equality and justice, there can be no hope for democracy and all their rights which they may

now have are held only by precarious tenure. Other
Negroes who thoroughly understand the inevitable result
from such a surrender give up the fight for democracy
in return for the profits of segregation. The extension
work of church organizations, social welfare agencies,
and institutions of learning controlled by white advocates
of caste have all been brought under the direction of
Negroes who have sealed their lips as to actual democracy.
Such Negroes are approached beforehand and thoroughly
tested as to their stand on race matters. If they conform to
the requirements of genuflecting toadyism they are placed
in these commanding positions to use their influence in
keeping the Negroes content with their lot. Most Negroes,
however, cannot be thus bought and paid for.

These very hopeful signs of vitality in the Negro, however, have caused reactionary whites to redouble their
efforts to keep the Negro down. Further legislation is
Unending unnecessary since the Negro has been socially
opposition. and politically proscribed in the South. The
new step toward repression, then, has been characterized
by personal methods. Negroes known to have radical views
have been dismissed from positions. Negro business men
regarded as thus inclined have been refused the coöperation
of whites. Negroes seeking loans to buy property in
desirable districts or to conduct a business interfering with
the trade of the whites have not been given any consideration in the larger business world. This has forced upon the
race a crisis, to meet the exigencies of which Negro financial
institutions are rapidly multiplying. In other words, the
struggle has become more intense on both sides—a discouraging aspect to some but a hopeful sign to those who
feel that in fighting it out the situation must become worse
before it becomes better.

All Negroes, however, have not permitted this crisis to

Courageous Efforts

SCHOLARS OF NATIONAL STANDING

ERNEST E. JUST
CHARLES H. TURNER

GEORGE W. CARVER
JULIAN H. LEWIS

diminish their interest in science, letters, and art.   The development of the race in the economic sphere has not

Achievements of the talented tenth.

meant the loss of intellectual and esthetic aspirations, but rather well-rounded growth unto full stature.   In music there have recently appeared men and women of prominence like Mrs. Florence Cole-Talbert, Marian Anderson, Hazel Harrison and Roland Hayes, performing their parts more beautifully than those of old.   Charles S. Gilpin and Egbert Austin Williams have become stars on the stage.   The poetry of Countée Cullen, Langston Hughes and Claude McKay has attracted nation-wide attention.   Scholars among Negroes, moreover, have steadily developed; and there has been an extensive recognition of their achievements.   The late Dr. Charles H. Turner of St. Louis made an all but universal reputation for himself in his studies of animal behavior.   Because of their unusual equipment, Dr. Elmer E. Imes, the physicist, and Dr. E. M. A. Chandler, the chemist, have been attracted by flattering offers in the commercial world, while Dr. St. Elmo Brady, another noted chemist, has continued as a teacher.   Dr. E. E. Just, a product of Dartmouth and Chicago, and an instructor at Howard University, has won professional standing as an authority in marine biology.   Dr. Julian H. Lewis, a specialist in pathology, has been appointed an assistant professor in pathology in a research institute connected with Chicago.   Mr. George Washington Carver, head of the Agricultural Experiment Station at Tuskegee, has made himself a world character by his achievements in the chemistry of agriculture.   He has developed more than a hundred products from the sweet potato, over a hundred and fifty uses for the peanut, upwards of sixty articles from the pecan, and extracted useful dyes from the clay of Southern soils.

Increasing interest in Negro education, moreover, has assured the growth of a larger number of Negroes unto the stature of this talented class. Systematic assistance has come from the General Education Board. This foundation, we were officially informed in 1925, has appropriated for the education of Negroes in the United States about $12,-000,000 during the past twenty-three years. A little more

Aid from the General Education Board.

A JULIUS ROSENWALD SCHOOL TAKING THE PLACE OF A RAM-SHACKLE STRUCTURE

than $8,000,000 of this sum had been paid at the close of the fiscal year 1924-25. About two-thirds went to colleges and secondary schools, approximately one-half of a million to Negro medical education and the remainder to public education, principally for rural work. These institutions include the group of independent and denominational institutes and colleges established by various Northern associations and churches and by boards of the Negro churches for the education of their own youth.

When the trying period of the recent war and the succeeding period of depression placed a difficult burden on Negro schools, the General Education Board's assistance

Special assistance. was largely devoted to annual grants for teachers' salaries and other current expenses. As the schools have become better established, this form of assistance has been gradually reduced. About $1,500,000 has been appropriated for endowment to insure the continuance of improved standards at a few schools; but, with the increasing support given by the state to its own schools of this type, the assistance given by the Board is gradually assuming other forms. The appropriations to medical education have been made to Meharry Medical

Medical education. College in Nashville, Tennessee, and to the Medical School of Howard University in Washington, D. C., principally for endowment purposes. A small part of these grants has been made for current purposes, and a portion has been appropriated for improved facilities for training Negro physicians, dentists, and nurses. When all appropriated has been paid the amount thus given will be considerable.

The General Education Board, in dealing with the problem of Negro education in the South, has consistently tried to aid the various educational agencies of the States

An educational policy. in their endeavors. In 1910 a State supervisor of colored schools was employed in the State of Virginia, through the financial aid of the Peabody Fund. A year later the support of this work was taken over by the General Education Board. A conference of the State Superintendents of Education was called at Hampton, the work was explained to them, and the offer was extended by the Board to each of the other States. Kentucky responded at once. North Carolina, Alabama and Arkansas quickly followed.

The work has grown steadily. In North Carolina, for

example, there is a Division of Negro Education employing nine people of both races. This Division is larger than the whole Department of Education twelve years ago. The State spends $15,000 a year for the support of this office. These men are well trained school men and have gone about the task of improving the Negro rural schools in a businesslike manner. From the beginning their services and counsel have been sought by school officers of the State and they have had a large share in all of the recent improvements.

The Julius Rosenwald Fund has been another factor in the rural education of Negroes. This gift has been used in building schoolhouses on the condition of getting the assistance of the State governments and the Negroes themselves. Schoolhouses have been thus built in Alabama, North Carolina, Mississippi, Louisiana, Tennessee, Virginia, South Carolina, Arkansas, Georgia, Kentucky, Texas, Maryland, and Oklahoma. These buildings numbering, July 1, 1926, as many as 3,433, vary in size from the one-teacher structure to that of one having the capacity for sixteen instructors. By July 1, 1926, 123 teachers' homes had been erected on the grounds of these schoolhouses. Schools are now in process of construction at the rate of a cost of $2,000,000 a year. Up to July 1, 1926, the Julius Rosenwald Fund had contributed $2,621,814 for this purpose, the Negroes $3,110,410, whites $694,142, and public school authorities $8,402,580, a total investment of $14,828,946.

Proceeding independently of these agencies, Mr. P. S. Dupont has all but revolutionized Negro education in Delaware by a grant of a million dollars which has been used to improve Negro rural schools. By the first of May in 1926, $1,113,258.98 had been spent in building 150 rooms in 84 schools. These buildings have capacity for 5,915 pupils and require 150 teachers. The result has been more than a mere stimulus to Negro education. Inasmuch as the improved facilities for Negroes excel those for whites in certain communities, more has been done for the latter.

The Laura Spelman Rockefeller Memorial has in recent years become interested in the interracial problems of **The Laura Spelman Rockefeller Memorial.** America and in the social and economic problems of the American Negro. It has given support toward certain researches and investigations in these fields and a limited support to certain social welfare organizations. It has made contributions to the general budgets of such organizations as the Commission on Interracial Coöperation, the National Urban League and the Association for the Study of Negro Life and History. It has encouraged research work in Negro folk studies, and in Negro social and economic studies at such institutions as the University of North Carolina and at Vanderbilt University at Nashville, particularly where these studies have been parts of systematic studies dealing with wider social groups. The Memorial has also recently made a contribution to the Department of Records and Research of Tuskegee Institute.

THE END

CHAPTER XXXII

NEGRO ART IN ITS NATURAL SETTING [1]

ON this side of the Atlantic where Americans are slowly emerging from the surfeit of material things we can see the beginning of an appreciation of art. Some few Americans have been making a small æsthetic contribution, but the atmosphere has been too cold to supply the required stimulus to persistent endeavor. People themselves may be artistic without knowing it. They sometimes go abroad in quest of art when they have it at home.

Art in its broad sense is the expression of beauty in form, color, sound, speech, and movement. It embraces, then, not only drawing, painting, sculpture and architecture, but poetry, music, dancing and dramatics. We refer to it sometimes as fine art, which is the creation of objects of imagination and taste for their own sake and without relation to the utility of the object produced. Art sometimes begins in such personal adornment as painting and tattooing the body. It expresses itself too in beautifully shaped designs as decorations on jewelry, clothing, utensils, furniture, the adornment of buildings and objects of worship. Finally, when more keenly appreciated, pictures, statutes and the like once used only for the ornamentation of objects are produced for their own sake by themselves separate and distinct from other things. Decorative art, then, becomes fine art. When these objects are produced also in conventional form according to our ideals of grace,

[1] For a more detailed treatment of Negro Art see the following: Guillaume and Munro's *Primitive Negro Sculpture*, Alain Locke's *New Negro*, pp. 19-25, and the Art Number of *Opportunity*, 1925.

ENTRANCE TO A PALACE

From the collection of works of art discovered at Benin by the Punitive Expedition in 1897, and now in General Pitt River's Museum at Farnham, Dorset. A few pieces of this art may be found in museums in Philadelphia, New York and Boston.

harmony, beauty, and the laws of perspective, we call it modern art. Modern art, then, does not rely so much upon imagination as it depends upon the imitation of nature.

The art of the African, however, is not imitative of nature. The African artist depends more upon his imagination. He is, therefore, more original. Without any training in the art of speech the African becomes a most dramtic orator; he easily expresses the rhythm of life in soul-stirring verse; and he pours out from his throat the richest of music. A study of the past of Africa, too, reveals all but wonderful paintings on its cliffs, and archæologists have found there sculptures in metal and stone which evoke the admi-

ration of the world. Among these are pointed out the ornamented pottery, the terra cotta decorations, the exquisite ivory carving, and the stone and metal productions like the megaliths of Gambia, the figures of Sherbro, and the antique works of art of Benin.

When the public began to hear of these things, some frankly said that the popular theory as to the inferiority of the African must be revised at least to the extent of conceding that he has excelled in the fine arts. Later those same observers have found so many other evidences of the significant contributions of the Negro that they have further revised their

ART AS THE AFRICAN
UNDERSTANDS IT

opinions. They now say that there is nothing in anthropology or psychology to support the theory of inferiority of people according to race. One race may have accomplished more than another, but this difference in progress is largely the result of a difference in opportunity offered by environment. It is generally agreed now, moreover, that the Negro has more of a spiritual makeup than other races. He has not permitted his mind wholly to dominate his body. He feels things deeply and he can express them emotionally. If a man is capable of deep impression he can give vivid expression. The explanation of Negro art, then, is found in his temperament or in his natural gifts.

A little study of the past of the Negroes will explain exactly why they have had little chance to make their art known. When they were carried away captive by

Negro Art Suppressed. the Europeans who did not understand their art they were dissuaded from following their native artistic bent. Negroes were encouraged to imitate their captors, and most of them are still doing it. Negroes suppressed the promptings of their own native religious instinct and ceased to give free exercise to their imagination. They were religiously taught by Europeans and Americans to forget their fondness for music, dancing,

AN AFRICAN IDEA

pageantry, and ceremony in general. Their education consisted solely of imitating the Caucasian. Negroes, then, lost their self-confidence and initiative.

Art, however, tends to reproduce itself. Nothing is ever destroyed altogether. All that the Negro accomplished in Africa was not lost. His art tended to revive in the slave on the American plantation. It appeared in the tales, proverbs and riddles of the plantation Negroes. The tribal chants of the African paved the way for the spirituals, the religious expression of the slave. The harmony of this music was in keeping with the aim of the lowly to satisfy the desire for another world better than this one of discordant note. John W. Work di- **Negro Art Returns.** rected the attention of the public to the spiritual and æsthetic value of this music. It has gradually grown upon the public until the people think of it as a work of art. Churches, schools and theaters now make a general

use of Negro music. Several have been ambitious enough to work certain fragments of it into an opera.

From the study of primitive African sculpture, moreover, art has recently received new life. Contemporary art, it is said, suddenly lost its creative powers. It was about to decline again as art did in **Negro Art a Stimulus.** Italy in the Sixteenth and Seventeenth Centuries. Fortunately at this juncture some artist

LESLIE PINCKNEY HILL

received from Negro primitive sculpture a new impetus for creative work in plastic art, in music, and in poetry. In the painting and sculpture of Picasso, Matisse, Modigliani, Lipchitz, and Soutine this influence is seen. The Negro spirit appears in the music of Satie, Auric, Honneger, Milhand, Poulenc and Talliaferro. This influence may be traced also to the works of Strawinsky and Diaghlieff. The same spirit is found in the prose and poetry of Guillaume Apollinaire, Jean Cocteau, Max Jacob, Blaise Cendrars, and Reverdy. The Negro motive in this sculpture has somewhat changed modern dress through its influence on decorative art. This is not a discovery of something entirely foreign but a recovery of an element in the past of European art. Some say that Greek art received its first stimulus from Africa.

Observing Negro sculpture, however, the layman would wonder why it is referred to as art. These figures do not show beauty as we understand it to-day. Human beings do not resemble them, and we are taught to look for imitation. They do not seem to express any high ideals. Their significance lies in *sculptural design*, a thing which the untrained observer is apt to miss. If one can learn to appreciate design he can understand African art. Thomas Munro, therefore, says: "As in other arts, it is achieved by taking certain basic themes or motifs, then repeating, varying, contrasting and interrelating them to form a unified, harmonious whole. In music, the composer takes as these certain melodic phrases and chord-progressions; the painter takes certain distinctive lines, color, spaces and areas of light and dark. What has the sculptor to use that is analogous to these themes? Sometimes he too uses color, but not often; mainly he depends on lines (grooves, ridges and contours of objects as seen in silhouette), on surfaces of different curvature, angularity, texture and degree of smoothness, and on masses of different shape, such as cylinders, spheres, and irregular approximations to these and other shapes. From these he can select a few particular forms, vary, and combine them in countless different ways.

"The repetition of similar lines, planes and masses tends to give an effect of rhythmic sequence, as of beats in music, which is satisfying to the instinctive craving for rhythm which all human beings, and even animals, possess innately.

How to Understand African Art.

IVORY UTENSILS FROM BENIN

"The real African," says Leo Frobenius, "need by no means resort to the rags and tatters of bygone European splendor. He has precious ornaments of his own, of ivory and feathers, fine plaited willowware, weapons of superior workmanship. Nothing more beautiful, for instance, can be imagined than an iron club carefully wound round with strips of metal, the handle covered with snake skin." And Dr. Franz Boas has recently called attention to the "dainty basketry" of the Congo and the Nile Lakes, the "grass mats of the most beautiful patterns" made by some of the Negro tribes, and "the beautiful iron weapons of Central Africa, which excel, in symmetry of form, and many of which bear elaborate designs inlaid in copper, and are of admirable workmanship."

A characteristic rhythm pervading the various parts of an object also tends to give it the appearance of harmonious unity, which satisfies another innate desire, that of order and equilibrium. Yet if the similarity of parts is too complete, the design tends to become monotonous, so an imaginative artist will introduce unexpected and surprising variations and contrasts, taking care at the same time not to let these destroy the underlying sense of harmony.

"Ordinary European and American sculpture, which imitates the Greek and Renaissance, shows comparatively little systematic use of rhythmic design. An occasional swirl is repeated in drapery; an angle of the elbow may be repeated in that of the knee; but these few conventional rhythms are used over and over again to the point of tiresome banality. Outside these few rhythms, many

The Use of Rhythmic Design.

R. NATHANIEL DETT

of the parts of an ordinary statue are plastically unrelated, thus destroying unity; many curves, features, limbs, have little definite resemblance to others. This must always be the case when art is dominated by the aim of exact representation, for if the artist must conform to the actual proportions of anatomy and clothing, including a host of details as they exist in nature, he can never bring them into a simple, harmonious and original design. Selection of certain aspects and elimination of others is the essence of all art, and the sculptor who merely copies nature, though he may astonish us with his technical skill, is no more creative than the maker of a plaster cast. In the interest of creative design, the sculptors of all great past traditions, such as the Egyptian, early Greek, Hindu and Chinese, have not hesitated to depart from natural anatomical proportions.

In other words, the "distortion" which perplexes many observers in Negro sculpture is not peculiar to the art of the Negro. In no other form of sculpture, however, is the body altered so freely and extensively, with the resulting achievement of a wealth of strik-   **Distortion an Art.** ing and different rhythms. Since these rhythms are composed of fully shaped masses as well as lines and surfaces, the typical Negro statue has an effect of vigorous three-dimensional solidity, and presents a variety of designs when seen from different points of view. Since in the best pieces every part is plastically related to every other with firm subordination of decorative detail to underlying structure, there results a high degree of harmonious unity and cohesive strength. These, in general, are the qualities for which Negro sculpture is to-day so highly prized. Such results, it should be needless to say, are never the outcome of mere savage crudity or lack of skill in accurate representation. The Negro's mastery of the medium is amply demonstrated by a complex unity of organization and a delicate precision of detail, which require quite as much purposeful technique as most accurate representation."

We are just beginning also to appreciate the Negro poet. The Negro is born a poet. He is not so much concerned with scientific precision as with things in the concrete, "the immediate and colorful." He likes the at-   **Poetry of Art.** mosphere of fancy. We were amused by Paul Laurence Dunbar. Few persons saw the depths of the philosophy which he presented in his lyrics

MASKS

A mask, as we understand it, is a cover for the face used for disguise or protection by dancers, fencers, and athletes. We know also that the Greek and Roman actors used the mask partly as a symbol of the character represented and partly to concentrate the sound of the voice. In the grotesque form, the mask has been widely used at carnivals. It seems that the African made all of these uses of the mask and in addition to this employed it in serious matters like worship. This probably accounts for the numerous works of this sort of art discovered in various parts of Africa. The unusual art displayed in making them may be explained by this extensive use.

of lowly life. The spirit of a great people was imbedded there, but we did not know it. The story is being told again by James Weldon Johnson, Angelina Grimké, Langston Hughes, Countee Cullen, Joseph Seaman Cotter, Georgia Douglas Johnson, Claude McKay, and others. As

LANGSTON HUGHES

Dr. A. C. Barnes says of this poetry of art: "The images are vivid and full of color; they express the personal sorrows, hopes and aspirations of the poet, transfigured by imagination and given universal human significance. They have the emotional harmony, the rhythmic surge, the poignancy and rapture which are the authentic note of poetic inspiration. In the work of the Negro novelists at its best, the same vivid realism is combined with imaginative vision. The modern literary movement among the Negroes is rapidly advancing; and, in conjunction with the new interest in Negro sculpture and music, is undoubtedly the chief agent in making the Negro aware of his actual spiritual stature. Through its investigations, reports, and publications the Association for the Study of Negro Life and History is doing much to bring this to pass. "When this consciousness is fully spread through his own race and the race of his oppressors, the Negro will be assured of the high place he deserves in American civilization."

APPENDIX

Speaking of the effect of the Missouri Compromise, John Quincy Adams, then Secretary of State, said:

I said that this confounding of the ideas of servitude and labor was one of the bad effects of slavery; but he (Calhoun) thought it attended with many excellent consequences. It did not apply to all kinds of labor—not, for example, to farming. He, himself, had often held the plow; so had his father. Manufacturing and mechanical labor were not degrading. It was only manual labor—the proper work of slaves. No white person could descend to do that. And it was the best guarantee to equality among the whites. It produced an unvarying level among them. It not only did not excite, but did not ever admit of inequalities, by which one white man could domineer over another.

I told Calhoun I could not see things in the same light. It is, in truth, all perverted sentiment—mistaking labor for slavery, and dominion for freedom. The discussion of this Missouri question has betrayed the secret of their souls. In the abstract they admit that slavery is an evil, they disclaim all participation in the introduction of it, and cast it all upon the shoulders of our old Grandam Britain. But when probed to the quick upon it, they show at the bottom of their souls pride and vainglory in their condition of masterdom. They fancy themselves more generous and noble-hearted than the plain freemen who labor for subsistence. They look down upon the simplicity of a Yankee's manners, because he has not habits of overbearing like theirs and cannot treat negroes like dogs. It is among the evils of slavery that it taints the very sources of moral principles. It establishes false estimates of virtue and vice; for what can be more false and heartless than this doctrine which makes the first and holiest rights of humanity to depend upon the color of the skin. It perverts human reason, and reduces men endowed with logical powers to maintain that slavery is sanctioned by the Christian religion, that slaves are happy and contented in their condition, that between master and slave there are ties of mutual attachment and affection, that the virtues of the master are refined and exalted by the degradation of the slave; while at the same time they vent execrations upon the slave-trade, curse Britain for having given them slaves, burn at the stake negroes convicted of crimes for the terror of the example, and writhe in agonies of fear at the very mention of human rights as applicable to men of color. The impression produced upon my mind by the progress of this discussion is, that the bargain between freedom and slavery contained in the Constitution of the United States is morally and politically vicious, inconsistent with the principles upon which alone our Revolution can be justified; cruel and oppressive, by riveting the chains of slavery, by pledging the faith of freedom to maintain and perpetuate the tyranny of the master; and grossly unequal and impolitic by admitting that slaves are at once enemies to be kept in subjection, property to be secured or restored to their owners, and persons not to be represented themselves, but for whom their masters are privileged with nearly a double share of representation. The consequence has been that this slave representation has governed the Union. Benjamin portioned above his brethren has ravened as a wolf. In the morning he has devoured the prey, and at night he has divided the spoil. It would be no difficult matter to prove, by reviewing the history of the Union under this Constitution, that almost everything which has contributed to the honor and welfare of the nation has been accomplished in despite of them or forced upon them, and that everything unpropitious and dishonorable, including the blunders and follies of their adversaries, may be traced to them. I have favored this Missouri Compromise, believing it to be all that could be effected under the present Constitution and from extreme unwillingness to put the Union at hazard. But perhaps it would have been a wiser as well as a bolder course to have persisted in the restriction upon Missouri, till it should have terminated in a convention of the States to amend and revise the Constitution. This would have produced a new Union of thirteen or fourteen States unpolluted with slavery, with a great and glorious object to effect, namely, that of rallying to their standard the other States by the universal emancipation of their slaves. If the Union must be dissolved, slavery is precisely the question upon which it ought to break. For the present, however, this contest is laid asleep.—Stedman and Hutchinson, *American Literature* (N. Y., 1888), IV, 213-233, *passim.*

On these restrictions in Missouri John Sergeant, Pennsylvania member of Congress and appointed commissioner to the Panama Congress, said:

It is time to come to a conclusion; I fear I have already trespassed too long. In the effort I have made to submit to the committee my views of this question, it has been impossible to escape entirely the influence of the sentiment that pervades this House. Yet I have no such apprehensions as have been expressed. The question is indeed an important one; but its importance is derived altogether from its connection with the extension, indefinitely, of negro slavery, over a land which I trust Providence has destined for the labor and the support of freemen. I have no fear that this question, much as it has agitated the country, is to produce any fatal division, or even to generate a new organization of parties. It is not a question upon which we ought to indulge unreasonable apprehensions, or yield to the counsels of fear. It concerns ages to come and millions to be born. It is, as it were, a question of a new political creation, and it is for us, under Heaven, to say what shall be its condition. If we impose the restriction, it will, I hope, be finally imposed. But, if hereafter it should be found right to remove it, and the State consent, we can remove it. Admit the State, without the restriction, the power is gone forever, and with it are forever gone all the efforts that have been made by the non-slaveholding States, to repress and limit the sphere of slavery, and enlarge and extend the blessings of freedom. With it, perhaps, is gone forever the· power of preventing the traffic in slaves, that inhuman and detestable traffic, so long a disgrace to Christendom. In future, and no very distant times, convenience, and profit, and necessity, may be found as available pleas as they formerly were, and for the luxury of slaves, we shall again involve ourselves in the sin of the trade. We must not presume too much upon the strength of our resolutions. Let every man, who has been accustomed to the indulgence, ask himself if it is not a luxury—a tempting luxury, which solicits him strongly and at every moment. The prompt obedience, the ready attention, the submissive and humble, but eager effort to anticipate command—how flattering to our pride, how soothing to our indolence! To the members from the south, I appeal, to know whether they will suffer any temporary inconvenience, or any speculative advantage to expose us to the danger. To those of the north, no appeal can be necessary. To both, I can most sincerely say, that as I know my own views on this subject to be free from any unworthy motive, so will I believe that they likewise have no object but the common good of our common country; and that nothing would have given me more heartfelt satisfaction than that the present proposition should have originated in the same quarter to which we are said to be indebted for the ordinance of 1787. Then, indeed, would Virginia have appeared in even more than her wonted splendor, and spreading out the scroll of her services, would have beheld none of them with greater pleasure, than that cries which began, by pleading the cause of humanity in remonstrances against the slave trade, while she was yet a colony, and embracing her own act of abolition, and the ordinance of 1787, terminated in the restriction of Missouri. Consider, what a foundation our predecessors have laid! And behold, with the blessing of Providence, how the work has prospered! What is there, in ancient or in modern times, that can be compared with the growth and prosperity of the States formed out of the Northwest Territory? When Europeans reproach us with our negro slavery, when they contrast our republican boast and pretensions with the existence of this condition among us, we have our answer ready—it is to you we owe this evil—you planted it here, and it has taken such root in the soil we have not the power to eradicate it. Then, turning to the west, and directing their attention to Ohio, Indiana, and Illinois, we can proudly tell them, these are the offspring of our policy and our laws, these are the free productions of the constitution of the United States. But, if, beyond this smiling region, they should descry another dark spot upon the face of the new creation—another scene of negro slavery, established by ourselves, and spreading continually towards the further ocean, what shall we say then? No, sir, let us follow up the work our ancestors have begun. Let us give to the world a new pledge of our sincerity. Let the standard of freedom be planted in Missouri, by the hands of the constitution, and let its

banner wave over the heads of none but freemen—men retaining the
image impressed upon them by their Creator, and dependent upon
none but God and the laws. Then, as our republican States extend,
republican principles will go hand in hand with republican practice—
the love of liberty with the sense of justice. Then, sir, the dawn,
beaming from the constitution, which now illuminates Ohio, Indiana,
and Illinois, will spread with increasing brightness to the further
west; until in its brilliant luster, the dark spot, which now rests
upon our country, shall be forever hid from sight. Industry, arts,
commerce, knowledge, will flourish with plenty and contentment for
ages to come, and the loud chorus of universal freedom, re-echo from
the Pacific to the Atlantic, the great truths of the declaration of
independence. Then, too, our brethren of the south, if they sincerely
wish it, may scatter their emancipated slaves through this boundless
region, and our country, at length, be happily freed forever from
the foul stain and curse of slavery. And if (may it be far, very far
distant!) intestine commotion—civil dissension—division, should
happen—we shall not leave our posterity exposed to the combined
horrors of a Civil and a servile war. If any man still hesitate, influenced by some temporary motive of convenience, or ease, or profit,
I charge him to think what our fathers have suffered for us, and then
to ask his heart, if he can be faithless to the obligation he owes to
posterity!—Moore, *American Eloquence* (N. Y., 1864), II, 531-532.

Calhoun, the champion of the slaveholding interests and
a fearless defender of the justice of slavery, thus com-
mented on abolition in 1837:

As widely as this incendiary spirit has spread, it has not yet in-
fected this body, or the great mass of the intelligent and business
portion of the North; but unless it be speedily stopped, it will spread
and work upwards till it brings the two great sections of the Union
into deadly conflict. This is not a new impression with me. Several
years since, in a discussion with one of the Senators from Massachusetts (Mr. Webster), before this fell spirit had showed itself, I then
predicted that the doctrine of the proclamation and the Force Bill,—
that this Government had a right, in the last resort, to determine
the extent of its own powers, and enforce its decision at the point
of the bayonet, which was so warmly maintained by that Senator,
would at no distant day arouse the dormant spirit of abolitionism. I
told him that the doctrine was tantamount to the assumption of
unlimited power on the part of the Government, and that such would
be the impression on the public mind in a large portion of the Union.
The consequences would be inevitable. A large portion of the Northern States believed slavery to be a sin, and would consider it as an
obligation of conscience to abolish it if they should feel themselves in
any degree responsible for its continuance,—and that this doctrine
would necessarily lead to the belief of such responsibility. . . .
They who imagine that the spirit now abroad in the North will
die away of itself without a shock or convulsion, have formed a
very inadequate conception of its real character; it will continue to

rise and spread, unless prompt and efficient measures to stay its progress be adopted. Already it has taken possession of the pulpit, of the schools, and, to a considerable extent, of the press; those great instruments by which the mind of the rising generation will be formed.

However sound the great body of the non-slaveholding States are at present, in the course of a few years they will be succeeded by those who will have been taught to hate the people and institutions of nearly one-half of this Union, with a hatred more deadly than one hostile nation ever entertained toward another. It is easy to see the end. By the necessary course of events, if left to themselves, we must become, finally, two people. It is impossible under the deadly hatred which must spring up between the two great sections, if the present causes are permitted to operate unchecked, that we should continue under the same political system. The conflicting elements would burst the Union asunder, powerful as are the links which hold it together. Abolition and the Union cannot co-exist. As the friend of the Union, I openly proclaim it,—and the sooner it is known the better. The former may now be controlled, but in a short time it will be beyond the power of man to arrest the course of events. We of the South will not, cannot, surrender our institutions. To maintain the existing relations between the two races, inhabiting that section of the Union, is indispensable to the peace and happiness of both. It cannot be subverted without drenching the country in blood, and extirpating one or the other of the races. Be it good or bad, it has grown up with our society and institutions, and is so interwoven with them, that to destroy it would be to destroy us as a people. But let me not be understood as admitting, even by implication, that the existing relations between the two races in the slaveholding States is an evil:—far otherwise; I hold it to be a good, as it has thus far proved itself to be to both, and will continue to prove so if not disturbed by the fell spirit of abolition. . . .

I feel myself called upon to speak freely upon the subject where the honor and interests of those I represent are involved. I hold then, that there never has yet existed a wealthy and civilized society in which one portion of the community did not, in point of fact, live on the labor of the other. Broad and general as is this assertion, it is fully borne out by history. . . . I fearlessly assert that the existing relations between the two races in the South, against which these blind fanatics are waging war, forms the most solid and durable foundation on which to rear free and stable political institutions. It is useless to disguise the fact. There is and always has been in an advanced stage of wealth and civilization, a conflict between labor and capital. The condition of society in the South exempts us from the disorders and dangers resulting from this conflict; and which explains why it is that the political condition of the slaveholding States has been so much more stable and quiet than that of the North. The advantages of the former, in this respect, will become more and more manifest if left undisturbed by interference from without, as the country advances in wealth and numbers. We have, in fact, but just entered that condition of society where the strength and durability of our political institutions are to be tested; and I venture nothing in predicting that the experience of the next generation will fully test how vastly more favorable our condition of society is to that of other sections for free and stable institutions, provided we are not disturbed by the interference of others, or shall have sufficient intelligence and spirit to resist promptly and successfully such interference. It rests with ourselves to meet and repel them. I look not for aid to this Government or to the other States; not but there are kind feelings toward us on the part of the great body of the non-slaveholding States; but as kind as their feelings may be, we may rest assured that no political party in those States will risk their ascendance for our safety. If we do not defend ourselves none will defend us; if we yield we will be more and more pressed as we recede; and if we submit we will be trampled under foot. Be assured that emancipation itself would not satisfy these fanatics;—that gained, the next step would be to raise the negroes to a social and political equality with the whites; and that being effected, we would soon find the present condition of the two races reversed. . . . Calhoun, *Speeches* (N. Y., 1856), II, 628-633 *passim.*

The beginnings of the *Liberator* are well set forth in this extract:

To the Public.

In the month of August I issued proposals for publishing the *Liberator* in Washington city; but the enterprise, though hailed in different sections of the country, was palsied by public indifference. Since that time, the removal of the *Genius of Universal Emancipation* to the Seat of Government has rendered less imperious the establishment of a similar periodical in that quarter.

During my recent tour for the purpose of exciting the minds of the people by a series of discourses on the subject of slavery, every place that I visited gave fresh evidence of the fact, that a greater revolution in public sentiment was to be effected in the free States— *and particularly in New England*—than in the South. I found contempt more bitter, opposition more active, detraction more relentless, prejudice more stubborn, and apathy more frozen, than among slave-owners themselves. Of course, there were individual exceptions to the contrary. This state of things afflicted, but did not dishearten me. I determined, at every hazard, to lift up the standard of emancipation in the eyes of the nation, *within sight of Bunker Hill and in the birthplace of liberty.* That standard is now unfurled; and long may it float, unhurt by the spoliations of time or the missiles of a desperate foe—yea, till every secret abettor tremble— let their northern apologist tremble—let all the enemies of the persecuted blacks tremble. . . .

I shall not array myself as the political partisan of any man. In defending the great cause of human rights, I wish to derive the assistance of all religions and of all parties.

Assenting to the "self-evident truth" maintained in the American Declaration of Independence, "that all men are created equal, and endowed by their Creator with certain inalienable rights—among which are life, liberty, and the pursuit of happiness," I shall strenuously contend for the immediate enfranchisement of our slave population. In Park Street Church, on the Fourth of July, 1829, in an address on slavery, I unreflectingly assented to the popular but pernicious doctrine of *gradual* abolition. I seize this opportunity to make a full and unequivocal recantation, and thus publicly to ask pardon of my God, of my country, and of my brethren, the poor slaves, for having uttered a sentiment so full of timidity, injustice, and absurdity. A similar recantation, from my pen, was published in the *Genius of Universal Emancipation*, at Baltimore, in September, 1820. My conscience is now satisfied.

I am aware that many object to the severity of my language; but is there not cause for severity? I *will be* as harsh as truth, and as uncompromising as justice. On this subject, I do not wish to think, or speak, or write, with moderation. No! no! Tell a man whose house is on fire to give a moderate alarm; tell him to moderately rescue his wife from the hands of the ravisher; tell the mother to gradually extricate her babe from the fire into which it has fallen,— but urge me not to use moderation in a cause like the present. I am in earnest—I will not equivocate—I will not excuse—I will not retreat a single inch—and I will be heard. The apathy of the people is enough to make every statue leap from its pedestal, and to hasten the resurrection of the dead.

It is pretended that I am retarding the cause of emancipation by the coarseness of my invective and the precipitancy of my measures. The *charge is not true*. On this question my influence,—humble as it is,—is felt at this moment to a considerable extent, and shall be felt in coming years—not perniciously, but beneficially—not as a curse, but as a blessing; and posterity will bear testimony that I was right. I desire to thank God, that he enables me to disregard "the fear of man which bringeth a snare," and to speak his truth in its simplicity and power. And here I close with this fresh dedication:

> Oppression! I have seen thee face to face,
> And met thy cruel eye and cloudy brow;
> But thy soul-withering glance I fear not now—
> For dread to prouder feelings doth give place
> Of deep abhorrence! Scorning the disgrace
> Of slavish knees that at thy footstool bow,
> I also kneel—but with far other vow
> Do hail thee and thy herd of hirelings base:—
> I swear, while life-blood warms my throbbing veins,
> Still to oppose and thwart, with heart and hand,
> Thy brutalizing sway—till Afric's chains
> Are burst, and Freedom rules the rescued land,—
> Trampling Oppression and iron rod:
> *Such is the vow I take*—so help me God!
> —W. L. Garrison, *Works* (Boston, 1905), pp. 70-73.

The constitution of the American Antislavery Society was:

Whereas, the Most High God "hath made of one blood all nations of men to dwell on all the face of the earth," and hath commanded them to love their neighbors as themselves; and whereas, our National Existence is based on this principle, as recognized in the Declaration of Independence, "that all mankind are created equal, and that they are endowed by their Creator with certain inalienable rights, among which are life, liberty, and the pursuit of happiness"; and whereas, after the lapse of nearly sixty years, since the faith and honor of the American people were pledged to this avowal, before Almighty God and the World, nearly one-sixth part of the nation are held in bondage by their fellow-citizens; and whereas, Slavery is contrary to the principles of natural justice, of our republican form of government, and of the Christian religion, and is destructive of the prosperity of the country, while it is endangering the peace, union, and liberties of the States; and whereas, we believe it the duty and interest of the masters immediately to emancipate their slaves, and that no scheme of expatriation, either voluntary or by compulsion, can remove this great and increasing evil; and whereas, we believe that it is practicable, by appeals to the consciences, hearts, and interests of the people, to awaken a public sentiment throughout the nation that will be opposed to the continuance of Slavery in any part of the Republic, and by effecting the speedy abolition of Slavery, prevent a general convulsion; and whereas, we believe we owe it to the oppressed, to our fellow-citizens who hold slaves, to our whole country, to posterity, and to God, to do all that is lawfully in our power to bring about the extinction of Slavery, we do hereby agree, with a prayerful reliance on the Divine aid, to form ourselves into a society, to be governed by the following Constitution:

Article I.—This Society shall be called The American Antislavery Society.

Article II.—The objects of this Society are the entire abolition of slavery in the United States. While it admits that each State, in which Slavery exists, has, by the Constitution of the United States, the exclusive right to *legislate* in regard to its abolition in said State, it shall aim to convince all our fellow-citizens, by arguments addressed to their understandings and consciences, that Slaveholding is a heinous crime in the sight of God, and that the duty, safety, and best interests of all concerned, require its *immediate abandonment*, without expatriation. The Society will also endeavor, in a constitutional way, to influence Congress to put an end to the domestic Slave trade, and to abolish Slavery in all those portions of our common country which come under its control especially in the District of Columbia,—and likewise to prevent the extension of it to any State that may be hereafter admitted to the Union.

Article III.—This Society shall aim to elevate the character and condition of the people of color, by encouraging their intellectual, moral, and religious improvement, and by removing public prejudice, that thus they may, according to their intellectual moral worth, share an equality with the whites, of civil and religious privileges; but this Society will never in any way countenance the oppressed in vindicating their rights by resorting to physical force.

Article IV.—Any person who consents to the principles of this

Constitution, who contributes to the funds of this Society, and is not a Slaveholder, may be a member of this Society, and shall be entitled to vote at the meetings.

The text is in a pamphlet, entitled *Platform of the American Anti-slavery Society and Its Auxiliaries* (New York, 1855), pp. 3, 4. The fullest account of the convention is in *William Lloyd Garrison: Story of His Life Told by His Children*, I, pp. 392-415, where is also a copy of the Declaration. The Declaration is also in the pamphlet above cited. For Whittier's account, see *Atlantic Monthly*, Vol. XXXIII, pp. 166-172. (February, 1874.)

This appeal of a Southern Matron for patience is a case in evidence of the thinking element in the South:

Shut your eyes no longer, my countrymen—the Union is threatened; and all the blessings it confers, and which our fathers suffered and died to attain, must perish with it. Scorn not the feeble voice of a woman, when she calls on you to awake to your danger, ere it be forever too late. We are told that the citizens of the North would arouse our slaves to exert their physical force against us—but we cannot, we will not believe the foul, shocking, unnatural tale. What! have the daughters of the South inflicted such injuries on their Northern brethren, as to render them objects of their deadly, exterminating hate? Have helpless age, smiling infancy, virgin purity no claims on the generous, the highminded and the brave? Would they introduce the serpents of fear and withering anxiety into the Edens of domestic bliss; bathe our peaceful hearths with blood, and force us to abhor those ties which now unite us as one people, and which we so lately taught our sons to regard as our pride? We cannot believe it. We cannot be so unjust to the enlightened and humane citizens of the Northern States, as to suppose for a moment that they approve of the course pursued by those reckless agitators who seek to inflict such cruel calamities on the South. The poor slave himself merits not at their hands the mischief and woe which his mistaken advocates would heap on his devoted head; for even they cannot imagine that an exertion of physical force on their part could result in aught but his destruction. No—the Northern people are too well acquainted with historical facts, to condemn us for evils which we deprecated as warmly as themselves, but which were ruthlessly imposed on us by the power of Great Britain.

So far from condemning, they must sympathize with us; for they well know that slavery was forced upon us, and that as early as 1760 the Southern colonies earnestly sought to avert it by passing acts imposing duties on slaves, and even prohibiting their importation. In spite of sectional prejudices (alas, too often fostered for the worst ends by the unprincipled and ambitious)—in spite of conflicting interests, the people of the North are our brethren. Together our fathers shared many a peril. Side by side, they fought and bled in defense of their common country. Their united wisdom was exerted to form our glorious Constitution, and these republican institutions, which so justly are our boast, and the safeguard of our liberties.

Would the sons overthrow the noble fabric their fathers assisted to rear, even now, when towering aloft in its majesty and beauty, it attracts the admiration of the world?—We cannot believe they are prepared for so suicidal an act. The States are all more or less dependent on each other. Let one portion be weakened and depressed, the whole must ultimately suffer. Oh! that a spirit of compromise, forbearance, and brotherly love could be infused into our councils, and animate the bosoms of our public men. Then the voice of contention would be hushed into silence. The insidious treachery of the incendiary would meet the contempt it merits, and factious demagogues would shrink abashed beneath the deep, stern voice of a nation's censure. Then the daughters of America could look joyfully on their sons and indulge the proud hope that they and their children would live and die the free and happy citizens of the great, flourishing and United States of America.

Deluded emancipators of the North, we now appeal to you! We deprecate slavery as much as you. We as ardently desire the liberty of the whole human race; but what can we do? The slow hand of time must overcome these difficulties now insurmountable. An evil, the growth of ages, cannot be remedied in a day. Our virtuous and enlightened men will doubtless effect much by cautious exertion, if their efforts are not checked by your rash attempts to dictate on a subject on which it is impossible that you can form a correct judgment. Forbear your inflammatory addresses. They but rivet the fetters of the slaves, and render them ten thousand times more galling. You sacrifice his happiness, as well as that of his owner, for, by rendering him an object of suspicion and alarm you deprive him of the regard, confidence, and, I may add, with the utmost truth, the affection of his master. You render a being now light-hearted and joyous, moody, wretched—yes, hopelessly wretched. You wreak on the innocent and helpless, who, had they the will, possess not the power to bid the slave be free from all his imagined wrongs. You agonize gentle bosoms, which glow with Christian charity towards the whole human race, of whatever color they may be: Fearful forebodings mingle with all a deep, imperishable love, as the matron bends over the infant that smiles in her face, and with more shuddering horror, she trembles as she gazes on the daughters, whose youthful beauty, goodness and grace shed the sunshine of joy and hope over the winter of life. I appeal to you as Christians, as patriots, as men, generous, highminded men, to forbear. By all you hold sacred—by your own feelings or the wives of your bosom and the children of your love, pause and reflect on the mischief and woe you seek to inflict on both the white and colored population of the Southern States. . . .

"A Southern Nation," *The Colonizationist* (Boston, 1834), 75-77.

The following speech of John Quincy Adams shows his later attitude on slavery and the like:

The inconsistency of the institution of domestic slavery with the principles of the Declaration of Independence was seen and lamented by all the Southern patriots of the Revolution; by no one with deeper and more unalterable conviction than by the author of the Declaration himself. No insincerity or hypocrisy can fairly be laid to their charge. Never from *their* lips was heard one syllable of attempt to justify the institution of slavery. They universally considered it as a reproach fastened upon them by the unnatural stepmother country; and they saw that, before the principles of the Declaration of Independence, slavery, in common with every other mode of oppression, was destined sooner or later to be banished from the earth. Such was the undoubting conviction of Jefferson to his dying day. In the memoir of his life, written at the age of seventy-seven, he gave to his countrymen the solemn and emphatic warning that the day was not distant when they *must* hear and adopt the general emancipation of their slaves. "Nothing is more certainly written," said he, "in the book of fate, than that these people are to be free. My countrymen! It is written in a better volume than the book of fate; it is written in the laws of Nature and of Nature's God."

We are told, indeed, by the learned doctors of the nullification school, that color operates as a forfeiture of the rights of human nature; that a dark skin turns a man into a chattel; that crispy hair transforms a human being into a four-footed beast. The master-priest informs you that slavery is consecrated and sanctified by the Holy Scriptures of the Old and New Testament; that Ham was the father of Canaan, and all his posterity were doomed, by his own father, to be hewers of wood and drawers of water to the descendants of Shem and Japhet; that the native Americans of African descent are the children of Ham, with the curse of Noah still fastened upon them; and the native Americans of European descent are children of Japhet, pure Anglo-Saxon blood, born to command, and to live by the sweat of another's brow. The master-philosopher teaches you that slavery is no curse, but a blessing! that Providence—Providence! —has so ordered it that this country should be inhabited by two races of men,—one born to wield the scourge, and the other to bear the record of its stripes upon his back; one to earn, through a toilsome life, the other's bread, and to feed him on a bed of roses; that slavery is the guardian and promoter of wisdom and virtue; that the slave, by laboring for another's enjoyment, learns disinterestedness and humility; that the master, nurtured, clothed, and sheltered, by another's toils, learns to be generous and grateful to the slave, and sometimes to feel for him as a father for his child; that, released from the necessity of supplying his own wants, he acquires opportunity of leisure to improve his mind, to purify his heart, to cultivate his taste; that he has time on his hands to plunge into the depths of philosophy, and to soar to the clear empyrean or seraphic morality. The master-statesman—ay, the statesman in the land of the Declaration of Independence, in the halls of national legislation, with the muse of history recording his words as they drop from his lips, with the colossal figure of American Liberty leaning on a column entwined with the emblem of eternity over his head, with the forms of Washington and Lafayette speaking to him from the canvas—turns to the image of the father of his country, and, forgetting that the last act of his life was to emancipate his slaves,

to bolster up the cause of slavery, says, *"That* man was a slaveholder."

My countrymen! these are the tenets of the modern nullification
school. Can you wonder that they shrink from the light of free
discussion—that they skulk from the grasp of freedom and of truth?
Is there among you one who hears me, solicitous above all things for
the preservation of the Union so truly dear to us—of that Union proclaimed in the Declaration of Independence—of that Union never to
be divided by any act whatever—and who dreads that the discussion
of the merits of slavery will endanger the continuance of the Union?
Let him discard his terrors, and be assured that they are no other
than the phantom fears of nullification; that, while doctrines like
these are taught in her schools of philosophy, preached in her
pulpits, and avowed in her legislative councils, the free, unrestrained
discussion of the rights and wrongs of slavery, far from endangering
the Union of these States, is the only condition upon which that
Union can be preserved and perpetuated. What! are you to be told,
with one breath, that the transcendent glory of this day consists in
the proclamation that all lawful government is founded on the
inalienable rights of man, and, with the next breath, that you must
not whisper this truth to the winds, lest they should taint the
atmosphere with freedom, and kindle the flame of insurrection?
Are you to bless the earth beneath your feet because she spurns
the footsteps of a slave, and then to choke the utterance of your
voice lest the sound of liberty should be reëchoed from the palmetto
groves mingled with the discordant notes of disunion? No! no!
Freedom of speech is the only safety-valve which, under the high
pressure of slavery, can preserve your political boiler from a fearful
and fatal explosion. Let it be admitted that slavery is an institution of internal police, exclusively subject to the separate jurisdiction of the States where it is cherished as a blessing, or tolerated as
an evil as yet irremediable. But let that slavery which intrenches
itself within the walls of her own impregnable fortress not sally
forth to conquest over the domain of freedom. Intrude not beyond
the hallowed bounds of oppression; but, if you have by solemn
compact doomed your ears to hear the distant clanking of the chain,
let not the fetters of the slave be forged afresh upon your own
soil; far less permit them to be riveted upon your own feet. Quench
not the spirit of freedom. Let it go forth, not in panoply of fleshly
wisdom, but with the promise of peace, and the voice of persuasion,
clad in the whole armor of truth, conquering and to conquer.

Josiah Quincy, *Memoir of the Life of John Quincy Adams* (Boston,
1858), 272-275.

In the following speech Joshua R. Giddings attacked the policy of yielding ground to slavery:

It is well known, Mr. Chairman, that, since the formation of this
confederacy, there has been a supposed conflict between the southern
and the northern States. I do not say that the conflict is *real;* I
only say that, in the minds of the people, both North and South, and
in this hall, such a conflict exists. This has given rise to a differ-

ence of policy in our national councils. I refer to the tariff in particular, as being a favorite measure of the North, while free trade is advocated more generally by the South. I refer also to our harbor improvements, and the improvement of our river navigation, as another measure in which the Northwest and West have felt great interest, and to which the South have been constantly opposed. But so equally balanced has been the political power, between these opposing interests, that for five years past our lake commerce has been entirely abandoned; and such were the defects of the tariff, that for many years our revenues were unequal to the support of government.

By the fixed order of nature's law, our population at the North has increased so much faster than it has in the slave States, that under the late census the North and West hold the balance of political power; and at the present session we have passed through this body a bill for the protection of our lake and river commerce, which awaits the action of the Senate to become a law. But let us admit Texas, and we shall place the balance of power in the hands of Texas. They, with the southern States, will control the policy and the destiny of this nation; our tariff will then be held at the will of the Texan advocates of free trade.

Are our friends of the North prepared to deliver over this policy to the people of Texas? Are the liberty-loving democrats of Pennsylvania ready to give up the tariff? To strike off all protection from the articles of iron and coal and other productions of that State, in order to purchase a slave-market for their neighbors, who, in the words of Thomas Jefferson Randolph, "breed men for the market like oxen for the shambles?"

I do not argue to the policy of protecting our American manufactures. I only say, that at this time, New England and the free States generally are in favor of it, while the slave States are equally opposed to it. And I ask are the mechanics and manufacturers of the North prepared to abandon their employments, in order that slave-markets may be established in Texas, and a brisk traffic in bodies, the flesh and blood of our southern population may be maintained? Are the farmers of the West, of Ohio, Indiana, and Illinois, prepared to give up the sale of their beef, pork, and flour, in order to increase the profits of those who raise children for sale, and deal in the bodies of women? Are the free States prepared to suspend their harbor and river improvements for the purpose of establishing this slave-trade with Texas, and to perpetuate slavery therein?

But, if Texas be admitted to the Union, it is to be a slaveholding State, out of which several States are hereafter to be admitted, with the advantages over our free States of holding a representation on this floor, and a vote in the election of president and vice-president, and in the administration of the federal government, in proportion to the number of slaves they shall hold in bondage. In other words, their influence on all these subjects is to be proportioned to their contempt of liberty. The Texan, who holds five slaves, is to wield an influence over our national interests equal to four of our northern freemen. If each holds fifty slaves, his influence will be equal to that of *thirty-one* of the independent electors of the free States. I ask the learned gentleman from Indiana (Mr. Owen) if he really estimates the political worth of his constituents so low as to require thirty-one of them to form an aggregate of political influence equal to that of the piratical owner of fifty "human chattels" in Texas? Or does he estimate his own political worth at one-fourth part of that which he attaches to the holder of five slaves in Texas? I wish gentlemen here would speak out, and let us know the real estimate which they put upon the moral and political worth of northern men? Would to God I were able to speak to every man of every party, north of Mason and Dixon's Line. I would demand of them as *men*, as *freemen*, to come forward, and let the country understand whether any one of them is willing thus to degrade himself; or whether any one of them is willing to be thus degraded by his representatives in this hall. This proposition, come from whom it may, from persons high in office, or from those *wishing* to be high in office, is insulting to northern feeling and northern honor. Sir, why not propose at once that our people shall surrender themselves as slaves to the Texan planters? Why not advise the people of our free States at once to leave their homes, to go to Texas, and become the voluntary "hewers of wood and drawers of water" to those fugitive criminals, who, within the last fifteen years, were driven from the United States to avoid punishment for their crimes? . . .

Joshua R. Giddings, *Speeches in Congress* (Boston, 1853), 104-106.

As the following extract from his speech shows, Sumner believed in the equality of all men before the law. He said:

The way is now prepared to consider the nature of Equality, as secured by the Constitution of Massachusetts. The Declaration of Independence, which followed the French Encyclopedia and the political writings of Rousseau, announces among self-evident truths, *"that all men are created equal;* that they are endowed by their Creator with certain unalienable rights; that among these are life, liberty, and the pursuit of happiness." The Constitution of Massachusetts repeats the same truth in a different form, saying, in its first article: *"All men are born free and equal,* and have certain natural essential, and unalienable rights, among which may be reckoned the right of enjoying and defending their lives and liberties." Another article explains what is meant by Equality, saying: "No man, nor corporation or association of men, have any other title to obtain advantages, or particular and exclusive privileges, distinct from those of the community, than what arises from the consideration of services rendered to the public; and this title being in nature neither hereditary, nor transmissible to children, or descendants, or relations by blood, the idea of a man being born a magistrate, lawgiver, or judge is absurd and unnatural." This language, in its natural signification, condemns every form of inequality in civil and political institutions.

These declarations, though in point of time before the ampler declarations of France, may be construed in the light of the latter. Evidently they seek to declare the same principle. They are declarations of *Rights;* and the language employed, though general in character, is obviously limited to those matters within the design of a declaration of *Rights.* And permit me to say, it is a childish sophism to adduce any physical or mental inequality in argument against Equality of Rights.

Obviously, men are not born equal in physical strength or in mental capacity, in beauty of form or health of body. Diversity or inequality in these respects is the law of creation. From this difference springs divine harmony. But this inequality is in no particular inconsistent with complete civil and political equality.

The equality declared by our fathers in 1776, and made the fundamental law of Massachusetts in 1780, was *Equality before the Law.* Its object was to efface all political or civil distinctions, and to abolish all institutions founded upon *birth.* "All men are *created* equal," says the Declaration of Independence. "All men are *born* free and equal," says the Massachusetts Bill of Rights. These are not vain words. Within the sphere of their influence, no person can be *created,* no person can be *born* with civil or political privileges not enjoyed equally by all his fellow-citizens; nor can any institution be established, recognizing distinction of birth. Here is the Great Charter of every human being drawing vital breath upon this soil, whatever may be his condition, and whoever may be his parents. He may be poor, weak, humble, or black;—he may be of Caucasian, Jewish, Indian, Ethiopian race,—he may be of French, German, English, or Irish extraction; but before the Constitution of Massachusetts all these distinctions disappear. He is not poor, weak, humble, or black; nor is he Caucasian, Jew, Indian, or Ethiopian; nor is he French, German, English, or Irish; he is a *MAN,* the equal of all his fellow-men. He is one of the children of the State, which, like an impartial parent, regards all its offsprings with an equal care. To some it may justly allot higher duties, according to higher capacities; but it welcomes all to its equal hospitable board. The State, imitating the divine justice, is no respecter of persons.

Here nobility cannot exist, because it is a privilege from birth. But the same anathema which smites and banishes nobility must also smite and banish every form of discrimination founded on birth,—

"Quamvis illc niger, quamvis tu candidus esses."

Charles Sumner, *Works* (Boston, 1875), II, 340-342.

Voicing a strong protest against the theory that the rightfulness of slavery must not be publicly discussed or questioned, Joshua R. Giddings said:

Sir, certain Senators in the other end of the capitol have for months been endeavoring to convince the people of the necessity of passing the "omnibus bill," as it is called. No arguments could be raised in favor of that measure, for it was not founded on reason. One consideration alone was pressed upon the public mind. The cry was raised that *"the Union was in danger!"* The newspapers here

responded, *"the Union is in danger!"* The country press repeated
the alarm. The cry was caught up and echoed by every timid, fal-
tering poltroon of the North. Petitions to *"save the Union"* were
circulated. Public meetings were held in our commercial cities
where Texas scrip was mostly influential, and resolutions were
adopted *"to save the Union."* The supplications were not that we
"may legislate in righteousness," deal out justice and mercy to
those who are oppressed and degraded by our laws. These were
regarded as objects of trifling importance, when compared with the
pending danger that *Texas would dissolve the Union.* Indeed, they
are never mentioned by our chaplain.

Sir, I am nauseated, sickened at this moral and political effem-
inacy; this downright cowardice. It is unworthy of American statesmen. Our constituents sent us here to maintain and defend their
rights; not to surrender them; not to make ourselves and our people
tributary to Texas. In electing us, they had no expectation that
we would turn upon them and violently thrust our hands into their
pockets and take therefrom ten millions of dollars, and hand it over
to the slave-holders of Texas, for territory which belongs to us, and
to which Texas never had any title whatever.

Sir, gentlemen here may say what they please; the people have no
fears of a dissolution of the Union. They understand this kind of
gasconade. The cry of "dissolution" has been the dernier ressort of
southern men for fifty years, whenever they desired to frighten
doughfaces into a compliance with their measures. It may alarm
gentlemen here; but I do not think you can find in northern Ohio an
equal number of nervous old women or of love-sick girls, who could
be moved by it.

Again, it is said that we must stop this agitation in relation to
slavery! The people see us here passing laws to enslave our fellow-
men; to sell women in open market; to create a traffic in the bodies
of children. They know this to be opposed to the self-evident truth
that "all men are created equal," "that governments are constituted
to sustain that equality of rights"; and they converse on the subject, examine the reasons on which such traffic is based, and vote
for men who will oppose such barbarous practices. This is called
agitation; and gentlemen here talk of suppressing it by passing
such laws as that on your table. This is the manner in which we
are to stop the progress of truth; to seal the lips of philanthropists;
and to silence the voice of humanity. Yes, Sir, it is gravely proposed
that we should set bounds to the human intellect, and to limit
political investigations by statute laws.

Sir, the great founder of our holy religion, when he proclaimed the
Heaven-born truths of his Gospel, was denounced as an *"agitator."*
He was arrested, condemned, and executed for asserting truths which
the Scribes and Pharisees were too stupid to comprehend. It was
done to stop *agitation;* but truth, emanating from "the Holy One,"
has extended, spread, and progressed, and will "go on conquering and
to conquer," in spite of all the political Scribes and Pharisees in
Congress, and the quaking and trembling of doughfaces here and
elsewhere.

This progress in morals and in political intelligence is in strict
accordance with the law of our being, and cannot be prevented. The

idea of setting bounds to the human intellect, of circumscribing it by statute law, is preposterous. Why not limit the arts and sciences by conservative legislation, as well as moral and political progress? Why not follow the example of those who attempted to stop the agitation of Galileo, when he proclaimed the truth of our solar system, and the laws by which the planets are retained in their orbits? He caused great agitation, and was excommunicated for his *infidelity*, in thus daring to proclaim truths which the *conservatives* of that age were too ignorant to comprehend. It required two hundred and fifty years for the stupid clergy of that day to understand the truths for which he had been expelled from their Christian fellowship. How long it will require certain theological professors of the present day to comprehend the "self-evident truths" of man's equality, is not yet determined. Or how long it will require our political doctors to comprehend the very obvious fact that an educated and reflecting people *will think and act for themselves,* is yet to be ascertained.

But, if we are to have conservative legislation, let us tear down the telegraphic wires, break up our galvanic batteries, and imprison Morse, and stop all agitation upon the subject of your "magnetic" railroads of thought." Lay up your steamboats, place fetters upon your locomotives, convert your railroads into cultivated fields, and erase the name of Fulton from our history. Go down to yonder Institute, drive Page from his laboratory, break in pieces his galvanic engines, and unchain the imprisoned lightning which is there pent up; then pass an act of Congress prohibiting all further agitation on these subjects, and thus carry out your conservative principles, of which some men are continually boasting. . . .

Joshua R. Giddings, *Speeches in Congress* (Boston, 1853), 409-411.

Giving great offense to Jefferson Davis and other Southern friends, William H. Seward spoke thus for *The Higher Law than the Constitution:*

There is another aspect of the principle of compromise which deserves consideration. It assumes that slavery, if not the only institution in a slave State, is at least a ruling institution, and that this characteristic is recognized by the Constitution. But *slavery* is only *one* of many institutions there. Freedom is equally an institution there. Slavery is only a temporary, accidental, partial, and incongruous one. Freedom, on the contrary, is a perpetual, organic, universal one, in harmony with the Constitution of the United States. The slaveholder himself stands under the protection of the latter, in common with all the free citizens of that state. But it is, moreover, an indispensable institution. You may separate slavery from South Carolina, and the state will still remain; but if you subvert freedom there, the state will cease to exist. But the principle of this compromise gives complete ascendency in the slave states, and in the Constitution of the United States, to the subordinate, accidental, and incongruous institution, over its paramount antagonist. To reduce this claim of slavery to an absurdity, it is only necessary to add that there are only two states in which slaves are a majority, and not one in which the slaveholders are not a very disproportionate minority.

But there is yet another aspect in which this principle must be examined. It regards the domain only as a possession, to be enjoyed either in common or by partition by the citizens of the old states. It is true, indeed, that the national domain is ours. It is true it was acquired by the valor and with the wealth of the whole nation. But we hold, nevertheless, no arbitrary power over it. We hold no arbitrary authority over anything, whether acquired lawfully or seized by usurpation. The Constitution regulates our stewardship; the Constitution devotes the domain to union, to justice, to defense, to welfare, and to liberty.

But there is a higher law than the Constitution, which regulates our authority over the domain, and devotes it to the same noble purposes. The territory is a part, no inconsiderable part, of the common heritage of mankind bestowed upon them by the Creator of the universe. We are his stewards, and must so discharge our trust as to secure in the highest attainable degree their happiness. How momentous that trust is we may learn from the instructions of the founder of modern philosophy:

"No man," says Bacon, "can by care-taking, as the Scripture saith, add a cubit to his stature in this little model of a man's body; but, in the great frame of kingdoms and commonwealths, it is in the power of princes or estates to add amplitude and greatness to their kingdoms. For, by introducing such ordinances, constitutions, and customs, as are wise, they may sow greatness to their posterity and successors. But these things are commonly not observed, but left to take their chance."

This is a state, and we are deliberating for it, just as our fathers deliberated in establishing the institutions we enjoy. Whatever superiority there is in our condition and hopes over those of any other "kingdom" or "estate" is due to the fortunate circumstance that our ancestors did not leave things to "take their chance," but that they "added amplitude and greatness" to our commonwealth "by introducing such ordinances, constitutions, and customs, as were wise." We in our turn have succeeded to the same responsibilities, and we cannot approach the duty before us wisely or justly, except we raise ourselves to the great consideration of how we can most certainly "sow greatness to our posterity and successors."

And now the simple, bold, and even awful, question which presents itself to us is this: Shall we, who are founding institutions, social and political, for countless millions; shall we, who know by experience the wise and the just, and are free to choose them, and to reject the erroneous and unjust; shall we establish human bondage, or permit it by our sufferance to be established? Sir, our forefathers would not have hesitated an hour. They found slavery existing here, and they left it only because they could not remove it. There is not only no free State which would now establish it, but there is no slave State, which, if it had had the free alternative as we now have, would have founded slavery. Indeed, our revolutionary predecessors had precisely the same question before them in establishing an organic law under which the states of Ohio, Indiana, Michigan, Illinois, and Wisconsin, have since come into the Union, and they solemnly repudiated and excluded slavery from those states forever. I confess that the most alarming evidence of our degeneracy which has yet been given is found in the fact that we even debate such a question. . . .

The senator proposes to expel me. I am ready to meet that trial, too; and if I shall be expelled, I shall not be the first man subjected to punishment for maintaining that there is a power higher than human law, and that power delights in justice; that rulers, whether despots or elected rulers of a free people, are bound to administer justice for the benefit of society.

William H. Seward, *Works* (N. Y., 1853), I, pp. 74-129.

The following speech from Lincoln exposed the fallacy of the so-called reasonableness of slavery:

Equality in society alike beats inequality, whether the latter be of the British aristocratic sort or of the domestic slavery sort. We know Southern men declare that their slaves are better off than hired laborers among us. How little they know whereof they speak! There is no permanent class of hired laborers amongst us. Twenty-five years ago I was a hired laborer. The hired laborer of yesterday labors on his own account to-day, and will hire others to labor for him to-morrow. Advancement—improvement in condition—is the order of things in a society of equals. As labor is the common burden of our race, so the effort of some to shift their share of the burden onto the shoulders of others is the great durable curse of the race. Originally a curse for transgression upon the whole race, when, as by slavery, it is concentrated on a part only, it becomes the double-refined curse of God upon his creatures.

Free labor has the inspiration of hope; pure slavery has no hope. The power of hope upon human exertion and happiness is wonderful. The slave-master himself has a conception of it, and hence the system of tasks among slaves. The slave whom you cannot drive with the lash to break seventy-five pounds of hemp in a day, if you will ask him to break a hundred, and promise him pay for all he does over, he will break you a hundred and fifty. You have substituted hope for the rod. And yet perhaps it does not occur to you that to the extent of your gain in the case, you have given up the slave system and adopted the free system of labor.

If A can prove, however, conclusively, that he may of right enslave B, why may not B snatch the same argument and prove equally that he may enslave A? You say A is white and B is black. It is color, then; the lighter having the right to enslave the darker? Take care. By this rule you are to be slave to the first man you meet with a fairer skin than your own. You do not mean color exactly? You mean the whites are intellectually the superiors of the blacks, and therefore have the right to enslave them? Take care again. By this rule you are to be slave to the first man you meet with an intellect superior to your own. But, you say, it is a question of interest, and if you make it your interest you have the right to enslave another. Very well. And if he can make it his interest he has the right to enslave you.

The ant who has toiled and dragged a crumb to his nest will furiously defend the fruit of his labor against whatever robber assails him. So plain that the most dumb and stupid slave that ever toiled for a master does constantly know that he is wronged. So plain that no one, high or low, ever does mistake it, except in a plainly selfish way; for although volume upon volume is written to prove slavery a very good thing, we never hear of the man who wishes to take the good of it by being a slave himself.

Most governments have been based, practically, on the denial of the equal rights of men as I have, in part, stated them; ours began by affirming those rights. They said, some men are too ignorant and vicious to share in government. Possibly so, said we; and, by your system, you would always keep them ignorant and vicious. We proposed to give all a chance; and we expected the weak to grow stronger, the ignorant wiser, and all better and happier together.

We made the experiment, and the fruit is before us. Look at it, think of it. Look at it in its aggregate grandeur, of extent of country, and numbers of population—of ship, and steamboat, and railroad. . . .

Thus we see that the plain, unmistakable spirit of that age toward slavery was hostility to the principles and toleration only by necessity.

But now it is to be transformed into a "sacred right." Nebraska brings it forth, places it on the highroad to extension and perpetuity, and with a pat on its back says to it, "Go, and God speed you." Henceforth it is to be the chief jewel of the nation—the very figurehead of the ship of state. Little by little, but steadily as man's march to the grave, we have been giving up the old for the new faith. Nearly eighty years ago we began by declaring that all men are created equal; but now from that beginning we have run down to the other declaration, that for some men to enslave others is a "sacred right of self-government." These principles cannot stand together. They are as opposite as God and Mammon; and whoever holds to the one must despise the other. When Pettit, in connection with his support of the Nebraska bill, called the Declaration of Independence "a self-evident lie," he only did what consistency and candor require all other Nebraska men to do. Of the forty-odd Nebraska senators who sat present and heard him, no one rebuked him. Nor am I apprised that any Nebraska newspaper, or any Nebraska orator, in the whole nation has ever rebuked him. If this had been said among Marion's men, Southerners though they were, what would have become of the man who said it? If this had been said to the men who captured André, the man who said it would probably have been hung sooner than André was. If it had been said in old Independence Hall seventy-eight years ago, the very doorkeeper would have throttled the man and thrust him into the street. Let no one be deceived. The spirit of seventy-six and the spirit of Nebraska are utter antagonisms; and the former is being rapidly displaced by the latter.

Fellow-countrymen, Americans, South as well as North, shall we make no effort to arrest this? Already the liberal party throughout the world express the apprehension "that the one retrograde institution in America is undermining the principles of progress, and fatally violating the noblest political system the world ever saw." This is not the taunt of enemies, but the warning of friends. Is it quite safe to disregard it—to despise it? Is there no danger to liberty itself in discarding the earliest practice and first precept of our ancient faith? In our greedy chase to make profit of the negro, let us beware lest we "cancel and tear in pieces" even the white man's charter of freedom.

Our republican robe is soiled and trailed in the dust. Let us repurify it. Let us turn and wash it white in the spirit, if not in the blood, of the Revolution. Let us turn slavery from its claims of "moral right" back upon its existing legal rights and its arguments of "necessity." Let us return it to the position our fathers gave it, and there let it rest in peace. Let us readopt the Declaration of Independence, and with it the practices and policy which harmonize with it. Let North and South—let all Americans—let all lovers of liberty everywhere join in the great and good work. If we do this, we shall not only have saved the Union, but we shall have so saved it that the succeeding millions of free, happy people, the world over, shall rise up and call us blessed to the latest generations.

Abraham Lincoln, *Early Speeches* (N. Y., 1907), 216-264.

Some of the thoughts of *The Irrepressible Conflict of Freedom and Slavery* were:

This African slave system is one which, in its origin and in its growth, has been altogether foreign from the habits of the races which colonized these states and established civilization here. It was introduced on this continent as an engine of conquest, and for the establishment of monarchial power, by the Portuguese and the Spaniards, and was rapidly extended by them all over South America, Central America, Louisiana, and Mexico. Its legitimate fruits are seen in the poverty, imbecility, and anarchy which now pervade all Portuguese and Spanish America. The free-labor system is of German extraction, and it was established in our country by emigrants from Sweden, Holland, Germany, Great Britain, and Ireland. We justly ascribe to its influences the strength, wealth, greatness, intelligence, and freedom, which the whole American people now enjoy. One of the chief elements of the value of human life is freedom in the pursuit of happiness. The slave system is not only intolerant, unjust, and inhuman, toward the laborer, whom, only because he is a laborer, it loads down with chains and converts into merchandise, but is scarcely less severe upon the freeman, to whom, only because he is a laborer from necessity, it denies facilities for employment, and whom it expels from the community because it cannot enslave and convert into merchandise also. It is necessarily improvident and ruinous, because, as a general truth, communities prosper and flourish, or droop and decline, in just the degree that they practice or neglect to practice the primary duties of justice and humanity. The free-labor system conforms to the divine law of equality, which is written in the hearts and consciences of men, and therefore is always and everywhere beneficent.

The slave system is one of constant danger, distrust, suspicion, and watchfulness. It debases those whose toil alone can produce wealth and resources for defense, to the lowest degree of which human nature is capable, to guard against mutiny and insurrection, and thus wastes energies which otherwise might be employed in national development and aggrandizement.

The free-labor system educates all alike, and by opening all the fields of industrial employment and all the departments of authority, to the unchecked and equal rivalry of all classes of men, at once secures universal contentment, and brings into the highest possible activity all the physical, moral, and social energies of the whole state. In states where the slave system prevails, the masters, directly or indirectly, secure all the political power, and constitute a ruling aristocracy. In states where the free-labor system prevails, universal suffrage necessarily obtains, and the state inevitably becomes, sooner or later, a republic or democracy. . . .

Hitherto the two systems have existed in different states, but side by side within the American Union. This has happened because the Union is a confederation of states. But in another aspect the United States constitute only one nation. Increase of population, which is filling the states out to their very borders, together with a new and extended network of railroads and other avenues, and an internal commerce which daily becomes more intimate, is rapidly bringing the states into a higher and more perfect social unity or consolidation. Thus, these antagonistic systems are continually coming into closer contact, and collision results.

Shall I tell you what this collision means? They who think that it is accidental, unnecessary, the work of interested or fanatical agitators, and therefore ephemeral, mistake the case altogether. It is *an irrepressible conflict* between opposing and enduring forces, and it means that the United States must and will, sooner or later, become either entirely a slave-holding nation or entirely a free-labor nation. Either the cotton or rice fields of South Carolina and the sugar plantations of Louisiana will ultimately be tilled by free labor, and Charleston and New Orleans become marts of legitimate merchandise alone, or else the rye-fields and wheat-fields of Massachusetts and New York must again be surrendered by their farmers to slave culture and to the production of slaves, and Boston and New York become once more markets for trade in the bodies and souls of men. It is the failure to apprehend this great truth that induces so many unsuccessful attempts at final compromises between the slave and free states, and it is the existence of this great fact that renders all such pretended compromises, when made, vain and ephemeral. . . .

At last, the Republican party has appeared. It avows, now, as the Republican party of 1800 did, in one word, its faith and its works, "Equal and exact justice to all men." Even when it first entered the field, only half organized, it struck a blow which only just failed to secure complete and triumphant victory. In this, its second campaign, it has already won advantages which render that triumph now both easy and certain.

The secret of its assured success lies within that very characteristic which, in the mouth of scoffers, constitutes its great and lasting imbecility and reproach. It lies in the fact that it is a party of one idea; but that is a noble one—an idea that fills and expands all generous souls; the idea of equality—the equality of all men before human tribunals and human laws, as they all are equal before the Divine tribunal and Divine laws.

I know, and you know, that a revolution has begun. I know, and all the world knows, that revolutions never go backward. Twenty Senators and a hundred Representatives proclaim boldly in Congress to-day sentiments and opinions and principles of freedom which hardly so many men, even in this free state, dared to utter in their own homes twenty years ago. While the Government of the United States under the conduct of the Democratic party has been all that time surrendering one plain and castle after another to slavery, the people of the United States have been no less steadily and perseveringly gathering together the forces with which to recover back again all the fields and all the castles which have been lost, and to confound and overthrow, by one decisive blow, the betrayers of the Constitution and freedom forever.

William H. Seward, *The Irrepressible Conflict: A Speech Delivered at Rochester*, Oct. 25, 1858 (no title page, New York, 1858), 1-7 *passim*.

This review of the struggle by Senator Benjamin F. Wade, an Ohio antislavery senator who frequently assailed slavery, shows how the sentiment in the South had drifted toward secession:

There is no principle held to-day by this great Republican party that has not had the sanction of your Government in every department for more than seventy years. You have changed your opinions. We stand where we used to stand. That is the only difference. . . . Sir, we stand where Washington stood, where Jefferson stood, where Madison stood, where Monroe stood. We stand where Adams and Jackson and even Polk stood. That revered statesman, Henry Clay, of blessed memory with his dying breath asserted the doctrine that we hold to-day. . . . As to compromises, I had supposed that we were all agreed that the day of compromises was at an end. The most solemn compromises we have ever made have been violated without a *whereas*. Since I have had a seat in this body, one of considerable antiquity, that had stood for more than thirty years, was swept away from your statute books. . . . We nominated our candidates for President and Vice-President, and you did the same for yourselves. The issue was made up and we went to the people upon it. . . . And we beat you upon the plainest and most palpable issue that ever was presented to the American people, and one that they understood the best. There is no mistaking it; and now when we come to the capitol, I tell you that our President and our Vice-

President must be inaugurated and administer the government as all their predecessors have done. Sir, it would be humiliating and dishonorable to us if we were to listen to a compromise (only) by which he who has the verdict of the people in his pocket should make his way to the Presidential chair. When it comes to that you have no government. . . . If a State secedes, although we will not make war upon her, we cannot recognize her right to be out of the Union, and she is not out until she gains the consent of the Union itself; and the chief magistrate of the nation, be he who he may, will find under the Constitution of the United States that it is his sworn duty to execute the law in every part and parcel of this Government; that he cannot be released from that obligation. . . . Therefore, it will be incumbent on the chief magistrate to proceed to collect the revenue of ships entering their ports precisely in the same way and to the same extent that he does now in every other State of the Union. . . . What must she do? If she is contented to live in this unequivocal state, all would be well perhaps, but she could not live there. No people in the world could live in that condition. What will they do? They must take the initiative and declare war upon the United States; and the moment that they levy war, force must be met by force; and they must, therefore, hew out their independence by violence and war. There is no other way under the Constitution, that I know of whereby a chief magistrate of any politics could be released from this duty: If this State, though seceding, should declare war against the United States, I do not suppose there is a lawyer in this body but what would say that the act of levying war is treason against the United States. That is where it results. We might just as well look the matter right in the face. . . .

I say, sir, I stand by the Union of these States. Washington and his compatriots fought for that good, old flag. It shall never be hauled down, but shall be the glory of the Government to which I belong, as long as my life shall continue. . . . It was my protector in infancy, and the pride and glory of my riper years; and although it may be assailed by traitors on every side, by the grace of God, under its shadow I will die.

Nicolay and Hay, *Arbaham Lincoln: A History* (New York, 1890), Ch. II, pp. 412-414.

These last words of John Brown show exactly how radical the antislavery movement had become:

I have, may it please the Court, a few words to say.

In the first place, I deny everything but what I have all along admitted—the design on my part to free the slaves. I intended certainly to have made a clear thing of that matter, as I did last winter, when I went into Missouri, and there took slaves without the snapping of a gun on either side, moved them through the country, and finally left them in Canada. I designed to have done the same thing again, on a larger scale. That was all I intended. I never did intend murder, or treason, or the destruction of property, or to excite or incite slaves to rebellion, or to make insurrection.

I have another objection: and that is, it is unjust that I should suffer such a penalty. Had I interfered in the manner which I admit, and which I admit has been fairly proved,—for (I admire the truthfulness and candor of the greater portion of the witnesses who have testified in this case)—had I so interfered in behalf of the rich, the powerful, the intelligent, the so-called great, or in behalf of any of their friends, either father, mother, sister, brother, or wife, or children, or any of that class, and suffered and sacrificed what I have in this interference, it would have been all right, and every man in this Court would have deemed it an act worthy of reward rather than punishment.

This Court acknowledges, as I suppose, the validity of the Law of God. I see a book kissed here which I suppose to be the Bible, or at least, the New Testament. That teaches me that all things whatsoever I would that men should do unto me I should do even so to them. It teaches me further, to "remember them that are in bonds as bound with them." I endeavored to act up to that instruction. I say, I am yet too young to understand that God is any respecter of persons. I believe that to have interfered as I have done, in behalf of His despised poor, was not wrong, but right. Now, if it is deemed necessary that I should forfeit my life for the furtherance of the ends of justice, and mingle my blood further with the blood of my children, and with the blood of millions in this slave country whose rights are disregarded by wicked, cruel, and unjust enactments—I submit; so let it be done.

Let me say one word further:

I feel entirely satisfied with the treatment I have received on my trial. Considering the circumstances, it has been more generous than I expected. But I feel no consciousness of guilt. I have stated from the first what was my intention and what was not. I never had any design against the life of any person, nor any disposition to commit treason, or excite slaves to rebel, or make any general insurrection. I never encouraged any man to do so, but always discouraged any idea of that kind.

Let me say, also, a word in regard to the statements made by some of those connected with me. I hear it has been stated by some of them that I have induced them to join me. But the contrary is true. I do not say this to injure them, but as regretting their weakness. There is not one of them but joined me of his own accord, and the greater part at their own expense. A number of them I never saw, and never had a word or conversation with, till the day they came to me, and that was for the purpose I have stated.

Now I have done.

James Redpath, *The Public Life of Capt. John Brown* (Boston, 1860), pp. 340-342.

The Act to Establish a Bureau for the Relief of Freedmen and Refugees was:

Be it enacted . . . That there is hereby established in the War Department, to continue during the present war of rebellion, and for one year thereafter, a bureau of refugees, freedmen, and abandoned lands, to which shall be committed, as hereinafter provided, the supervision and management of all abandoned lands, and the control of all subjects relating to refugees and freedmen from rebel states, or from any district of country within the territory embraced in the operations of the army, under such rules and regulations as may be prescribed by the head of the bureau and approved by the President. The said bureau shall be under the management and control of a commissioner to be appointed by the President, by and with the advice and consent of the Senate, . . . And the commissioner and all persons appointed under this act, shall, before entering upon their duties, take oath of office prescribed in . . . (the act of July 2, 1862). . . .

Sec. 2. *And be it further enacted*, That the Secretary of War may direct such issues of provisions, clothing, and fuel, as he may deem needful for the immediate and temporary shelter and supply of destitute and suffering refugees and freedmen and their wives and children, under such rules and regulations as he may direct.

Sec. 3. *And be it further enacted*, That the President may, by and with the advice and consent of the Senate, appoint an assistant commissioner for each of the states declared to be in insurrection, not exceeding ten in number, who shall, under the direction of the commissioner, aid in the execution of the provisions of this act. . . . And any military officer may be detailed and assigned to duty under this act without increase of pay or allowances. The commission shall, before the commencement of each regular session of Congress, make full report of his proceedings with exhibits of the state of his accounts to the President, who shall communicate the same to Congress, and shall also make special reports whenever required to do so by the President or either house of congress; and the assistant commissioners shall make quarterly reports of their proceedings to the commissioner, and also such other special reports as from time to time may be required.

Sec. 4. *And be it further enacted*, That the commissioner, under the direction of the President, shall have authority to set apart, for the use of loyal refugees and freedmen, such tracts of land within the insurrectionary states as shall have been abandoned, or to which the United States shall have acquired title by confiscation or sale, or otherwise, and to every male citizen, whether refugee or freedman, as aforesaid, there shall be assigned not more than forty acres of such land, and the person to whom it was so assigned shall be protected in the use and enjoyment of the land for the term of three years at an annual rent not exceeding six per centum upon the value of such land, as it was appraised by the state authorities in the year eighteen hundred and sixty, for the purpose of taxation, and in case no such appraisal can be found, then the rental shall be based upon the estimated value of the land in said year, to be ascertained in such manner as the commissioner may by regulation prescribe. At the end of said term, or at any time during said term, the occupants of any parcels so assigned may purchase the land and receive such title thereto as the United States can convey, upon paying therefor the value of the land, as ascertained and fixed for the purpose of determining the annual rent aforesaid.

Sec. 5. *And be it further enacted,* That all acts and parts of acts inconsistent with the provisions of this act, are hereby repealed.

Approved, March 3, 1865.

Text in *U. S. Statutes at Large,* XIII, 507-509. For the proceedings see the *House and Senate Journals,* 38th Congress, 1st and 2d Sess., and the *Cong. Globe.* On the work of the bureau see *Senate Exec.* Doc. 28, 38th Cong., 2d Sess.; *House Exec. Docs.* 11, 70, and 120, 39th Cong., 1st Sess.; *House Exec. Doc.* 7, 39th Cong., 2d Sess.; *House Report* 30, 40th Cong., 2d Sess.; *House Exec. Doc.* 329, *ibid.; House Exec. Doc.* 142, 41st Cong., 2d Sess.; *House Misc. Doc.* 87, 42d Cong., 3d Sess.; *House Exec. Doc.* 100, 43d Cong., 1st Sess.; *House Exec. Doc.* 144, 44th Cong., 1st Sess. On the condition of Freedmen see *Senate Exec. Doc.* 53, and *Senate Report* 25, 38th Cong., 1st Sess.; *House Exec. Doc.* 118, 39th Cong., 1st Sess. Southern State legislation respecting freedmen is summarized in McPherson, *Reconstruction,* 29-44. See also Cox, *Three Decades,* chap. 25.

It may be interesting to note Abraham Lincoln's prophetic protest against lynch law uttered in 1830. He said:

In the great journal of things happening under the sun, we, the American people, find our account running under date of the nineteenth century of the Christian era. We find ourselves in the peaceful possession of the fairest portion of the earth as regards extent of territory, fertility of soil, and salubrity of climate. We find ourselves under the government of a system of political institutions conducing more essentially to the ends of civil and religious liberty than any of which the history of former times tells us. We, when mounting the stage of existence, found ourselves the legal inheritors of these fundamental blessings. We toiled not in the acquirement or establishment of them; they are a legacy bequeathed us by a once hardy, brave, and patriotic, but now lamented and departed, race of ancestors. . . .

At what point then is the approach of danger to be expected? I answer, if it ever reach us it must spring up amongst us; it cannot come from abroad. If destruction be our lot we must ourselves be its author. We must live through all time or die by suicide.

I hope I am over wary; but if I am not, there is even now something of ill omen amongst us. I mean the increasing disregard for law which pervades the country—the growing disposition to substitute the wild and furious passions in lieu of the sober judgment of courts, and the worse than savage mobs for the executive ministers of justice. This disposition is awfully fearful in any community; and that it now exists in ours, though grating to our feelings to admit, it would be a violation of truth and an insult to our intelligence to deny. . . .

Turn then to that horror-striking scene at St. Louis. A single victim only was sacrificed there. This story is very short, and is perhaps the most highly tragic of anything of its length that has ever been witnessed in real life. A mulatto man by the name of McIntosh was seized in the street, dragged to the suburbs of the city, chained to a tree, and actually burned to death; and all within a single hour from the time he had been a freeman attending to his own business and at peace with the world.

Such are the effects of mob law, and such are the scenes becoming more and more frequent in this land so lately famed for love of law and order, and the stories of which have even now grown too familiar to attract anything more than an idle remark.

But you are perhaps ready to ask, "What has this to do with the perpetuation of our political institutions?" I answer, "It has much to do with it." Its direct consequences are, comparatively speaking, but a small evil, and much of its danger consists in the proneness of our minds to regard its direct as its only consequences. . . . But the example in either case was fearful. When men take it in their heads to-day to hang gamblers or burn murderers, they should recollect that in the confusion usually attending such transactions they will be as likely to hang or burn some one who is neither a gambler nor a murderer as one who is, and that, acting upon the example they set, the mob of to-morrow may, and probably will, hang or burn some of them by the very same mistake. And not only so; the innocent, those who have ever set their faces against violations of law in every shape, alike with the guilty fall victims to the ravages of mob law; and thus it goes on, step by step, till all the walls erected for the defense of the persons and property of individuals are trodden down and disregarded. But all this, even, is not the full extent of the evil. By such examples, by instances of the perpetrators of such acts going unpunished, the lawless in spirit are encouraged to become lawless in practice; and having been used to no restraint but dread of punishment, they thus become absolutely unrestrained. . . . Thus, then, by the operation of this mobocrat spirit which all must admit is now abroad in the land, the strongest bulwark of any government, and particularly of those constituted like ours, may effectually be broken down and destroyed—I mean the attachment of the people. Whenever this effect shall be produced among us; whenever the vicious portion of (*our*) population shall be permitted to gather in bands of hundreds and thousands, and burn churches, ravage and rob provision stores, throw printing presses into rivers, shoot editors, and hang and burn obnoxious persons at pleasure and with impunity, depend upon it, this government cannot last. By such things the feelings of the best citizens will become more or less alienated from it, and under such circumstances, men of sufficient talent and ambition will not be wanting to seize the opportunity, strike the blow, and overturn that fair fabric which for the last half century has been the fondest hope of the lovers of freedom throughout the world. . . .

The question recurs, "How shall we fortify against it?" The answer is simple. Let every American, every lover of liberty, every well-wisher to his posterity swear by the blood of the Revolution never to violate in the least particular the laws of the country, and never to tolerate their violation by others. As the patriots of seventy-six did to the support of the Declaration of Independence, so to the support of the Constitution and laws let every American pledge his life, his property, and his sacred honor—let every man remember that to violate the law is to trample on the blood of his father, and to tear the charter of his own and his children's liberty.

Let reverence for the laws be breathed by every American mother to the lisping babe that prattles on her lap; let it be taught in schools, in seminaries, and in colleges; let it be written in primers, spelling-books, and in almanacs; let it be preached from the pulpit, proclaimed in legislative halls, and enforced in courts of justice. And, in short, let it become the political religion of the nation; and let the old and the young, the rich and the poor, the grave and the gay of all sexes and tongues and colors and conditions, sacrifice unceasingly upon its altars. While ever a state of feeling such as this shall universally or even very generally prevail throughout the nation, vain will be every effort, and fruitless every attempt, to subvert our national freedom. . . .

A. Lincoln, *Early Speeches* (N. Y., 1907), 14-21 *passim.*

INDEX

Abbott, A. R., a Negro surgeon, 374

Abbott, R. S., 552

Abdy's observation on interbreeding, 231

Abolition, Societies for, 131-133, 306-331; the movement in the South, 320-321; quelled in the South, 323; rise of, in the West, 320-322

Abolitionists, achievements of, 326-329

Abraham, Negro, 194

Absentee ownership of slaves, 74

Achievements of Negroes in freedom, 446-473

Adams, Henry, a leader of Negro migrants, 429

Adams, John, fear of, 119

Adams, John Quincy, the champion of free speech, 332-333; comment of, on the Missouri Compromise, 565-566; on slavery, 575-576

Africa, the Negro in, 1-70; unknown parts of, 1-21; stone age in, 17-18; features of, 10; civilizations of, 10-11; slavery in, 12-13; institutions of, 22-36; peoples of, 15-21; empires in, 37-52; Negro colonists in, 299-305

African background, 1-70

African colonization in the Niger Valley, 298

African M. E. Church, 147-148, 225

African M. E. Zion Church, 150-152

Aggression in Africa, 53-70

Alabama, peonage in, 435

Albert, A. B., an inventor, 462

Aldridge, Ira, an actor, 274

Alexander, W. W., 550

Alexandria, fugitive slaves in, 366

Alien and Sedition Laws, the bearing of, on secession, 358

Allen, Richard, founder of the A. M. E. Church, 147-148, 272

Allen, William G., 270

Alton, Illinois, the murder of Lovejoy at, 352

American Antislavery Society, the constitution of the, 572-573

American Federation of Labor, the, and the Negro, 539-543

Anderson, Marian, 560

Angolas, the, 70

Anthony, Susan B., an abolitionist, 313

Anti-abolition riots, 328-329

Anti-Lynching Bill, 551

Antislavery argument, 94-99

Antislavery cause during the American Revolution, 128-129; in the South, the decline of, 206-207

Antislavery movement restricted to the North, 323-325

Appeal, the, of a Southern Matron, 573-574

Appleton, Nathaniel, an advocate of the rights of man, 118

Apprenticeship enforced, 394-397

Arkansas, the reconstruction of. 392

Arming Negroes, the, advised, 123-124, 372

Armstrong, Gen. S. C., 385

Art, African, 23-24, 25, 31, 39-41, 43, 44, 565 et seq.

Artisans, Negro, 235-236

Ashanti, the state of, 48

Ashmun, Jehudi, 301-303

Association for the Study of Negro Life and History, the, 546, 547; Introduction

Attacks on slavery through the mails, 336

Attucks, Crispus, a martyr for freedom, 121

Augusta, A. T., a Negro surgeon, 374

Ayers, Eli, 300, 302

Back-to-Africa movement, the, 554

Bacon, Ephraim, 300

Bacon, Samuel, 300

Bacon, Thomas, interest of, in the instruction of Negroes, 102

Baldwin, William H., a philanthropist, 456

Ball, Thomas, a Negro contractor in Ohio, 260

Ball, W. S., 292

Ballou, General, a commander of Negro troops, 523

Baltimore, colonization in, 290, 292

Bancroft's opinion as to the valor of Negro soldiers quoted, 126

Banks, General, opinion of, as to Negro troops, 376

Banks controlled by Negroes, 459

Bankson, John, 300

Banneker, Benjamin, the mathematician and astronomer, 137-140

Bannister, E. M., a painter, 467

Bantu, the, 20-21

Baptists, early churches of, 146, 153-154, 226

Barclay, Arthur, 492

Barrow, David, an antislavery man in Kentucky, 203-204

Bassett, E. D., a reconstruction officeholder, the education of, 407

Beard, Andrew J., an inventor, 464

Beers, Captain, the killing of, by slaves, 91

Bell, Phillip A., an editor, 270

Benezet, Anthony, a friend of the Negro and promoter of Negro colonization, 98-99, 133; belief of, in the mental capacity of the Negro, 134

Bennett, Miss Belle H., 500, 550

Benson, S. A., 304

Bentley, George, a Negro preacher, 226

Benton, J. W., an inventor, 464

Berea College, antislavery, 319

Berkeley, William, 305

Bethune, Mrs. Mary McLeod, 550

Bias, J. G., an advocate of colonization, 296

Biased investigators, 544-545

Bibb, Henry, a colonizer, 296

Binding a State, 238-239

Birney, James G., an abolition editor, 320, 321; the employment of Matilda by, 343

Birth of a Nation, The, 490

Black Corsair, the, 76

Black, Jeremiah, opinion of, on granting slaves patents, 231

Blair, Henry, an inventor, 230

Blazing the way on free soil, 259-278

Blease, Cole, a leader of the poor white, 535, 550

Bold slander, a, 528-529

Bond, James, 550

Boston, the rising of slaves in, 93; colonization in, 290

Bowditch, William J., an abolitionist, 310

Bowman, Henry A., an inventor, 466

Boyd, Henry, a successful manufacturer, 261

Bradley, Senator, effort of, to stop the slave trade, 172-173

Brady, St. Elmo, 560

Braithwaite, W. S., a literary critic, 472-473

Brannagan, Thomas, the interest of, in colonization, 133

Brazil, the Negro Numantia in, 79-81

Bremer, Fredrika, an abolition writer, 322

British, the arming of Negroes by, 122-123

British America, sought as a place for colonization, 295

British American Manual Labor Institute, the establishment of, 278

Brown, Mrs. Charlotte Hawkins, 550

Brown, George D., a social worker among Negroes, 453

Brown, John, underground railroad efforts of, 235; the martyrdom of, 359-360; the last words of, 589-590

Brown, John L., 325

Brown, William Wells, a Negro historian, 268; an antislavery lecturer, 316

Bruce, B. K., United States Senator, 403; education of, 406

Bryan, Andrew, a pioneer preacher, 131

Buchanan, James, a weak president, 356-357

Buchanan, Thomas H., 303

Bureau for the Relief of Freedmen, the, 590-591

Burgess, Ebenezer, 300

Burke, the imprisonment of, 325

Burleigh, Charles C., an abolitionist, 313

Burleigh, Harry, a musician, 467

Burnaby, Andrew, comment of, on slavery, 94

Burns, Anthony, the return of, 263

Burr, the imprisonment of, 325

Burroughs, Nannie H., 550

Burton, Belfast, 272

Bushmen, the, 17-18

Business, the progress of Negroes in, 459

Business League, 459

Butler, General B. F., the contrabands of, 363-364

Cain, Richard H., a member of Congress, 405; education of, 406

Calabar, Eboes, from, 70

Caldwell, Elisha B., a promoter of colonization, 285-286

Calhoun, John C., the defense of slavery by, 334, 336, 337; effort of, to have mails searched, 336

California, a free State, 350

Camden, Negro insurrection at, 178

Campbell, Jabez, a churchman, 272

Canaan Academy, the breakup of, 207-208

Canada, exodus to, 295; progress of Negroes in, 296; colonization in, 295-296

Canterbury, Ct., the Prudence Crandall affair in, 208, 312

Capability of Negro officeholders, 405-408

Capers, Bishop, interest of, in the religious instruction of Negroes, 207

Cardozo, F. L., a reconstruction officeholder, the education of, 407; honorable record of, 408

Carnegie, Andrew, a philanthropist, 456

Carver, G. W., 560

Cary, Lott, a colonizationist, 287, 301

Cassey, James, opposition of, to colonization, 291

Cassey, Joseph, a successful Negro, 273

Caste of color, 258

Central America, 298

Chamberlain, Alexander F., quotation from, 135-136

Chandler, E. M. A., 560

Channing, W. E., an abolitionist, 322; opinion of, on miscegenation, 324; interpretation of the Constitution by, 331

Chapman, Professor Charles E., quoted, 79-81

Chapman, Maria Weston, an abolitionist, 310

Charleston, South Carolina, refugees in, 167; the free Negroes of, 246-247; the prosperity of, 248

Chase, S. P., construction of the Constitution by, 331; counsel in the Van Zandt case, 343

Chastellux, Marquis de, opinion of, as to the valor of Negro soldiers, 126

Chavis, John, 159-160

Cheatham, H. P., a member of Congress, 403

Cheesman, J. J., 492

Chester, T. Morris, honorable record of, 408

Chicago, race riot in, 533; segregation tendencies in, 538

Child, Lydia Maria, an abolitionist, 310

Choise, Garret, escape of, with a Negro woman, 110

Christian slavery, 61, 96-97

Christiana tragedy, the, 262

Church, the Negro in, 145-160; proslavery attitude of, 226-227

Churches, Negro, broken up by the Fugitive Slave Law, 262; the progress of, 382-390, 452

Cincinnati riots in, 208; the free Negroes in, 259-261

Cinque, Joseph, the leader of the rising on *L'Amistad*, 346

Citizenship of Negroes, 239-240

Civil Rights Act declared unconstitutional, 484-485

Civilization of Africa, 1-70

Clark, Edward V., a successful business man, 255

Clarkson, Thomas, efforts of, for abolition, 133; a discourse on, 275; for colonization, 281

Clay, Cassius M., an antislavery editor, 319; expulsion of, from Kentucky, 323

Clay, Henry, interest of, in colonization, 285; the evasive position of, 335-336; the compromiser, 350

Clayton, M. C., 274

Clergy, the attitude of, toward the blacks, 102-103

Coast, Gold, the Dutch traders on, the, 64

Codman, John, slaves of, put to death because of insurrection, 92

Coffin, Levi, the promoter of the Underground Railroad, 264

Coker, Daniel, 300

Cole-Talbert, Mrs. Florence, 560

Coleman, W. D., 492

Collins, Henry M., a successful business man, 255; an advocate of colonization, 296

Colonization, African, 279-305; other schemes of, 294-305; revival of by Lincoln, 367, 381; by Turner and Morgan, 434

Colonizationists not interested in Africa, 294-305

Columbus, segregation tendencies in, 538

Comet, The, freedom of slaves of, 345

Compensated emancipation proposed, 361

Compromise of 1850, the, 350

Compromises on slavery by the Convention of 1787, 163-164

Confiscation of property, an act for, 368-370

Conflict of races in cities, 537-538

Congoes, the, 70

Congress, the action of, on the memorial from the Quakers and from the Pennsylvania Abolition Society, 164; report of, adopted, 164-165; lack of interest in the Negro, 165

Congress of the Confederation, silence of, on slavery, 162

Congressional reconstruction, 401-402

Constitution of the American Antislavery Society, the, 572-573

Constitutional questions, 377-378

Contrabands, 363-364

Control of white men in reconstructed States, 407

Convention of 1787, the attitude of, toward slavery, 163-164

Convicts as teachers of Negroes and whites, 104

Cook, John F., a minister and teacher, 273-274

Cook, Will Marion, a musician, 467

Corbin, J. C., honorable record of, 408

Cornish, Samuel E., an editor, 273

Coromantees, 69

Corruption explained, 421

Cotter, Joseph Seaman, a writer, 472

Cotton, the increase in the production of, 209-212

Cotton gin, the invention of, 171; the effect of, 171

"Courageous Efforts," 548-564

Cowley, Robert, 272

Craft, Ellen, a fugitive, 262-263

Craft, William, the escape of, 262-263

Crandall, Prudence, the imprisonment of, 208, 312

Crandall, Reuben, imprisonment of, 323

Craney Island, fugitives in, 366

Credit system for the freedmen, 427

Creeks, the Negroes with, 190

Creighton, a Negro slaveholder, 247

Creole Case, the, 347-348

Crime, the decrease in, 449

Crisis of 1850, the, 350

Crisis, The, 443-444

Criticism of Negroes in the army, 527-528

Crittenden, Gov. John, pardon of C. Fairbank by, 325

Croft, C., slaves of, burned alive, 92

Cromwell, Isaac, escape of, with a white woman, 110

Cromwell, J. W., an historian, 469

Crothers, Samuel, an antislavery leader in the Western Reserve, 320

Crum, W. D., appointment of, 481

Crummell, Alexander, a churchman, 274, 275

Cuffe, Paul, the interest of, in colonization, 283-285

Cullen, Countee P., 560

Culture of Negroes, 1-70

Curry, J. L. M., efforts of, for Negro education, 455

Dabney, Austin, a soldier of distinction during the American Revolution, 128; the pension of, 128; standing of, 128

Dahomey, the State of, 48

Daniel, the fugitive, arrested, 262-263

Davidson, S. J., an inventor, 462

Davis, Hugh, a white man charged with lying with a Negro woman, 111-112

Davis, Joseph, attitude of, toward his slaves, 223

Declaration of Independence, the, and the Negro, 120

Decline of the Seaboard Slave States, 219

De Grasse, John V., a Negro surgeon, 374

Delany, Martin R., an editor, 270, 274; a colonizationist, 297, 298; an officer, 374

DeLarge, R. C., a member of Congress, 405

Delaware, aid to Negro schools in, 563-564

De Mello, Caetano, expedition of, sent against Palmares, 79-81

Deportation schemes, 295-305

De Niza, Fray Marcos, Estevanecito with, 59-60

Des Moines, the training camp for Negro officers at, 521-522

Desalines, child of the rebellion in Haiti, 169

Dett, Nathaniel, a musician, 467

Diaguillo, the Black Corsair, 76

Dias, John, 270

Dickinson, J. H., an inventor, 462

Dickinson, S. L., an inventor, 462

Dillard, J. H., efforts of, for Negro education, 455, 505

Discovery of America by Negroes, 58-59

Discrimination against Negroes in the army, 520-529

District of Columbia, emancipation in, urged, 350; slave trade in, abolished, 350

Dix, General, attitude of, toward Negro fugitives, 364

Donato, Martin, a Negro slaveholder, 248

Douglas, Stephen A., popular sovereignty of, 351

Douglass, Frederick, an editor, 270; an opponent of colonization, 296-297; an antislavery lecturer, 317; an officeholder, 408, 430

Douglass, H. F., a Negro officer, 374

Douglass, William, a churchman, 274

Douglass, William, an inventor, 464

Dowd, Jerome, interest of, in the study of the Negro, 547

Downing, Thomas, a successful Negro, 255

Doyle, James, an inventor, 464

Drake, Sir Francis, the plundering of, 58

Drayton, D., the imprisonment of, 325

Dred Scott decision, 353

Dresser, Amos, the punishment of, 324

Du Bois, W. E. B., opposition of, to Booker T. Washington, 442; a controversial writer, 443, 469, 554

Dubuclet, the excellent record of, 410

Dulin, John, intelligent slave of, 107-108

Dunbar, Paul Laurence, a poet, 469-471

Duncan, William, 272

Dupont, P. S., aid of, to Negro rural schools, 563-564

Duprey, Louis, an antislavery man, 203

Durham, Plato T., 550

Dutch West India Company, 64

Dyer, L. C., 550, 551

Early, of Georgia, the effort of, in favor of the slave trade, 173-174

Eboes, 70

Economic condition of the freedmen, 425-427; remedies for, proposed, 428

Economic problem of the Negro after the migration, 539; with respect to slavery after the reaction, 241-242

Edenton, disturbance at, 178

Education, African, 26

Education of Negroes in the Eighteenth Century, 104-107; prohibition of, in the South, 228; of slaves, 229, 230; trial of, in solving the Negro problem, 431

Educational advantages of Negro reconstruction officeholders, 405-407

Egypt, 45, 46

Ellicott, George, the friend of Benjamin Banneker, 137

Elliott, Robert B., a member of Congress, 405; education of, 406

Ellis, William, a Negro surgeon, 374

Ellsworth, Oliver, attitude of, toward slavery, 163

Emancipation by enlistment during the Revolutionary War, 124, 125; by statute, 128-129, 199; the check of, 170-174; proclamation of, by Fremont during the Civil War, 368; the same by Hunter, 369

Emancipation Proclamation, the, the issuance of, 371; the constitutional aspect of, 378

Emlen Institute, 260

Encomium, The, freedom of slaves of, 345

Enfranchisement of Negroes, the question of, 411

Enlightenment of slaves, 228

Enterprise, The, the freedom of the slaves of, 345

Environment, the effect of, 12

Equality before the law advocated by Sumner, 578-579

Estevanico, exploration of, 59-60

Ethiopia, the rise of, 45, 46

Evans, Henry, a preacher, 155-156

Exceptional slaves, 105-109

Exodus of 1879, the, 428-430

Explorers, Negroes with, 58-60

Fairbank, Calvin, the imprisonment of, 325

Faulkner, R. P., 492

Fauset, Jessie R., a writer, 472.

Featherstonaugh, comment of, on the internal slave trade, 216-217

Fee, John G., an abolitionist, the founder of Berea College, 319

Ferdinand, King, and the slave trade, 62

Fessenden, W. P., reconstruction ideas of, 393

Fifteenth Amendment, 398, 419

Fighter, the Negro as a, 530

Finding a way of escape, 425-445

Finley, Robert, a promoter of colonization, 285

First Regiment Infantry Corps d'Afrique, 373

First Regiment of Louisiana Heavy Artillery, 373

First Regiment of Louisiana Native Guards, 373

Florida, the purchase of, 214; peonage in, 435

Follen, Eliza Lee, an abolition poet, 310

Force, the use of, to check the exodus of Negroes, 429

Forten, James, an inventor, 230; a successful business man, 273; opposition of, to colonization, 291

Fortress Monroe, fugitive slaves at, 366

Foss, Andrew T., an abolitionist, 313-314

Foster, Abby Kelly, an antislavery lecturer, 312, 313

Foster, Stephen, an abolitionist, 312-313

Fothergill, interest of, in colonization, 133

Fourteenth Amendment, 397-398

Francis, Henry, a teacher and minister, 131

Franklin, Benjamin, interest of, in emancipation, 132

Fraternal organizations, 459

Fraud, 421-422

Fray, Marcos de Niza, Estevanico with, 60

Free Negroes, 243-278; owners of slaves, 246-247; relations with slaves, 252-253; a disturbing factor, 253-254; opposition of, to colonization, 288-292

Freedmen among the Latins, 75; in Guatemala, 75-76; maltreatment of, in the South, 394

Freedmen's Bureau, the, 398, 400

Fremont, John C., the emancipatory order of, 368-369

French and Indian War, social forces following, 117

French generals, the praise of, for Negro soldiers, 526

French traders of the Senegal, 64

Frissell, H. B., 500

Fugitive Slave Law, the effect of, 262, 265, 343, 344

Fugitives, among Indians, 187-198; among the British, 122-123, 201-202; in the United States, 233-235; reactionary measures dealing with, 350; in the army camps, 365-366; Lincoln's policy with respect to, 367; sent North, 366

Fuller, Meta V. W., a sculptor, 467

Gaboons, 70

Gabriel's Insurrection, 177-178, 281

Gag rule, the adoption of, 334-335

Gage, Sir Thomas, quotatio; from, concerning the Blac Corsair, 76

Gambia, the megaliths of, 40; English traders in, 64; Negroes from, 70

Gardiner, A. W., 491

Garnett, Henry H., an editor, 270; a churchman and educator, 275

Garrett, Thomas, an abolitionist, 310

Garrison, William Lloyd, supposed connection with Nat Turner, 184, 307; in Negro convention, 272; on colonization, 289; the antislavery efforts of, 306-309; humiliation and imprisonment of, 328-329; comment of, on the Constitution, 331; reward offered for, 340, 342; extracts from *The Liberator* of, 570-571

Garvey, Marcus, 554

Gaston, William, an antislavery man in North Carolina, 205

Gay, Sydney Howard, an abolitionist, 310

General Education Board, 506, 561-562

George, David, 281

George, James, an intelligent slave of, 109

George III and the slave trade, 120

Georgia, uprising of slaves in, 92; peonage in, 435

Germans, competition of, with Negro laborers, 207-208

Gerry, Elbridge, attitude of, toward slavery, 163

Ghana, the kingdom of, 47

Gibbs, M. W., honorable record of, 408

Giddings, Joshua R., an antislavery congressman, 330, 337; resolutions of, on the mutiny of the Creole slaves, 348-349; the censure of, 349; the resignation of, 349; the return of, to Congress, 349; remarks of, on slavery, 577-578, 580-581

Gilpin, Charles S., 560

Gloucester, John, 156

Godkin, E. L., comment of, on the internal slave trade, 218-219

Gold Coast, slave trade on, 54-56, 64, 66, 67, 68, 69, 70

Gomez, Sebastian, 136

Goodell, William, report of, on miscegenation, 232; an abolitionist, 314

Goodloe, Daniel R., position of with reference to teaching Negroes, 207; a southern abolitionist, 319-320

Goodrich, William, a business man, 255

Goodwyn, Morgan, appeal of, in behalf of slaves, 102

Gordon, Robert, a successful Negro coal-dealer in Cincinnati, 261

Gordon, William, interest of, in freedom, 99

Gorsuch, the, killing of, 262

Goybet, General, praise of, for Negro soldiers, 526

Grant, U. S., attitude of, toward fugitive slaves, 364-365; the use of Negroes in the army by, 370; report of, on the South, 394-395

Greeks and the Negro, 14-15

Green, Augustus R., an advocate of colonization, 296

Green, Beriah, 275

Green, Samuel, imprisonment of, 324

Greene, Anna, a white woman escaping with a Negro man, 110

Greene, Colonel, defended by Negro soldiers, 126

Greene, General, interest of, in the enlistment and freedom of the Negroes, 124; Negro soldiers under, during the Revolutionary War, 126

Greener, R. T., a reconstruction officeholder, the education of, 407, 430

Greenleaf, Professor, 303

Greer, Allan J., an officer arrayed against Negroes, letter of, to Senator McKellar, 526

Grew, Mary, 314

Grimké, A. H., a protagonist in the struggle for social justice, 443

Grimké sisters, abolitionists, 314

Guatemala, a Negro freedman in, 75; maroons in, 75-76

Guinea Coast, slave trade on, 64

Gurley, R. R., 302

Haiti, insurrection in, 167; refugees from, 167; exodus to, 298; condition of, 491; mission to, 491

Hale, John P., an antislavery senator, 330

Hale, Joseph, slave of, able to read and write, 106

Hall, Basil, comment of, on the internal slave trade, 217

Hall, Prince, 143-144

Hall v. *De Cuir*, 419

Halleck, General, attitude of, toward Negro fugitives, 364

Hamburg massacre, 415-416

Hamilton, Alexander, interest of, in the freedom of the Negro, 124

Hamilton, Thomas, 270

Hamlet, the fugitive, arrested, 263

Hammon, Jupiter, a writer of verse, 469

Hammond, Mrs. L. H., 500, 550

Hampton, fugitive slaves in, 366

Hampton Institute, the progress of, 455

Hancock, John, opposition of, to the enlistment of Negro troops, 121

Haralson, Jere, a member of Congress, 403, 406

Hardships of Negroes in the North, 249

Harlan, Robert, a successful Negro in Ohio, 260

Harper, Chancellor, position of, on the teaching of Negroes, 206-207

Harper, Frances E. W., a writer of verse, 469

Harper, William A., a painter, 467

Harris, Dr., opinion of, as to the valor of Negro soldiers in the American Revolution, 126

Harrison, Hazel, 560

Hartford, Connecticut, secession convention at, 242; colonization in, 291

Hausa, the state of, 48

Hawkins, Sir John, exploits of, 56, 58

Hawkins, John R., 459

Hawkins, William, 56

Hayes, R. B., the withdrawal of the Federal troops by, 416, 418

Hayes, Roland, 560

Hayne, Robert Y., 184

Haynes, George E., head of the Bureau of Negro Economics in the Department of Labor, 521, 550

Haynes, Lemuel, a patriot and preacher of the American Revolution, 157-158

Hayward, Colonel, a commander of Negro troops, 523

Helper, H. H., 355

Henry, Patrick, an advocate of freedom, 120

Henson, Josiah, comment of, on the internal slave trade, 217-218; a promoter of the Underground Railroad, 235, 264, 278

Hermosa, The, freedom of the slaves of, 345

Higginson, T. W., a leader of Negro troops, 375

Higher pursuits, slaves in, 109

Hill, of Chillicothe, a successful Negro, 259

Hill, L. P., a writer, 472

Hillsboro, Negro insurrection at, 178

Hilyer, A. F., an inventor, 462

Hispaniola, slave traders, 56

Hodges, Willis A., 270

Hoffman, Frederick L., interest of, in the study of the Negro, 547

Hollie, Sallie, an abolitionist, 314

Holly, J. T., 274, 297-298

Holsey, Bishop L. H., 410

Homes of Negroes, in Africa, 38; improvements in the United States, 454

Hooter, H. E., an inventor, 464

Hopkins, Samuel, interest of, in freedom, 99

Hottentots, the, 18-19

House, Grace Bigelow, 500

Hovey, Charles F., an abolition merchant, 310

Howard, O. O., head of the Freedmen's Bureau, founder of Howard University, 400, 455

Howard University, the establishment of, 400; aid to, 562

Howells, W. D., a friend of Dunbar, 470

Hubbard, George W., 500

Hughes, Langston, 560

Humphries, Solomon, a wealthy Negro, 248

Hunter, Alexander, the purchase of a slave by, 247

Hunter, Major General, the emancipatory order of, 369-370; Negroes armed by, 372

Hunton, William A., first Negro International Young Men's Christian Association Secretary, 453

Hurst, Bishop John, 487

Hyman, John A., a member of Congress, 403

Imes, Elmer E., 560

Impending Crisis, The, 355-356

"In the Court of the Gentiles," 474-493

Independent efforts, 141-160

Indianapolis, segregation tendencies in, 538

Indians, Negroes among, 187-198

Industrial arts, 38-39

Industrial revolution and the reaction, 170-172

Industrial Schools, Negro, the progress of, 456

Industrialism in the South, 355

Inferiority of races, question of, 544-545

Institutions of Africa, 22-36

Institutions of learning founded, 431-432

Insult to Negro army officers, 522-525

Insurance companies controlled by Negroes, 459-460

Insurrection of the Negroes during the early period, 78-79, 90-93; in the United States, 177-185

Interbreeding, 252

Interests differing, of the sections, 237-238

Internal improvements, the question of 242

Internal slave trade, 220-222

International entanglements, 345-349

Interracial movement, 499-502

Interstate slave trade, the regulation of, 221

Intimidation of Negroes in the South, 393-397

Inventions of Negroes, 230, 231; the difficulties of, 466

Investigators, biased, 544-545

Irish Nell, marriage of, to a Negro slave, 111

Irish in the North, competition of, with Negro laborers, 207-208

Irrepressible Conflict, The, of William H. Seward, 353

Isabella, Queen, attitude of, toward slavery, 62

Jackson, Andrew, address of, to Negro soldiers, 200-202

Jackson, Benjamin F., an inventor, 464

Jackson, Francis, an abolitionist, 310

Jackson, May Howard, a sculptor, 467

Jacobs, Governor R. T., pardon of Fairbanks by, 326

Jamaica, Francis Williams, the scholar, in, 77; agents from, in quest of Negro immigrants, 294-295

James, David, an illegitimate mulatto bound out, 113

Jameson, J. F., interest of, in the study of the Negro, 547

Jay, William, the enemy of colonization, 207; thought of, on miscegenation, 324; opinion of, as to the Constitution, 331

Jefferson, Thomas, an opponent of slavery, 120; correspondence of, with Banneker, 137; message to Congress concerning, 172-173; his fear of the evil, 206; interest of, in colonization, 283

Jenkins, David, a successful Negro in Ohio, 259

Jenne, the state of, 47

Jennings, Thomas L., 272

Jerry, the fugitive arrested in Syracuse, 263

Jocelyn, S. S., 272

Johnson, a hero of the World War, 530

Johnson, Andrew, acceptance of Lincoln's reconstruction plan by, 392

Johnson, C. S., 550

Johnson, Elijah, 301

Johnson, General, the attitude of, toward fugitive slaves, 364

Johnson, Georgia Douglas, a poet, 472

Johnson, H. R. W., 492

Johnson, James Weldon, a writer, 550-551

Johnson, Mrs. Luke, 550

Johnson, Oliver, an abolitionist, 314

Johnson, William H., an inventor, 464

Johnston, Sir Harry H., 492

Jones, C. C., interest of, in the instruction of Negroes, 207

Jones, E. K., 550

Jones, M. Ashby, 550

Jones, Thomas Jesse, 503-505

Judson, Andrew T., the decision of, in the *Amistad Case*, 346

Just, E. E., 560

Kansas-Nebraska question, 351, 359

Kansas Colored Volunteers, 373

Kebby, Lahmen, 175

Keith, George, interest of, in the instruction of Negroes, 97; in colonization, 280

Kemble, Frances, an antislavery writer, 322

Kench, Thomas, interest of, in the enlistment of Negroes, 125

Key, Francis Scott, a promoter of colonization, 285

King, C. D. B., 493

Koch, Bernard, the agent of the colonizationists of the Civil War period, 367-368; governor of the Vache colony, 367

Kreamer, Henry, an inventor, 464

Ku Klux Klan, the operations of, 413-415, 435; recrudescence of, 531, 547

Labor a factor in the Negro situation, 512, 514

Lafayette, Marquis de, opinion of as to the valor of Negro soldiers, 126

Lafon, Thomy, wealthy Negro, 248

Lago, William, the indictment of, in Kentucky, 340

Lambert, William, a colonizationist, 296

L'Amistad, the freedom of the slaves of, 346

Lane, Lunsford, an antislavery lecturer, 313

Lane Theological Seminary, antislavery, 320

Langston, J. M., a member of Congress, 403; the education of, 406; on the exodus, 430

Last words of John Brown, 589-590

Latimer Case, the, 343

Latins, the enlightenment of slaves among, 62

Latrobe, J. H. B., a factor in colonization, 287

Laura Spelman-Rockefeller Memorial, 564

Laurens, Henry, the proposal of, for enlisting and freeing Negroes, 124-125

Law, Josiah, interest of, in the instruction of Negroes, 207

Lawrence, Samuel, rescue of, by Negroes, 121

Lay, Benjamin, attack of, on slavery, 97-98

Leavitt, Joshua, an abolitionist, 308

Lecky's opinion of the valor of Negro soldiers mentioned, 128

Lecturers, antislavery, 312-318

Lee, Joseph, an inventor, 464

Lee, J. R. E., 550

Le Jeune, Paul, a missionary, 102

Leonard, James, an intelligent slave of, 109

Le Petit, a missionary, 102

Lewis, Edmonia, the artist, 274

Lewis, Julian H., 560

Lewis, William H., 494

Liberator, The, the influence of, 307-308; beginnings of the, 570-571

Liberia, the exodus of Negroes to, 287, 293, 298, 299-305; the situation of, 491-492

Liele, George, a pioneer preacher, 131

Lincoln, Abraham, the slavery issue by, 351-353; interest of in compensated emancipation, 361; policy of, in dealing with fugitive slaves, interest of, in freedmen, 367-368, 379-381, 392; emancipation by, 371; powers of, 377; plan of, for reconstruction, 390-391; comment of, on lynching, 591-593

Long, Jefferson F., a member of Congress, 403

Longfellow, H. W., antislavery writings of, 322

Louisiana, slaves in, 86-87; reconstruction of, 392

Louisiana Purchase, the, and slavery, 170

Louverture, Toussaint, leader of the insurrection in Haiti, 167-169

Lovejoy, Elijah P., the murder of, 330

Lowden, Fred J., an inventor, 464

Lowell, J. R., the antislavery writings of, 322

Loyalty of Negroes, 518, 519, 521

Lundy, Benjamin, an abolitionist, 319; a gradual emancipationist, 272; a colonizationist, 319

Lynch, John R., a member of Congress, 403; the education of, 406

Lynching, remarks of Lincoln on, 591-593

Macaulay, Zachary, interest of in the Negro, 133

McCook, General, attitude of, toward the fugitive slaves, 364

McCoy, Elijah J., an inventor, 465-466

McCrummell, James, the opposition to colonization, 291

McHenry, James, a friend of Benjamin Banneker, 137

McKay, Claude, 560

McKellar, Senator K. D., the letter of Allan J. Greer to, 526

McKim, an agent of the Underground Railroad, 314

Madison, James, suggestion as to emancipation, 124; the complaint of the sister of, as to miscegenation, 231-232

Madison, W. G., an inventor, 464

Mahan, Asa, an antislavery student at Lane Seminary, one of the founders of Oberlin College, 320

Mahan, Joseph P., 340

Mail, the use of, in reaching Negroes, 342

Major, John, the murder of, by slaves, 91

Malone, Mrs. A. E., 461

Mansfield, Lord, the Somerset decision of, 101

March, Charles, a colonizationist, 285

Marcy, Governor, attitude of, toward the fugitive, 340

Maroons, the; elsewhere, 78-79; in Guatemala, 75-76

Marriage, in Africa, 27-28; among Negroes in the United States, 115-116

Martin, Asa, estimate of the extent of the internal slave trade by, 219

Martin, Samuel, a Negro slaveholder, 247

Martineau, Harriet, a case of miscegenation observed by, 232

Maryland, miscegenation in, 111; free Negroes sold in, 250

Maryville College, antislavery, 319

Mason, George, an advocate of freedom, 120

Masons, Negroes as, 143-144

Massachusetts, Negroes of, leave for Canada, 262

Massacres of Negroes, 415, 515

Matilda, the question as to the freedom of, 343

Matthews, W. D., a Negro officer, 374

Matzeliger, Jan E., a noted Negro inventor, results from patent of, 461-462

May, Samuel, Jr., an abolitionist, 310

May, Samuel J., an abolitionist, 310, 311

May, Thomas, an intelligent slave of, 106

Meade, Bishop William, 207

Mechanics, Negro, 108, 248

Mediterranean world, Negroes in, 43, 44, 45

Meharry Medical School, aid to, 562

Melle, the kingdom of, 47

Memphis, fugitive slaves in, 366

Menendez, exploits of, 58

Menial service of Negroes in the North, 439

Mental capacity of Negroes, 134-140

Mercer County, Ohio, the Negroes in, 260

Mercer, Charles Fenton, interest of, in colonization, 285

Merrick, John, a business man, 459

Metal workers in Africa, 39-40

Methodists, opposition of, to slavery, 118-119

Metoyer, Marie, a Negro slaveholder, 248

Mexico, the organization of territory acquired from, 350; Negro colonists in, 434

Mifflin, Ann, interest of, in colonization, 283-284

Migration of the Negroes to the North, 438-439; causes of, 514-517

Mild attack on slavery, 95

Military districts in the South, 401

Miller, Kelly, an educator, 432, 469, 556

Miller, Matthew, opinion of, as to Negro troops, 376

Miller, Thomas E., a member of Congress, 405

Mills, Elijah J., a promoter of colonization, 285, 300

Mills, Samuel J., a colonizationist, 285

Miner, Myrtilla, the work of, 265

Minor, Patrick, a Negro officer, 374

Miscegenation of the whites and blacks, 110-115, 231-232; cases of, 111, 231, 232

Mississippi, peonage in, 435

Missouri Compromise, 179, 206; comment on, by J. Q. Adams, 565-566; remarks of John Sergeant on, 566-568

Mobile, Alabama, the Negroes of, protected by the Louisiana Purchase Treaty, 170

Mohammed Askia, 49

Mohammedans in Africa, 49-50, 54

Molson, Richard, the escape of the slave of, with a white woman, 110

Monroe, President, interest of, in colonization, 287

Montgomery, Benjamin T., an inventor, 231

Montgomery, Isaiah T., experiences of, as a slave, 223; a business man, 459

Moore, William, intelligent slave of, 106

Morgan, John, an antislavery student at Lane Seminary, one of the founders of Oberlin College, 320

Morgan, Senator, interest of, in colonization, 434

Morrell, Junius C., 272

Morris, Thomas, an antislavery congressman, 334

Moton, R. R., the head of Tuskegee, 508

Mott, James, an abolitionist, 314

Mott, Lucretia, an abolitionist, 314

Mound Bayou, the home of a former slave, 223

Mulber, Luke, a successful Negro in Ohio, 259

Murray, George W., a member of Congress, 405; an inventor, 464

Mustees, 90

Nagoes, 69

Nash, Charles E., a member of Congress, 403, 405

National Association for the Advancement of Colored People, the work of the, 487, 550-551

National Association of Funeral Directors, 459

National Equal Rights League, 487

National Negro Bankers' Association, 459

National Negro Retail Merchants' Association, 459

Negro, the, enslaved, 100-115; the rights of man and the, 117-140; status of, reduced, 225, 231; in the Civil War, 361-381; in the World War, 512-533; the, and social Justice, 534-547

Negro, Abraham, 194

Negro contrabands, the record of, 363-364

Negro churches, 145-160, 388

Negro preachers, 145-160, 388

Negro soldiers enlisted, 121, 123, 125; opinions as to service of, 126

Negro units proposed for the American Revolutionary forces, 121; decision against, 121; fear of, 122; armed by British, 123

Negroes as refugees during the Civil War, 365-366; loyal to the United States, 518, 519 521

Negroes, murder of, 392-394

Nell, Irish, marriage of, to a slave, 111

Nell, William C., a Negro historian, 266, 268, 274

Newberne, Negro insurrection at, 178

New England and secession, 358

New Orleans, Haitian refugees in, 167; excitement in, 178, 184

New York City, the Negro riots in, 93; miscegenation in, 113; colonization in, 292; anti-abolition movement in, 328; the fugitive question in, 340

New York Fifteenth, 523

Niger, Martin R. Delany in the valley of, 297

Niles, Hezekiah, a promoter of colonization, 285

Niles, Nathaniel, interest of, in freedom, 99

Ninety-second Division, of Negro soldiers, 523

Norfolk, Haitian refugees at, 167; disturbance at, 178

North, reaction against the Negro in, 207-208; the free Negroes in, 249-250; fugitives in, 263; the migration of Negroes to, 429, 517; troubles of Negroes in, 515-516

North Carolina, miscegenation in 113; Negro voters in, 130; peonage in 435; education in, 562-563

Numantia, the Negro, 79-81

Oberlin College, the establishment of, 320

Officers, Negro, the demand for, 522; discrimination against, 523; training of, at Des Moines, 522; praised by French, 526

Ogden, Robert C., a philanthropist, 456

Ogden, Peter, 145

O'Hara, James E., a member of Congress, 403; the education of, 406

Ohio, the question of fugitives in, 340; anti-Negro laws of, 343

Opposition to slavery, 348-350

Oppression a cause of migration, 515

Ordinance of 1787, the emancipatory clause of, 162, 239

Ordingsell, Anthony, the sale of a slave by, 247

Oregon territory, 215

Osceola, a fighter, 194-198

Otis, James, an advocate of freedom, 119-120

Outcast, the free Negro an, 252

Overton, Anthony, 461

Paine, L. W., the imprisonment of, 325

Palmares, the Negro Numantia, 79-81

Palmyra, riot at, 209

Pan-African idea, the, 553-556

Parker, John T., an inventor, 464

Parrish, C. H., the efforts of, 509

Paw Paws, 69-70

Paxton, John D., the attack of, on slavery, 203-204

Payne, Daniel A., a churchman, 274

Payne, James S., 304, 491

Pearson, W. G., 461

Pelham, Robert A., an inventor, 462

Penn, William, the owner of slaves, 100

Pennington, J. W. C., a churchman, 276-277

Pennsylvania, miscegenation in, 113; anti-abolition riots in, 329

Pennsylvania Society for the Abolition of Slavery, memorial of, to Congress, action taken thereon, 164

Peonage, 435-437

Pernambuco and Palmares, 79-81

Personal liberty laws, 343

Petersburg, disturbance at, 178

Phelps, J. W., the arming of Negroes, undertaken by, 372

Phelps-Stokes Fund, 503-505

Philadelphia, miscegenation in, 110; riot in, 209; progress of free Negroes in, 255; segregation tendencies in, 538

Phillips, Wendell, an antislavery orator, 309, 310; attitude of, toward the Constitution, 309

Physicians, Negro, 452

Pickens, William, an orator, 432 437, 469

Pickering, J. L., an inventor, 464

Pinchback, P. B. S., a reconstruction officeholder, the education of, 407; record of, 408

Pinkney, William, assertion of, 134

Pittsburg, riot in, 209; segregation tendencies in, 538

Plantation system as a result from the industrial revolution, 216-242

Platt, William, a successful free Negro, 254

Plessy v. *Ferguson,* 419

Political institutions in Africa, 22-36

Politicians, Negro, leaving the South, 437-438

Polk, Bishop, interest of, in the instruction of Negroes, 207

Polk, James K. 215

Polygamy, in Africa, 29

Poore, Salem, exploits of, 121

Popular sovereignty, 351

Portsmouth, Ohio, riot at, 208

Port Royal, South Carolina, fugitive slaves in, 366
Portugal, slaves in, 62
Portuguese slave trade, 55-56, 61-62
Post, Louis F., 423
Potomac, the bravery of Negroes along, 376
Powell, William, a Negro surgeon, 374
Prejudice a factor in the South, 409; in the army, 528
Preparation of slaves for emancipation, 129
Presbyterians, opposition of, to slavery, 118-119
Presley, J., a successful Negro in Ohio, 260
Press, the Negro, 551-553
Price, J. C., an orator and educator, 432
Prigg Case, the, 343
Prince Henry, explorations of, 56
Privileges of free Negroes, 250-251
Proctor, Walter, 273
Professions, Negroes in, 449
Progress of the Negro race, statistics on, 446-459; of the Church, 452
Promoters of colonization, 279-288
Property of Negroes, the worth of, 446-447
Proslavery argument, 96-97
Proslavery victory in the mild prohibition of the slave trade, 174
Prosser, Gabriel, plot of, 177-178
Protest, further, 319-331
Proverbs, African, 50-52
Punishment of slaves, 225
Puritans, attitude of, toward slavery, 95
Pursuits, higher, slaves in, 109
Purvis, Charles B., a Negro surgeon, 374
Purvis, Robert, opposition of, to colonization, 273, 291
Purvis, W. B., an inventor, 462
Pushkin, A. S., 135

Quakers, attitude of, toward slavery, 95, 96-99; memorial of, to Congress, 164; opposition of, to slavery continued, 204-205; interest of, in colonization, 279
Quincy, Edmund, an abolitionist, 310
Quinn, William P., a minister, 274

Race riot in Washington, 532-533
Races in Africa, 1-21
Radical leaders of poor whites, 535
Rainey, J. H., a member of Congress, 405
Randolph, John, the attitude of, toward the slave trade, 173; comment of, on slavery, 204; on colonization, 285
Rankin, John, an antislavery leader in the Western Reserve, 320; comment of, on miscegenation, 324
Ransier, Alonzo J., a member of Congress, 405
Rapier, James T., a member of Congress, 403; the education of, 406
Rapier, John, a Negro surgeon, 374
Rappahannock River, the rising of slaves on, 91
Ray, Charles B., a churchman, 269; letter of, Gerrit Smith to, 323
Ray, Robert, opposition of, to colonization, 291
Raymond, Daniel, the opposition of, to slavery, 204
Reaction against the Negro, 161-175; in the North, 202-203
Reason, Charles L., a scholar, 274
Rebellion of the Negroes in Haiti, 166-170
Reconstruction of the Southern States, 382-424; through schools and churches, 382-390; various theories about, 393,

401; the plan of Congress for, 401; the undoing of, 409-423; a success, 423

Redpath, James, a colonizationist, 298

Reed, William N., a Negro officer, 374

Refugees, Haitian, in United States, 167; influence of, 167-175

Relations of slaves and free Negroes, 252-253

Religion of the African, the, 31-36

Religious bodies opposed to slavery, 95-99, 102

Religious freedom, the bearing of, on the emancipation of the Negroes, 118

Religious instruction limited, 225-226

Remond, Charles Lenox, an antislavery lecturer, 315-316, 317

Removal of a slave to a free State, the effect of, 342

Rent system for the freedmen, 427

Resignation of Negroes to fate, 432-433

Restored South, 425; the cruelty of, 425-426, 433

Return of fugitives, the constitutional question of, 342-347

Return of Negroes to the South, 249-250

Revels, Hiram R., a member of the United States Senate, 403; the education of, 406

Rhett, of South Carolina, in the defense of slavery, 335

Ricard, Cyprian, a wealthy Negro, 248

Richards, Benjamin, a business man, 255

Richardson, Richard, the sale of a slave by, 247

Richey, Charles V., an inventor, 462

Riddell, W. R., interest of, in the study of the Negro, 547

Right of petition denied, 332-335

Rights of man and the Negro, 115-140

Rillieux, Norbert, an inventor, 230

Riots, 207, 208, 209, 394-395, 532

Rise, the, of the poor whites, 499

Roberts, a hero of the World War, 530

Roberts, Joseph J., 304

Robinson, E. A., an inventor, 466

Rockefeller, John D., a philanthropist, 456

Rockefeller, John D., Jr., interest of, in the study of the Negro, 547

Rogers, H. H., a philanthropist, 456

Rogers, N. P., an abolitionist, 314

Roosevelt, T. R., policy of, 481

Root, Elihu, warning of, 494

Roques, Charles, a Negro slaveholder, 248

Rosenwald, Julius, a philanthropist, 456; interest of, in the study of the Negro, 546

Rosenwald Fund, Julius, 563

Royal African Company, 64

Roye, E. J., 434

Ruffner, effort of, for Negro education, 455

Ruggles, David, a leader in the crisis, 270, 276

Rural Schools, aid to, 506-508

Rush of Negroes to cities, the, 438

Russwurm, John B., the first Negro college graduate in the United States, 269-270; a colonizationist, 303

Rutherford, S. W., a Negro business man, 459

Rutledge, Governor, a Negro slave of, distinguished by his valor, 128

Ryland, Robert, 207

Said, Omar Ibn, 175

Saint-George, the Chevalier de, 135

Sale, George, 492

Salem, Peter, the killing of Major Pitcairn, 121

Sandiford, Ralph, attack of, on slavery, 97

Sandoval, Alphonso, protest of, 102

Sandy Lake, the settlement of, broken up, 262

Santo Domingo, Negro insurrection in, 167-169

Savannah, Georgia, the uprising of slaves at, 92-93

Schools, Negro, first establishment of, 104; the progress of, 455, 561, 562

Schurz, Carl, report of, on the South, 394

Scott, Emmett J., mission of, to Liberia, 492; Special Assistant to the Secretary of War, 523

Scott, George, the self-assertion of the slaves of, 91

Scott, Henry, a successful Negro, 255 ·

Scott, William E., a painter, 467

Seamen Acts of South Carolina, 338, 340

Searching the mails, 342

Secession, 358

Secret Information concerning Black American Troops, 528-529

Segregation, 419-420, 475-493, 557-558

Seminole Wars, 193-198

Senegal, traders on, 56

Sergeant, John, remarks of, on the Missouri Compromise, 566-568

Servants indentured, 103-104, 110

Service of Negro troops, 375-376, 524-526

Settlements of Negroes broken up, 262

Seville, slaves in, 62

Seward, W. H., attitude of, toward the fugitive, 338; counsel in the John Van Zandt case, 343; an antislavery leader in Congress, 351-352; *Higher Law* *than the Constitution* of, 581; *Irrepressible Conflict* of, 585-587

Shadd, Abraham D., 272

Shadrach, the fugitive, arrested, 263

Sharp, Granville, attorney in the Somerset case, 101; interest of, in the Negro, 133, 281

Shaw, John, refusal of, to grant a writ for the freedom of a fugitive, 343

Shaw, R. G., a commander of Negro troops, 375

Shellabarger, reconstruction plan, of, 393

Sherbro, the figures of, 40

Sierra Leone, 300

Simms, Thomas, the fugitive arrested, 263

Simpson, William H., a painter, 274

Singleton, Benjamin, a leader of Negro migrants, 429

Sipkins, Henry, 273

Skilled labor, 447

Slade, William, an antislavery congressman, 334

Slander, a bold, 528

Slave-breeding, 219-220

Slave trade, 54, 56, 61-67; the horrors of, 67-68; in the South, 171-172, 212-214; efforts to stop the, 306 et seq.

Slave trading corporations, 64

Slavers, 65

Slavers, 64, 66, 67; source of, 61, 62, 69-70; hardships of, 67-68; the enlightenment of, among the Latins, 75; able to read and write, 106; brought to the West Indies, 105-106; well-dressed, 107; in good circumstances, 108; slaves in higher pursuits, 109; relation with poor whites, 110

Slavery, ancient, 53-54; Mohammedan, 54; Christian, 61; European, 61-62; the introduction of, in America, 64, 82; in its mild form, 82-116; in the North, 100; in England, 101; in the eighteenth century,

82-115; early objections to, 84-85, 94-99; as affected by the Louisiana Purchase Treaty, 170

Smalls, Robert, a member of Congress, 405

Smart, Brinay, an inventor, 464

Smilie, of Pennsylvania, the effort of, against the slave trade, 173

Smith, Gerrit, the antislavery efforts of, 322-323

Smith, James, an inventor, 464

Smith, James McCune, a Negro physician in New York, 266; letter of G. Smith to, 322

Smith, Stephen, a lumber merchant, 255

Social justice and the Negro, 534-547

Social relations of Negroes and whites, 231

Social upheaval, fear of, 411

Society for the Propagation of the Gospel in Foreign Parts, 102-103

Soldiers, Negro, in the Revolutionary War, 121-128; in the War of 1812, 199-202; in the World War, 518-530; restriction of, in the service, 520; assignment of, to labor divisions, 520; the abuse of, 527

Somerset decision, 101

Songhay, the empire of, 49

Soni Ali, 49

Soudan, the empires of, 46-47

South, the situation in, after the reaction, 216-220

South America, 298

South Carolina, uprising of slaves in, 91-92; the reopening of the slave trade by, 172; peonage in, 435

Southern matron, the appeal of a, 573-574

Southern Sociological Congress, 499-501

Spain, African slaves in, 62

Spanish explorers, Negroes with, 59-60

Spingarn, J. E., a friend of the oppressed, 443, 529

State, limitations on a, 238

Statistics on free Negroes, 245-250

Stebbins, Charles B., an abolitionist, 314

Stephen, Little, 59-60

Steward, Austin, 272

Stewart, John, 156

Stiles, Ezra, interest of, in freedom, 99

Still, William, an agent of the Underground Railroad, 264

Stockton, Robert F., 300

Stone age in Africa, 17-18

Stone, Daniel, an opponent of slavery, 352

Stone, Lucy, an abolitionist, 313

Storey, Moorfield, a friend of the oppressed, 443

Stowe, Harriet Beecher, the writings of, 278

Stringent measures in the South, 185

Study of the Negro, the, undertaken, 546-547

Suffolk, fugitive slaves in, 366

Sugar industry and slavery, 209-210

Sumner, Charles, opinion of, on the mutiny of the Creole slaves, 347-348; reconstruction ideas of, 393; interest of, in the freedmen, 393; on equality before the law, 578-579

Superiority of races, a myth, 4-5

Supreme Court of the United States, decisions of, 484-487

Suttle, Charles F., claimant of Anthony Burns, 263

Taft, W. H., policy of, 481, 494

Talbert, Mary B., 550

Talmadge, James, effort of, to prevent slavery in Missouri, 237-238

Tanner, H. O., a renowned painter, 467-469; paintings of, 468; prizes of, 468

Tappan, Arthur, an abolitionist, 272, 308; a reward offered for, 340

Tappan, Lewis, an abolitionist, 322
Tarboro, Negro insurrection at, 178
Tariff and slavery, 240-241; opposition to the tariff, 241
Taxation during the Civil War, 377-378
Ten per cent governments, 391
"Tender Mercies of the Wicked," 494-510
Tennessee, the reconstruction of, 392
Terrell, Judge Robert H., 495
Terrell, Mary Church, 550
Terrorism in the South, 413-415, 425
Texas, slavery and, 214-215
Thirkield, W. P., 500
Thirteenth Amendment, 378
Thompson, A. V., a successful Negro in Ohio, 260
Thompson, George, lecture of, stopped by mob, 328
Thompson, the imprisonment of, 325
Tilghman, Richard, the escape of the slave of, with a white woman, 110
Tillman, Benjamin, a leader of the poor whites, 499
Timbuctoo, the city of, 48
Toleration and the Negro, 118
Topp, Henry, a successful Negro, 254
Torrey, C. T., imprisonment of, 326
Town slaves, 235
Traders, slave, 54-70
Trades unions and the Negro, 438-439, 539-543
Trinidad, colonization in, 294
Troops, Federal, in the South, the withdrawal of, 416
Tropical America, Negroes in, 71-81
Trotter, W. M., a leader opposed to Booker T. Washington's policies, 442; the humiliation of, 442; protest of, 490
Truth, Sojourner, an antislavery lecturer, 316

Tubman, Harriet, the career of, 235; a promoter of the Underground Railroad, 264
Tucker, Alpheus, a Negro surgeon, 374
Turner, Benjamin, a member of Congress, 403; education of, 406
Turner, Bishop H. M., interest of, in colonization, 434
Turner, C. H., 560
Turner, Franklin, an advocate of colonization, 296
Turner, Nat, insurrection of, 180-185, 186, 187
Tuscaloosa County, the indictment of R. G. Williams by, 340
Tuskegee, the progress of, 455-456

Uncle Tom's Cabin, 354
Underground Railroad, 264, 340, 343
Union, the nature of, 241, 357-358; the cause of, at first a failure, 370
Union Humane Society, 284
University Commission on Race Questions, 501-502
Unskilled labor, 447
Untoward condition of the freedmen, 425-427
Unwilling South, the, 394
Uprisings, Negro, 90-94

Vagrancy laws of the South, 395-396
Valladolid, Juan de, 62
Van Buren, attitude of, toward Jackson, 215; in the L'Amistad case, 346
Van Zandt, John, the fine of, 343
Vardaman, J. K., a leader of the poor whites, 499
Varick, James, founder of the A. M. E. Zion Church, 152
Varnum, General, enlistment of Negroes by, 125
Vasa, Gustavus, 135
Vashon, George B., a lawyer, 274
Vermont, the fugitive in, 343

Vesey, Denmark, leader of an insurrection, 178-180
Vicksburg, meeting at, to check the exodus of 1879, 429
Villard, O. G., grandson of William Lloyd Garrison, 443; interest of, in the study of the Negro, 546-547
Virgin Islands, mission to, 491
Virginia and Kentucky Resolutions, the bearing of, on secession, 358
Virginia, risings of slaves in, 91; miscegenation in, 111-113; Negro soldiers in, 125; insurrection in, 180-185; backwardness of, 305
Vogelsang, Peter, 272

Wade, Benjamin F., the defiant unionist, 358; attack of, on slavery, 587-589
Wage system for the freedmen, 427
Wainrite, Anne, escape of, with a negro woman, 110
Walker, Madame C. J., a business woman, 461
Walker, David, appeal of, 180, 184
Walker, John, suffering of, 325
Walker, Jonathan, 325
Wall, O. S. B., a Negro officer, 374
Walls, Josiah T., a member of Congress, 403
War of 1812, the Negro in the, 199-202
Ward, Joseph, the opposition of, to the enlistment of Negro troops, 121
Ward, S. R., a minister and orator of power, 277-278
Warner, David B., 304
Washington, Booker T., the policy of, 440; the Atlanta address of, 440-441; ideas of, accepted, 441; opposition to, 442; the results of the work of, 488, 498; a writer, 469
Washington, Mrs. Booker T., 550

Washington, Bushrod, a promoter of colonization, 285
Washington, George, interests of, in emancipation, 120; order of, to stop the enlistment of Negro troops, 121; revocation of the order, 123-124; the enlistment of Negroes by, 124
Washington, fugitive slaves in, 366; race riot in, 532-533; a lynching, 533
Watrum, F. P., a missionary, 102
Wayman, Alexander W., a churchman, 274
Webb, William, an advocate of colonization but not of African deportation, 296
Webster, Daniel, the evasive position of, 335-336; opinion of, on the Creole slaves, 347
Webster, Delia, the imprisonment of, 325
Webster, Samuel, interest of, in freedom, 99
Weld, T. F., an abolitionist, 314, 320
Wesley, Charles H., interest of, in the study of the Negro, 547
Wesley, John, opposition of, to slavery, 133-134
West Indies, slaves carried to, 68; the lot of slaves in, 71-81
Wheatley, Phyllis, a writer of verse, 136-137
Wheeler, John H., the escape of the slave of, 342
Whipper, William, the agent of the Underground Railroad, 264, 272
White, George H., a member of Congress, 403
White, Jacob C., 273
White, J. T., honorable record of, 408
White, Samson, 274
Whitfield, James M., an advocate of colonization, 297, 298
Whittier, John G., the antislavery writings of, 322
Whydahs, 69
Wilberforce, William, the antislavery efforts of, 281, 294

Wilcox, Samuel T., a Negro grocer in Cincinnati, 260-261

Williams, Egbert Austin, 560

Williams, Francis, the scholar, 77-78

Williams, G. W., an historian, 269, 469

Williams, John, intelligent slave of, 106

Williams, L. K., 483

Williams, Peter, mention of, 272; a churchman, 274

Williams, Roger, protest of, against slavery, 96

Williams, R. G., the indictment of, in Alabama, 340

Williams, W. T. B., 491

Williamsburg, Virginia, an insurrection of slaves in, 91

Williamson, Passmore, efforts of, to obtain the freedom of Jane Johnson, 342

Willis, Joseph, organizer of Baptist churches in Mississippi, 152

Wilmer, C. B., 550

Wilmot Proviso, the, 349

Wilson, Henry, reconstruction ideas of, 393

Wilson, Hiram, a worker among Canadian Negroes, 278

Wilson, Woodrow, attitude of, toward the Negro, 489, 494

Wilson, imprisonment of, 325

Winn, J. B., 300

Winslow, Sydney W., the purchaser of Matzeliger's patent, 462

Wise, Henry A., the defense of slavery by, 333-334

Woods, Granville T., an inventor, 464-465.

Woods, Lyates, an inventor, 465

Woods, Robert C., the efforts of, 510

Woodson, C. G., founder of the Association for the Study of Negro Life and History, 546-547; *Introduction*

Woodson, George H., 491

Woolman, John, a Friend pleading the cause of the Negro, 98

Work, F. W., a musician, 467

Work, J. W., a musician, 467

World War, the Negro soldiers in, 512-533

Wright, Elizur, an abolitionist, 308; an instructor, 320

Wright, Henry C., an abolitionist, 314

Wright, Theodore S., letter of Gerrit Smith to, 322

Wythe, George, an advocate of freedom, 120

Yazoo Lands, 213-214

Yorktown, fugitive slaves in, 366

Young, Colonel Charles, the proscription of, 492, 522-523

Young Men's Christian Association, the work of, among Negroes, 453, 480

Young Women's Christian Association, the work of, among Negroes, 454, 480

Zambezi, the, 3, 10

THE END